SOEHARTO

THE LIFE AND LEGACY OF INDONESIA'S SECOND PRESIDENT

Dear Frank,

Wati Knapp spent Good Valuable time with Pak Harto.

11 March 2009

SOEHARTO

THE LIFE AND LEGACY OF INDONESIA'S SECOND PRESIDENT

AN AUTHORISED BIOGRAPHY

RETNOWATI ABDULGANI-KNAPP

Marshall Cavendish
Editions

Photos from the collections of Saidi and the author

© 2007 Marshall Cavendish International (Asia) Private Limited
Reprinted 2007

Published by Marshall Cavendish Editions
An imprint of Marshall Cavendish International
1 New Industrial Road, Singapore 536196

Other Marshall Cavendish Offices:
Marshall Cavendish Ltd. 119 Wardour Street, London W1F 0UW, UK • Marshall Cavendish Corporation. 99 White Plains Road, Tarrytown NY 10591-9001, USA • Marshall Cavendish International (Thailand) Co Ltd. 253 Asoke, 12th Flr, Sukhumvit 21 Road, Klongtoey Nua, Wattana, Bangkok 10110, Thailand • Marshall Cavendish (Malaysia) Sdn Bhd, Times Subang, Lot 46, Subang Hi-Tech Industrial Park, Batu Tiga, 40000 Shah Alam, Selangor Darul Ehsan, Malaysia

Marshall Cavendish is a trademark of Times Publishing Limited

National Library Board Singapore Cataloguing in Publication Data
Abdulgani-Knapp, Retnowati.
Soeharto : the life and legacy of Indonesia's second president / Retnowati Abdulgani-Knapp.
–Singapore : Marshall Cavendish Editions, c2007.
p. cm.
Includes bibliographical references and index.
ISBN-13 : 978-981-261-340-0
ISBN-10 : 981-261-340-4

1. Soeharto, 1921 – 2. Soeharto, 1921- – Political and social views. 3. Soekarno, 1901-1970 – Political and social views. 4. Presidents – Indonesia – Biography. 5. Indonesia – Politics and government – 1966-1998. I. Title.

DS644.1.S56
959.8037092 — dc22   SLS2006045621

Printed in Singapore by Fabulous Printers Pte Ltd

In loving memory of:
my parents,
Sihwati Nawangwulan and Roeslan Abdulgani
and
Ibu Siti Hartinah Soeharto

To Hubert,
who is always there as my inspiration

ACKNOWLEDGEMENTS

I first met Pak Harto when he was Indonesia's second president, a few days before my wedding in August 1985. At that time, Pak Harto had achieved a life beyond his wildest dreams as he had become the most powerful man in the country. This book is more than a portrait of a famous person because Pak Harto has personally granted me permission and access to capture the essence of his life, a most captivating life and one which many would agree is larger than life itself. Pak Harto is taking a gamble of trust in allowing me to write about his remarkable life in spite of his declining health and in the midst of public controversy over his court trial. For this very reason, I would, first and foremost, like to express my deepest gratitude to Pak Harto.

My gratitude goes beyond those who are still alive. My beloved father taught me to always seek the best in each human being; the example he has set will stay with me until the end of my days. The loving memories of my mother and Ibu Tien, two women who stood firmly through thick and thin with their partners cum soul mates, stayed with me as I put pen to paper. The memory of the late Ibu Soetamtitah Soedjono Hoemardhani was present as well, guiding me to use intellect with sentiments of the heart in writing this book. Radius Prawiro, who when alive, candidly portrayed the true spirit behind Pak Harto's economic policies, their successes and failures, strengths and weaknesses. Mbah Dwidjo Kartono, who passed away in April this year and yet only a few months ago accepted me graciously amongst her family members in Klaten. Soewito, who left this world recently, opened a new horizon to my knowledge of Pak Harto's early childhood.

Tutut, Sigit, Bambang, Titiek and Mamiek—and Tommy Soeharto, whom I did not have the opportunity to meet—have supported my work on this book. For this, I am indebted to their kindness and support. Their deep dedication to their father is matched only by their deep desire for his legacy to be viewed in the right perspective.

This book would not have required the assistance of the whole village in Kemusuk to write, but without the help of Probosutedjo, Soehardjo Soebardi and Bu Bress, I would have encountered difficulties in completing the manuscript. Furthermore, they trusted me and had confidence in what I was doing, but above all, I admire their steadfast stand during the lowest ebb in Pak Harto's life. I extend my special thanks to Mbah Hardjoso and her family in Wuryantoro, and also the people in Kalitan, for their warmth and hospitality during my visit in September 2005.

To Hari Sabardi, Suweden, Maliki and those who are by Pak Harto's side daily, I must express my gratitude for their extreme patience in helping to clarify my understanding of the various issues I have discussed in this book. I would have been lost without their guidance. Yuniarti and her husband, Hatta, who were there in Kemusuk and Mangadeg during my visit in September 2005, lifted my spirit with their cheerful nature during those wonderful days.

Try Sutrisno, Ali Sadikin, Des Alwi, Abdul Madjid, Mochtar Buchori, Ismail Saleh, Moerdiono, JB Sumarlin, R Soerjo, S Wiryono, Hariadi Darmawan, Maryanto Danusaputro, Winarto Soemarto, Franz Magnis Suseno, Aristides Katoppo, Hariman Siregar, Sri Bintang Pamungkas, Amir Santoso, Amin Aryoso, Bob Hasan, Harjono Kartohadiprodjo, Susmanto, Waluyo, Bambang Ismawan, Syahrir and Faisal Basri are a few amongst those in my thoughts who have contributed towards helping me to move forward after my beloved father passed away in June 2005. For this, I owe a special 'thank you' to Try Sutrisno, Ali Sadikin, Des Alwi and Ismail Saleh.

Although I missed the chance to interview Ibu Nasution, I do thank her for her encouragement on my first book and her wisdom on this present one. My deepest appreciation for the encouragement from Ibu Kardinah Soepardjo Roestam, Ibu Herawati Diah, Ibu Ratmini Sudjatmoko, Meutia Hatta, Ibu Muktiah Mashud, Ibu Waluyo, Sylvia Ismawan, Mely Tan, Rosita Noer, Astrid Soerjo, Titiek Budhisantoso, Sri Rahayu Poernomo, Yuli Ismartono, Mimis Katoppo, Clara Juwono, Ika Wardhana, Ibu Anna, Daisy Ratna and many others; without their moral support, I might have been unable to complete this book.

The management of the Yayasan deserve my highest regard and praise, as without their help, a crucial chapter of this book would not have been possible to write. From Yayasan Dakab: Rusmono, Subono, Soewarno, Tb M Sulaeman. From Yayasan Trikora: Syaukat Banjaransari and Syahfruddin. From Yayasan Supersemar: Arjodarmoko, Soebagyo, Abdul Rahman, Herno Sasongko and Guritno. From Yayasan Dharmais: Indra Kartasasmita and Zarlons Zaghlul. From Yayasan Gotong Royong: M Yarman, M Djaeni, Ali Wathon and Istikomah. From Yayasan Amalbakti Muslim Pancasila: Sulastomo, to whom

I also owe so much more than his explanation about the Yayasan. From Yayasan Damandiri: Haryono Suyono and Subiakto Tjakrawerdaja.

There is no doubt that there are more ideas about the Yayasan that I wanted to write about than space and time would allow. After my discussions with them, a new phase in my understanding of Pak Harto was opened. This was combined with a humbling and daunting responsibility to make the Yayasan's deeds known to the public at large.

To Eddy Djauhari, the secretary general of Supersemar Alumni, my appreciation and high hopes that alumni members will follow my example in writing about their lives' achievements as a result of having received their Supersemar scholarships.

A book of this nature requires a mammoth amount of reading, writing and checking of facts. My smartest decision was to ask Anita Teo-Russell, whom I had worked with on my first book, to help with this project. A major share of the work was done by Anita, who persistently asked for clarification of facts and along the way, she taught me how to be a good author. To my assistant, Luthfi Ikhwani, I cannot thank him enough for his patience as I repeatedly asked for his help.

My father once said that a book is a light for the next generation. To Dita, Dinda and other Indonesians of the younger generation whom this book is intended for, I hope that this book will be a source of valuable lessons, which will provide them with some of life's wisdom. Pak Harto's presidency cannot be separated from the lives of millions of the *wong cilik*. For those *wong cilik* whom I have interviewed, I want to relay my sincere appreciation: Suratin, Masbukin, Mira, Susi, Supri, Mien, Poer, Donni and others too numerous to mention.

To my husband, Hubert, who sustained me when I went through the lowest point in my life when my father passed away on 29 June 2005. There are no words sufficient to convey my gratitude for his ideas, encouragement and inspiration. He was the one who, from the start, had the foresight to look for the positive traits in President Soeharto. Hubert is right: without President Soeharto in the country's driving seat, he might never have come to Indonesia for his work assignment and we would never have met.

In conclusion, I would suggest that Indonesians keep in mind what Bill Clinton wrote in the Prologue of his book, *My Life* (Hutchinson, London, 2004): "Whether I'm a good man is, of course, for God to judge."

CONTENTS

AUTHOR'S NOTE

"Our greatest glory is not in never falling, but in rising every time we fall," said Confucius. This axiom aptly describes leaders such as Indonesia's former first and second presidents, Soekarno and Soeharto. As complex as their lives might have been, there is no doubt that they were both extraordinary men, their leadership deserving credit and their failures empathy, from my point of view.

In embarking on this book project, I agreed with and was inspired by an article I read in the Thai newspaper, *The Nation*:[1]

> Asians, with the exception of very few, are writing for narrow audiences and like some of their counterparts in other professions have failed to raise their work to international standards. We have past kingdoms and all the grandiose ceremonies … And we have also grand literary treasures from the past. Yet, with all of our rich culture and history we rarely make an effort to develop and create world-class writing. Much of our history, especially political, social and economic, are written by foreign scholars. … We need to develop and express our philosophy and history based on our own identity, experience and knowledge that will reveal in writing of an international standard and universal appeal. We should not allow our knowledge of our own country to be overshadowed by international writers because our education system has crumbled.

My late father, Roeslan Abdulgani, had wanted me to put into writing ex-presidents Soekarno and Soeharto's policies in the appropriate context and perspective. In this book, I portray the human side of both men and offer a perspective of events from my privileged situation as an Indonesian whose father had held positions in the governments of both presidents and who had been personally and professionally close to both of them. In the book, I refer to ex-president Soeharto as "Soeharto" in his youth, "President Soeharto" when he was in power and simply as "Pak Harto" after he stepped down from the presidency. Soekarno is referred to as "Bung Karno", or brother. Accordingly, I refer to our first vice president, Mohammad Hatta, as "Bung Hatta". This is the Javanese way to show respect to one's elders and leaders.

A few scholars, journalists and politicians have, in their works, simply noted the differences between ex-president Soekarno and ex-president Soeharto and ignored the common ground that both men stood for. Future generations can learn from the lives of these two men by looking for and learning from their successes and mistakes. It would be an achievement if future generations of Indonesians are able to study the road that Indonesians, as a nation, have travelled thus far and avoid making the same errors in the future.

Both President Soekarno and Bung Hatta had proclaimed Indonesia's freedom with a missionary zeal to achieve their dream of a better world where justice and prosperity exist. Reality has revealed, however, that these ideals are not easy to attain even when freedom is in our hands. Hard work and sacrifice are the costs we have to bear as freedom does not come cheap. President Soekarno was not faultless; however, Indonesia might not exist today without his valour in proclaiming its independence in 1945. President Soeharto may not have been perfect, but the Indonesia which stands in the 21st century is one which the international community can no longer ignore. He not only continued the dream, he also contributed to making part of the dream come true.

To govern over 200 million people from such diverse backgrounds, languages, traditions and religious beliefs is not an easy job. It takes exceptional ability to be able to lead Indonesia for such a long period of time. "A country that appreciates its leaders is a country that can move forward" was one of President Soekarno's strong beliefs. President Soeharto followed a Javanese philosophy of "*mikul dhuwur, mendhem jero*" or "to look for the best in mankind and to try to forgive the trespasses of those whom we respect highly". He put this philosophy into action when he dealt with his predecessor, President Soekarno, in 1966.

President Soekarno has often been described by his critics as having been influenced by a variety of half-learnt European ideas. I believe the same could be said of non-Indonesian writers who claim to know and understand Indonesia well—the "instant Asian experts" or "paratroopers" in their understanding of the Indonesian psyche. Henry Kissinger once aptly wrote: "Continents interact, but they do not necessarily understand each other. Especially the long-established nations of the West have fallen prey to the temptation of ignoring history and judging every new state by the criteria of their own civilization".

At the time of writing this book, the Republic of Indonesia had passed 61 years of independence, albeit comprising both years of turmoil and triumphs. President Soekarno may have had many failures, but in the final analysis, it was he who had brought Indonesia to independence from the Dutch in 1945. When President Soeharto took charge in 1965 amidst speculations on the manner in which he had come to office, he managed to move Indonesia forward. In three decades, Indonesia has slowly but surely progressed from being a backwater, poor and unstable nation. Along the way, many things have gone wrong. The climb up the mountain of prosperity has not been free of hiccups as Indonesians stumbled on big stones and gravel. The journey to a better life has taken us on a slippery road where temptations grew strong and, in the interests of self, the less privileged were undeniably left behind.

President Soeharto, born a commoner, was to govern Indonesia for more than 30 years. His upbringing as a traditional Javanese and his belief that everything is predestined rather than the result of choice were a great influence on him. He came to power at a time of hyperinflation when the country's economy was on the verge of collapse. He introduced several economic and fiscal policies and allowed foreign investment into the country. By 1967, Indonesia's budget deficit had been reduced from nearly 7 per cent of GDP in 1965 to 0.3 per cent in 1967. President Soeharto's triumph has been to hold the fragile nation together. Unlike his predecessor, President Soeharto is a closed, quiet and enigmatic person. His public statements have not been viewed as forceful, fiery or open. His environment is limited to the arena of national boundaries. His first biography was written by two Indonesians.[2] It is not easy for a Westerner to evaluate him. In his book, *Suharto, A Political Biography*, RE Elson wrote:[3] "together with his public mask and evasive, undemonstrative manner, it makes the task of attempting to understand the man elusive in the extreme."

As president, Soeharto rejected Western democracy and introduced "Democracy Pancasila"—a democracy based on the people's sovereignty. He was a firm believer that people had a moral duty to respect the order of existence: they had to respect the order of society, and honour the elderly and their superiors because development could only take place in the presence of stability. Growth could not take place if political and social instability abounded.

Faced with the choice of driving the economic engine slowly and taking everyone along on the ride of development or driving fast and taking along only a selected few, he chose the latter and, in so doing, widened the gap between the "haves" and the "have-nots". President Soeharto, in the driver's seat, did not see the real picture, blinded by the praise from the happy set on the ride. They convinced him of his success, of his tremendous popularity, and of the huge respect he received.

Was President Soeharto a man with good intentions when he came to power? I believe there had never been any bad intentions on his part. However, as a result of increasing power and self-confidence, and escalating age, he was pushed and slipped over a dangerous cliff. Nevertheless, when I saw him from 2000 onwards, he seemed to have accepted his past glory and tragic fall with composure and dignity. His footprints remain imprinted solidly in Indonesia's history.

Of course, we should not and cannot close our eyes to the mistakes made, but the problems have to be examined in the context of the day. This book, while focusing on Soeharto's life and legacy, will also draw parallels with President Soekarno's style of governing. It will give an insight into President Soeharto's charitable foundations (Yayasan) which have been accused of misappropriating funds for his personal wealth and benefit. In fact, one positive finding of my research is that over 950 mosques have been built, thousands of orphanages have obtained financial assistance and thousands of students have received scholarships, in addition to contributions towards the building of hospitals, schools, health centres and the like. However, there has also been abuse of trust along the way.

My father was an active player in Indonesia's fight for independence and was one of President Soekarno's close confidantes. He felt that both men gave their best for their country. In my father's view, leaders are like actors in a drama. He wrote:[4]

> The actor would not be able to see the whole stage performance from the stand where he has performed. Nor could he see it from the technical level. The audience without doubt is in a better position than the actor. A player's impression of our history would certainly differ from the onlookers'. Therefore, it is almost impossible for a player to make appraisals, let alone form criticisms. Appraisals and criticisms are undeniably well reserved for the benefit of a spectator.

ENDNOTES
1   Thailand's national newspaper, *The Nation*, 8 October 2004.
2   G Dwipayana and Ramadhan KH, *Soeharto, Pikiran, Ucapan dan Tindakan Saya* (PT Citra Lamtoro Gung Persada, 1988).

3   RE Elson, *Suharto, A Political Biography* (Cambridge University Press, 2001), p 297.
4   Roeslan Abdulgani, *Three Public Lectures in Australia*, 1972 (Yayasan Idayu, Indonesia, 1974).

Chapter 1

DISTANT DREAMS IN KEMUSUK

To be a philosopher is not merely to have subtle thoughts
nor even to be found in a school,
but so to love wisdom,
as to live according to its dictates,
a life of simplicity, independence,
magnanimity, and trust.
— Henry David Thoreau

My father once told me that to understand President Soeharto, one has to learn about the Javanese people, the farming culture and the military. These elements of Indonesian life undoubtedly shaped Soeharto's character from childhood through to his career as president of the country.

UNDERSTANDING THE JAVANESE

The Javanese people are those whose mother tongue is the Javanese language and whose ancestors come from Central or East Java. The Javanese differentiate themselves into three social groups: the *wong cilik* or the poor (mostly farmers), some of whom live in the city on minimum income; the *priyayi*, who are the bureaucrats and intellectuals; and the aristocrats or *ndara*.

The Javanese have a strong belief in spiritual forces and religious rituals. Offerings are made before crop harvests or long journeys, after a promotion and on all occasions when cosmic happiness is sought or has been bestowed. They consult the *primbon* or registration book to choose the best time and place for important events. Even Javanese kings, queens, presidents and prime ministers would not be happy to make a change once the *primbon* has put forth a view. Bung Karno, for example, decided to proclaim Indonesia's independence on 17 August 1945 after consulting the *primbon*.

The Javanese also believe that legend plays an important role in educating and developing the minds of the young. *Wayang* performances with puppets or actors based on stories from the Hindu epics of the *Ramayana* and the *Mahabhrata* convey a peculiarly Javanese set of values to their audience. It is important to learn about *wayang* if one wants to understand the Javanese.

To a Javanese, a leader has to be *alus* or refined, elegant, soft-spoken, polite, adaptable and sensitive, with an inner strength to give indirect and polite commands that appear to be submissions. Emotions such as happiness, sadness, disappointment, anger, submission, hope and pity were not to be displayed in public. President Soeharto was very good at demonstrating the *alus* quality, and above all, self-control.

Personal and social tensions, conflicts and confrontations were studiously avoided by the Javanese for whom *rukun* or being harmonious was a very important quality. Harmony meant living in agreement, in "peace and tranquility without conflict and disagreement" or "to be united so that people could help one another". I believe President Soeharto governed with an iron fist to establish a harmony that was vital in order to achieve stability which was a prerequisite for development. In its absence, progress could not even begin. The lack of growth would not have made equality feasible. Wealth could be accomplished through development, without which there was only poverty to be shared. These ideals were key to his establishment of the charitable foundations in later years.

Growing Up in Kemusuk

In the middle of Central Java, the nucleus of the ancient Javanese kingdoms, lies an insignificant village named Kemusuk. Scant attention was paid to this small and peaceful community until one of its sons became the second president of Indonesia.

To understand the modern history of Indonesia, one has to understand the thinking of a person born and raised in a village setting like Kemusuk. Above all, one must have a sense of empathy with the heartbeat of a place which lies within the shadow of the mighty Borobudur. There were no paved roads, electricity or modern conveniences in that area in 1921. Yet, the largest Buddhist monument in the world had been in existence there since the eighth century. There was a vast difference between the magnificence of the monument and the simplicity with which the people lived. Life must have been much simpler back then and the simplicity no doubt influenced the outlook of the community. This was reflected in the people's behaviour and their way of life. In contrast, Borobudur was a landmark that would challenge modern technology in the years to come. The relationship between these two distinct features on the landscape would mirror what Soeharto's life was to become: a man of simple origins and simple tastes, who would rise to rule the nation and attain iconic status.

The former Kemusuk was divided into Kemusuk Lor (North) and Kemusuk Kidul (South). It is now integrated under one village administration. Soeharto's great-grandfather, Demang Wongsomenggolo, was amongst those who founded Kemusuk. Soeharto's paternal line was from the southern part of the village, while his maternal bloodline came from Northern Kemusuk. In those days, it was customary for people within the same vicinity to marry. It would have been hard to meet outsiders as travel was difficult. Soeharto's paternal grandfather was Kertoirono. He had two children, a son named Kertoredjo, who was Soeharto's father, and a daughter later known as Mrs Prawirowihardjo. It was in the house of Mrs Prawirowihardjo that Soeharto lived during his early adulthood.

In Central Javanese tradition, it is common that men change their names when they get married. Hence, Kertoredjo adopted his wife's family name, Kertosudiro. Kertosudiro worked as the village *ulu-ulu or* irrigation official. It was a high-ranking job within a village setting. He already had two children from an earlier marriage when he met the girl who would later become Soeharto's mother. Soeharto's mother was the daughter of Notosudiro. Arranged marriages were known in the old Javanese tradition. Obviously, arranged marriages had their ups and downs; it worked for some but failed for others. For Soeharto, it had worked extremely well, but not in his mother's case. His mother's name was Sukirah. At the time Sukirah met Kertoredjo, she was only 16 years old. Nevertheless, for Sukirah, she was in her prime to be wed, as girls were married very young in that era. She was also known for her beauty. It was not long after the wedding that Sukirah became pregnant.

In those days, there was no radio or television and the common entertainment was *wayang*, which was performed only when there were special occasions such as births or weddings. Probably as a result of this, Kertosudiro spent his free time gambling and smoking. These were common activities for men of his standing, but he needed a lot of money to support these habits. Soon, Sukirah was forced to sell her jewellery. Faced with this predicament at such a tender age, Sukirah became increasingly frustrated. Heavily pregnant and unhappy, she decided to return to her parents' home. However, tradition frowned upon a wife who left her husband and marital home thus, her family did not welcome her with open arms. Upset by her family's unreceptive behaviour, she hid in one of the many rooms of their house and fasted. By the time her family found her, she had become unconscious and very ill. When she recovered, her parents made her return to her husband. Not long thereafter, she gave birth to a healthy baby boy, whose destiny was to be the second president of Indonesia.

This son was born on 8 June 1921. As Sukirah was still weak from her illness, she was not able to breastfeed her newborn baby. The infant was given the name "Soeharto" by his father. "Soe" stands for "better" and "harto" means "wealth". Kertosudiro had hoped that his son would grow up to be a man of wealth and high position. Soeharto was their only child as the marriage did not last. When Sukirah's health deteriorated, the baby was handed over to the village midwife, the one who helped bring him into this world. The midwife, Mbah Kromodiryo, was the younger sister of Soeharto's paternal grandmother. The infant was only 40 days old when he was handed over into the care of Mbah Kromodiryo. Mbah Kromodiryo took Soeharto everywhere and taught him to stand and take his first steps. If she had to do her work as a midwife, her husband would take him to the rice field. There were times when the little boy would sit on his granduncle's shoulders as the old man dug up the soil. Pak Harto vividly remembers how happy he had been when he was old enough to instruct the water buffalo to move forward or to make a right or left turn. He remembers the pleasure of being able to jump into the rice field and play in the muddy water. That was the time when he learnt to catch eels, which remain his favourite food.

The village life suited Soeharto well. He recalls how he had an accident while cutting down a banana tree when the knife had dropped on his toes. He realised how much his grandaunt loved him as she tended to the wound lovingly. For Soeharto, this period was one of the best in his life. He loved the village life, where playing with water buffalos and catching eels in the river brought him real happiness. Those early years have had a great impact on him—until today, Pak Harto prefers simple food and dresses modestly. His simple habits have differentiated him from those Indonesians who like to be "Westernised". To this group, someone like Pak Harto is considered too Javanese and is sometimes even looked down on.

The burden of the marriage became too great for Sukirah to carry and she soon asked for a divorce. As in all divorces, there was rivalry for custody between man and wife. Both Sukirah and Kertosudiro wanted to keep the little boy. Sukirah finally decided to let her former husband take charge of their son. It was not an easy decision, but being young and physically unfit, she knew she could not take good care of the baby. This did not mean that Sukirah was irresponsible or unstable, as a few books have described her. The young Soeharto stayed with Mbah Kromodiryo and her husband until he was four years old.

After the divorce, Kertosudiro remarried and had four more children. Sukirah also remarried, to Atmopawiro with whom she had seven more children. One of them, Probosutedjo, became very loyal to Soeharto and was later to stand by him through thick and thin, in glory and in pain.

Soeharto was taken back by Sukirah when he was four years old. Atmopawiro grew very fond of his stepson and even bought him a goat. This spoke much of his affection for Soeharto as a goat is a precious animal in Indonesia. Goats are sacrificed during one of the Muslim holy days. Goats are also given when babies are born: one goat for a girl and two for a boy. A few writers think of Soeharto as a lone ranger. Although Soeharto might have been lonely and a loner as an only child, his close relatives did pay attention to his well-being and genuinely cared about him.

As he grew older, Soeharto spent his free time as a shepherd. After school, he would look after the goats and sheep, and when he was old enough, he took care of the water buffalo. One day, young Soeharto was asked by his maternal grandfather, Mbah Atmosudiro, to take the water buffalo to the paddy field. On the way, the water buffalo fell into a small stream. Soeharto thought that the animal would know which way to go, but the creature was not as smart as he had thought. The stream became narrower and deeper and it was impossible to move forward or go back. The only thing the little boy could do was cry. Fortunately, his grandfather who had become worried when he failed to show up, soon found him. This incident has remained etched in his mind—the memory of a small, lost child crying helplessly in the middle of nowhere.

By the time Soeharto was eight years old, his mother had had more children and Kertosudiro decided to put his son in the care of his sister, Mrs Prawirowihardjo, who lived in Wuryantoro, a more prosperous place. Married to a *mantri tani* or land official, she could give Soeharto a better education. Kertosudiro, however, was afraid to tell Sukirah about his plan, so he "kidnapped" his son instead. Little Soeharto was taken quietly from his classroom and they travelled by train to Jogjakarta (Yogya). Arriving in that big city, he was taken to a shop and given new clothes. They then continued by bus via Solo to Wonogiri and by taxi to Wuryantoro. Mrs Prawirowihardjo and her family immediately welcomed the little boy into their midst. The Prawirowihardjos had nine children of their own— one of them was Sudwikatmono who would later join a business that flourished as Soeharto became president.

A year after the "kidnapping", while Soeharto was on his school holidays, Atmopawiro took him to his home. Atmopawiro promised to return the boy once the school vacation was over, but Sukirah did not want to let her son go. Mrs Prawirowihardjo had to go and collect her foster son herself. Sukirah subsequently gave in as she saw that the Prawirowihardjos had taken care of Soeharto as one of their own children and treated him as the eldest amongst them. This built Soeharto's character and inculcated in him the responsibility of taking care of his siblings' interests when he became president. He stayed with the Prawirowihardjos until adulthood.

As a devout Muslim, Mrs Prawirowihardjo taught Soeharto not only the importance of school but also of religious education and spirituality. Soeharto spent his evenings in a small mosque, and learnt to recite the Qur'an. It was during this period that Soeharto developed his passion for the teachings of his ancestors, an important development that influenced him throughout his life. Soeharto took his spiritual training seriously. Part of it was fasting on Mondays and Thursdays, and sleeping under the eaves of the roof outside the house. The Javanese believe that by fasting and meditation, one developed personal strength to overcome the burdens of life.

He also joined Hizbul Wathan, a religious group. The training that he received from his family to respect his ancestors, the sense of nationalism he learnt in school and the religion which he studied in the mosque undoubtedly shaped his future well-being.

UNDERSTANDING THE FARMING CULTURE

As Indonesia is an agricultural nation where rice is the main staple food, farming is one of the main driving forces of the country's economy. The psychology of the farming community hinges on the notion of people helping each other. This was one aspect of Javanese life that would influence Soeharto tremendously in making decisions as the president. Understanding the psychology of farmers, their hopes, fears and needs was invaluable to his political career.

Living with the Prawirowihardjos was an opportunity for him to gain first-hand knowledge about farming. On analysis, this was one of the keystones of his later success in leading Indonesia. He accompanied his uncle on visits to lands that were cultivated for farming. While there, he would listen to his uncle explaining the art of farming in detail to the farmers. Soeharto admired his uncle's commitment to his job. His uncle's determination and creativity inspired Soeharto deeply and became the guiding principles in his later life. In the evenings, he often stayed overnight in the mosque with his fellow students. One important principle he strongly believed in was: "*hormat kalawan Gusti, Guru, Ratu, lan wong atuwo karo*", that is "to honour God Almighty, teacher, government and parents", later to be seen in his treatment of President Soekarno and his other critics.

This was the period that he felt most loved. He loved and was loved by those who took care of him and his siblings from different mothers and fathers. His dealings with his parents, siblings, extended families and friends during his childhood affected the ways he chose to make important decisions as the president. The love of Mbah Kromodiryo and the attention of Atmopawiro influenced his decision to take good care of his relatives. The achievements of the Prawirowihardjos no doubt inspired the way he looked at various issues.

It is indeed natural for a Javanese family to take care of the less fortunate members of the family. In the early days, it was common for children to be separated from their families for economic reasons and, more significantly, to train them in life skills. For example, when they lived with their relatives, children were expected to help with household chores—make their own beds, clean the bathroom, sweep the floor and wash dishes. It is entirely within the spirit of *gotong royong* or mutual assistance. There are no written laws about "payback", but the tradition continues from generation to generation.

Contributing towards sending children to school, paying for medical treatment or contributing towards home maintenance is also common. Families are told to distribute what they have and excess of wealth is to be divided, and to give more to the more deprived. There is a saying "*ada sedikit dibagi sedikit, ada banyak dibagi banyak*", which means that "when you have little, divide it in small portions and if you have a lot, divide it in big portions". These principles must not be ignored completely if one wants to understand the traditional Javanese mental state. This is also the concept inherent in extended families.

Early Life

After completing five years in elementary school, Soeharto continued his studies in Schakel School, a junior high school in Wonogiri. He moved to Selogiri, 6 km away from his new school, and shared a room with Sulardi, a classmate of his future wife. They lived with Sulardi's elder sister, whose husband was an official in the agriculture office and this gave him the opportunity to expand his knowledge of farming. During the holidays, he cycled to Kemusuk on Sulardi's bicycle to visit his parents. At the age of 14, he was circumcised, rather old for a boy of his age. Unfortunately, Sulardi's sister's marriage soon broke down and he moved to Wonogiri where he stayed with Hardjowijono, a pensioner and a friend of his father's.

Hardjowijono was a pupil of Kyai Darjatmo, a famous religious teacher who healed the sick and predicted the future. Soeharto learnt philosophy from him and often joined him in the mosque where he taught. Kyai Darjatmo's followers included intellectuals, bureaucrats, traders, farmers and peddlers. During this time, Soeharto learnt to prepare traditional medicines from plants that grew only in the parish.

Soeharto completed his education in Yogya. Around this time, he heard the beginnings of protests against Indonesia's Dutch colonial rulers. Before long, the winds of war began to sweep throughout the Pacific region. Obviously confused and preoccupied with warfare, the Dutch left the Indonesian movement alone. There had been political meetings held by upcoming Indonesian politicians to fight for the nation's freedom from the Dutch. Soeharto had not been too involved as he had been focusing on completing his education in 1939. After attending Muhammadiyah (an Islamic education institution), he had to look for a job as his father could not afford to let him continue his education.

Soeharto decided to return to Wuryantoro, hoping that having acquaintances there would be helpful. He was right, as he was soon accepted as a clerk in Bank Desa or Village Bank. He did not particularly care for the work, but it was better than being unemployed. As a bank employee, he had to wear full Javanese dress, which included a traditional hat, traditional shirt and *sarong*. He cycled to meet farmers, small traders and stall owners who needed loans to run their businesses. When the one *sarong* he had wore out, he had to borrow another from his aunt. His banking career came to an end abruptly when the *sarong* got caught in his bicycle one day and was torn. It was his aunt's best *sarong*.

Jobless once again, he moved to Solo to try his luck as a friend had told him of an opening for a cook in the Dutch Navy. It was his last resort but in Solo, there was no job opening. He decided to return to Wuryantoro. While looking for work, he filled his time with *gotong royong*, which included helping to build a mosque and cleaning the gutters and rice depot.

MILITARY LIFE

Soeharto's career as a combat soldier did not come about intentionally. There was an opening in the Dutch Military Army (KNIL). He joined them on 1 June 1940 and this was the first step in his long military career. He started basic military training in Gombong, west of Yogya. Military education appealed to him, and its impact remained with him for the rest of his life. His earlier unsettled years might have made him appreciate the strong discipline and orderliness in military life. Certainly, his leadership and strategic thinking skills were honed here.

The Royal Dutch Army had two types of training: a long one and a short one. He chose the short one where the training was very tough. It started in the early morning and ended late at night. It was very different from his job as a bank clerk. After graduating as the best in his class, he was sent to Battalion XIII, in Rampal, Malang. On 2 December 1940, he received the rank of corporal. Soeharto contracted malaria when he was young and it recurred several times. Later, he was sent back to Gombong for further training and soon after, he was promoted to the rank of sergeant. The Japanese were approaching when he went to Bandung as a reserve in the army headquarters in Cisarua. He stayed for just one week as on 8 March 1942, the Dutch surrendered to the Japanese. Although he had been a member of the Royal Dutch Army, he was fortunate not to have been arrested.

As soon as the Dutch were defeated, he travelled back to Yogya. As his train approached Tugu railway station, however, he heard on the radio that all former military personnel were to report in Jetis. He decided not to disembark and risk capture by the Japanese. He changed his plans and took a train in the direction of Sleman. After a one night stay, he took the bus to Wonogiri, then to Wuryantoro.

The country's situation had worsened. Soeharto decided to look for a better job. Yogya became his choice, as he thought that he would have better prospects in the city. He started to take typing lessons, but stopped when he fell ill. One day, he read a police announcement that the police, the *Keibuho*, had an opening. Hesitant at first as he wondered whether the Japanese would find out about his previous work, he finally decided to register. Luckily, he cleared his health test. After three months' training, he was assigned to be a courier and had to learn the Japanese language. He was encouraged by the head of the police to join the Pembela Tanah Air (PETA), the embryo to the later Indonesian armed forces. Once he passed the examination, he was trained as a *Shodancho*, a platoon commander, for four months. For him, it was relatively easy to pass because of the training he had had in the KNIL.

In 1944, he took up the officer training course to be a *Chudancho* or Company Commander in Bogor. The training as a *Chudancho* and a *Daidancho* or Battalion Commandant was less severe and more relaxed. His lessons on military tactics and strategy were completed in 1944 and he was assigned to Seibu, the PETA headquarters in Solo, to take charge of its training. His sense of patriotism grew while he was in PETA.

PETA later formed the core of the new Indonesian army. It was not a continuation of the Dutch or the Japanese occupation armies, but was formed during the country's revolution by young men and independent freedom fighters. Thus, PETA was a social force which became a state institution.

In 1945, a PETA battalion mutinied against the Japanese in Blitar in East Java. After the rebellion, which was led by a young PETA lieutenant named Supriyadi, was put down, the Japanese planned to "purify" the PETA officers. There were also rumours that Soeharto would be dismissed. The Blitar rebellion created a vacuum in the leadership as many of the *Shodancho* and *Bundancho* (non-commissioned officers), who had been involved in the uprising, were captured and put on military trial. But the Japanese felt Soeharto was useful and assigned him to Brebeg, at the foot of Gunung Wilis, the southern part of Madiun. The Japanese formed defence units in the *kampongs*, regions and cities. The defence units were called *Keibodan* and *Seinandan*. Women were recruited to establish Fujin Kai. Soon after, *Romusha* or the compulsory work force, was enforced at the village level. At Brebeg, Soeharto trained the PETA members from the Blitar battalion to become *Bundancho*.

Following the Japanese surrender to the Allied Forces on 14 August 1945, Bung Karno and Bung Hatta proclaimed Indonesia's independence on Friday, 17 August 1945 at 10 am. It was the fasting month, the holy month for Muslims. Soeharto was in Brebeg when he learnt about the proclamation, the new constitution and the election of Bung Karno as the country's first president and Bung Hatta as the vice-president from the daily newspaper *Matahari*. Sultan Hamengkubuwono IX and Paku Alam VIII from Yogya sent their congratulations to the new government. Sultan Hamengkubuwono IX pleaded to all to make sacrifices for the country's common goal and to guard and maintain the freedom that had been declared. President Soekarno pleaded for PETA, *Heiho* (the local Japanese army comprising volunteers and the militia), *Kaigun* (the Japanese navy) and all KNIL former members to join and unite under the Badan Keamanan Rakyat (BKR), which was established by the Committee for the Preparation of Indonesia's Independence on 22 August 1945. Soeharto complied and he and his former PETA colleagues joined them although, secretly, they had doubts over the real intentions of the Japanese.

President Soekarno decreed the formation of the Indonesian armed forces, Tentara Keamanan Rakyat (People's Safety Army) or TKR, on 5 October 1945, just nearly two months after the declaration of independence and Soeharto registered himself as a member that same day. All BKR troops became TKR troops. On 7 January 1946, TKR was renamed Tentara Kedaulatan Rakyat (People's Sovereign Army); two weeks later, the name was again changed to Tentara Republik Indonesia (Republic Indonesian Army). Tentara Republik Indonesia was the embryo of TKR, which was to later become Tentara Nasional Indonesia (TNI) through a Presidential Decree announced by President Soekarno on 3 June 1947. TNI later came to be called Angkatan Bersenjata Republik Indonesia (ABRI), incorporating the navy, police and air force. Since the mid-950s, the names TNI and ABRI have been used synonymously.

Five years later in 1950, President Soekarno highlighted the following:[1]

> The name has been TKR or Tentara Keamanan Rakyat—Soldier of People's Safety. Since then, the name has been changed several times. The role has remained the same. That is to defend the safety of Indonesia from internal and external attacks. War is a part of our army's duty, when our country is attacked. If our people's safety is not being taken care of, it also means that our armed forces have not carried out their duty at their best.

In the same speech, President Soekarno reminded all that the armed forces, the ABRI, originated from the people and its status was aligned with that of the Indonesian citizens. The ABRI became a significant player in domestic politics and its role took centre stage in 1965 and reinforced Soeharto's authority during his presidency. ABRI's main functions were to maintain the nation's security and to defend the country against external and internal aggression.

However, the Dutch did not recognise the new Republic's independence and a series of battles broke out with the Indonesians defending their newly-gained freedom from the Allied Forces, the Dutch who wanted to regain their colonial power and the Japanese who wanted to hold on to their power. On 31 October 1945, open conflict started in Semarang and then in Magelang. Soeharto, who had been promoted to the rank of Major, was in charge of Battalion X, the battalion which assaulted Ambarawa and Banyubiru. That brought Major Soeharto's name to the attention of General Gatot Subroto. General Gatot Subroto was from Division V/Purwokerto. He was the foster father of Mohamad (Bob) Hasan who became Major Soeharto's close friend. The Allied Forces withdrew to Semarang. On 18 December 1945, Colonel Soedirman, the TKR leader who was promoted to the rank of General, came to know of Major Soeharto's success. In December 1945, General Soedirman appointed Major Soeharto the Commander of Regiment III, Yogya and upgraded his rank to Lieutenant Colonel. Soeharto was now in charge of the Yogya region and responsible for overseeing four battalions.

MARRIED LIFE

By this time, Lieutenant Colonel Soeharto had moved and was living on his own. In fact, while in Yogya, his half-brother Probosutedjo had moved in with him. For both, life in the city was a far cry from life in Kemusuk. Their house was now much bigger and more luxurious and cars were a part of their better lifestyle. Sadly, Atmopawiro did not get to see this as he had been killed in Kemusuk when the Dutch invaded Yogya. Sukirah had also died in 1946, the year Lieutenant Colonel Soeharto became Commander of Battalion X in Yogya. She never saw her eldest son rise to the highest position in the country. During her final days, her eldest son had not even been able to stay by her side; he had been fighting on the frontline. Soeharto's father, meanwhile, had changed his name to Notokariyo and died in 1951.

At the time of the Dutch and Indonesian negotiations, Soeharto's single status became a matter of discussion. Lieutenant Colonel Soeharto was then 26 years old, a ripe age to start a family. One day, the Prawirowihardjos paid Soeharto a visit. He was asked about the future of his personal life and he replied that his mind was very much preoccupied with his military career and the ongoing fighting in the country. However, his foster parents emphasised that marriage should not be delayed because of the war. To a question on whom he should marry, Siti Hartinah's name was brought up. She was the daughter of a *wedana* and an employee of Mangkunegara. Mangkunegara was the smallest and the youngest *kraton* in Solo. Employees of a *kraton* had to have royal blood. After being persuaded that Siti Hartinah's social status as royalty and his as commoner would not be an obstacle, he agreed. Deep in his heart, he doubted if her parents, Soemoharjono and Hatmanti, would be ready to give their daughter's hand to a commoner. After all, they were *priyayi*.

Mrs Prawirowidihardjo convinced him that she knew of someone close to the family. She would ask this person to be the go-between. Soemoharjono and Hatmanti appeared to have no objections and consented to have him as their son-in-law.

On 26 December 1947, Lieutenant Colonel Soeharto married the second daughter of RM Tumenggung Soemoharjono. The marriage had not been a case of love at first sight or love as we know it today. Soeharto wrote that love developed through years of being together. In Javanese, the phrase *"witing tresno jalaran kulino"* means love nurtured through habit. Three days after the wedding, he took his new bride to Yogya. For Ibu Tien, as Siti Hartinah became known, it was a completely new experience, a new life as a military wife.

To help supplement the meagre family income, Ibu Tien planted vegetables in their backyard. To support her husband's military career, she founded and became the chairman of Ikatan Kesejahteraan Keluarga Hankam (IKKH). This was the association of wives from the Ministry of Defence. Her husband encouraged her to follow his keen interest in charitable organisations and she pursued it dutifully. Ibu Tien was known in later years as the promoter of Taman Mini Indonesia Indah (TMII) and Yayasan Harapan Kita. Their long-lasting marriage was blessed with six children—three sons and three daughters: Tutut, Sigit, Bambang, Titiek, Tommy and Mamiek.

When they grew up, the daughters became more outgoing than the sons. Titiek admitted that her brothers hardly spoke and were not as extroverted as her two sisters. Amongst them, Tutut is looked upon as the one who is closest to Soeharto, including in the political arena. When I asked her about this in 2005, Tutut replied that everyone received the same treatment from her parents, while Pak Harto gave his benign smile listening to Tutut's reply. They are a very close-knit family. They all live in the vicinity of Jalan Cendana. In fact, Mamiek, the youngest, lives just across the road from her parents and after Ibu Tien's passing, she stayed with her father every night. Mamiek has the same birth date as her mother: on her 41st birthday on 23 August 1964, Ibu Tien gave birth to her youngest child.

Why did Siti Hartinah agree to marry Soeharto in the first place? Maybe she had a sixth sense for success. Her decision also mirrors Javanese pragmatism and reflects tolerance. Ibu Tien became his strongest pillar. The couple had a solid marriage for 49 years until Ibu Tien died in 1996. When criticisms against Soeharto mounted, Ibu Tien had her share of criticisms: she was nicknamed "Mrs Ten Percent", a reference to the fee she allegedly received from various projects.

In the early 1970s, career opportunities for women were limited. Many engaged in small trading businesses to help keep their families afloat financially. Ibu Tien had also traded in *batik* when Soeharto was a mid-ranking soldier. Just as for President Soeharto, the core of family existence for Ibu Tien was the Javanese custom for compassion (*tresno*). Ibu Tien was a good wife and mother. She lived simply and was friendly, inquisitive and concerned for the well-being of others.

The Javanese believe in cosmic forces. Many Javanese still practise meditation and fasting on mountain tops, in caves and in dense forests and rivers to reinforce their inner strength so as to receive a bequest. President Soeharto subscribed to this Javanese outlook on life, and Ibu Tien's background also influenced this. Like President Soeharto, Ibu Tien felt that power or success was not a result of wealth, influence, relationship, military strength, astuteness or birthright. There was only one way to obtain power and that was through cosmic forces. A leader was believed to have received a bequest or *wahyu*, but this bequest need not be given directly to that person, it could be bestowed to the one closest to him or her. In the case of President Soeharto, many people believed that the bequest was bestowed upon Ibu Tien and that after she passed away, President Soeharto was unable to retain his power.

BATTLE FOR THE NATION

As the Netherlands Indies Civil Administration (NICA) stepped up their offensive in the capital, Jakarta, President Soekarno felt that not only was the critical situation growing dangerous for the leaders, it also endangered the existence of the infant republic. Thus, on 4 January 1946, President Soekarno announced that the seat of the government was to be relocated to an area clear of Dutch influence. Yogya was chosen, as it was central and the government stronghold could be based there. Lieutenant Colonel Soeharto's task became more difficult as he was now responsible for the safety of the new state and government. New political parties mushroomed. The negative consequence of this was that each new Cabinet did not survive for long.

My father referred to the years 1950 to 1955 as the period of Indonesia's survival. He summarised the negotiations with the Dutch from the declaration of freedom in 1945 into three stages, which he named as the halting stations.

The first negotiation was on 25 March 1947 in the hills of north Cirebon, Linggarjati, which took four months to conclude. President Soekarno chose the high altitude to cool down the Dutch temperament. My father said the Linggarjati Agreement, which comprised 17 articles, was not meant to be a good solution, but it was the best option at that time. It did not work. The Dutch, who were not happy with losing their former colony, attacked the new territories. On 21 July 1947, the Dutch commenced the first belligerence towards Yogya from Semarang. They invaded the republic by land, sea and air. This was the first attack from the country's former colonial ruler in its attempt to recapture it. President Soekarno declared that the nation would fight the Dutch until the last drop of blood was shed.

On 1 August that year, the United Nations Security Council called upon both parties to cease fighting and settle the dispute by arbitration.

The second negotiation with the Dutch was the Renville negotiation, which took place on board *USS Renville* on 8 December 1947. After the conclusion of the Renville Agreement, the Republic's territory in Java was reduced to a mere one-third of its previous size. Those loyal to the new Republic moved to Yogya. The city became overly crowded as newcomers moved in. They had to live in cramped houses, schools, boarding schools and warehouses, even train wagons. An Indonesian, Abdul Kadir Widjojoatmodjo, had astonished Lieutenant Colonel Soeharto as he saw him as the leader of the Dutch delegation. In addition, there were members such as Tengku Zulkarnaen and Dr Soumokil, who later planned to establish a separate Republik Maluku Selatan (RMS) or Republic of South Maluku. How could these Indonesians take the enemy's side?

In 1948, as the situation became more uncertain, President Soekarno decided to conduct "Rekonstruksi-Rasionalisasi" or restructuring and streamlining. Consequently, many military personnel resigned and those who stayed had their ranks downgraded. General Soedirman and General Urip Sumohardjo were relegated to the ranks of Lieutenant General and Major General, respectively.

The Dutch took Malang, Besuki and West Java. The value of the country's currency dropped because of acute food shortages. Further puppet states were created in Madura, Bandung, East Sumatra and South Sulawesi. Well-known leaders were kidnapped and murdered and the Communist

Party became more active. It was a time of turmoil. It created a class of people who took up opportunities for deceit, betrayal and self-fulfilling egos. While on a trip to East Java, Lieutenant Colonel Soeharto met Muso, the rebellious Partai Komunis Indonesia (PKI) or Indonesian Communist Party leader. Muso confided that he had never been against the country's freedom. He had disagreed with the continuing negotiations with the Dutch, which President Soekarno and Bung Hatta had favoured. Soon, Muso declared Madiun as a separate state on 18 September 1948. President Soekarno appealed for the public to choose between President Soekarno-Bung Hatta or Muso-Amir Syariffudin. Madiun was recaptured on 30 September 1948 and on 31 October, Muso was killed. Such was the situation during the early stages of the infant republic.

The worst took place on 19 December 1948, when the Dutch aggressively ambushed Yogya. President Soekarno said, "The Dutch dropped a Christmas package down my chimney." That eventful Sunday morning became an unforgettable day for my family. After attending the extraordinary Cabinet meeting that morning, my father was on his way home when a low-flying Dutch Spitfire shot him while he was riding his bicycle. He was the Secretary General of the Ministry of Information at that time. My father lost two and a half fingers on his right hand. While visiting my father in hospital, President Soekarno said, "It is your best contribution for our freedom."

Lieutenant Colonel Soeharto and his troops tried unsuccessfully to recapture Yogya on 30 December 1948. It was only on 1 March 1949 that Yogya was finally back under Indonesian control. Even then, the army managed to hold the city for just six hours. The Dutch had asked for help from their troops in Semarang. In the end, Lieutenant Colonel Soeharto decided once again to retreat. This battle had been so widely covered in international news that it caught the United Nations' attention. Soon after, negotiations with the Dutch resumed on 7 May 1949. Called the Roem-Royen, it was named after the heads of Indonesia and the Dutch. The Dutch had to leave and Yogya was restored as the Indonesian capital. Initially, the police force was placed in command, which Lieutenant Colonel Soeharto objected to. Lieutenant Colonel Soeharto decided to meet Sultan Hamengkubuwono and persuaded him that once the enemy had left, the military would enter to assist the police force. The Dutch completed their troops' withdrawal on

30 June 1949. President Soekarno and Bung Hatta were released and returned to Yogya. The Indonesian government started to function again. On 27 December 1949, the Dutch legally recognised the country's sovereignty. A few historians have recorded Indonesia's independence as having taken place in 1950, five years after the declaration of freedom. For the Indonesian people, freedom had been in existence since 1945. Thirty years later, President Soeharto formed an association to commemorate the attack in 1949. In October 1986, he formed Pagujuban Wehrkreise III Yogyakarta and built a foundation, Yayasan Serangan Umum 1 Maret 1949. His opponents claimed that the foundation had been for self-promotion.

In April 1950, Lieutenant Colonel Soeharto was appointed as Commander of Brigade Garuda Mataram and was sent on expedition to Makassar, Sulawesi to fight the Andi Azis rebellion over there. He managed to quell this rebellion in a short time more, by *musyawarah* or negotiation than by brutal force. At the end of September of the same year, Lieutenant Colonel Soeharto's Brigade Mataram returned to Java. He was very pleased to be back with his family. In 1953, he became the commander of Infantry Regiment 15 in Solo.

In the midst of the upheavals, Indonesia hosted an international conference in Bandung to launch the Non-Aligned Movement. The conference conducted in 1955 was also to promote African and Asian solidarity. Lieutenant Colonel Soeharto's role in the political arena during that period was not spectacular. Soon, discontent from the army against the central government came from other islands as well. There were rebellions in Dewan Banteng in West Sumatra in 1956, Dewan Gajah in Medan, North Sumatra, Dewan Garuda in South Sumatra, Dewan Manguni in Menado, North Sulawesi and Dewan Lambung Mangkurat in South Kalimantan, where the army commanders in a few of the local regions either supported or started the rebellions against the president's rule.

Similar to President Soekarno, Lieutenant Colonel Soeharto stood firmly behind the country's unity. One reason for his promotion to Chief Commander was his successful efforts at curbing these episodes of unrest. The territory he was in charge of was not involved in any of these episodes. He had no empathy for those who rebelled against the lawful government. He showed no qualms and was always ready to go after the rebels. It was for this same reason that he did not trust the Indonesian Communist Party which argued that the "Indonesian revolution is not over." For him, the communists were using this as an excuse to put an end to imperialism and feudalism in order to generate social disorder.

Unlike the gentle royal cities of Yogya and Solo, Semarang sits on Central Java's hot northern plain and has the only port open to large ships on that stretch of the coast. Under the Dutch, it became a busy trading and administrative centre. Once when President Soekarno came to visit, Lieutenant Colonel Soeharto voiced his anxiety about the communist situation. President Soekarno advised him to focus on his job and mind his own business, as political issues were for President Soekarno to look after. Sure enough, the friction between the communists and the army reached its peak within a decade. Lieutenant Colonel Soeharto's rank was raised to Acting Colonel on 1 November 1956.

The first smears on his integrity took place when he was the head of army logistics in Diponegoro Division in Semarang, where his main task was to provide sufficient supplies to meet the army's needs. In January 1957, he was promoted to the rank of Colonel. Critics accused him of being a smuggler, but smuggling in the feudal perspective was sometimes looked upon as an appendage to rank. As the Chief of Staff of Diponegoro Division in Semarang, he was aware that harvest had been dreadful and the people were in near total starvation. He saw that, with many sugar factories, the city had substantial stocks of sugar on hand. Thus, Colonel Soeharto gathered the governor, local leaders and the representatives from political parties to discuss the serious situation. He suggested alternatives: let the people starve to death or have porridge instead of rice to eat, and drink with less or no sugar. To eat porridge was the consensus reached and they agreed to barter sugar for rice. In a war-like situation, Colonel Soeharto felt he had the right to take emergency action. Bartering was against government regulations and President Soekarno had imposed a cap on sugar prices. Colonel Soeharto knew of the government's low budget and the huge needs of the army. He asked close friends such as Lieutenant Colonel Munadi, Major Soedjono Hoemardhani and Bob Hasan for help. This was also the beginning of a venture to combine the private sector and the military. This method continued in his future charitable organisations when he would ask Ibu Tien and his other family members to join the various ventures he helped to develop.

He suggested that Bob Hasan buy out the dilapidated sugar factories, formerly owned by the Dutch. Bob Hasan agreed and bought the sugar factories very cheaply. To circumvent the cap on sugar prices, they shipped and sold the sugar in Singapore. Bob Hasan had gone to Singapore to arrange the barters. However, the rice was to be shipped in first to Indonesia before the sugar was shipped out. They exchanged sugar for medical supplies, army equipment, agricultural tools and fertilisers. Nevertheless, bartering was still forbidden and illegal.

It was at this time that Colonel Soeharto embarked on his idea to build his many foundations. The basis of the foundations was to raise cash by imposing levies on goods and services, for example, radio ownership or electricity consumption. One of the earliest was The Fourth Territory Foundation established in June 1957. The foundation raised funds to help improve the troops' living standards and to provide them with additional income after retirement. The Fourth Territory Development Foundation was founded in July 1957 to help farmers. Indeed, social welfare, as known in the West, was almost non-existent in the country. The scope of the activities of the foundations expanded into ventures like marketing, transportation and small industries. In 1958, he started similar undertakings in Solo. He saw only the positive impact of the foundations and the benefits of such solidarity. Nevertheless, a few thought that Colonel Soeharto had become too "enthusiastic" and had crossed the line into outright smuggling.

There were other reasons for his foundations, which were due to political considerations. Colonel Soeharto did not want to stay neutral in the political struggle being waged in Central Java. During the regional elections in July 1957, the communists had won across the country. The communists held majorities in the assemblies of nine out of the 34 regions in Central Java, including Semarang. The city he was in control of became a battleground between the nationalists and the communists. Once in total power, Colonel Soeharto not only provided his loyal followers with cash funding for village developments but also used it as a mechanism for his political interests. Ali Moertopo, one of his early friends, encouraged self-development in *kampongs* and villages like Kemusuk.

His dislike of the communists was one thing, but rebellions against President Soekarno were entirely different issues. Colonel Soeharto publicly denounced the rebels of PRRI-Permesta at a national conference in September 1957. In fact, his division helped to defeat the insurgents by sending troops. On 1 September 1957, Colonel Soeharto was appointed a member in the Curator Council of the National Military Army, Magelang. This prestigious Military Academy was temporarily closed after the Dutch attacked Yogya.

Towards the end of 1958, General Nasution, then Minister of Defence and Security, introduced the military into politics; they were to be neither totally in control nor simply just a professional fighting force. It had to be something in-between. General Nasution, known as "Mr Clean", was very worried about the corruption that existed in the military. In August 1959, he announced that the army had to cleanse itself from this bad reputation. Mindful of public criticism about the alleged sleazy practices, he established an inspectorate general to clear the army's tarnished standing. He considered smuggling a violation of military discipline that brought dishonour to the army. He ordered investigations into the regional commands, with Colonel Soeharto's region being one of those chosen. The budgetary controller found that Colonel Soeharto was involved in the smuggling of sugar. In asking for cash contributions from the industrialists, Colonel Soeharto was named as the person who had instituted corrupt practices. On 13 October 1959, the Inspector General, Brigadier General Sungkono, announced the unauthorised levies that took place in Colonel Soeharto's region had not been found in other places. Colonel Soeharto was relieved of his command and he made his last appearance as Diponegoro Commander on 16 October. He was posted to the Sekolah Staff Komando Angkatan Darat (SSKAD) or the Army Staff and Command School in Bandung.[2]

It was suggested that General Nasution had prematurely moved Colonel Soeharto from his post. It was also suggested that the motive behind the decision had been General Nasution's disapproval of Colonel Soeharto's dealings. The difference in the nature of their outlooks strained their relations in the years to come; the peak was when General Nasution joined Petition 50 when Colonel Soeharto was president. Colonel Soeharto left all his family behind in Semarang and admitted that while attending SSKAD, there were issues of his corruption and that he had enriched himself from the barter of sugar. Gatot Subroto, Deputy Chief of Army, confronted him with these charges. The charges were found unproven and he was not guilty, so Colonel Soeharto was ordered to finish his training. By then, the political role of the army had become more important as President Soekarno launched "Guided Democracy" in 1959.

Having completed his training, Colonel Soeharto was promoted to Brigadier General and assigned to the army headquarters in Jakarta (MBAD). Soon after, he became its Deputy Commander. In this new position, he accompanied General Nasution on his overseas trip to Yugoslavia, France and West Germany. This was his first trip to Europe. While in Germany, he met BJ Habibie (whom he had first met in 1953 and whose family lived across from his Brigade Mataram) once again. BJ Habibie had been a student there and the meeting this time left Brigadier General Soeharto with an everlasting impression.

From 1950 until 1953, Indonesia tried to resolve the West Irian issue through direct negotiations, but the Dutch did not want to give in. Hence, in 1954, the issue was brought to the United Nations. Ellsworth Bunker, the American diplomat, had proposed to the United Nations General Assembly in 1961 that the Dutch should return West Irian back to Indonesia. The United Nations forces would stay for one to two years. Indonesia agreed with a note to reduce the two-year transition period. Typically, the Dutch proposed something to the contrary: they wanted to establish a Free State of Papua once the United Nations left. In response to such a suggestion, Indonesia opted to use cannons. On 19 December 1961, President Soekarno announced *Trikora* or *Tri Komando Rakyat*, the Three People's Commands: first, to crush the Dutch in their plan to form a puppet Papuan state; second, to raise the nation's flag in West Irian as part of Indonesia's lawful territory; and third, to mobilise all Indonesia's fighting resources. On 2 January 1962, a command for the Liberation of West Irian was formed, nicknamed "Mandala". Brigadier General Soeharto was appointed to be in charge and he was promoted to Panglima Komando Mandala or Mandala Commander.

In February that year, he was promoted to Deputy Commander for the East Indonesia Region. His military career moved relatively fast as his past achievements had been impressive. His appointment to lead the liberation of West Irian received positive reactions as newspapers praised his past military success. His headquarters was in Makassar. Once again, he had to leave his family behind. The couple was by then blessed with five children and it would not have been easy to take the young children around. On 12 March 1962, Brigadier General Soeharto was awarded the title of Mandala Military Governor. In a true sense, it gave him authority under martial law. His tasks included increasing the food supply and preparing for civil administration after liberation. His strategy was to combine all the forces and build a solid base for the region. They had to take stock of the terrain and, above all, to find the strongholds of the Dutch. They had to penetrate West Irian by land, sea and sky. The first infiltration was by air. The most important attack was amphibian in nature while the city of Biak was besieged by air. Brigadier General Soeharto's target was to raise the Indonesian flag on 17 August 1962, exactly 17 years after the nation's independence. It was hoped that after 17 years of freedom, Indonesia would be united as it should have been.

By now, his achievement in Mandala had gained him prominence at the national level. His military success had been impressive and he became a figure hard to ignore. In addition, the Mandala assignment gave him the opportunity to inspect the vast island. He was sad to see how backward the people were. The region was 17 years behind the rest of the country. Brigadier General Soeharto promised to build West Irian through provincial development funding. When elected as president, he issued an "Instruction President" or "Inpres Desa" to develop this province. There was no doubt that West Irian would open up a huge opportunity to do business.

Indonesian-American relations was at its lowest ebb in 1963. Washington was convinced that President Soekarno's major objective was to dominate the Southeast Asian nations. President Soekarno felt that the Americans had pressed him to stay put within their orbit, but he wanted Indonesia to maintain a free and active foreign policy. While in this mood, President Soekarno became aggravated by the United Nations resolution to incorporate Sarawak and Sabah into the Federation of Malaysia. In his opinion, this alliance was nothing more than a form of neocolonialism. Resentment increased as Malaysia complained to the Security Council of the United Nations in September 1962 about the "blatant and inexcusable aggression" by Indonesia.

In September 1963, a summit organised by Indonesia, Malaysia and the Philippines took place in Manila. There was agreement for the Secretary General of the United Nations to conduct a fact-finding mission. However, the outcome was a total disappointment. Indonesia embarked on a semi-military confrontation with Malaysia. Branded as "Ganyang Malaysia", "Crush Malaysia"or referred to as "Dwikora", President Soekarno declared Indonesia's resistance to the alliance. He announced it during a mass congregation for voluntary militia on 3 May 1964. The final straw for him came when Malaysia was endorsed by the great power as a non-permanent member on the Security Council.

President Soekarno was getting older and he had been blinded by the hunger for power. He had been in control for almost two decades and not only was he older, but he had also been in power for too long and had become over-confident. As a person close and loyal to President Soekarno, my father looked on helplessly as President Soekarno refused to listen to dissenting points of view. For him, President Soekarno was no longer the man he used to be from 1963 to 1965. My father said: "President Soekarno is no longer the vigorous young Bung Karno of the 1930s. Nor is he the mature adult President Soekarno of the 1950s with a realistic and cautious approach." By then, President Soekarno was growing old and had suffered from the immense burden of the presidency of a turbulent nation.

CHANGE OF DESTINY

In the political showground, President Soekarno became disillusioned with the parliamentary system of government after the 1955 general elections. (I recall stories about how good the communists had been during the campaign. In a classroom, pupils were asked to close their eyes and pray for books and pencils. Of course, none were there when they opened their eyes. Once again, they were asked to close their eyes and to pray to PKI for books and pencils. To their bafflement, there were books and pencils laid neatly on top of their desks.) From 1956, the concepts of *musyawarah* and *mufakat* were applied, whereby government was based on agreement through consultation and consensus. This was translated to mean that the majority seldom ruled; neither were decisions simply passed down from the top. Rather, the people were expected to reach agreement on chosen courses and implement decisions accordingly. This method might have seemed sluggish but it was in fact effective because everyone stood behind it.

Early in 1958, the Revolutionary Government of the Republic of Indonesia (PRRI) in Padang challenged President Soekarno. PRRI fascinated Masyumi, the Council of Indonesian Muslim Associations or the Muslim Party, and Partai Sosialis Indonesia/Partai Serikat Islam (PSI) or the Indonesian Socialist Party/Indonesian Islamic League Party, whose concepts for modernisation had been let down by President Soekarno. The West often felt that President Soekarno was leaning towards the communist bloc. In addition, there had been evidence that the CIA had sent arms to Sumatra. The Americans' combat aircrafts had flown from US bases in the Philippines to support the rebels. Bung Karno, imprisoned most of the time throughout his youth, had been continuously worried that the former colonial powers would try to return. When the British brought an additional 40,000 troops to help the Malayan police crush an insurgency that broke out in 1948, President Soekarno doubted the real motives behind it. It worsened as the British introduced the concept of the Federation of Malaysia.

The main players in Indonesian politics during the Cold War had been the coalition of the nationalists, Muslims, Christians and Catholics, but the coalition did not survive for long. In December 1956, Masyumi formed the opposition while PKI played a passive role outside the government despite the considerable votes they had won in the 1955 elections. Thus, President Soekarno believed it was time to reinforce the concept of National Harmony (*Kerukunan Nasional*). By then, a power play between the president, PKI and other parties, had come into the picture. The failure of Western-style democracy convinced the president that it was necessary for him to take the role as the centre of power. PKI increased their position as President Soekarno introduced the concept of *Nasakom*: nationalism, socialism and communism. To tap the energy of Islam and communism, President Soekarno gave both equal footing with the nationalist group. He allowed the three factions to compete in mobilising mass support, but the strained relations between the communists, the Muslims and the army endangered the unity of the nation.

President Soekarno announced martial law in 1957. In July 1959, he decreed the return to the 1945 Constitution. Two major opposition parties,

Masyumi and PSI, were banned. Critics viewed Guided Democracy as a tool to return to a system of personal rule. One of them had been Bung Hatta. He claimed the decree of July 1959 was a violation of the 1945 Constitution itself. In a system that grew more akin to ancient Javanese kingship, President Soekarno became the ruler who showed his mystic grace by including three contradictory elements—the army, PKI and the Muslims—in his court. The accord shaped under the name of *Nasakom* did not survive for long.

By 1962, PKI made a strong point to have the 1960s land ownership system reformed. This was targeted at the countryside, to enhance PKI popularity among the poor. However, the rich Muslim traders and property owners were against it as they had large holdings. In the meantime, inflation skyrocketed and the economy was in deep trouble. Economic affairs had played second fiddle under President Soekarno. He had focused on keeping the country afloat and united. Indonesia was heading for disarray. It was fuelled by the ideological passion of the old hostility and political rivalry. The 14 January 1965 edition of *Sinar Harapan*, a leading local paper, quoted Dipa Nusantara Aidit, the PKI chairman: "ABRI plans to train ten million farmers and five million labourers as the fifth armed forces." *Berita Yudha*, an army-backed paper, published reports indicating that General Nasution, General Yani and President Soekarno were aware of public frustration over the corrupt practices of the armed forces. Just before 30 September 1965, the paper printed that the political situation was explosive. Behind the curtain and in the corridors of power, ambition and opportunity wrestled to take over when the president's ill health became public. That was the state of Indonesia's politics as the stage was set for the modest, quiet and unpretentious man whose name was Soeharto.

Major General Soeharto, too, had become frustrated at the political tension, so much so that it had crossed his mind to give up his career. He wanted to be just a taxi driver or go back to farming, perhaps even to be a cook. The Communist Party became increasingly powerful and had no effective opposition. The army, very much against communism, refrained from entering the political arena. It was President Soekarno's interest to keep the status quo. In 1965, as the vote to seat Malaysia on the Security Council of the United Nations was confirmed, Indonesia withdrew its membership from this international organisation in anger. It was with anxiety that the

Malaysian Federation was founded on 16 September 1966. A creation by the British, the new Federation of States consisted of the Malaysian Peninsula, Sarawak, Sabah and Singapore. Against such a backdrop, the PKI raised the idea to build a fifth force. It was to be a collection of farmers and workers. The army openly and strongly opposed this notion. To strengthen their stand, PKI started rumours about the existence of a Dewan Jenderal or Council of Generals, which the army denied. PKI claimed a document named "Gilchrist" had been found in the house of American film importers. "Gilchrist" was the name of the British Ambassador in Indonesia and Bill Palmer was an American film importer who was a good friend of President Soekarno's. President Soekarno often visited his residence in the tea plantation in the high hills of Puncak. President Soekarno liked the Americans, but not their policies. He chose an attractive American lady, Cindy Adams, to write his biography. This was the main difference between Bung Karno and Pak Harto: President Soekarno loved the West but the West became suspicious of his ambition, while Pak Harto had never been at ease with the West, yet the CIA was alleged to have backed his rise to power. Until now, Pak Harto stays away from the West and the West, too, has abandoned him.

The alleged document was a confidential telegram sent by "Gilchrist" to the Home Office in London. In it was reportedly this sentence: "… our future cooperation with local army friends". The words "local army friends" were interpreted by PKI as a reference to Dewan Jenderal, which intended to push President Soekarno out of power. President Soekarno, who had also heard of these rumours, asked General Yani for clarification. Was it true that Dewan Jenderal's programme was to assess President Soekarno's policies? General Yani replied that it was untrue. There was Wanjakti (Dewan Jabatan dan Kepangkatan Perwira Tinggi), a committee to evaluate promotions for ranks and positions of higher army officers, but Aidit, the chairman of PKI, pointed to Dewan Jenderal as a plot to carry out a *coup*. As President Soekarno's foreign policies threatened the American position during the Cold War, PKI had made use of the situation to the fullest. Today, it is public knowledge that the CIA was indeed involved in removing President Soekarno.

President Soekarno fell ill suddenly in August 1965, and being the person at the top, it made the political situation very uncertain. Those who were hungry for power tried their luck. Aidit, just returned from his trips to

Moscow and Peking, felt the urgency to expedite his plan to seize President Soekarno's power, in case he died. He thought it was better to make the first move rather than wait around. Meanwhile, Major General Soeharto was busy preparing the Armed Forces Day celebration due on 5 October. However, something more dramatic and lasting took place.

The early hours of 1 October 1965 were some of the darkest hours in Indonesia's history. The Cold War was still on. From the early 1960s, the international mood was dominated by the United States' fear that the Southeast Asian nations would fall to communism one by one. If this happened, Indonesia would become one of the largest communist countries in the world.

Istana Olahraga Senayan is a stadium built with the assistance of the Soviet Union. The stadium can accommodate up to 100,000 people and be used for major sports tournaments. When football is played, the whole area becomes frenzied, as thousands throng the site. Located in the centre of the capital, any major event would block traffic for hours. On the night of 30 September 1965, President Soekarno gave a speech in front of Mubestek (Musyawarah Besar Teknik) at the stadium. His speech was broadcasted by all the radio stations. President Soekarno was a great orator and was able to captivate thousands of listeners for hours. People would go enthusiastically to listen to his speeches, with some climbing on trees to get a vantage point. At times like these, Bung Karno was like a rock star giving his best performance.

All the important leaders were there, but one general was missing. The missing figure was Major General Soeharto, who, in a matter of hours, would change the face of Indonesia's history. When he had finished his speech, President Soekarno decided not to return to Merdeka Palace; instead, he stayed at the house of his young Japanese wife, Ratna Sari Dewi. President Soekarno's protection was undertaken by the Cakrabirawa.[3] The Commander was Colonel Untung. Colonel Untung had been a parachute trooper during the West Irian conflict when Major General Soeharto was the Commander of Mandala and they knew each other fairly well. Colonel Untung, a good combat soldier, had been selected to join the elite Cakrabirawa in January 1965.

The next morning, Colonel Saelan, the Deputy Commander of Cakrabirawa, heard that gunshots had been fired in front of General

Nasution and Deputy Prime Minister Leimina's homes, both located in Jalan Teuku Umar. Jalan Teuku Umar, like Jalan Diponegoro, is a prime street in Menteng. Other gunshots were fired in the house of Brigadier General Panjaitan. Meanwhile, in front of Merdeka Palace, troops in war-like stance had gathered. It was soon discovered that President Soekarno was not in Merdeka Palace and Colonel Untung instructed his troops to look for the president. At first, they thought President Soekarno had been in the house of his other wife, Haryati. President Soekarno had four wives by that time, and it was not easy to locate him.

Soon, news broke out that Colonel Untung had instructed his troops to kidnap the highest ranking officers in the army: General Nasution, Lieutenant General Ahmad Yani, Major General Soeprapto, S Parman, Harjono, Brigadier General Panjaitan and Sutoyo Siswomiharjo. During the kidnap attempt, General Nasution had managed to escape but his young daughter, Ade Irma Suryani, had been badly wounded. His adjutant, a young Lieutenant Pierre Tendean, was killed during the raid.

At that time, Major General Soeharto was living in Jalan Haji Agus Salim 98, in a relatively simple house not too far from Jalan Cendana, where he lives today. On the night that President Soekarno was giving his speech at the Istana Olahraga Senayan, Major General Soeharto and Ibu Tien were visiting their son Tommy at the Military Hospital, RSPAD. It was a nightly routine. Tommy had been scalded when he ran into Ibu Tien carrying a pot of hot soup while playing hide and seek in the kitchen with his sister Mamiek. Major General Soeharto hence did not attend President Soekarno's speech. At around 10 pm, he saw Colonel Abdul Latief passing by. He knew Latief since 1948 during his assignment with Brigade X in Yogya. He and Ibu Tien had visited Latief in the past. Major General Soeharto found the accusation that his friendship with Latief had something to do with the *coup* incredible. Of course, he had visited Latief's family on special occasions. That was a common practice when subordinates invited their bosses for significant family events.

On 30 September, Major General Soeharto had gone straight home and slept a little after midnight. After the first prayer of dawn, a technician, Hamid Syamsuddin, from the national television station, TVRI, came by. On his way home after a day's filming, Hamid had heard gunfire in several places. Half an hour later, Mashuri SH, his neighbour, came by as well. Mashuri, too, had heard of several shootings. Shortly thereafter, Major General Soeharto put on his uniform and went to his office. Komando Strategis Angkatan Dasat (Kostrad) or the Army Strategic Command was not too far from Merdeka Palace. He drove himself as his driver and adjutant had not arrived. He noticed soldiers in green berets as he drove by. Suddenly, he felt uneasy with the whole atmosphere. A little after 6.30 am, he entered his office. He soon received information of what had happened. President Soekarno was not at the Palace but had gone instead to Halim. Halim was the landing field for the Air Force. At 7 am, the government radio station, Radio Republic Indonesia (RRI), issued a statement from Dewan Revolusi, or the Revolutionary Council. The Dewan Revolusi chairperson was Colonel Untung. The broadcast related to an attempt of *coup d'etat* by Dewan Jenderal.

The announcement is summarised as follows:

On Thursday 30th September 1965 in the capital of the Republic of Indonesia, Dewan Jenderal, a group within the army supported by other forces attempted to take over the government. Colonel Untung, Commander Battalion 1 of Cakrabirawa, personal bodyguard of President Soekarno, is now to lead the G30S (Gerakan tiga puluh September), the 30 September Movement, to defy them. A few generals have been captured and vital communication, as well as important entities, is now under the control of G30S. Dewan Jenderal is a subversive act, sponsored by the CIA and has been active since President Soekarno was seriously ill in the beginning of August this year. However, their expectation that President Soekarno would die has not come true. For this purpose, Dewan Jenderal plans to carry out a show of force during the Armed Forces Day on 5th October. They have asked our troops from East, Central and West Java to participate. Jakarta is chosen as the centre point. Dewan Jenderal is in fact a contra-revolutionary *coup*. Colonel Untung has successfully taken the right steps. Dewan Jenderal consists of a few army officers who want to damage the army's reputation. They have bad intention towards the Republic and President Soekarno. As a member of Cakrabirawa, whose duty is to protect the safety of the President and the Republic, Colonel Untung feels it is therefore his duty to stop their suit. G30S will be followed in similar manner in every part of our country. We will act against the followers of and those who have sympathy with Dewan Jenderal. As a follow-up, we will form Dewan Revolusi, while in the regions it will be named as the Dewan Revolusi Propinsi, from the regional level down to village level. The members of Dewan Revolusi will consist of civilians and the military, which has no reservation about the Dewan Revolusi. All political parties, mass organisations, newspapers and magazines should carry on their activities until a decision is made on a later date. But they have to pledge loyalty to Dewan Revolusi. This Council, established on 30 September, would ensure "Panca Amanat Revolusi" or the Fifth Revolution Order.

We will endorse the People Assembly decision, resolution of DPR-GR (Parliament) and DPA (National Advisory Council). The Revolutionary Council will not change our free and active foreign policy. We would stand against neocolonialism and aim for peaceful existence in Southeast Asia and the rest of the world. Similarly, the policy of Asia-African Conference 11, Conefo and our confrontation against Malaysia will not change. Our roles in international relations remain unchanged. Let Colonel Untung as the Commander of G30S plead for all citizens to increase vigilance and help G30S to save the Republic from Dewan Jenderal. By this, we will stop miseries and meet our people's demand (*Ampera*).

Colonel Untung extended his plea to every soldier to stop Dewan Jenderal and its followers, who were power hungry and ignoring the well-being of their subordinates. They were the ones who lived in luxury and were exploiting the country's wealth. They had to be expelled from the army and punished accordingly. The army was not just for the generals but belonged to every soldier loyal to the Revolution of 1945. To other members of the armed forces, Colonel Untung asked that they distance themselves from Dewan Jenderal.

This sounded like an announcement which was leftist in orientation. Colonel Untung's leftist ideology convinced Major General Soeharto that G30S was a *coup d'etat* attempt from the left or PKI. Meanwhile, the Armed Forces Day celebration on 5 October was on its way and Battalion 454 from Central Java and Battalion 530 from East Java had arrived in Jakarta. After he heard the radio announcement at 7.30am, Lieutenant Ali Moertopo and Brigadier General Sabirin Mochtar came to advise him that the two battalions were on their way to the Palace. They were under the command of Captain Kuntjoro and Suradi, who were loyal to President Soekarno, therefore it was very crucial to arrange a meeting with them. When they met, Captain Kuntjoro and Suradi reaffirmed that their duty was to safeguard the president from the forthcoming *coup* by Dewan Jenderal. "That is not true. The president is not in the palace and there is no such Dewan Jenderal. There is Wanjakti, of which I am also a member. It is not possible and Wanjakti will not attempt a *coup*. I am positive PKI is behind Colonel Untung's movement," Major General Soeharto explained. After hours of dialogue, the two battalions finally gave in, except one division from Battalion 454, which had decided to go to Halim. A staff meeting to discuss the radio broadcast that morning soon took place. "I have known Untung since 1945 and he is a student of the PKI leader, Alimin," explained Major General Soeharto. "Wanjakti never discusses politics, only promotions from Colonel's rank up to General. Untung is wrong and in my opinion, this is not only a movement against the so-called Dewan Jenderal but a *coup* to take over the government. It is certainly backed by PKI," he said further.

Soon thereafter, at 10 am, Major General Soeharto asked for Colonel Sarwo Edie, Laksamana Martadinata and Sutjipto Judodihardjo, the latter two being the chiefs of the navy and the police. He also tried to contact Commander Omar Dhani of the air force, but it was Leo Wattimena, his deputy, who answered his call. The kidnapping of the higher-ranking officers in the army was discussed. He also advised them that he had taken over the lead within the army to avoid a vacuum of power. His reasoning was that whenever General Yani was absent, he would always be the one in charge.

Major General Soeharto did not want bloodshed and tried to persuade the rebels to come over to his side. He asked the other armed forces for their understanding and help. He suggested that they coordinated their actions to differentiate those for and against G30S. Consolidation amongst all the armed forces was crucial and all troop movement should be coordinated with Kostrad. All troop movement would take place only on Kostrad's instructions. Soon, Colonel Sarwo Edie arrived on a panzer at 11 am. They discussed strategies on how to take the radio station and telecommunications building under their control. Both buildings had fallen under Colonel Untung's control by that stage.

A decision was made to distinguish the two opposing groups. A white band was placed on the uniform of those on the army's side. At midday, Leo Wattimena came for clarifications, while stating that he had no knowledge of G30S, although the fact remained that G30S had chosen the Halim Air Force landing field as its headquarters. A few of the insurgent leaders were also members of the air force. Major General Soeharto decided to postpone the assault of RRI and the communication building, as there would be innocent victims if the attack was to take place in the day. Most importantly, as long as Colonel Untung was in control, more broadcasts would undoubtedly be aired. That way, more people could listen to G30S's announcements. Major General Soeharto was right; within a short time, Colonel Untung announced Decree Number 1 of the Revolutionary

Council. This announcement downgraded the army's ranking and expounded Colonel Untung's ideas about Dewan Revolusi.

The second broadcast repeated that Dewan Revolusi had concluded that G30S was solely an act within the army to stop Dewan Jenderal. The members of G30S would give further details of the organisations they had in mind. Until the general elections took place, Dewan Revolusi would hold the power in the country. They would form a presidium to manage the day-to-day operations. The present Cabinet, Dwikora, would cease to work but the ministers were asked to continue their jobs. They were not allowed to appoint new staff. They were now accountable to Dewan Revolusi and were prohibited from making any policy or decision. A regional council would be established with no more than 25 members, 10 in *Kabupaten* (county), 10 in *Kecamatan* (sub-district) and in the villages. On 1 October, they announced the members of the Council, which consisted of 45 members, including two well-known figures: Soebandrio and Leimina. Interestingly, from that list, only a few were from the PKI. The rest were from religious circles and the military, which, in fact, knew nothing.

Another staff meeting took place in Kostrad to draw plans to attack Halim. Halim was not only the G30S headquarters but also where President Soekarno and a few of his ministers were staying. However, they needed President Soekarno to be on their side or at least staying within a territory controlled by them. After all, President Soekarno was still the legal Head of State. President Soekarno's adjutant, Colonel Bambang Widjanarko, arrived in Kostrad and confirmed that the president was indeed still at Halim. Major General Soeharto appealed for President Soekarno to move before midnight, as Halim would be attacked that night. Bambang Widjanarko relayed this message to Leimina, who then advised the president to move immediately to Bogor Palace. The president took this advice and left Halim within a short time.

At 3 pm, Major General Soeharto prepared and recorded his announcement that would be aired once the radio station was back under their control. Battalion 454 and 530 returned to Kostrad at 8 pm that evening. In the early evening, General Nasution showed up with his wounded leg. Exhausted, he quickly recounted what had happened. His wounded daughter was still alive and hospitalised. The army attacked the radio station and the telecommunications headquarters after 6 pm with no resistance from Colonel Untung and his troops. In fact, Colonel Untung was nowhere to be found. The chairman of PKI, Aidit, had flown to Yogya by Air Force Dakota. The Chief of Air Force, Omar Dhani and his family, were given refuge in Bogor Palace. Once the radio was safely under their control, Brigadier General Ibnu Subroto put on air Major General Soeharto's recorded announcement:

> On 1 October 1965, G30S kidnapped six army generals. Lately, radio-RRI and headquarters of telecommunications have been under G30S control. President Soekarno is safe and in good health. I have temporarily taken over command of the army. The army, navy and police force have reached an understanding and have decided to work together to defeat the G30S. G30S has formed Dewan Revolusi, which in fact, has seized power illegally or conducted a *coup*. They have declared that Cabinet Dwikora should stop work and kidnapped high-ranking army officers. As a consequence, it is clear that this is contra-revolutionary and is to be defeated.

This statement was in total contrast to Colonel Untung's earlier announcement. It was also clear that the Air Force was not mentioned. A little before midnight, Halim was attacked. The Kostrad headquarters was moved that night to Senayan, as Major General Soeharto had received information that the air force had planned to bombard it. The next day, at around 11 am, he received a telephone call that President Soekarno wanted him to go immediately to Bogor Palace. Arriving in Bogor, he soon noticed that Leimina, Chaerul Saleh, Pranoto, Leo Wattimena and Omar Dhani were among those present. After they shook hands, President Soekarno asked him to take a seat and said: "This kind of incident is common in a revolution. We have to understand and the army should not accuse the other armed forces. Omar Dhani has informed and convinced me that the Air Force had no knowledge of this."

Soon, a gun similar to those used by the air force was found in Halim and was brought to the president's attention. President Soekarno asked Leo Wattimena to examine the firearm in question. Leo acknowledged that it looked like an Air Force weapon, but there was a possibility it had been stolen from their warehouse. President Soekarno soon said that he had taken over the command of the army and appointed General Pranoto to manage the day-to-day operations. Major General Soeharto commented that he had also temporarily taken over the command since whenever Yani was not available, he was in charge. In addition, he had announced it over the radio. To avoid dualism of power, he was prepared to hand control over. President Soekarno decided that Major General Soeharto should stay in charge of security and defence, while General Pranoto managed the administration and this was later announced at 6 pm through Radio RRI.

Looking back, it is clear that President Soekarno had made a wise decision by saving the faces of all parties concerned. The statesmanship that President Soekarno possessed was clear; he did not want to create friction. The country's unity had to be preserved at all cost, especially when the situation was so fragile. President Soekarno did not want to blame Major General Soeharto for the important decision he had made without the Head of State's knowledge since the president was also the Supreme Commander of the Armed Forces. It showed that Bung Karno had, in his own style, protected Pak Harto from blame in making his own decision without consulting his superior.

While looking for the missing generals, a police officer who had been captured by G30S managed to escape. He reported to Kostrad on 3 October 1965. He had been kept in a place called Lubang Buaya or Crocodile Hole, situated on a small lane off the main street leading to Halim airport. It was tucked away in the midst of the military installation, dormitory and hangar, with small *kampongs* and rice fields in the background. It was the site where 2,000 voluntary youths and women were trained in preparation for attacking the Federation of Malaysia. It could not have been just a mere coincidence that the Revolutionary Council used Halim as its headquarters.

The bodies of the murdered generals were found together on 4 October 1965 in an old well. Major General Soeharto was there when they removed the corpses: first, it was Lieutenant Pierre Tendean, who was young and extremely handsome, and popular amongst the young ladies; next were the bodies of Major General Soeprapto and S Parman; followed by the bodies of Lieutenant General A Yani, Major General MT Harjono and Brigadier General Sutoyo Siswomiharjo; and finally that of Brigadier General DI Panjaitan. Trembling, frustrated, full of anger and deeply hurt as he saw the corpses of his peers, Major General Soeharto promised to seek revenge on those who had shown such cruelty to his fellow officers. Furthermore, the rebels had accused the six murdered generals of being "too western and corrupt as they put more importance on lifestyle instead of ideology".

G30S EVENTS

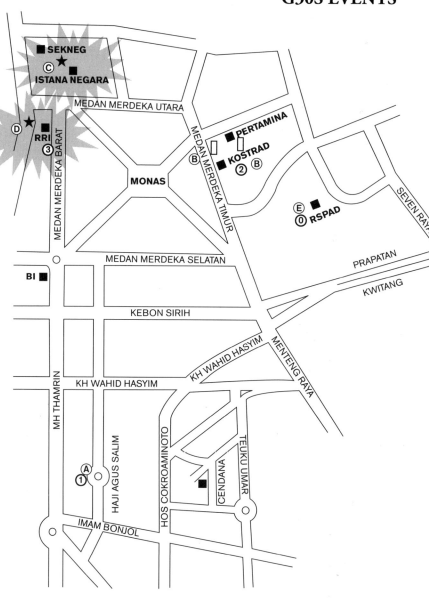

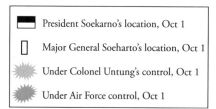

President Soekarno's location, Oct 1

Major General Soeharto's location, Oct 1

Under Colonel Untung's control, Oct 1

Under Air Force control, Oct 1

TROOP DEPLOYMENT

★ Cakrabirawa Batallion

RPKAD (Army Parachute Commando Regiment)

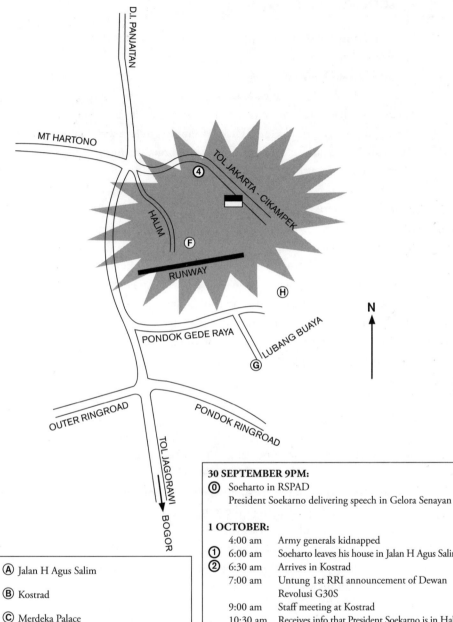

30 SEPTEMBER 9PM:

Ⓞ Soeharto in RSPAD
President Soekarno delivering speech in Gelora Senayan

1 OCTOBER:

	4:00 am	Army generals kidnapped
①	6:00 am	Soeharto leaves his house in Jalan H Agus Salim
②	6:30 am	Arrives in Kostrad
	7:00 am	Untung 1st RRI announcement of Dewan Revolusi G30S
	9:00 am	Staff meeting at Kostrad
	10:30 am	Receives info that President Soekarno is in Halim
③	14:00	Untung 2nd RRI announcement of the names of the members of the Dewan Revolusi
④	18:00	RPKAD attacks and takes control of RRI
	After 18:00	President Soekarno leaves Halim for Bogor Palace Soeharto broadcast announcing that President Soekarno is safe and that the army is in control
	23:30	Kostrad moves to Senayan to avoid possible attacks by the Air Force
	23:30	RPKAD secures Halim

Ⓐ Jalan H Agus Salim

Ⓑ Kostrad

Ⓒ Merdeka Palace

Ⓓ **RRI** = Radio Republic Indonesia

Ⓔ **RSPAD** = Military hospital

Ⓕ Halim Airfield

Ⓖ Lubang Buaya

Ⓗ PKI Volunteer Training Ground

The bodies were taken to the Military Hospital, RSPAD Gatot Subroto, and were kept there for one night. They were then moved to the army headquarters where Major General Soeharto kept vigil all night. The next day, on 5 October 1965, to coincide with the 20th anniversary of the Armed Forces Day, the remains were taken in panzers to their last resting place. The burial took place in the National Heroes Cemetery in Kalibata. Unfortunately, President Soekarno was absent from an emotional memorial service which caught the world's attention.

What had occurred in Jakarta also took place in similar style and manner in other major cities such as Semarang, Yogya and Solo. Radio Semarang was taken over by Colonel Sahirman, a member of G30S. In Yogya, they brutally murdered Colonel Katamso and Lieutenant Colonel Giyono. Lieutenant Colonel Giyono had been Major General Soeharto's adjutant and operational officer as he led the attack on Yogya on 1 March 1949. By this time, Major General Soeharto realised he had no choice but to move in fast in order to go after, clean up and bring an end to G30S.

Major General Soeharto was very disappointed that President Soekarno had a different viewpoint on the degree of the communists' involvement in G30S. The president commented on the event as "small waves in the ocean". Major General Soeharto's feelings worsened at the Cabinet meeting convened in Bogor Palace on 6 October. The atmosphere was far from sorrowful. President Soekarno told Nyoto, Aidit's deputy: "Nyoto, you are stupid to start this condemned affair. This episode has clearly destroyed the communist party's standing. The whole thing is so childish." These words gave an indication that the president knew that something had been brewing between the communists and the army. Obviously, President Soekarno knew about the involvement of foreign powers with those who wanted to overthrow him. He knew also that as long as he could use the communists to balance his opponents, his power would stay intact. When he had fallen ill, the communists were afraid of being too late in grabbing power from the right, which might have made the initial move. Therefore, they had made the first move. History would show that they had miscalculated their chances.

Major General Soeharto's spirit weakened further as he learnt about an innocent life cruelly taken away at a very young and tender age. General

Nasution's five-year-old wounded daughter died six days after the shooting. Meanwhile, reports of the murdered generals had spread like wildfire. Demonstrations by thousands took place and demonstrators burnt the PKI office in Kramat. Banners that read "Dissolve PKI", "Hang Aidit" and "PKI is against God" suddenly appeared everywhere. The students formed KAMI, a student organisation, and KAPPI, a new high school organisation, and many other such organisations sprouted. The year of living dangerously had started.

Colonel Untung was captured on 11 October 1965 and after a military tribunal, he was sentenced to death. Aidit was killed in Yogya as he tried to escape on 22 November 1965.

For his involvement in G30S, Colonel Latief was imprisoned on 11 October 1965. Regretfully, for reasons unknown, his case was only brought to trial after 13 years of his captivity. In his defence, Colonel Latief asserted that he was visiting Tommy in RSPAD on 30 September to advise Major General Soeharto that the next morning, there would be a movement of the Dewan Jenderal. He claimed that on 28 October 1965, he had also visited the Major General in his house while Ibu Tien and his in-laws were there. Colonel Latief claimed that during the visit, he had asked him whether Dewan Jenderal existed. Colonel Latief said that Major General Soeharto had received the same query put forward by one Bagyo, another soldier whom they both knew. Colonel Latief stated that Major General Soeharto promised to find out more information on this issue of Dewan Jenderal.

Unfortunately, it was not possible to seek clarification on this as at the time of writing, Colonel Latief had just died. However, Pak Harto and Probosutedjo admitted it was true that Colonel Latief had come to visit. It was also true that Dewan Jenderal was discussed. This did not provide a strong link between Major General Soeharto and his involvement in the alleged Dewan Jenderal.

President Soekarno decided to pay homage to the massacred generals at their graves during the Hero's Day commemoration on 10 November 1965. As the riots continued, the Chinese Embassy near Chinatown was completely burnt to the ground. The demonstrators insisted on the suspension of PKI, which President Soekarno vigorously refused. People were disappointed that President Soekarno maintained his stand, even under heavy pressure from all sides. Under the watchful eye of Colonel Sarwo Edie, the student demonstrators milled around the State Secretariat in January 1966. The protesters voiced three demands (*Tritura*): first, to ban PKI; second, to reform the Cabinet from the leftist-orientated and incompetent individuals; and lastly, to reduce the price of essential commodities. As the Commander of Kostrad, Major General Soeharto knew that the Army had to safeguard the country from the communists and bloodshed. For all that he had done during those trying times, on 1 February 1966, his rank was raised to Lieutenant General.

On 21 February 1966, President Soekarno retooled the Dwikora Cabinet. General Nasution no longer held the position of Minister of Defence and Security. Lieutenant General Soeharto was assigned to the post of Minister/ Commander of the Army and Chief of Staff. As the Cabinet installation day approached, students with yellow jackets mounted a siege on Merdeka Palace. The youths sacked nearby government offices and immobilised traffic. As the ceremony proceeded inside, troops fired on the demonstrators, killing a medical student, Arief Rachman Hakim. His funeral was attended by thousands and became another rallying point.

While the demonstrations continued, General Soeharto met and conducted a dialogue with President Soekarno. Left alone, President Soekarno had asked him in Javanese: "Harto, what do you actually want to do with me?" To which the General replied: "Bapak Presiden, I am a son of a poor farmer, but my father always reminded me that I have to respect my elders. *Mikul dhuwur, mendhem jero* (placed highly and buried deeply)." Loosely translated, *mikul dhuwur* is "to respect and keep the good name of one's elders"; *mendhem jero* means "not to expose the deficiencies of one's elders, but it is more important not to repeat their mistakes".

President Soekarno seemed pleased with his answer and instructed him to stop the ongoing protests. General Soeharto argued that it would be impossible, unless President Soekarno was willing to dissolve PKI. President Soekarno refused, giving arguments such as "I am already recognised as a world leader and I have sold the concept of *Nasakom*. If I have to ban PKI, where shall I hide my face?" To which General Soeharto replied, "Pak, if the issue is one for foreign consumption, it is easy—I can be your buffer. I can dissolve PKI, but nationally, you have to approve my action." President Soekarno stood firm and refused.

Even today, Pak Harto is still very sad about this incident, as he was when he recounted that conversation to my father. Thereafter, President Soekarno banned KAMI. The army kept guard on the University of Indonesia campus. Destructive and violent rioting by both sides spread throughout the city in the following days. On 8 March, the students broke into and pillaged the Foreign Ministry while a counter demonstration damaged the US Embassy. Attacks on Chinese Representative Offices followed in the next two days. General Soeharto asked the students to come to Kostrad on 10 March 1966. The late meetings weakened him and he was unable to attend a Cabinet meeting on 11 March 1966. That day became the most important day in the life of the man who was born in Kemusuk 45 years ago.

General Soeharto was ill at home when the three generals, Amir Machmud, Andi Muhammad Yusuf and Basuki Rachmat came to visit. They were the Jakarta Commander, the Minister of Industry and the Minister for Veteran Affairs, respectively. With the city brought to a standstill, President Soekarno summoned party leaders to Merdeka Palace on 10 March for a tongue-lashing session. By then, the president was advised that unidentified troops had surrounded the palace and he abruptly left by helicopter for Bogor Palace. President Soekarno had left with Soebandrio and Chaerul Saleh. The three generals wanted to go to Bogor Palace to meet President Soekarno and their visit that day was to find out whether General Soeharto had any message to relay to the president. General Soeharto only sent his regards and asked them to inform the president that he was ill, but to assure the president that he would try his best to control the situation.

The three generals proceeded to Bogor Palace and they returned the same evening. They reported the outcome of the meeting to General Soeharto. It was the birth of the famous Supersemar, the document that transferred presidential power from President Soekarno to General Soeharto. The original Supersemar document is missing to date and has since become the centre of debate as it related to the validity of the transfer. The speculation was whether President Soekarno had dictated the draft or whether the generals had prepared one and forced him to sign it. Knowing President Soekarno's unquestionable courage and fiery temperament, it is very hard to believe that he was willing to give in, even at gunpoint, as a few have suggested. President Soekarno would rather have died than give in. It is highly improbable that the generals could have bullied a man who had spent most of his youth in prison. It had to have been his choice as a statesman to sign Supersemar in good faith.

General Amir Machmud's own account read that when the generals arrived, President Soekarno was asleep. Awakened by his adjutant, Sabur, the president wanted to find out how the situation had developed. The generals convinced him that it would be better for the nation if the president agreed to govern jointly with General Soeharto. After that, the wording of Supersemar was prepared. When it was finished, President Soekarno called the member of the Presidium and it was read out.

The resolution primarily involved three main issues. First, General Soeharto, as Minister and Chief of Army, was to take necessary steps and action in governing and to ensure the personal safety and dignity of the president. Second, General Soeharto was to coordinate the execution of these tasks with the other Chief of Armed Forces. Third, General Soeharto was to report on and be accountable for all the above actions. General Soeharto was in Kostrad to receive commanders from the regions. After careful reading, the first decision General Soeharto had in mind was to ban PKI. Sudharmono and Moerdiono were asked to prepare the draft late that night using Supersemar as the legal basis. Later, Supersemar was used to execute several more changes. From then on, President Soekarno no longer signed the subsequent orders. General Soeharto's signature on behalf of the president emerged although President Soekarno's full title of "President/Supreme Commander/Revolution Leader/Mandatory of the People's Assembly" remained. The most important decision made under this power was on 12 March 1966, when PKI and its affiliations were outlawed.

President Soekarno soon gave an address to the highest ranks of the military forces in Merdeka Palace:

> I am a part of the revolution. I am also the Supreme Commander of the Armed Forces. The Armed Forces are tools for the revolution. Our understanding of a revolution is a process, a social political process that will take years to finish. And our target is to abolish feudalism. Now we are in political conflict with different groups; between Nahdlatul Ulama (Muslim) and PNI (Nationalist Party). Even among the armed forces there are political differences, which is natural. The demonstrations to include small children are in fact organised or supported by neocolonialist forces such as the CIA to topple the government. And at this moment my leadership is being tested.

The same day, General Soeharto persuaded businessmen to help save the economy. The next day, he gave another announcement for the state's apparatus to keep the government functioning. The Army Parachute Commando Regiment (RPKAD) staged a victory parade through the streets of Jakarta on 13 March, as General Soeharto formally banned PKI. On 14 March, strong appeals were made to leaders, cadres and activists of PKI and its affiliates to report to the authorities. Directives had been issued prohibiting political parties from taking in the former communists as members. Strong measures would be taken against those who acted to the contrary. Next, active PKI members were exiled to remote places, the famous one being Pulau Buru.

On 18 March, they announced names of old ministers who had strong indications of their involvement in G30S. Fifteen had been taken into custody; the most important and well-known were Soebandrio and Chaerul Saleh. The hardest attack was against Soebandrio, as many were aware he had been Soekarno's evil advisor. Nicknamed "Durno" (bad and hated *wayang* character), his effigy was burnt by students and schoolchildren. A presidium with Sultan Hamengkubuwono IX, Adam Malik, Roeslan Abdulgani, Idham Chalid, J Leimina and General Soeharto as members was created. They each held the position of Deputy Prime Minister. In this composition, Sultan Hamengkubuwono, Adam Malik and Soeharto represented the new team, while Roeslan Abdulgani, Idham Chalid and Leimina epitomised President Soekarno's old regime. Thus, the transition was a compromise between the old and the new government. The reformed Dwikora Cabinet announced on 27 March 1966 was only the first step and not the final one that could be attained. This was a typical Indonesian solution in making a compromise and taking the middle road. General Nasution was appointed Minister/Deputy Supreme Commander to crush Malaysia (Wapangsar KOGAM).

The Islamic Students' Association (HMI) declared that they did not want President Soekarno to be replaced in an unconstitutional way. HMI was well aware that when President Soekarno had been at the peak of his power, he never wanted to stop HMI's existence. Instead, President Soekarno had asked Roeslan Abdulgani to guide HMI so that HMI could have a more progressive political outlook. The president thought of HMI not only as Islamic intellectualism, but perceived them as having the potential to possess considerable nationalist spirit. It had been President Soekarno's long-held dream to have an amalgamation of Islam and nationalism in the country. A seasoned politician, President Soekarno did not want to outlaw HMI just for the political consumption of other political groups. General Soeharto, too, had no intention of taking President Soekarno's power in an unconstitutional way.

The position of President Soekarno had weakened, even though there were students and schoolchildren in early 1966 who had formed *Barisan Pendukung Soekarno* for those still loyal to his leadership. This took place from October 1965 to mid-1966. Nevertheless, in his speeches, the president was still very forceful in his accusation that there had been an attempt of a "constitutional" *coup d'etat* backed by the CIA. It was during this time that a finger had been pointed, at least in silence, to General Soeharto being possibly amongst those who had wanted to unseat the president from his legal post. General Soeharto had been appointed as Minister and Commander of the Army by then. In close coordination with the Navy Commander, Muljadi, Air Force Commander, Rusmin Nurjadin and the Police Chief, Sutjipto Judodihardjo, he had performed the day-to-day management of the country. As the wheel had turned full circle, almost all political parties, the media and the students were suspicious about the involvement of President Soekarno in G30S. They blamed President Soekarno for the country's declining moral values and economic catastrophe.

In an extraordinary meeting on 22 June 1966, the Provisional Consultative People's Assembly (MPRS) wanted to ask President Soekarno to provide accountability. However, General Soeharto warned the Assembly not to make a drastic decision. He felt that in the political sphere, this would only create physical conflict if the army was involved. Such a scenario would endanger national life and only benefit the former communist party, whose spirit was still very much alive even though the PKI had been officially banned. General Soeharto said, "Let it not be that our generation is blamed by the next one because of the wrong treatment of a patriotic leader." General Nasution was elected as the Chairman of MPRS. The MPRS was the only body that could remove a president, hence, by naming General Nasution as its Chairman, civilians felt that the military really wanted to push President Soekarno out.

In the meantime, President Soekarno emphasised his plea that Indonesia needed to be independent in politics, culture and economics. "The crown of independence is the ability to stand on one's own feet," he said. The speech was known as *Nawaksara*, meaning "nine words" in Sanskrit. However, the MPRS rejected the speech he read on 22 June 1966. In his speeches on 17 August 1966 and 5 October 1966, the president condemned G30S. In addition, he demanded that those in the wrong be punished. He also stated the need to establish Extraordinary Military Tribunal or Mahmilub (Mahkamah Militer Luar Biasa). Led by Panji Suroso, for the first time, the MPRS disagreed with President Soekarno. Based on its Decision No XVIII/MPRS/1966, the MPRS resolution outlawed PKI and proclaimed the party illegal, including the teachings of communism/Marxism, Leninism. Soon, President Soekarno's titles of "The Big Leader of Revolution" and "President for Life" were declared to be of no legal basis. The meetings between the armed forces and members of the Presidium Cabinet from December 1966 until the beginning of January 1967 were continually tense.

The MPRS decided that general elections were to take place on 5 July 1966, and until then, President Soekarno would remain the lawful president, but the students kept up their pressure for President Soekarno to resign. General Soeharto tried to calm them down and said, "In Bung Karno's case, it is not a matter of for or against. We should stand on justice." On 28 July 1966, General Soeharto's rank was promoted to full general. The Cabinet formed after the MPRS meeting was called *Ampera* and General Soeharto became Chief of the Presidium. However, the students' demands for a total change did not stop. Again, General Soeharto reminded them that President Soekarno was still the lawful president in line with that written in the 1945 Constitution. Furthermore, he said that the people should keep their high regard for President Soekarno. General Soeharto did not want to push President Soekarno out from the presidency by force, as many had wanted him to do. He also refused to bring President Soekarno into the Extraordinary Military Tribunal. In his speech of *Isra Mi'raj*, General Soeharto convinced the audience: "After I tried to analyse the president's speeches on 17 August, 5 October and other occasions, I have come to the conclusion that the president did condemn G30S."

In June 1966, Adam Malik reached a tentative agreement to call off the confrontation with Malaysia. This symbolised a complete turnaround from being anti-West to being friendly with the Americans and European nations. The first trial against the former Minister of Central Bank, Jusuf Muda Dalam opened on 30 August 1966. During the trial, the issue of Dana Revolusi or Funds of Revolution was raised. Jusuf Muda Dalam said he was ordered to set up this fund by President Soekarno to finance prestigious projects. Monumen Nasional was identified as one of those. The funds were supposedly collected from trades that were out of the government's control. They came from private entrepreneurs who were asked to contribute in exchange for profitable import licenses. A similar method was later used by President Soeharto when he asked conglomerates to give contributions to his foundations. General Soeharto, in his meeting with the Minister of Justice and other high-ranking figures, declared that investigations would have to be carried out. The outcome provided no real evidence of *Dana Revolusi*. He warned that he would not tolerate slander and libel, especially towards the Head of State.

BERKELEY MAFIA

As the protests continued, intellectuals, politicians and soldiers who sought the New Order came together at a seminar to discuss the economic strategy. It was held in the University of Indonesia and lasted for several days. Participants included the American-educated economists Widjojo Nitisastro, Emil Salim, Moh Sadli, Ali Wardhana and Subroto and the Dutch-educated Radius Prawiro, as well as the social scientists Selo Soemardjan and Fuad Hassan. Prominent figures such as Sultan Hamengkubuwono IX, Adam Malik and Nasution were also there. Inflation had reached 500 per cent in 1965; the price of rice had gone up by 900 per cent. The national budget had a deficit of 300 per cent. This meant that almost all of the country's revenue would be used to pay the outstanding foreign debt by the end of 1966.

In August 1966, the army conducted a seminar in Bandung which gave birth to the name of "New Order". A message from General Soeharto was read out:

> The New Order would be more pragmatic and realistic without leaving out the ideals of freedom. The New Order wants to put our national interest in the driving seat while continuing with our ideology to fight against colonialism and imperialism. The New Order is not against a strong leadership and government; to the contrary, it is

the intention to have this characteristic in this transitional period and development. The New Order wants to implement democracy in economy. It is an order to achieve a social, political, economic and cultural society with Pancasila and Belief in God Almighty, as our moral values.

Those were the words in General Soeharto's speech. One of the crucial efforts was to get help from abroad. Firstly, the country had to pay its external debts and then add new ones. There were negotiations to be done with the Western countries, followed by the Eastern countries. General Soeharto entrusted economic affairs to the experts in restoring the country's relations with the Western powers. Ali Moertopo introduced the new leadership's goals and tapped the desperately needed funds from overseas Chinese in Singapore, Hong Kong and Taiwan. Sultan Hamengkubuwono, who was the new economic coordinator, announced on 12 April 1966 that the country expected to collect a total of US$430 million in foreign exchange. The debt service obligation that year alone was US$530 million. The largest portion of the international debt was US$2.358 million, to China, USSR and its allies. The most important step was clearly the need to delay repayments and to reschedule the debts. On the other hand, new credit had to be found to cover the vital imports. Adam Malik flew to Moscow and other East European countries. Other senior officials had to negotiate with the Western lenders.

In June 1966, the International Monetary Fund (IMF) delegation arrived in Jakarta to set up an office in the Central Bank. Their main task was to assess Indonesia's foreign exchange position. Late in September that year, Sultan Hamengkubuwono went to Tokyo and met with the non-communist creditors. Sultan Hamengkubuwono explained the government strategy for economic recovery. On his return, Sultan Hamengkubuwono announced a drastic stabilisation policy. Priority was given to curb inflation, which, for the whole of 1966, reached a peak of 640 per cent. By late October, the government managed to secure commitments of new credit totalling some US$174 million.

On 3 October 1966, less than seven months in office and following weeks of intensive preparation, the government stabilisation programme was launched. It was the first major set of economic policies. The public was at best hopeful but skeptical. The economic team was not convinced that the measures they had decided to take up would work. It was a gamble at best as

Radius wrote, "The policies were created with equal measures of science and faith." In December 1966, the People's Representative Council (DPR) ratified the first budget of the new government. The 1967 budget was a balanced budget, which in short meant that government expenditure had to be restricted in relation to its revenue. In taking such a course of action, the government was hopeful that the deficit could be eliminated. The government also measured foreign aid as revenue and not as new debt. In reality, the government would have placed anything beyond the collection of taxes (for example, foreign aid and revenue from oil and state-owned enterprises) into their budget.

In February 1967, Indonesia held a more formal meeting with the Western and Japanese creditors and potential new lenders in Amsterdam. It was attended by delegations from Australia, Belgium, France, West Germany, Italy, Japan, the Netherlands, the United Kingdom and the USA. Observers were from Canada, New Zealand, Norway and Switzerland. International agencies such as the IMF were also present, including the World Bank (IBRD), the United Nations Development Programmes, the Organisation for Economic Co-operation and Development and the Asian Development Bank. The IMF delegation presented a report on Indonesia's economic potential to support her request for aid totalling US$200 million in 1967. However, it was not until a second Inter-Governmental Group on Indonesia (IGGI) meeting in June that the request was fully agreed to, with the USA and Japan each meeting one-third of the total amount.

In the beginning, the foreign aid rendered was very much in the nature of an emergency affair. It only dealt with essential imports including consumer goods, raw materials and equipment required for building domestic industries. With eventual rescheduling of the debts and together with stable economic conditions, the foreign aid sought became more geared towards a long-term development strategy instead of economic first-aid. However, the government's heavy reliance on foreign aid became a persistent and intensely controversial issue throughout Soeharto's tenure as president.

Up to that point in time, there were four local bourgeoisie in Indonesian society. First, there were the traditional indigenous capitalists or petty capitalists as found mainly in petty trade or commodity production, such as the type of business that my grandfather had in Kampung Plampitan in the early part of 1900. Second, there were the Chinese traders, retailers, commodity producers and those engaged in small-scale service industries. In the past, the Dutch considered these groups the chosen ones as they received privileges unknown to the indigenous people. Third, there were the medium to large-scale indigenous groups, with political connections and often doing business in partnership with Chinese capital. Finally, there were the Chinese capitalists who ran businesses in the medium and large-scale sectors, with access to state resources and, in many cases, receiving overseas finance. The latter group, in the years to come, would become conglomerates. This was the group that later became one of the most serious reasons for President Soeharto's downfall.

ENDNOTES

1   President Soekarno's speech delivered on Army Day, 5 October 1950. This quote is extracted from the book *Bung Karno dan ABRI, Kumpulan pidato Bung Karno di hadapan ABRI 1950–1966* (CV Haji Masagung, Jakarta 1989).

2   The abbreviated name was later changed to Seskoad.

3   Presidential bodyguards who were chosen from the very best members of the Armed Forces during President Soekarno's regime.

Chapter 2

BUILDING THE NATION

The main thing is, that one has a soul
that loves truth and that accepts it
where it is to be found.
— Johann Wolfgang von Goethe

President Soekarno's contribution to Indonesia's freedom is considered by many to be an indisputable fact, and similarly President Soeharto's role in transforming Indonesia in terms of the country's economic development and industrialisation. The latter was aware that 85 per cent of the Indonesian people still depended on the cultivation of the land to grow rice, and this knowledge was the key to his success. He is perceived by some to have been the right man in the right place at the right time, and this summarises one view of how General Soeharto came to power and succeeded in keeping it for three decades, which many do not believe was entirely the result of an accident. In the case of President Soeharto, it was augmented by his practical mind. From the start, President Soeharto was aware of the risks if he took drastic action against President Soekarno, which would not have helped the country's unity. Hence, he had to find an equilibrium, and the country could move forward only if such an equilibrium was found and maintained.

The first move was to appoint economic experts to take stock of the country's immense problems and to propose a strategy for managing these problems. As in a war situation, they had to understand the urgency of the situation facing the country. This sense of crisis was the key to success in the implementation of their economic policies. President Soeharto knew that time was a luxury they could not afford to waste. Indonesia was on the brink of disaster and he needed the economic team's help in assessing the country's strengths and weaknesses before embarking on a strategy. They needed to analyse risks in order to take the next step forward. The team concluded that rice cultivation was the nation's lifeline as the majority of the population was involved in farming. Rice was the country's main staple food, yet the system used in rice growing was outdated. The state apparatus and policies supporting the economy were dilapidated, but luck was on President Soeharto's side: the oil bonanza and the windfall profit from oil revenue in the early 1970s enabled him to improve agriculture in the country.

PUSHED TO THE TOP

Political developments took place very quickly. Pressure came from political parties, students and the armed forces, urging him to take the lead. He said, "In the midst of conflict, I was pushed to step forward. There were groups who wanted to change our leadership immediately. Some tried to force me to take over but I rejected them." His reply to this latter group: "If this is the only way, then it is better for me to withdraw. This is not the right way. To take over a government through military force would create instability and it would not last for long. I do not want to leave a legacy of having taken over the government through military means. It has never occurred to me to have a *coup d'etat*. This will not be successful. If that is what you want, please go ahead but I will not be involved." Those were his words, but not everyone believed him and many have accused him of orchestrating a *coup*.

Why did President Soekarno refuse to outlaw PKI? My father said that as far as PKI was concerned, President Soekarno had been overconfident. My father was quoted in recounting what Bung Karno had said:[1]

> I am convinced PKI can be tuned as a nationalist group. What is the meaning of *Nasakom*? Nationalism should not refer only to nationalism that uses incense. Religion does not mean that Indonesia has to be an Islamic state, which is what Kartosuwiryo had wanted Indonesia to be. Communism should not be what Muso had in mind. Indonesian communism should respect and honour religion and our nationalism.

President Soekarno even introduced Aidit, Chairman of PKI, to then US President Ike Eisenhower in 1957, during his state visit to Washington DC and he jokingly said, "Aidit is a good communist since he believes in Pancasila."

In fact, up to the time of his downfall, President Soekarno had gone through three rounds of constitutional changes. The 1945 Constitution, announced on 18 August 1945, consisted of 37 articles. Some consider this Constitution to have given too much power to the president. Several months later, a decree was announced for a change of direction to a parliamentary system. In 1949, following negotiations with the Dutch, a Federal Constitution was drafted.[2] A year later, another new version came into being. The 1950 Constitution consisted of 146 articles and appeared to contain comprehensive individual freedom. The role of the president, for the most part, was reduced to a ceremonial one. Nevertheless, it lasted only until 1959, when President Soekarno decreed the reinstatement of the 1945 Constitution.

What was the general observer's opinion of General Soeharto at that stage? General Soeharto was barely on the same level as the six generals who had been killed. Colonel Latief insisted that General Soeharto had his feet in two camps, one in Dewan Jenderal and the other in G30S. Professor Wertheim, a Dutch scholar from Leiden University in the Netherlands, viewed the whole episode as a detective story. He questioned General Soeharto's role from 1965 and beyond. He pointed to General Soeharto's association with Colonel Untung and General Soepardjo, both of whom held key roles in the drama of G30S. Professor Wertheim has also questioned General Soeharto's relationship with Colonel Latief before G30S. Most importantly, he questioned why General Soeharto was not captured like the other high-ranking officers. Why was the Kostrad headquarters left alone while the buildings nearby were taken under Colonel Untung's control? Further, he raised doubts over General Soeharto's efficiency and tactical foresight. General Soeharto's quick decision to assume temporary command of the army and the trust he obtained from the other key commanders was another uncertain issue. Why did General Soeharto refuse when President Soekarno named General Pranoto as the national caretaker? All of these areas were considered to be unclear. Professor Wertheim suspected that Ali Moertopo and Soedjono Hoemardhani were the men behind the scenes as the tragedy was being played out.

Observers have a right to express their evaluations and analyses, as is required by their profession. However, such evaluations and analyses must be based on evidence, not just plainly on theory and expectations. In real life, friendships and even family relationships can often change dramatically. The fact that Colonel Latief was once close to General Soeharto did not guarantee his friendship for life. Once, when my father was the Minister of Foreign Affairs, he had been impressed with Soebandrio's skills and intelligence, and had invited him to take the position of Secretary General in the Ministry of Foreign Affairs. Soon thereafter, Soebandrio replaced him as the Foreign

Minister and took over his position as one of President Soekarno's closest contacts. Soebandrio then became my father's strongest adversary. Yet, by the time Soebandrio was 80 years old and had been in prison for 30 years, my father started a motion for him to be officially pardoned. President Soeharto granted Soebandrio amnesty at Ramadan in 1996, but rejected Colonel Latief's appeal. These are examples of how relationships can change in politics. If General Soeharto had wanted to take over President Soekarno's power, it was unlikely that he would have waited for such a long time. As a strong military commander, he could have easily joined the rebels such as the Darul Islam/Tentara Islam Indonesia (DI/TII), a movement of disgruntled soldiers in South Sulawesi led by Colonel Kahar Muzakkar, which violently fought for an Islamic state in the 1950s. Instead, he carried out President Soekarno's order to crush the rebellion.

Another Dutch scholar, Professor (Dr) Antonie CA Dake concluded, during the launch of his book, *Sukarno Files. Berkas-berkas Sukarno 1965-1967* in November 2005, that President Soekarno was the one behind the communists as he allowed G30S to take place. This accusation is now being contested by Soekarno's youngest daughter, Sukmawati. President Soekarno was perceived as leaning too much towards the Russian/Peking axis by the West. President Soekarno's fear of the return of neo-colonialism was understandable. During the first few months of the country's independence, defectors of the Dutch troops had supported a federalist rebellion. The unrelenting Dutch presence in West Irian was viewed as interference in the country's domestic affairs. Republik Maluku Selatan (RMS) or Republic of South Moluccas received help from the West. In 1958, the US Seventh Fleet, which was to evacuate oil workers and their families from Sumatra, was seen as a cover for providing support to the Revolutionary Government of the Republic of Indonesia (PRRI). Such operations were believed to be sufficient proof that the United States had supplied arms to the rebels. Finally, the shooting down of an American pilot near Ambon in May 1958 and the recovery of weapons sent by and made in the United States proved beyond doubt that indeed, the United States had provided backing to the rebellion in Sulawesi. President Soekarno was an intelligent person and there was no need for him to initiate a *coup* as he was in total control. More importantly, President Soekarno did not have the slightest intention of breaking the country he had helped to set free.

Sulastomo, the chairman of Himpunan Mahasiswa Islam (HMI) or the Islamic Students' Association, wrote that there were five analyses of this episode. First, G30S was the outcome of internal fighting within the army. Second, it was a *coup* by General Soeharto to topple President Soekarno. Third, President Soekarno had been the mastermind behind the whole tragedy. Fourth, it had been a conspiracy between the chairman of PKI, Aidit, President Soekarno and Mao Tse Tung. Fifth, it was a foreign conspiracy by the West against President Soekarno.

Indonesia had been caught up in the Cold War. The capitalist countries had been worried that Indonesia would lean towards communism. The communists wanted Indonesia to be within their sphere. President Soekarno, a true nationalist, did not want the country to be a puppet of these two opposing forces, but he was also a first-class statesman who valued the people's choice. It had been possible for PKI to become a major force only because the country's economic situation was so bad. General Soeharto, with his nationalistic and pragmatic approach, knew that PKI was up to no good. It only wanted to take advantage of the Cold War situation and make Indonesia a communist country. Both President Soekarno and President Soeharto strongly believed that Pancasila was the only way to unite the multi-racial and multi-faith Indonesian society. Hence, if PKI won, the sacrifices of the pioneers of Indonesia's independence would have been for nothing and the country would have fallen apart.

On 10 January 1967, President Soekarno clarified in writing the speech he had delivered on 22 June 1966, entitled *Nawaksara*. He demanded that a judicial body should conduct investigations on his involvement or knowledge of G30S. Again, the MPRS rejected it. In the early stages of the transferring of power, the battle of wits between President Soekarno and General Soeharto was intense. At that stage, General Soeharto became the rallying point of groups who nursed a silent opposition against President Soekarno, seen as part of the Old Order. Those against President Soekarno were the more right-wing elements of the armed forces, particularly officers of the Siliwangi Division of West Java. They had been strongly influenced by the ideas of the banned Partai Sosialis Indonesia (PSI) or the Indonesian Socialist Party, the Army and Command School's staff in Bandung and the ex-Siliwangi officer, General Kemal Idris, who had been brought down from North Sumatra to replace General Soeharto's position in Kostrad. The Resimen Para Komando Angkatan Darat (RPKAD) or the Army Parachute Commando Regiment remained as the movement spearheaded by General Soeharto's forces around Jakarta. The month of February 1967 was a tense period full of tragedy. President Soekarno, a great leader in the eyes of many, became the target of allegations for causing the country's failure and even corruption. A few students even called him a traitor. To me, it did not seem right that the younger generation who had not been present during their fight for freedom should accuse President Soekarno of being a traitor. I felt that the fact that he chose to stay in Indonesia after he had fallen from power and "swallowed" the insults hurled at him was a proof of his patriotism.

In this context, it is useful to look into the nature of the relationships between the country's leaders. President Soekarno and General Nasution's relationship had often blown hot and cold. Born in December 1918, General Nasution was one of Bung Karno's early supporters, but he later came to think of President Soekarno as being much too involved when an internal struggle took place within the army in 1952. General Nasution was behind the demonstration that took place at the Parliament Building (DPR) and which proceeded to the Palace on 17 October 1952. The demonstrators, arguing that Members of Parliament were not representing the true ideals of the people, demanded that President Soekarno should dissolve Parliament and requested for an election. President Soekarno refused, thus creating a split in the army. General Nasution was then the Army Chief of Staff and as a reprimand, he was dismissed from service. Yet, in 1955, immediately after the PRRI-Permesta situation took place, General Nasution was reappointed as the Army Chief of Staff. He was even asked by President Soekarno to join the Cabinet in the late 1950s. However, the relationship soured again, as General Nasution felt that President Soekarno had given too many chances to PKI in the 1960s. In fact, General Nasution was one of the supporters of the New Order after he survived the G30S killings. He was the chairman of the Majelis Permusyawaratan Rakyat Sementara (MPRS) or the Provisional People's Consultative Assembly when they made the decision to take President Soekarno's power away. Yet, General Nasution once said to an American journalist, "Bung Karno had already spent his time in prison when I did not even understand what freedom was all about."

General Nasution's relationship with President Soeharto also went through the same ups and downs. He was against the smuggling activity going on in Semarang under General Soeharto and later he signed the petition *Petisi 50*.[3] He was unhappy that his original concept of the *Dwi Fungsi* of ABRI, the dual function of the armed forces, was misused during the New Order. As he signed *Petisi 50*, however, he became an outcast in the New Order. Nevertheless, President Soeharto made him a Five-Star General before he passed away in 2000. These events in the country's history provide an important lesson for the younger generation of Indonesians—that in politics, there is nothing permanent but self-interest; that a friend can be an enemy and an enemy can be a friend.

On 7 February 1967, the president sent a letter through Hardi SH, a nationalist figure, to General Soeharto. In President Soeharto's biography,[4] it was written that there had been two letters. One contained a job assignment and the other was personal in nature. The personal note elaborated on the duty assigned in Supersemar. There was a plan for President Soekarno to explain Supersemar to the MPRS. Most importantly, General Soeharto had to consult with him so that his rights and duties could be carried out in the best possible way. In fact, at that time, some political leaders had pleaded with him to replace President Soekarno. General Soeharto replied that he had no interest to be the president. He argued that he had no qualifications to hold the highest position in the country. Nevertheless, the pressure continued.

Finally, General Soeharto gave in on the assurance that it was to be on a trial basis. He wanted to start as an acting president first. A compromise was reached that he would be the acting president for one year and should he fail within the year, another candidate would be selected. General Soeharto relied on his philosophy of "*alon-alon asal kelakon*" or "slowly but surely". This did not refer to moving slowly at all times, but to take action in well-calculated stages. For him, the contrary would be "*cepat-cepat, tetapi kelewat*" or "fast but merely passing by", in short, "things done quickly would turn out to be a mistake". He sought Ibu Tien's support at times like this. He wrote that no matter what happened, any decision he made would have a big impact on his family. Ibu Tien gave her concurrence, which for him was very important. He needed her full support in order to carry the huge responsibility.

On 10 February 1967, General Soeharto met President Soekarno to discuss the best way to resolve the transfer of power. It was not until 20 February that President Soekarno, with support from the Commander of the Armed Forces, except the Army which had decided not to give any opinion on the matter and stayed neutral, agreed to transfer his power to General Soeharto. On 22 February 1967, an announcement was read out to the effect that, as the President of the Republic of Indonesia and as mandated by the MPRS, President Soekarno would transfer his power to General Soeharto. This was in line with the spirit of the MPR and within the context of the 1945 Constitution. As mandated, General Soeharto was to provide the president with reports if deemed necessary. He also pleaded with the nation to intensify its efforts to unify. After that, the outgoing president watched a *wayang* performance while Acting President Soeharto started to take stock of the heavy burden on his shoulders. In retrospect, the country had been fortunate that the political conflict was resolved in an amicable manner without any occurrence of a civil war.

On 8 March 1967, as he left to attend the MPRS meeting, President Soeharto's mind was focused on the three wisdoms of "*ojo kagetan, ojo gumunan, ojo dumeh*" or "do not be troubled (startled or shocked), do not be surprised and do not be arrogant"—three basic notions he learnt a long time ago in Kemusuk. He even admitted to me that he always did and still does pray for God's guidance especially when he is in despair or comes face to face with difficulties. He believes that there is never a need to be surprised with any turn of events as everything is determined by God's will. The MPRS meeting was very tense that fateful day. It had been critical not only for him personally but also crucial for the survival of the country. President Soeharto admitted that, as usual, he did not show his emotions. He only spoke of facts and tried to choose words that would not lead to public debates. He announced that there had been no indication of President Soekarno's knowledge of, and more so involvement with, G30S. Further, he said that there were two groups within the New Order, one rational and one irrational. The rational group comprised those who understood and respected President Soekarno for what he had done for the country's freedom, for Pancasila and his role in proclaiming Indonesia's independence. Those who were irrational were also there within the armed forces. He did not want the irrational ones to turn to the Old Order. This would happen if he disappointed them.

After tough debating, the MPRS concluded that President Soekarno's accountability could not be accepted. Consequently, President Soekarno was no longer able to carry out the duties as outlined in the Constitution. The MPRS terminated President Soekarno's power and transferred it to Acting President Soeharto. The MPRS decided to revoke his title of "*Pemimpin Besar Revolusi*" or "The Great Revolutionary Leader" and appointed President Soeharto as Acting President on 12 March 1967. The politics manifesto was replaced by the Broad Outlines of State Policy (GBHN). Another MPRS resolution was for the Acting President to make a decision about legal judgment on private citizen Dr Ir Soekarno. It had not been an easy situation for the newly appointed Acting President as his mind turned to President Soekarno. For him, whatever the situation, Bung Karno was an extraordinary man with huge charisma. Bung Karno was a true statesman. The Acting President realised that due to his strong principles, Bung Karno did not want to budge from his opinion on the Indonesian communist party. A true leader would pay for his values with his life. For other human beings, this would be perceived as stubbornness. He was certain that Bung Karno had no bad intentions in letting the PKI develop, but it had not been his intention to allow PKI to make Indonesia a communist state; PKI had taken advantage of Bung Karno's good intentions.

By then, Acting President Soeharto had decided to use "*ilmu katon*" in his leadership. *Katon* is that which is seen/visible. It refers to what is happening around us and for us to learn from it. Soon after, he gave his message through the radio and television. He also asked a team of doctors to oversee President Soekarno's state of health. From that time on, the government also did not allow President Soekarno to be involved in political affairs until the next general elections took place. This verdict was viewed as a "political assassination"; after all, what is a president without power? The Acting President's first job was to deal with the government apparatus and the armed forces. He needed the continuity and the military's strong support. The most important thing was for the political groups to stop bickering. Hence, he pleaded for the political parties to accept Pancasila as a whole. In May 1967, he made up his mind on how to treat President Soekarno. President Soekarno no longer kept his title as Head of State, President of the Republic of Indonesia and Chief of the Armed Forces. He could no longer use the presidential flag, but he was still allowed to wear his uniform with all the medals when attending official or government events. In reality, this treatment was intended for retired Heads of State.

The country's standing in the international arena was achieved by following a pragmatic route. In August 1967, the Association of South-east Asian Nations (ASEAN) was formed through the Bangkok Declaration. Jakarta was the chosen site for the office of the secretariat. In September of that year, the Acting President made changes to the Chief of the Armed Forces who no longer sat as a Cabinet Minister but was accountable to him in his position as Minister of Defense and Security. Indonesia's relations with the People's Republic of China worsened and the decision was made to close the embassy in China in October 1967. The Acting President's duties were those outlined by the MPRS. For this, he had the prerogative to choose ministers. For him, qualifications would be the most important criteria in selecting his ministers. He took into account any backing from political parties or social forces, but this would have been the last consideration in selecting a minister. This was in total contrast to the Cabinets which were to come after him. Nowadays, the first and foremost consideration would be one's backing from political parties. Perhaps that was the reason why President Soeharto took a military approach. He felt more comfortable in his own group. He knew that the general elections would not be able to take place on 5 July 1968 as a decision had not been made about the ruling for the elections. Finally, everyone agreed that the elections would have to be postponed. His mandate as Acting President would expire on 5 July 1968, but for him, it did not really matter, as an acting president would have to remain in this position. In fact, he was content, as this would provide him with time and opportunity to learn the ropes.

As Acting President, he met with President Soekarno on several occasions. He genuinely wished that President Soekarno would agree to outlaw PKI and openly condemn G30S, but the latter steadfastly refused and this led the way for Acting President Soeharto to forge his own path in resolving the situation. The students' protests did not stop. He had called them and explained at length that changes had to be made in a constitutional way. He agreed that from that time on, the students representation in Parliament would no longer be via appointment through the president's privilege. The students' representation in Parliament would be through the newly formed Partai Karya Pembangunan.

The democracy that was to be pursued was the next important issue to be confronted. There were few models available, none of which could be applied or imitated blindly. The country needed to find one that would guarantee national stability in order to commence its development plan. Democracy Pancasila was viewed as the best choice. Acting President Soeharto followed President Soekarno's stand against capitalism, feudalism, dictatorship, colonialism and imperialism. In addition, poverty, backwardness, conflict and extortion were to be eradicated. On 27 March 1968 he left an MPRS meeting at almost midnight. That day, he had been appointed to the full presidency. It had been a long journey for a humble man from Kemusuk.

By this time, former president Soekarno had given in graciously. President Soeharto was pleased to read congratulatory notes from Bung Karno, who stayed in Bogor Palace. Bung Karno did not wish to be president any more and, if allowed, wanted to move to his private house in Bogor. The new president gave his consent. In July 1968, amidst debates on whether he had been a hero or traitor, Bung Karno left Bogor Palace. The Legion of Veterans declared Bung Karno a non-member. The football game to compete for the Soekarno Cup was discontinued. Critics claimed that if President Soekarno had used the vociferous slogans of Guided Democracy, President Soeharto came to replace them with "stabilisation, rehabilitation and dynamic stability". President Soeharto had to use a strong hand as he wields his authority. He had to walk a tightrope, knowing that his predecessor was a very well-loved and respected leader. He knew that Bung Karno had been left out in the cold by some. He was aware of those who were truly devoted to as well as those who had deserted the former president. That was the main reason he had to take a moderate path in his dealings with Bung Karno: he had to satisfy two different camps—one against Bung Karno and which wanted to prosecute him, and one which accused President Soeharto himself of being the mastermind of the *coup*. The compromise reached had been to remove his predecessor from the political arena. At the same time, he wanted to maintain Bung Karno's dignity as a national leader. Both had been gentlemen of commendable behaviour during the transfer of power. In spite of everything that had taken place, in public, they followed the old traditional etiquette of politeness and decency.

A FAMILY MAN

President Soeharto epitomised everything that was good about the country's character and almost everyone developed a great rapport with him. He was always hospitable, kind, polite, generous, caring, gallant and respectful both of his elders and his subordinates. He was a good Muslim, but very tolerant of all faiths. His handsome and typical Javanese features, with soft brown eyes and simple dressing, delighted the people. He lived with a modest wife—Ibu Tien portrayed nothing more than a similar simplicity. They refused to make Merdeka Palace their private residence and moved from Jalan Haji Agus Salim No 98 to Jalan Cendana in the suburb of Menteng, where they have lived since. The house itself was not a picture of luxury as was normal amongst the homes of the rich.

One of the main reasons for the move was security. There was a high-rise building behind Haji Agus Salim No 98. Merdeka Palace had not been the president's choice because he wanted his children to have freedom. In his biography, he claimed that he had never spoilt his children and had trained them to be humble. On the issue of humility, he had been right. He remembered the hardship of his early life which led him to think of others less fortunate, and he imparted this to his children as well. One of the problems he faced was having less time with them as he took up the presidency, a common problem faced by many famous parents. This might have made it easier for opportunists to influence his children negatively.

Every morning, he would wake up around the same time, between 4.30 to 5am, have a cup of coffee and read the papers left on his desk. On regular days, after a short break with his family, he would read again until 7pm, and on some days until past midnight. To keep fit, he played golf three times a week. There were times for family gatherings, such as *selamatan* for birthdays and the like. On holidays, he liked to go fishing. He spent time in Tapos, West Java, where crossbreeding of cows from Australian and local stock took place. He liked to cook and kept up this hobby during the first years of his presidency. Before he became president, he visited the family graveyard regularly but was not able to continue doing so. He asked his relatives to undertake the rituals on his behalf. He and Ibu Tien decided that all gifts he received as president would be recorded and kept in a museum, as the residence in Jalan Cendana was too small to keep them.

The military budget was insignificant and not sufficient to build a strong defence for the country, nor to make a career in the armed forces attractive. As the defence budget was minimal, it hardly created a serious political issue for President Soekarno. When President Soeharto came to power, it became the most criticised and sore point of his government. However, the military and bureaucrats welcomed the New Order, as it was in line with the paternalistic ways and populist elements in the country's culture, which served their interests. It also complied with the Javanese principles of compassion and submission. Under President Soeharto, the Indonesian bureaucracy managed everything from the production of soap to the running of steel mills.

This culture could be traced back to the time of the Hindu Mataram kingdom, when the general pace of growth in such a system follows in the wake of the central authority: when the central power is strong, the local bureaucracy acts as a hand to that power; when the central power is in the decline, there is great political freedom for the bureaucracy to become self-ruling. In the village sphere, too, the function of a leader is very much to dominate and rule. A strong leader's role is to create unity and move the society forward.

President Soeharto took up the mantle of leadership much in the same way as an eldest son would have done so in a family. This was how he treated his subordinates. The loyal ones would be given almost endless help. When he moved from one place to another as he was growing up, he had been looked upon as the eldest in each family. Being the eldest son, one had to ensure the well-being of the younger family members, with "younger" not necessarily referring only to age but to one's position within the family as well. Within his own family, this was his approach as well.

ECONOMIC DEVELOPMENTS

Memories of the 1966 carnage soon faded away, as President Soeharto managed gradually to achieve measurable economic growth. There had been a minority who claimed that the new president had suppressed the people's voice and had deprived them of the chance to be a democratic society. The legality of Supersemar and the way President Soeharto had replaced his predecessor remained major points of debate. For President Soeharto, a regime based on military discipline was not entirely bad. One should not judge his situation at that time based on present-day standards. For whatever reason, President Soekarno's rule had reached its peak and he had already given his best for the country. The revolution was a thing of the past and the country had to move forward.

Until the mid-1960s, Indonesia was known, under the World Bank's standards, as the poorest country in Asia and amongst the poorest in the world. When President Soeharto came to power, inflation was running at over 650 per cent per annum and the currency had lost its worth. By early 1960, Indonesia had become "a nation of hoarders". This meant that consumers were hoarding as prices were outpacing their wages. Shopkeepers hoarded so that they could maximise their profits by holding goods as long as possible and selling at the highest bid. The only party who stood to gain any benefit under such a situation was the speculator. President Soeharto opted for unpopular actions by using strong military discipline and applied the term "those for us or those against us". The Cold War was still raging with the roots of communism steeped in poverty. He had to beat poverty if he wanted to defeat communism. His early public speeches specifically asked for public awareness of the nation's own fate: did the people want to be communists, capitalists or none of the two?

The country's structure featured decaying systems that were still valid but irrevocably damaged. This was through intentional neglect due to other concerns such as security issues which had commanded greater priority. The first Development Cabinet from 1968 to 1973 was formed on 10 March 1968. President Soeharto chose 23 ministers. Key economic posts such as Minister of Finance was given to Ali Wardhana and the Minister of State for Economy and Finance to Sultan Hamengkubuwono IX. The stabilisation that President Soeharto achieved during the late 1960s, although substantial, was still insufficient to meet the needs of the growing population. An overhaul was needed in almost every aspect of the country's economic life. The population was growing at a yearly rate of 2.4 per cent. The farmers continued to rely on traditional cultivation methods that had been used for centuries. Agricultural produce was inadequate for export. Domestic industries were not able to absorb the country's abundant workforce and there was virtually no industry to speak of. The foreign exchange revenue was insignificant.

President Soeharto's early attempt at gaining the people's trust was to choose low profile policing. After the formation of the economic team, the government introduced the first important step in price stabilisation. It related to restructuring of the government apparatus. President Soeharto needed to put the house in order. A few ministries were merged and others streamlined—the Ministry of Basic and Light Industries and Energy was dissolved and the State Ministry on Economy, Finance and Industry took over; the Ministry of Plantation and the Ministry of Maritime Affairs were dissolved as well. Inflation had to be tackled very quickly. Instead of a gradual approach, the government moved decisively to restore conditions conducive to the growth of the private sector. In the area of politics, except for PKI, President Soeharto continued mostly with his predecessor's policies but in the economic area, there was a complete turnaround. The previous government had tightly regulated or controlled every aspect of public services, including manufacturing and trade. Private enterprises were left to sink or flounder. The rotting infrastructure was the outcome of parasitism in the bureaucratic circle and harassment from the regulatory bodies.

Under President Soeharto, a significant portion of the budget came from foreign aid, especially from the capitalist nations. This was considerably greater than in the past when foreign aid came mostly from Moscow or Peking. In addition to the ministers, President Soeharto also appointed two special expert advisory groups. One of these advisory groups was for political affairs and the other for economic matters. The first one comprised prominent intellectuals, national figures and the military. The other group consisted of intellectuals from the Economic Faculty of the University of Indonesia. The political advisory group was dissolved in 1968 while the economic advisory group continued its role for many years to come.

Amongst the members of the economic group were Widjojo Nitisastro and Ali Wardhana, who remained at the forefront of policy-making for a remarkably long period. They stayed on in later years when their influence had waxed and waned. Widjojo based himself at the National Development Planning Board (Bappenas), where he drew up the basic guidelines for economic policy, while at the same time nurturing a generation of economists. Ali Wardhana served as Finance Minister for three terms and then as Coordinating Minister for the Economy during President Soeharto's fourth term. From 1988, they were retained as President Soeharto's advisors on economic policy. Regretfully, the economists who worked closely with him for years rarely put pen to paper to record their policies and experiences for international consumption. One book which can be found on this area is published abroad by Radius Prawiro.[5] In 2005, Pak Harto also revealed his disappointment in this lack of printed records on this crucial phase of the country's development.

Widjojo Nitisastro, small in stature, was always a very low-key and unassuming figure. He was polite and able to make everyone he met feel at ease as he was not snobbish. He was not unlike President Soeharto, quiet and did not speak much. Widjojo was the demographics and economics expert in his team as well as a brilliant strategist with a vision for long-term focus. He was also an excellent listener who did not try to dominate his subordinates. Further, he had the talent to bring out the best from each member of his team. Amongst the technocrats, he was credited as an excellent and natural leader. The team felt that if there was one person who deserved the title of being the architect of Indonesia's economic development, it would be him. To President Soeharto he did not pose a threat; he had no political ambitions and he was content with the job he was best at. He knew how to counter his boss on sensitive issues, for instance, knowing that President Soeharto considered him an equal, he sent only his juniors to relay messages that President Soeharto might not like to hear such as the economic advisors' desire to devaluate the rupiah.

This is one way through which the Javanese avoid confrontation. In short, the relationship between President Soeharto and Widjojo had been one of mutual understanding and respect. Both of them could draw a line between facts and emotions. When he became Chairman of Bappenas, Widjojo was only 35 years old. East Javanese by birth and Muslim by religion, he fought in the students' army in the 1940s before he began to teach economic studies. He obtained his PhD from the University of California, Berkeley. When he returned to Indonesia, he joined the University of Indonesia as a lecturer.

Two other members of the economic team—Ali Wardhana, who came from Central Java and Emil Salim, a Western Sumatran and grandson of Haji Agus Salim—also obtained their doctorate degrees from Berkeley. Two other members who studied in the United States were Moh Sadli and Subroto, who came from Central Java, and obtained his doctorate degree from North America. Hence, the phrase "Berkeley Mafia" was coined. Over a period of time, others joined the team, including JB Sumarlin, a Roman Catholic from East Java; Radius Prawiro, a Protestant from Yogya, who was among the 100 ministers in Soekarno's final Cabinet and served as Governor of Bank of Indonesia in 1966; Frans Seda, a Catholic from Flores, who had his formal education in Holland just like Radius and was appointed to the Cabinet to be in charge of the economic portfolio in 1966. President Soeharto soon reinforced his powerful team with figures like Rachmat Saleh, Arifin Siregar and Professor Sumitro Djojohadikusumo. President Soeharto had wholehearted faith in these experts and he gave them a free hand to do their work. This liberty, however, did not mean that he allowed them to function like loose cannons. With his instincts, he watched over them with an eagle eye.

The group carried out their duties on par with managers in private institutions. The first issue facing them was how to tackle the country's outstanding debts. Renegotiation for debt rescheduling was the first step taken. At the same time, guidelines were designed to attract international funds. The priorities were clear-cut and they were to stop hyperinflation, to overcome the balance of payment problems and to restore production, especially in export industries. With a high degree of presidential and public support, the technocrats introduced a stringent set of economic measures. Soon, they successfully met their objective of stabilising the fragile economy. Inflation was reduced from 640 per cent in 1966 to 113 per cent in 1967, and down to 85 per cent in 1968. In 1969, the country entered a period of price stability in which the Jakarta cost of living index rose by only 22 per cent over the next three years. President Soeharto was happy with his choice of the economic team members and their achievements.

With the technocrats, too, President Soeharto was not an autocratic leader. He was willing to learn what he did not know. He was always willing to listen and reach his own judgment based on what he heard. He listened to their arguments carefully. He rarely imposed his will on the team. He gave them a free hand with one condition: if there was a disagreement, he did not want to be confronted with it in public. He would take any argument in private and in a non-confrontational manner. When a tricky situation arose, Widjojo would send a colleague to speak directly to the president. That way, he could preserve their good relations. Being a Javanese himself, Widjojo was known for his skill in persuading President Soeharto have to trust in the merits of the technocrat-supported measures. It was a skill which was not necessarily present amongst the nationalist group. The technocrats kept President Soeharto on a razor's edge and that was how they managed to get their way. They politely reminded him that if he did not take their advice, there would be no food and clothing for the people. The economy would remain stagnant. On economic issues, he remained in the backseat. President Soeharto was sharp enough to understand the crucial pillar on which his power rested. If the economy was bad, a communist-led move to start a *coup* would be impossible to stop. PKI might not have won if the people had been well-fed and clothed in 1955. PKI thrived because poverty had been rampant. The same situation applied to other extremists like the fanatic Muslims.

If in politics President Soeharto used his comrades in arms, in economics it was a completely different matter. His choice of the technocrats was very impressive as the team were very much different from his own background. The men behind the economic progress were highly-educated. President Soeharto had come across these experts during his long military career, but they were not his close friends. The New Order used rational thinking as the basis of its strategy. Those who thought that President Soeharto's milieu and his strong outlook on Javanese culture would override his *raison d'être* were wrong. His intellect ruled his emotions. Thus, macro economic policies were delegated entirely to a group of economists who had been trained in the United States and other Western countries. The Bappenas cluster later held key positions as the economic ministries.

To ensure that foreign aid and loans were wisely spent, Bappenas needed reinforcement. Bappenas was the cornerstone of the country's budget planning process. The history of Bappenas went back to President Soekarno's era. At that time, Bappenas was not run by trained economists. There was a shortage of economic experts as there were not many who were Western-educated in the early years of the country's freedom. President Soeharto's first principle was to develop Indonesia based on the country's own strengths. A pragmatist, he knew only too well the limitations the country faced. To develop Indonesia, there was a need for long-term loans, with low interest and instalment repayments spanning 10 to 15 years. In the financial world, it was almost impossible as the longer the credit period stretched, the higher the interest rates that would be charged. The Eastern bloc loans were for no longer than 10 years and they could not agree with interests of 2 per cent to 3 per cent. Then, the Inter-Governmental Group in Indonesia (IGGI) came up with favourable terms.

President Soeharto's choice of economic specialists did not stand on political considerations but was based on individual expertise. The team successfully convinced him to introduce a set of new economic policies and philosophies, but it took place only after he had won political victory and had strong military support on his action against PKI. This in turn secured his success against the threat posed by the landless and urban workers, previously a stronghold of the PKI. His former economic team members confirm that he was far from autocratic, at least not in matters he knew little or nothing about. On areas where he had less knowledge, he had been willing to listen, learn and carefully follow the decisions made. He took time in reaching a decision—and only after he had taken into account all options available and digested them. His Javanese philosophy of "*alon-alon asal kelakon*" or "slowly but surely" was also practised here.

The experts suggested going after a free market economy for the country to rise above its fiscal and monetary dilemmas. Such open market policies were a complete turnaround from President Soekarno's economic strategy which had a strong nationalistic base. The liberated market strategies aimed at rehabilitation, entrenchment and expansion of all that had been established. These included those whose power had been fixed through political connections. President Soeharto realised that a free market was not the best solution, but it was the best way to start growth. Growth could not be achieved at once, especially with an increasing population. Infusions in large amounts from foreign capital investment, aid and new technology were needed. There were three solid foundations for development without the need to redistribute wealth or power. International capital through the inflow of funds from abroad fitted in well as a vital element in forming a new capitalist cluster. Ideally, the newcomers would enter into agreements with a mixture of companies from both the international and national sectors.

The Japanese, Americans, Chinese and the indigenous, in large and small scales, struggled to shape the country's new face of capitalism. Until the mid-1970s, Indonesia adhered to open-door policies as advised by the Western liberal economic viewpoints from the International Monetary Fund (IMF), the World Bank, the International Bank for Reconstructions and Development (IBRD) and in particular, the IGGI. The relatively strong standing of IMF, IBRD, IGGI and other international bodies have since increased substantially. Along with these liberal economic policies came an additional number of technocrats. Some people saw the economic policies as a sign of the government surrendering the country's autonomy over economic planning. For that reason, President Soeharto needed a strong foothold in the political arena. For the same reason, he used an iron fist in the political game. On the other hand, there had been free will in his economic policies, while he managed to get political support in an intensely nationalistic country.

The IMF office was set up within the Central Bank building. The World Bank established a local mission in 1968. Its large expert staff were involved in Indonesia's planning in the important sectors from the beginning. The two agencies helped to prepare the country's annual loan submission to the IGGI. The IMF and the World Bank published annual reports which were always in high demand. These were based on inside information and data that were not accessible to the public. It soon became the most important source of information for evaluating the country's economic standing. Every year, bankers domestic and foreign, competed to obtain the first copy. In the days leading to the distribution of the official reports, the data were constantly leaked to the newspapers. In most cases, these were reported by foreign correspondents. Somehow, they always managed to get the first few copies. By this time, the demand for foreign newspapers had skyrocketed and sales reached a peak. These are just a few examples of the difference in the way the foreign and the local press were treated and how foreign interest in the vital affairs of the country seemed to be viewed with greater importance than domestic interest.

The negative impact of such incidents was the reluctance of the country's leaders to trust educated Indonesians. The experts, too, admitted that they had to learn the hard way. They soon learnt that an impulsive use of foreign aid would lead to economic disaster. The blunder occurred in the case of the Pertamina Affair under Ibnu Sutowo in the 1970s and BJ Habibie's pet projects in the 1980s. In both cases, it appeared that President Soeharto had consciously allowed them to happen, bringing forth the question as to why he did so—because both had a streak of nationalism, which was the one element no leader in Indonesia dared to challenge. BJ Habibie had managed to leave President Soeharto with a deep impression and admiration for his technical skills. Technology was the country's weakest link, hence President Soeharto accepted BJ Habibie's strategy as Indonesia approached industrialisation.

President Soeharto never showed an inferiority complex to those he thought of as being more of an expert. On the contrary, he was proud when the experts admired his fast learning skills. He had a high level of self-confidence and had no qualms about not having academic titles. Perhaps, the only time he felt insecure was in the early days when he and President Soekarno had to govern together, but then who would not have felt inferior against President Soekarno's charisma and fame? President Soekarno once said, "Go to hell with your aid," to the Americans and Western donors. President Soeharto was astute enough to comment on this incident by saying: "Maybe Bung Karno's politics had confused them. Or else they wanted to help in such a way that pushed Bung Karno into saying "go to hell." He said that even for himself, if help was being extended with political strings attached, he too would have said "go to hell."

In this context, President Soeharto wrote that mutual benefit was important but not to the extent of having a foreign nation meddling in the country's domestic affairs, or to forgo Indonesia'a sovereignty. He further stated that this had been an accepted principle and within the spirit of the Asia Africa Conference in 1955. He skilfully and carefully designed remarks to avoid conflict, knowing the importance and sensitivity of President Sockarno's place in Indonesia's history. Still, some felt that President Soeharto was self-centred and had used it as a disguise for his own interests. My father did not think so. President Soeharto genuinely wanted to keep President Soekarno's legacy intact. If his policies later reflected the opposite, they were the product of changing times. Different times call for different methods of management, as all good leaders are aware of.

BEHIND THE GUN

The new president needed a system of security in place more than anything else as he chose those whom he trusted to be members of his team to work as his personal assistants. Unlike in economic matters where he was not afraid to make a U-turn, in military and political issues it was the other way around. He did not believe in a drastic realignment of power since it could have been potentially dangerous and might lead to instability. A first-class strategist, President Soeharto had the ability to anticipate the future. He believed in and used the principle that every problem could be resolved by finding its roots. The main problem in Indonesia when he took power was inflation and the high cost of basic necessities. This was the reason he started his Repelita (Five-Year Development Plan) with the three basic human needs: food, clothing and housing—once their stomachs were full, the people would be happy and they would leave him alone to his other plans. He realised that some members of his chosen inner circle, his *Aspri* or personal assistants, might not have been popular choices and were far from perfect, but he had no time to look for perfection. Since 1968, he had heard criticisms about his *Aspri*. He was surprised by the lack of understanding that he needed a team he could trust to help him carry out his monumental tasks. When he was in West Irian, he had gathered a wide circle of military connections into a tight military clique based on his old Diponegoro Division links. This proved to be one of the best networks he ever had. One of them was Ali Moertopo, who was assigned to be in charge of testing a new combat intelligence unit attached to Strategic Reserve and Special Operations (Opsus). Many felt that Ali Moertopo could impress people with his energetic and broad intellect, all hidden behind a mask of joviality and earthiness. He often showed a broad smile as he ruthlessly pressured and enticed his opponents into meek submission.

Born in Blora on the north coast of Central Java in 1924, Ali Moertopo was the son of an impoverished *priyayi*. His father was a *batik* trader and his education in Central and West Java had been disrupted in his early teens. He joined the Hisbullah, the Islamic force set up by the Japanese in parallel with PETA. He grew close to General Soeharto when the latter held the position of Deputy Chief of the Diponegoro territory in 1957. The president listened to him on political matters and accepted his recommendations for key political appointments.

Soedjono Hoemardhani was born in Sunan Palace in Solo on 23 December 1919. He was of true royal blood and attended a Dutch business school in Semarang and later an advanced finance course at Fort

Benjamin Harrison in the United States. He then joined the Military Academy Seskoad, which General Soeharto had also attended. He started his military career in Division VII/Diponegoro and became a Member of Parliament. When General Soeharto was elected president, he was appointed into his *Aspri* for overseeing economic and trade affairs. He was chosen to be the Inspector General of development projects and Honorary Chairman of the Center for Strategic and International Studies (CSIS). He was often thought of as the president's mystic guru. Soedjono Hoemardhani considered life to be a blessing from God which had to be preserved. He believed that God gave a few humans *daya luwih* or greater ability, some to heal and a few to rule. He had an aristocratic, kind and serene nature, and it was easy to understand why a person like President Soeharto often listened to his spiritual advice.

President Soekarno had fallen out of power not just because of PKI. During that time, the people were restless due to hunger. Life was hard and the future was bleak. In addition, there were internal and external forces pushing for President Soekarno to fail. The internal struggle was between the left- and the right-wing political forces. The external forces were the Central Intelligence Agency (CIA) and the like, who had been anxious about President Soekarno's inclination towards the communists. President Soeharto did not want to repeat Soekarno's mistakes. He knew that economics, politics and security were closely connected. Hence, economic problems were one of his main concerns. He decided that long-term planning had to be instituted over a period of 25 years before the country could be industrialised. Within this time frame, stages of development were planned in five-year phases. Therefore, the first long-term planning phase started in 1969 and was completed in 1994. On 1 April 1969, he announced the government's goals in the country's first Repelita. It contained a set of goals with measurable success. Benchmarking was clear-cut. Priorities were set to overcome the country's acute economic breakdown. In order to do this, it was necessary to turn to the free market. The government slowly carried out a limited undertaking of improving the economy.

In the political arena, President Soeharto did not want to rock the boat and tried to maintain balance with his own ideas of how to run the country with what was there before. The changes were not to be too radical. He also knew that a strong economic nationalist sentiment still existed among those in public administration. They clung on to an inefficient network of bureaucracy. The New Order was aware that economic development could turn into a double-edged sword. On one hand, it could generate wealth to cement national unity and lift the country's standing and status in the international community. On the other hand, if it provided benefit to only a select group, jealousy and hatred would arise.

The main objectives of Repelita from 1 April 1969 to March 1974 were, first and foremost, food and clothing. The people also needed jobs. The second Repelita from April 1974 to March 1979 aimed at food and clothing sufficiency at an affordable rate for all, and housing for the majority. The basic infrastructure was to be further extended and enhanced. Job creation was to be widely spread and wealth more equally distributed. The third Repelita from April 1979 to March 1984 called for a higher standard of living, better education and affluence for all, on an equal and fair basis. As rice was the main staple, priorities were given for improving agricultural products and achieving self-sufficiency. The country had to be able to export agriculture-related products, the production of which could absorb more manpower. To this end, there was a need to produce tools and machinery that would keep agriculture and industry in balance. The priorities in economic growth should also be accompanied by development in the country's political, social and cultural life.

The objectives of the second long-term plan of 25 years were further development in the economy, social welfare, education and culture. Failure to improve these areas would undoubtedly provide an opportunity for the extremists to return. To prepare the country for modernisation in the field of science and technology, it was necessary to anticipate the next new knowledge area that would arise. The law, state apparatus and mass communication had to be upgraded. Overall, there was a need to overhaul the whole system. In addition, there was a need for security and defence to function as the foundation for the country's development. Building the nation was like building a new house from the ground up. The country needed a blueprint of how its house was supposed to look. Once it was clear how many bedrooms, bathrooms, kitchens and other facilities were needed, one had to calculate the number of pillars to support the building. The pillars were the judicative and legislative institutions. The kitchen was the executive body ensuring that everything fitted in well with the needs of the people and in compliance with the law and regulations. What the people needed was food, clothing, housing, schools, hospitals and so forth.

Meanwhile, the pressure for a national state-led capitalist movement came from a loose coalition comprising Ibnu Sutowo together with Ali Moertopo and Soedjono Hoemardhani, the dominant figures in Opsus. President Soeharto's few statements typically stressed the need for unity and harmony. He relied on Javanese philosophy to navigate his path in life. Repelita would have provided the right steps had it not been for the blatant show of wealth by a number of rich individuals. The first Development Cabinet began on 10 March 1968 and continued until 1973 with 23 ministers. President Soeharto did not appoint a vice-president during his first term, while the Minister of State for Economy and Finance was Sultan Hamengkubuwono IX. The political parties formerly banned under President Soekarno wanted to get their status back but President Soeharto did not agree to it. For President Soekarno and President Soeharto, the outlawed parties followed extreme Islam and their loyalty to Pancasila was questionable. When it came to extremists, both presidents had no empathy and Pancasila was considered the appropriate tough weapon to counter such a movement.

Western democracy serves the interests of individuals at the expense of society. It emphasises individual freedom and it works perfectly well in a nation where the people are already well-educated, know the boundaries of freedom and are aware of their as well as other people's rights. In Indonesia's case, however, we are convinced that many, if not all, of Indonesia's political problems were the outcome of the country being "too liberal". In the late 1950s, the army responded well when President Soekarno called for it to bring down the multi-party system, but in the early 1960s, they watched in dismay as President Soekarno turned to the Communist Party, which had more than 20 million members and supporters at that stage, for political support. Those who responded to nationalism dutifully recorded their votes for Golongan Karya or Golkar (Functional Group), which was considered to be the army's political organisation. The organisation was formed on 20 October 1964 with the original name Sekretariat Bersama Golongan Karya or Sekber GOLKAR. It was the federation of 97 functional organisations and non-political associations, whose members continued to rise in number. In the beginning, the idea of Golkar was for a socio-political force and it was not meant to be a political party. Golkar was a coalition of professionals which focused more on shared interests and national harmony than power or ideology. While the political parties emphasised ideology and political self-interest, Golkar stood for common understanding and its focus was to serve the government and state. Golkar was supposed to rise above ethnic, social, religious and ideological interests.

When President Soeharto took control, many jobs were especially created for ethnic and regional constituencies whose political support was needed by his ruling Golkar party. Golkar became his most important political vehicle. On 4 February 1970, Golkar announced its participation in the general elections in 1971, with a logo that has remained the same to date. In later years, critics claimed that one of the most devastating and enduring part of President Soeharto's legacy was not in the bureaucratic and high membership numbers he had created in Golkar, but in the system of cash contributions expected from the industrialists. The money—millions of dollars—went into the coffers of Golkar, allegedly for election purposes. Everything had a price: licence for industrial expansion, obtaining passports for travelling abroad, among others. Only a few were granted exemptions. Hence, within a short period, every official—from the lowliest peons to Cabinet ministers—began demanding his share. Even federal civil servants had to bribe their ministers for positions they wanted. Yet, Golkar managed to keep its position as the leading frontrunner during President Soeharto's reign.

In 1971, Golkar won more than 62 per cent of votes during the first parliamentary elections. Golkar had been fortunate because immediately after they emerged the winner, the economy entered its best period due mainly to the oil boom in early 1973. With the best of luck in his hands, President Soeharto was re-elected for the second term on 23 March 1973. This time around, he chose Sultan Hamengkubowono IX as his vice-president. It was a very commendable move, as the sultan's figure was integral with President Soekarno's success in maintaining the country's unity when the Dutch tried to reclaim Indonesia as their colony. The sultan had welcomed President Soekarno's move to shift the seat of government to Yogya. The sultan had made many sacrifices to aid the country's survival during its infancy and for this he was highly respected. Meanwhile, Bung Karno passed away on

21 June 1970, making a sense of continuity from the early days of freedom very crucial.

Sultan Hamengkubowono IX was born a prince under the name of Dorodjatun in Yogya on 12 April 1912. His parents were of royal blood from the *kraton* of Yogya. He received his early education from the Dutch schools and continued to study Indologie (Indonesian) and economics in Rijkuniversiteit, Leiden, in the Netherlands. This progression was customary for children born in a *kraton*. From 1946 onwards, the sultan held the position of State Minister in different Cabinets. In 1950, he became the Deputy Prime Minister. On 23 March 1978, he resigned from his vice-presidency due to ill health. He died 10 years later on 1 October 1988 at the George Washington Hospital in the United States. In the second Development Cabinet formed on 27 March 1973, there were 21 ministers, most notably Ali Wardhana as the Minister of Finance and Widjojo Nitisastro as the Minister of State for Economy and Finance/Chairman of Bappenas.

During that period, in addition to the physical progress achieved, such as roads, harbours, and transportation, President Soeharto also managed to keep uprisings under control. Golkar managed to win over 62 per cent of the votes for the second time during the general elections held in May 1977. President Soeharto took stronger control as he ordered the closure of a leading newspaper and the close monitoring of the student movement. He was set for his third term on 22 March 1978. This time around, he chose Adam Malik as his vice-president, another veteran in the political arena and an old player under President Soekarno. Twenty-four ministers assisted him during the period of the third Development Cabinet, which had been formed on 29 March 1978. The Cabinet remained until 1983. The Minister of State for Economy and Finance/Chairman of Bappenas was still under the leadership of Widjojo Nitisastro, while Ali Wardhana remained the Minister of Finance.

Unlike the sultan, Adam Malik was not a Javanese, less so a *priyayi*. Born on 22 July 1917 in Pematang Siantar, Sumatra, he began his political career by joining Partindo, a youth movement in Sumatra, and in 1934, became its regional chairman. Unlike the sultan, Adam Malik only completed his primary education and had no further formal schooling. He was a self-made man like President Soeharto. In 1946, he formed Partai Rakyat and Partai Murba.

During President Soekarno's time, he had been a Member of Parliament, a member of the Supreme Advisory Council (DPA) and even an ambassador in the Soviet Union and Poland. Before becoming vice-president, he was chairman of Dewan Perwakilan Rakyat (DPR) or the People's Representative Council and he was at the United Nations. His positions during the transition from President Soekarno to President Soeharto had been the sixth Deputy Prime Minister and Minister of Foreign Affairs.

RICE—THE HEARTBEAT OF INDONESIA

From 1965 to 1968, there was little doubt that President Soeharto's economic team intended to follow the IMF/IBRD ideology of free market economics. The government curbed fiscal and monetary spending for capital accumulation. It was believed that the market would be able to generate maximum growth and efficiency. The first crucial problem was to overcome rice shortages. Rice remained the staple food in the country. A few years after gaining freedom, President Soekarno had tried to change the people's eating habits by suggesting that they replace rice with corn or potato, but this never worked as Indonesians felt that corn or potato could not satisfy them as much as rice did.

President Soeharto understood that shortage of rice could cause social upheaval. Rice served as the unofficial barometer of national well-being and amongst many of the country's problems, it remained the key issue in the government's setting of priorities. At the same time, the economic team felt it would be wrong to reduce the agricultural sector production to just rice alone. Commodities such as rubber and coffee had been the country's principal exports and therefore played an important role in restoring the unstable economy. Revenue from foreign exchange was so low that the country barely had the ability to import rice. Above all, the correlation between rice shortages and inflation was unnervingly direct. When the demand for rice went up, the price increased and everything followed suit. When something like this happened, speculators used rice shortages as an excuse to hoard and make quick profits. In the end, public discontent, disorder and, in a worst case scenario, riots happen. Social unrest and endangered security could lead to instability, which in turn would delay the development process. Hence, from 1967 onwards, the government set rice-sufficiency as one of its most vital objectives. For many years, the country's agricultural policies were almost single-mindedly geared towards attaining self-sufficiency in rice output.

The government had, from 1963, initiated a number of programmes to improve rice productivity. The Faculty of Agriculture at the University of Indonesia, which later became the Agriculture Institute of Bogor (IPB), piloted the task for improvement of seed strains and new techniques for crop cultivation. It involved improvement of irrigation, enhancement of seed selections and use of fertilisers and pesticides. Cultivation methods were expanded and cooperatives were reinforced. In coaching the new skills, IPB's students had to live in the villages and work alongside the farmers. This method was very effective. To expand this programme on a national scale, the government employed a group of experts who were well-trained and dedicated tutors to the farmers. They used new technology. The programme started in Java and soon spread throughout the entire country. Over the years, government reliance on new varieties of seeds, techniques, and the like, helped to increase crop yields. To obtain higher rice production, the technique of reducing strains of rice was the key factor.[6] In the Philippines, the International Rice Research Institute (IRRI) embarked on a wide research on this with financial and technical support from the United States and Japan. For many years, Indonesian researchers worked closely with IRRI, which was (and still is) one of the foremost institutions undertaking research in rice cultivation.

In 1970, new strains of rice (referred to as New Rice or Padi Baru Nos 5 and 8) were introduced. These were more disease resistant than what farmers used to know. Land on a large scale was needed for planting thus, the total area for crop growing was increased by nearly 50 per cent. Due to the previous rice damage from 1965 to 1969, the country could only produce 1.25 tonnes per hectare. By using the new method, it was possible to double the output to 3 and 4 tonnes per hectare. The positive correlation between the use of fertilisers and rice output became clearly evident. The Bimbingan Massal (Bimas) projects for the rehabilitation of irrigation systems, financing of fertilisers and pesticides carried a price tag of Rp380 billion in the budget under the first Repelita. Bimas was a set of social guidelines designed to give credit as working capital to the farmers. So was Instruksi Massal (Inmas), a set of instructions to the community on how to use the working capital to start improving their farming method. The success of Bimas made Indonesia self-sufficient in rice in 1984. The programme was discontinued as the government introduced a set of banking deregulations in 1988. Bimas was yet another example of President Soeharto's in-depth knowledge of farming and awareness of the level of skills among the farmers. Above all, he understood that their limitations were based on what he himself had seen during his days in Kemusuk.

The period from 1965 to 1974 characterised a clear-cut benchmark in the development of the country's economic policy. Luck was on President Soeharto's side as the influx of state revenue came from an unexpected increase in the price of oil. The unforeseen oil boom helped President Soeharto to fund the country's development. The oil boom was meant to be a blessing but due to over-expansion and uncontrollable growth, it only helped the government to a certain extent before the collapse of Perusahan Tambang Minyak Negara (Pertamina), the state-owned oil company. Pertamina's failure led to an important modification in President Soeharto's economic policy.

There were complaints that the economic team granted a protective framework for the emerging domestic capital dominated by state corporations, which were owned by the military and their local Chinese partners. Meanwhile, President Soeharto emphasised that industrial development had to go hand in hand with agriculture. Since then, there had been improvements to rice yields through the use of chemical fertilisers. To this end, the government drew upon the country's natural wealth, which had not been fully utilised: the abundant supply of natural gas. Natural gas is an essential component in fertiliser production. This method proved successful for supplying the growing demand for fertiliser from 1969 to 1984, when fertiliser production increased by 49 times. For many years to come, fertiliser received the biggest subsidy from the national budget.

However, the biggest problem remained the nation's pervasive poverty. One of the fundamental questions was how to create public purchasing power from almost nothing. The public had very little disposable income. As a result, bank credit was given on a very selective basis. To qualify for credit, a borrower had to project a quick return on his investment or it had to be related to food production or export. Credit priorities were also given to the rehabilitation of an existing facility, rather than new projects.

Poverty, combined with a lack of infrastructure, made the shortage of rice even worse. Therefore, the immediate need in the mid-1960s was to get hold of and distribute fertiliser to improve rice output. There was only one fertiliser factory with a production capacity of 100,000 tonnes per year. It was clearly inadequate to meet the growing demand. Moreover, the country needed foreign exchange to finance the importation of fertiliser. It was an additional headache for the economic team because even if there was adequate fertiliser, the infrastructure remained poor, and the fertiliser had to be distributed to thousands of farmers spread out in many locations across the vast archipelago. One of the new solutions was to get the rice supply primarily through the PL 480 food aid scheme, which was special aid from the United States, Japan and other IGGI member countries.

The strategy and policy of the New Order were not executed all at once but through well-calculated stages. It was taken step by step to enable assessment of public reaction. From 1966 until 1975, the government followed the *laissez-faire* or open door economic policy, based on the maximisation of economic growth through heavy reliance on foreign investment. By 1970, significant fractures were evident. It was soon followed by the resurgence of economic nationalism. During this period, the state played a more aggressive and active role in financing, protecting and subsidising domestic capital as well as direct investment. This economic nationalism focused heavily on the creation of industrial sectors based on the country's natural resources such as steel, natural gas, oil and aluminum refining and import-substitution. During this period, growth faltered as the country moved to a state-led economy. This resulted in a decline in interest by foreign investors which reduced the country's ability to finance or attract financing for the government's industrialisation programme. In fact, a struggle emerged within the capitalist class and the state apparatus. The scuffle took place within the centres of political bureaucracy, particularly amongst the Kostrad/Opsus/Palace alliance. Attention shifted to more strategic and lucrative state-owned corporations such as the Pertamina, Bulog and PT Timah. After the 1965 episode, the military clearly did not want to relinquish their control over selected state corporations that were established since the late 1950s.

At the same time, President Soeharto watched closely the development of village cooperatives. The original concept of cooperatives was written in the

1945 Constitution. However, it had not taken off on a large scale until 1972, when the country faced the rice crisis. There were two forms of cooperatives: at the village level, there was Badan Usaha Unit Desa (BUUD), the village unit for business; at the district or regency level was the Koperasi Unit Desa (KUD), the village cooperatives. These cooperatives were the distribution centres for agriculturally related products such as seeds and fertilisers. In some cases, the rice processing facilities were also in the hands of the cooperatives. It was within this context that Bulog, the National Procurement Logistics Board, used BUUD and KUD as intermediaries for selling agicultural products to the end buyers.

PASAR KLEWER

On 9 June 1971, President Soeharto opened a monument in Pasarean Ageng (Life-size Tomb), where there is an inscription from Sri Mangkunegoro I from Solo. It is believed that Mangkunegoro had received *Tjakraningrat*, a divine charge from the Almighty. The monument encrypts his dedication to the court and the people he ruled. Known as the *Tri Dharma* or Three Commitments (*Rumongso melu handarbeni*), it expounds the sense of ownership in the community: *wajib melu hangrungkebi*, which refers to an obligation to preserve and defend the community, and *mulat sarira hangrasawani*, which means to be perceptive. This establishes the viewpoint from our Javanese forefathers and reflects the ethics pursued by President Soeharto.

One of his extraordinary talents was clearly demonstrated in his speech at the opening of Pasar Klewer, a must-see destination for visitors and tourists who want to experience and understand what Solo is all about, on 9 June 1971. The general elections were scheduled to take place on 3 July 1971, less than a month later. This was to be the first elections after he came to power.

In Pasar Klewer, President Soeharto delivered an impromptu speech which demonstrated his abilities, thoughtfulness and brilliant policy-making skills. My father believed that this was the best communciation he had ever made to the people. He illustrated his economic development plan which was to be the basis of the country's progress. It was relayed at the right time and place. Pasar Klewer was a mirror reflecting how development should take place for Indonesia to become a prosperous nation. Pasar Klewer had started through the cooperation between the local government and local investors. It was an exchange market for buying and selling textiles, mostly *batik*. Its main function was that of a service provider. Pasar Klewer played an important role in maintaining price stability and acted as a catalyst between sellers and buyers. Textiles are the prime materials for clothing, the second most important essential need after food. Acting as the bridge between sellers and buyers, Pasar Klewer respected both the producers' need to make a profit and the need to protect consumers from being overcharged.

To President Soeharto, this was an illustration of how democracy should work. There were three components in this equation: the producers, the consumers and the service providers, who acted as the intermediary between the other two. These three components determined the extent to which fair pricing could be achieved. They had to cooperate so that no one party would feel that they had more rights than the other two. Producers were not to overcharge consumers to get the highest profit. Farmers were not to be forced to push their prices down during harvest time. However, speculators could, and would, purchase in large quantities and keep the stocks for months, waiting for market demand to reach a higher level before selling—in other words, hoarding to manoeuvre prices. This was not the type of financial system the government had in mind. Democracy in the economy meant that all players had to work together without making it a burden on consumers. This was where the service providers played a crucial role. They monitored fair dealing through implementation of cost-cutting measures. In Pasar Klewer, they asked for fairness. Both producers and consumers would set the selling and buying prices in realistic figures. The middlemen, namely shopkeepers, were not to take advantage by speculating. It was acceptable to achieve a profit, but it had to be a reasonable one.

Unfortunately, along the way, the system faced problems and accumulated mountains of bad debts. The traders, mostly women, young and old, bought and sold in "Solo style"—well-dressed and using their flirtatious smiles, they enjoyed the fun of bargaining for good deals. When Pasar Klewer encountered problems, the ladies decided to see the mayor. They persuaded the mayor to get involved. However, they did not envisage that it would catch the president's attention and that was the reason the president came and gave his speech.

The MPRS mandate in 1968 did not set the state directives or GBHN. President Soeharto was asked to prepare his own Five-Year Plan and to streamline the political parties. In addition, he had to carry out the general elections before the end of 1971. His team outlined the first Five-Year Development Plan with simple objectives: food, clothing, housing, job creation and education. In Pasar Klewer, he said that the country needed to balance farming and industry. GBHN was to be linked to the nation's short-term and long-term development programmes. The long-term plans would focus on industries that supported agricultural businesses. The fast pace of growth in science, communication and information technology could not be ignored. Hence, the Five Year Development Plan or Repelita was born.

Each stage was well-calculated as a platform to support growth step by step. Development in farming was not too difficult as the country already had the infrastructure. However, for industrialisation, the infrastructure was not established. Foreign currency earnings were needed to pay external debts. At the same time, industrial development required capital, not only domestically but also in terms of foreign currency in order to import machinery and the like. Furthermore, skilled labour was required for industrial growth. In the area of technology, the country had hardly any experts, and it was impossible to industrialise without the relevant expertise. Farming and industry had to be on equal footing. The distribution of manufactured goods needed transportation; in short, land and sea transportation were needed. The country had to be able to market its goods for domestic and overseas consumption. This meant storage place and warehouses were needed.

Subsequently, other needs requiring multi-faceted actions arose which cost more money and energy. Therefore, the country needed to exploit its natural resources, which further required the necessary machinery for exploration. In Bintan, there was bauxite, which had to be separated from the mud before it could be exported. On the islands of Bangka, Beliton and Singkep, there was sand, which also had to be separated from the mud before it could be exported. The same applied to wood—if only cut wood was sold abroad, the income would be minimal. The more appropriate approach would have been to manufacture aluminum by using the country's own bauxite. Sand should be processed to become tin and wood used to produce pulp. Pulp could be used to produce paper, textile and the like. If each stage required four to five years, then the country's long-term development would take from 20 to 25 years. President Soeharto declared that the loan the country had managed to secure was to be used for development and not for the normal budget, more so not to buy weapons. He warned of the danger of former wrong practices, where loans had been used to finance consumption and prestige projects. It was here in Pasar Klewer that he emphasised the national interest and had no reservations about taking strict action against those who went against him.

If challenged, President Soeharto could remain calm and calculative, but once a decision was made, he was decisive and shrewd. It was also in Pasar Klewer where he said that if the 1971 general elections was not fair, there would be a *jihad*. For him, this meant that the nation would suffer chaos. He stated firmly: "In the name of security for development and in the interest of Pancasila and our 1945 Constitutions, we have no choice but to undertake *jihad* together with ABRI." *Jihad* referred to a struggle, not fighting or committing suicide for political reasons as the term has come to be commonly known. He also noted and denied the accusation that he wanted the forthcoming general elections to be used as a camouflage for being elected as president for life. He confirmed that the presidency was to be filled through an election process once every five years. His opponents later charged that he intended to manipulate the MPR as he succeeded in being elected seven times.

In retrospect, it was in Pasar Klewer that he had openly explained what he had in mind for the country's economy, security and politics.

BULOG

After the issue of rice production had been dealt with, in line with his speech at Pasar Klewer, the price equilibrium had to be addressed. One solution for resolving the logistical problems was through money supply management and the creation of a national food agency or logistics board, which later came to be known as Bulog. Bulog was a merger between the two areas of food distribution (Badan Pelaksana Urusan Pangan) and national logistics (Kolognas). Officially founded on 10 May 1967, it was responsible for coordinating all entities responsible for the supply and distribution of essential commodities such as fertiliser and rice. It developed the system of delivery and distribution of rice to civil servants, personnel in state enterprises and members of the armed forces, whose wages were supplemented with essential foods, especially rice. Bulog's main mandate was to build and maintain a buffer stock of rice. It also managed distribution throughout the country, and engaged in market intervention in order to preserve price stability.

The government was aware that Bulog's intervention was a paradox in a free market situation. However, it helped to safeguard food supplies and hence, maintained political stability. It also presented President Soeharto's pragmatism and practicality in choosing the right solutions in spite of the controversial nature of the policy taken. The government, through the cooperatives, also gave credit from time to time. The cooperatives acted as a bridge between Bulog and the farmers. Most importantly, the cooperatives also assisted with communications and mobilising farmers on a nationwide basis. Bulog soon expanded its activities to the logistics of other staples like sugar and flour, although rice remained the main commodity.

Bulog's policy adopted in 1968 remained in effect until 1998. In the beginning, Bulog's impact was positive. Unfortunately, in later years, it ran into problems. Through its authority to appoint distributors and contacts, Bulog was often looked upon as a major cushion for domestic corporate capital. The negative impact was that Bulog became a major resource for funding the bureaucrats who controlled it. It became a hotspot for the creation of wealth for those in charge. In the early years, the military was considered the closest group to the president, especially when Kostrad and Opsus had been assigned to manage Bulog. In late 1966 and early 1967, Bulog was directly accountable to the president, who was himself commander of Kolognas, one of Bulog's predecessors. From 1967 to 1973, the Head of Bulog was General Achmad Tirtosudiro, a former Kostrad officer.

Up to 1971, about 80 per cent of Java's rice was hand-pounded to remove the husks. Within two years, the percentage was brought down to 50 per cent. Typically, the women pounded the rice in wooden troughs, but the practice was replaced by hundreds of mechanical mills. A small pair of scissors called *ani-ani* was used to harvest rice. To increase rice production, the government needed to induce the big landowners to use the new methods available and for this purpose, the government took a lenient policy towards larger landowners who were willing to introduce mechanised tools. The risks, though, included the loss of jobs for thousands of women. The negative impact of using mechanised tools was that only a few of the people were able to find work in the mills. There was no doubt that the change to the use of modern technology hit the female workforce hardest in the rural areas, but this policy led to the quick recovery of the country's rice production. It was a risk President Soeharto had to take—in making any changes, there would inevitably be a few sacrifices which had to be made. At the end of the day, he made a decision which was considered best for the majority. The country produced more rice for its people's consumption in return for sacrificing a few jobs. The solution to this was to train the workforce with new skills.

Several government agencies were involved when it came to securing the food supply. Most notable was the Co-coordinating Ministry for the Economy, Industry, Finance and Development Supervision followed by the Ministry of Agriculture, Bulog, Bappenas, the Ministry of Trade, the Ministry of Cooperatives, the Ministry of Finance and Bank Indonesia. Each was acutely aware of the high stakes for the government's success in improving the country's agricultural sector. To this end, all ministries contributed to policy formulation and the provision of manpower. Nevertheless, all felt that if there was any one institution which should be singled out for the success of rice self-sufficiency in the country, it had to be Bulog. Bulog was not directly implicated in farming activities, it merely administered supplies and price control. Bulog's main task was to help the farmers and push them into the formal market economy. To do this, the most important step was the creation of a functioning market for agricultural products, rice in particular. "Bulog is Indonesia's middleman par excellence," wrote Radius Prawiro. It had to create a buffer stock through nationwide storage facilities. It had to set two key prices: firstly, a minimum floor price for farmers to sell, and secondly, the maximum ceiling price for consumers to pay. The margin between selling and buying was for the government. Setting the right pricing was not an easy job. If the price was set too high, consumers would not have been able to afford it; if the ceiling was set too low, traders would have had little incentive to sell, as the profit would be marginal, and even worse, the farmers would not have been encouraged to grow rice beyond what they needed for their own consumption. Hence, Bulog had to establish a floor price at which the cooperatives would buy on its behalf. If the farmers wanted to sell directly to wholesalers, the price set by the cooperatives would be within the same margin. Bulog's major strategy for stabilising the market was to store stocks in the warehouses that were built all over the country. When supplies fell and there was a rise in price, Bulog would instantly release the buffer stock. Conversely, when prices fell due to over-supply, Bulog would buy to re-build the buffer stock. Bulog had to rely on the international market in order to pressure the local market. If the domestic rice supply fell below the required level, Bulog would buy from the international markets. If the price of imported rice was more costly than local output, Bulog would subsidise the price difference. In the early 1970s, Bulog gradually raised the floor price and in the mid-1980s, when there was a rice surplus, Bulog started to sell abroad rather than allow the price to fall. These measures kept the market stable and the rice speculator at bay.

There were no problems until the mid-1970s, when Bulog was unable to control severe price fluctuations. Bulog had trouble operating within its budget and repaying its loans to the Central Bank. A significant aspect of Bulog's prerogatives was its ability to facilitate access to private companies in a sector of an economy which embraced the whole range of trade in basic commodities. It involved the importation, distribution and procurement of basic foodstuffs. As part of its duty, Bulog maintained monopoly for the purchase and distribution of certain crops. It was allowed to assign official distributors. Its crucial function was also to provide the basis for political and social order by sustaining stability in the supply and pricing of basic commodities. At times, Bulog's role was perceived as being political especially when a crisis arose. For instance, when there was a shortage and price increased, it intervened through the use of purchasing and pricing policies, including subsidies.

The negative consequence was that Bulog became well-placed to provide monopolies. The monopolies became a source of controversy. Bulog could decide which companies were allowed to have a monopoly and which were put on the blacklists for exclusion. Bulog became the window of opportunity for businesses to prosper. Under Bulog's patronage, several private companies very quickly took advantage of this opportunity. As always, the minority group that excelled was the Chinese capitalists who had a long-standing connection with Kostrad. This was a sample of the collusion which took place in the early stage of President Soeharto's rule. Soon, the nickname *cukong* became popular. It referred to Chinese businessmen who took the role of financiers for the military, in return for access to licences, trouble-free access to credit and, to a certain degree, political protection. In the late 1960s and early 1970s, business groups pushed for one of the organisations established by Bulog to import and distribute sugar, flour, wheat and rice. Among the early recipients was the Mantrust Group, headed by Tan Kiong Liep and Sjarief Margetan. For a long time, Mantrust was a major supplier of foodstuffs to the army.

Bulog's economic power and the nature of its relationship with the military and the private Chinese capitalists were probably best illustrated in the case of PT Bogasari. PT Prima, a Singapore company, was granted a licence to start milling in 1970. Liem Sioe Liong, a close friend of President Soeharto, had expanded his business in flour milling, for which he had formed PT Bogasari. PT Bogasari's partner and co-shareholder was Sudwikatmono. This was one of the first moves by a Chinese business group to pull President Soeharto's close relatives into their business ventures. This practice continued to grow until it became too much for public consumption. There were reports that 26 per cent of Bogasari's profits were set aside as contributions to the charitable foundations of Yayasan Harapan Kita, which was initiated by Ibu Tien. Yayasan Dharma Putra, Kostrad's foundation, was another recipient of the contributions. For President Soeharto, the contributions were considered the right way to re-distribute wealth from the rich to the poor. Looking back to the establishment of PT Bogasari, it was the blossoming of nepotism that would come to the fore in later years; so, too, the concept of the charitable organisations. Critics claimed that a few days after the establishment of PT Bogasari with a paid-up capital of only Rp100 million, it managed to obtain a credit of Rp2,800 million.[7]

Furthermore, PT Bogasari was granted a licence to mill flour for the whole of Western Indonesia, including Java and Sumatra. At the same time, PT Prima's original licence was revoked, with a new one allowing it to mill for the less lucrative market in the eastern part of the country, such as East and West Nusatenggara, Kalimantan, Sulawesi, Maluku and Irian Jaya.

From the beginning, people at PT Prima sensed that they were encountering difficulties in their relationship with Bulog. They felt that they were being discriminated against. PT Bogasari managed to secure Indonesia's US$400 million annual flour market. Between 1972 and the end of 1980, Bulog allocated wheat to PT Prima that merely covered half of its production capacity, whereas PT Bogasari was set to have flour to maintain its full production. Furthermore, there had been accusations that the wheat given to PT Bogasari was of higher quality. In 1980, PT Prima wanted to divest 25 per cent of its shares to a private businessman, Wirontono, but it did not obtain approval from Badan Koordinasi Penanaman Modal (BKPM) or Indonesia's Investment Coordinating Board, an investment service agency of the Indonesian government created for the purpose of implementing the enactment of law on foreign as well as domestic investments.

The decision coincided with the withdrawal of PT Prima's licence in Kalimantan. Supplies of wheat were also cut so that PT Prima could only sustain its operation at 20 per cent capacity. In the end, PT Prima sold 100 per cent of its shares to PT Berdikari. PT Berdikari, a trading group controlled by the military, was established in the early 1960s.

In 1972, Indonesia encountered its worst rice shortages. Bulog was caught completely off-guard. The long dry season on the island of Java at the end of 1972 caused widespread hardship in 1973 when the crisis continued. At the same time, corruption and inefficiency had been found in the way Bulog ran its business. Subsequently, Bulog was forced to buy rice in the international market during a world grain shortage. It brought a heavy import burden to meet the increasing demand. Bulog failed to take the necessary overseas procurement measures to avoid the acute domestic scarcity. It set off a quick increase in inflation that was difficult to control even during the oil and commodity boom in the next two years. The difficulties were caused by ineffective execution and the contradiction between Bulog's purchasing and marketing functions. The worst was its secret role in financing the interests of the top management officials of Bulog. The price of rice rose over 100 per cent and brought an immediate impact on the entire economy. It soon became public knowledge that Bulog's officials had deposited the proceeds of credit from Bank of Indonesia. The initial concept of borrowing from the Central Bank was to enable Bulog to withdraw last minute funds as dictated by market needs. This loan was charged a 3 per cent interest. However, Bulog's management used it as deposits at private banks, earning between 10 per cent to 15 per cent interest. The immense gap between the two rates was enough to make paupers become instant millionaires.

As public knowledge of Bulog's irregularities became widespread, Bulog found itself at the centre of scrutiny. People started to question the mystery behind its officials' wealth. Bulog had turned into something rather sinister. It became a venue of opportunities to make easy money. It was under such circumstances that three of Bulog's depository banks collapsed. It left Bulog with financial problems and, above all, exposed the manipulation that had been going on. A Commission of Four on Corruption, established upon the instructions of President Soeharto, was very critical of Bulog's operations. The commission recommended that the regional agencies be disbanded and for Bulog to be accountable to the Department of Agriculture. The press reported graphic examples of corruption, waste and incompetence. From that time, Bulog had various of its functions integrated, but the corruption charges lingered on for years. After the 1972 rice crisis, the government introduced the intensification programme called Bimas.

In 1973, the authorities tried to make up for the shortfall in rice stocks by acquiring more from the local market. A series of calls was sent out at the local level for district administrations to get hold of rice at government-determined prices. The price set by the government was significantly below that of the prevailing market price. It was understandable that the farmers were hesitant to sell. The tight hold on prices achieved by the technocrats was misplaced. It took them over a year before they were able to rebuild their strategy on rice reserves. On hindsight, Bulog was the starting point of collusion, one of three serious reasons for the demand for reform in the late 1990s.

FAMILY PLANNING

If Bulog tarnished President Soeharto's image, his success in the family planning programme was one of his major achievements. The roots of poverty are closely linked to the size of a country's population. With a population close to 100 million back in 1966, when inflation was skyrocketing and government coffers were empty, it was time for President Soeharto to take corrective measures. The national census in 1961 revealed that there were 97 million people with an annual growth rate estimated at 2.3 per cent. In such a situation, Indonesia would have a population of 236 million in the year 2000. The government forecasted that with a population growth of 1.8 per cent, it would lead to 180 million within the next decade. Indeed, as of 2004, the population was estimated to be 220 million.

Indonesia hosted the International Planned Parenthood event in 1969 and the government started to spend money on its family planning programme. The fast population growth, notably in Java and Bali, had strained the environment and created problems for the nation's natural resources. In 1971, Java had a population of 76 million, making it the most densely populated area in the world. In 1969, a woman of child-bearing years had an average of five or six children. This was closely related to the agrarian nature of the country as human labour was required for farming. The more children a family had, the better they were able to serve the family business. Therefore, having many children was considered good luck and a blessing.

In urban cities, the highest population growth was amongst the poor, such as amongst the blue-collared workers like servants and drivers. In most cases, married couples in the villages were forced to leave one spouse behind not only because of economic reasons, but also because the family needed help with the farming and to take care of the elderly. As time went by, the "single" husband or wife would find a second or even third or fourth spouse, and consequently produce more children.

The policy for population control was incorporated as early as in Repelita 1. A new culture and a good family image had to be created. First, the government launched the concept of family welfare, where having a small family with two children would increase the quality of life. The government explained the benefits by pointing out the relationship between mothers' health and having too many children, and the cost of a child's education. An institution called Badan Koordinasi Keluarga Berencana Nasional (BKKBN) or the Family Planning Co-coordinating Board was established in 1970. BKKBN started with a massive communication campaign to reach every level of the society. The motto was *dua anak cukup* or "two children is enough", accompanied by a picture of a man, a woman and two children. It was not an easy campaign to promote, as it involved changing the traditional mindset or mentality of "many children, much fortune" to "a happy small family; two children is enough".

Pelayanan Kesatuan Keluarga (PKK) or family centres were organised everywhere. In these centres, mothers gathered and discussed the benefits of small families. "BKKBN public communications could rival those of Coca-Cola and Sony in terms of public awareness," wrote Radius Prawiro. He was right, as in almost every corner of the main streets in the cities, there was a picture of the happy family with two children. The first priority was Java and Bali, as these two were the most densely populated regions. BKKBN achieved a remarkable result due to the combination of skillful methods in education and access to contraceptives. The community supported the radical change and the measures to regulate births. It was overwhelming to see a new concept being embraced so wholeheartedly. The success rested on the good job done by various social groups. It was not easy with conservative communities, regardless of whether the residents were Muslims or Christians.

The family planning programme was carried on a national level down to the remotest areas all around the vast archipelago. On centre stage and taking the role of the chief exponent was President Soeharto himself. He not only provided the programme with funding, he also gave moral support through noticeable and symbolic gestures. The president and Ibu Tien travelled from city to city, village to village, to personally promote the benefits of family planning. When he visited the first condom factory—PT Kimia Farma, located in Banjaran, Bandung—his pictures were splashed across newspapers all over the country. In early 1972, the armed forces supported and participated in the family planning programme. Several women's organisations soon joined the bandwagon and brought new ideas to women across the nation. The clergy also supported the programme, as long as it did not promote sterilisation or abortion, as abortion was illegal. The Muslim clergy's endorsement was crucial as the majority of the population were Muslims. Volunteer forces joined BKKBN and rendered their assistance. Without their help, the success of the family planning programme would have been minimal. The government had a restricted budget and welcomed the volunteers' participation. In Bali, the *Balinese Banjar* or community groups gave tremendous help. It was compulsory for married men to join the *Banjar*.

Finally, there was the participation of the village leaders. Teamwork between the head of the village and his wife was crucial. The village head acted as an unofficial sponsor while his wife assumed the role of organiser and facilitator for meetings and the distribution of contraceptives. The success should also be considered in view of the fact that the programme was not compulsory. There was freedom of choice. Those who agreed to family planning had several options: birth control pills, IUDs, implants, injections and condoms. For educational purposes, frequent meetings were organised to explain the benefits of each option.

With the help of voluntary organisations, a staggering total of 18.5 million women had been reached within a short period of time. These women understood and practised birth control thus, the average number of births dropped. The number of married couples who participated in the family planning programme substantially increased from 2.8 per cent in 1971-1972 up to 62.6 per cent in 1984-1985. Overall population growth fell from 2.3 per cent in the 1970s to 1.98 per cent in the mid-1990s. This is an astonishing achievement and even critics of President Soeharto agreed that the programme was a real success. The younger generation now chooses to have two or a maximum of three children. The success is, however, more evident amongst the educated who live in urban cities. The increasingly higher standard of living in big cites is the main reason. The cost of higher education and the temptation to enjoy a better lifestyle are other important factors. The new generation chooses quality over quantity of life.

In addition, every year, President Soeharto presented awards to couples who had successfully joined the programme. Medals and honours were given to those who had successfully embraced family planning at the Merdeka Palace. The icing on top of the cake was credit given as start-up capital in small businesses. Loans were also given for the planting of coconut trees that would bear fruit when a child was ready for school. These measures worked brilliantly and family planning became a huge success. This policy showed President Soeharto's skills in using the right strategies to solve a problem within a larger context and not in a piecemeal approach. For President Soeharto, it was simple. His childhood in Kemusuk taught him about the kind of mentality which existed in the village community. He absorbed his early life experiences and conscientiously took note of them as lessons from the past. He was aware of the importance of rewards for good performance or behaviour and achievements especially at the grassroots level at all times.

The government programme emphasised population growth and food demand, one closely linked to the other. The two are inter-linked with tremendous impact on each other. In the first decade of President Soeharto's rule, the population control programme was a success and self-sufficiency in rice production was also achieved. The production of rice had grown at an unparalleled rate in Asia over the past 20 years. Intensive food production programmes were geared to set Indonesia on the road to self-sufficiency in rice production by the early 1980s. In 1967, widespread poverty of around 60 per cent of the total population began to reduce slowly but surely.

In 1972, to balance the population among the many islands, the government embarked on a policy of transmigration. The aim of the policy was to reduce poverty in the heavily populated island of Java. At the same time, it gave an opportunity to those willing to work to fulfill the needs of labour in the outer islands such as in West Irian, Kalimantan, Sumatra and Sulawesi. Undang-Undang Republik Indonesia (Law of the Republic of Indonesia) No 3/1972 and Peraturan Pemerintah Republik Indonesia (Government Rules) No 42/1973 administered this policy, followed by Keputusan Presiden (Keppres) or Presidential Decree and Instruksi Presiden (Inpres) or Presidential Instruction. Yet, critics claimed that the government's transmigration programme was to replace the local inhabitants and to weaken the regional separatist movement.

SOCIAL WELFARE

President Soeharto's strategic concept was job creation as the best weapon to combat poverty. Poverty would be fertile soil for communism and other extreme elements to take root. In developed countries, basic education and healthcare provided by the ruling government would be considered a citizen's right and not a privilege. In Indonesia, basic education is clearly stipulated in Article 31 of the 1945 Constitution, while the government's task to provide healthcare is outlined in Article 34. As job creation could only be accomplished through investments, the flood of foreign investments and the fast growth of the domestic private sectors opened up job opportunities for thousands, if not millions, of the Indonesian people. Per capita income rose above US$200 in 1970 and it more than doubled to US$500 by 1980.

As foreign investments and lucrative oil revenues flowed in, the much neglected infrastructure had to be set up. Basic healthcare and education began to take form.

The country has one of the highest primary school enrolment rates in the developing world, for example, 93 per cent in 1987. Since the 1970s, thousands of elementary schools or *sekolah dasar* have been opened through Inpres. Inpres used special funds from the presidential office outside the government budget. The money came from the private sector contributions, voluntary or otherwise, in exchange for business. The private sector is now allowed and invited to join the field of education through government liberalisation policies. A few private schools and universities have been opened by the private sector. These schools vary from the very basic to the most exclusive in terms of curricular and extra-curricular activities. English is usually used in the classrooms of the expensive schools. One school even offers extra-curricular activities such as horseback riding. The government made sure that the rich got their luxuries, and the poor, their essential needs.

Another important area of progress was the literacy rate, which reached an estimated 88 per cent for men and 78 per cent for women. Over 94 per cent of school-going children are now enrolled in primary school. Women comprised 36 per cent of the total labour force. Many of these developments were achieved through simple, community-based activities.

After sufficiency in food and education had been achieved, the next important area requiring attention was healthcare. Since the turbulent years of the 1960s, healthcare services had deteriorated rapidly. There were shortages of medicines, hospitals and medical professionals. In 1969, the infant mortality rate was 132 out of every 1,000 births and average life expectancy was 47 years. The main cause for such early demise had been inadequate nutrition, poor hygiene and untreated illnesses. Diarrhoea and smallpox were rampant diseases. The average ratio of doctors to population had been 1:23,000 in urban cities and close to 1:100,000 in rural areas. The first step taken had been the rehabilitation of existing healthcare facilities. As the country's financial resources grew, the strategy was to focus efforts in the rural rather than urban areas. This made sense as the urban population was generally better off.

The government maximised its resources in low cost programmes by promoting prevention methods instead of finding cures. This was accomplished through the introduction of better nutrition. The people were also taught how to improve sanitation and families participated in various healthcare programmes. New graduates from medical schools were required to give training on nutrition and sanitation in rural areas. They had to spend several months in rural areas before they could start their own practice. Pusat Kesehatan Masyarakat (Pukesmas) or Community Health Centres were set up to provide medical treatments in villages and remote areas. To this day, hospitals such as Cipto Mangunkusumo in Jakarta charge very little for patients in its third-class wing. It is in this wing where all hospitals are required to treat the poor. A letter from the district chief certifying that one was poor would lead to a reduction of costs for medical treatment in state-controlled hospitals. It certainly did not mean that Indonesians obtained optimum medical care, but at least there were provisions, albeit less than sufficient, which helped to ease the financial burden. At the same time, modern and luxurious hospitals were also built for the rich.

In addition, at sub-district levels, the government opened Puskemas. Here, trained professionals, usually doctors and registered nurses, offered curative and preventive treatments. Auxiliary Puskesmas, staffed with two or three personnel with a nurse in charge, were established at the village level. The emphasis was on maternal and child healthcare. In addition, Pos Pelayanan Terpadu (Posyandu) or Combined Health Services was established to offer the following medical services: immunisations, information on nutrition, education on baby care, control of illness such as diarrhoea. It also introduced the benefits of family planning and maternal and pre-natal care. Posyandu could be found in almost every single town and village. Posyandu did not have any permanent staff; instead, the healthcare workers went around in a mobile unit. They travelled from one town to another, from one village to the next one. In addition, they organised periodical group meetings and individual consultations. All these came into being through the directives of Inpres.

The welfare of the underprivileged was managed by the PKK. The government wanted to provide a better life for children and women, especially in the rural areas. It was a sensitive issue for President Soeharto— his childhood years had been his best learning experience. This programme reduced the infant mortality rate. Life expectancy improved to an average of 60 years. Volunteers from each village had been mobilised through PKK. They also provided information based on *gotong royong* or mutual self-help. They taught the villagers the importance of good nutrition, clean clothing and housing maintenance. They also explained what home economics was all about and taught them about craft skills, cooperatives, protection and conservation of the environment and financially sound planning.

To improve the villagers' diet, they were urged to plant nutritious vegetables and fruits in their backyard. If they harvested more than what they needed, they could sell the rest. Cooperatives were there to help if they needed financing, for example, to buy seeds and the like. This concept is still implemented by Yayasan Dharmais and Yayasan Damandiri, foundations instituted by President Soeharto. Millions of PKK volunteers or cadres served as facilitators, implementers, motivators and communicators. These volunteers spearheaded community development. When asked, Ibu Soepardjo Roestam, one of its founding and prime movers, said it was pride that motivated the volunteers. The volunteers felt good that they were able to contribute and to see the improvement in someone else's life. It also inspired in them a feeling that they could make changes. Even President Soeharto's robust critics admitted that his biggest achievement was to give the people the ability to do things and get things done.

PKK managed hundreds of thousands of villages and took the lead role in income generation for poor families. It became the backbone of family planning. A key factor in the rapid progress made in the area of welfare for Indonesian society, it worked in close coordination with government agencies and local community organisations. Until the end of 1990, PKK was directly responsible for or took part in: immunisation exercises of at least 80 per cent of all infants; establishment of 255,209 Posyandus in 67,000 villages throughout the country; effective garden utilisation of 28,912,443 families to improve their nutrition; and establishment of 37,170 home industries and marketing units.

Another PKK programme was the Integrated Program for Enhancing the Role of Women. This was meant to enable women to take a more active role in improving their health. There was also a programme for less progressive villages or Inpres Desa Tertinggal (IDT). The IDT served to channel the World Bank funding through to the sub-district level to village self-help groups. The IDT was for the remotest places where communication and transportation hardly existed. For this, the IDT programme had to focus on community participation and village self-reliance. In areas with extreme difficulties in commuting, decentralisation was needed; it also required the participation of women and women's groups.

THE FALL OF THE PERTAMINA EMPIRE

The major risk during President Soeharto's rule had been the fact that the larger the state enterprises became, the more prone they were to mismanagement and corruption. Some of the negative effects of the rapid growth of the state enterprises began to take place in the mid-1970s. The nearly disastrous financial scandal of 1974, involving Pertamina's failure to pay its debts estimated at US$10 billion, exposed high levels of corruption during the first years of President Soeharto's rule. Nevertheless, it did not bring his regime down. The level of corruption and tarnished credibility did not change the minds of the hungry foreign investors. Indonesia had become the role model for Third World countries by then. Growth resulting from political stability with comparatively little social unrest improved the welfare of the majority of the people. The government welcomed initiatives and observations which aimed to improve the welfare of millions. In the past, there were fears that Indonesia could turn into one of the world's biggest communist nations, but through military discipline, the country had not fared badly after all. However, the oil bonanza resulted in the country's growth at an alarming rate. From 1974 to 1983, the size of the bureaucracy mushroomed at double the rate of the population growth, from 1.67 million to 2.63 million civil servants. Oil revenue was also used to finance the growth of state enterprises, which together with the bureaucracy, made it the largest single employer.

The state-owned oil company formed in 1957, known as Permina, controlled natural gas. It changed its name to Pertamina in 1968. The company managed oil and natural gas explorations. Pertamina kept the state petroleum monopoly. The insatiable appetite for energy amongst the world's industrialised nations created a huge demand for Indonesia's oil during the

1970s. As a result, Pertamina grew rapidly until 1975, when trouble suddenly erupted. The Pertamina crisis had a profound impact on President Soeharto's development efforts. Lessons derived from Pertamina's downfall are valuable but the costs have been extremely high. Just like Bulog, it was the prime player in the supply and distribution of basic commodities. At the epicentre of Pertamina was its President Director, Ibnu Sutowo, whose role has been indelibly entrenched in the history of Pertamina. The Pertamina story is not unlike a curse in the nation's life, where wealth, greed and success overtook humility, simplicity and moral ethics.

Ibnu Sutowo could have been considered a scholar since he was a graduate of Sorbonne in France and Leiden in Holland. Born in the shadow of the *kraton* in Yogya on 23 September 1914, Ibnu Sutowo was much more privileged than President Soeharto. His father was a regency head near Semarang. He was able to attend a superior Dutch school and later progressed to medical college in Surabaya. After his graduation in 1940, he was assigned to a new Javanese settlement in Belitung, South Sumatra. In 1945, he moved to Palembang, South Sumatra, where he became a combined staff and medical officer of the army. In 1949, Ibnu Sutowo worked in the region's civilian medical service, but remained on active army duty. He continued as commander of South Sumatra's Sriwijaya Division in 1955. General Nasution, who noticed his capabilities, brought him to Jakarta in 1956 as Chief of Logistics and concurrently Chief of Operations. That was the beginning of his career in the army.

Ibnu Sutowo's relationship with President Soeharto developed quickly as a work-related friendship. President Soeharto defined such relations as *tepo sliro* or mutual understanding. President Soeharto needed Ibnu Sutowo to get things done for Pertamina to back a threadbare army and to keep the troops away from regional commanders' conflicts. Pertamina was to carry political patronage and President Soeharto needed Ibnu Sutowo to maintain Indonesia's self-esteem. Pertamina was an outstanding example of a local enterprise keeping up with the big foreign corporations. To this extent, international corporations had bowed to its terms. Moreover, Ibnu Sutowo was a *pribumi*, not a Chinese, and yet was able to haul Pertamina into glory. Dressed immaculately in well-tailored suits, foreigners gave him the nickname "Black Diamond".

From early 1960 to 1970, oil revenue grew through a combination of increased volume, higher prices and new contracts. This brought large benefits to the country, and as the oil company came to take centrestage, so did Ibnu Sutowo's personal dominance grow. Ibnu Sutowo turned into a celebrity and gained the status of a movie star. Pertamina became a national treasure. Ibnu Sutowo was the first person of indigenous origins to succeed on such a grand scale as an entrepreneur. He was often called the "Indonesian Rockefeller". To his critics, however, he became the epitome of what had gone wrong under President Soeharto's rule. Ibnu Sutowo was beyond the reach of constitutional authority, accountable only to the president. As if untouchable, he ran a massive and expanding empire with little clarity of goals. The technocrats were skeptical and felt his priorities did not make good sense. He was literally the first amongst the government officials and a *pribumi* who set a bad example of personal extravagance. He was widely reported to have spent US$60,000 for the wedding of one of his daughters in the early 1970s. The houses built in his family compound, which was close to where President Soeharto lived, were amongst the first luxury houses built in Jakarta. His family scandals continued long after his fall from power. Bank Pacific became bankrupt under the leadership of one of his daughters. Hilton Hotel's land issues, under the management of Ponco Sutowo, remained in dispute. In 2004, another son, Adiguna Sutowo, shot a trainee waiter during the 2004 New Year party held at the Hilton Hotel in Jakarta, which coincided with the rest of the country mourning thousands of deaths in the *tsunami* catastrophe.

By the late 1960s, Ibnu Sutowo and a few of the chiefs of the state enterprises thought that they could use the state's economic powers to allocate licences for trade and manufacturing, and credits and contracts to build up conglomerates with Indonesian Chinese partners. These powers, like those of the Bulog, were considerable and a number of generals and top government officials were tempted by them. The *cukong* relationship also took place at that stage: those who held power stood in the background, while the Chinese entrepreneurs did the real work. It was seen as the best way to attain wealth.

In formal terms, Pertamina was to manage the country's oil resources through the allocation of drilling concessions, the administration of work and production-sharing contracts and the co-ordination of the oil industry as a whole. Pertamina, however, grew into the most powerful centre of economic strength as production and oil prices rose. It subsequently became the single most important source of wealth in Indonesia. Between 1969/1970 and 1974/1975, the country's revenue from oil jumped from Rp66.5 to Rp957.2 billion, or from 19.7 to 48.4 per cent. Ibnu Sutowo took the opposite stand from the technocrats who leaned towards IGGI, IMF and IBRD, and leaned more towards Japan. The issue of natural gas was a prime example. Japan became a natural choice, since the international lending organisation was not too keen about his nationalistic programme. Understandably, Japan, another Asian country with a high demand for natural gas, was the best choice to back Indonesia. Japan gave loans to Indonesia as the latter opened the doors for privileged access to a cheap energy source. The total official energy loan financing and direct investment from Japan represented nearly half of the total foreign investment in the country for the whole post-1966 period.

Over the next few years, Pertamina continued to grow in size, power and stature. Pertamina was exploited as an example of the creation of industrial capital accumulation. Ibnu Sutowo decided that Pertamina should expand its operations into investments in a wide range of activities. Pertamina formed subsidiary companies in PT Krakatau Steel. They were shareholders in petrochemicals, metal fabrication, engineering, telecommunications, real estate, air services and shipping. Their expansion included the development of Batam Island. It also expanded to very distant oil-related activities such as hospitals, hotels and even restaurants. In the early 1970s, Pertamina turned into a fast fiefdom active in dozens of industries, some of them bearing no relationship whatsoever to oil. Under President Soeharto's leadership, in the mid-1970s, Pertamina managed to top the two hundred largest international corporations. Nevertheless, beneath all of its success there was a lack of systems, control, management and experience. Pertamina became so large that it soon became the main focus of public interest. Pertamina came to be seen as the best choice and golden opportunity for starting a career, and even to pocket money and to embezzle funds! In the petroleum sector, the new style of production-sharing contract found a score of takers, which were mostly American oil companies.

The technocrats were not happy with such uncontrollable progress and felt that Pertamina had assumed the role of a quasi-national treasury and venture capitalists. As a quasi-treasurer, the organisation collected taxes but disbursed the funds in such high volumes that it made a direct impact on the supply of money. As venture capitalist, the organisation invested in steel production, hospitals and hotels, floating fertiliser factories, even restaurants in New York City. Thus, Pertamina drained the country's resources which should have been available to back the government in case of budget requirements. In retaliation, Ibnu Sutowo called the technocrats unimaginative, conservative and bookish. Contrary to criticisms, he felt that he was a great entrepreneur. However, Ibnu Sutowo had forgotten one thing: the money he had used for expansion was borrowed and the funds did not belong to Pertamina but were from the country's coffers. While entrepreneurs used their own resources, Pertamina had used government funds.

The costs of these projects were massive and none were included in the government's Five Year Plan. This created a real concern for the economic team and policymakers. The second thrust of Ibnu Sutowo's nationalist policies was the use of potential access to the country's oil and natural gas resources as a means to raise funds for the development of major projects in petrochemicals and natural gas. His ambition was very much the same as that of BJ Habibie's when he became Minister for Research and Technology. This was logical as BJ Habibie had begun his career under the supervision of Ibnu Sutowo. In both cases, President Soeharto had lost control of his wisdom, most probably over-ridden by the nationalist elements echoed by these two figures. The two had been successful in convincing President Soeharto that Indonesia would not be able to catch up with the developed nations unless the nation speeded up its industrialisation process and technology advancement. Sadly, President Soeharto had listened to them over his own passionate belief that industry was to be developed in Indonesia insofar as it related to agriculture.

The students, acting as a government watchdog, detected problems of fraud. The students' demonstration in 1970 expressed their unhappiness over the government decision to reduce oil subsidies on kerosene and petrol. In fact, they wanted to show that they knew what was going on. Corruption at the high-ranking management level became their main target. President Soeharto decided to appoint a special panel known as the "Commission of Four" to investigate these charges. Like in the case of Bulog, the findings were highly critical of Pertamina's management. One of the remedial actions imposed on Pertamina was to give 60 per cent of its net income, from both its own production as well as from production-sharing projects with foreign contractors, to the government treasury in 1971.

In January 1972, Soemantri Brojonegoro, the Minister of Mines, was appointed chairman of Pertamina's Board of Directors. In 1974, at the height of Ibnu Sutowo's career, presidential approval was granted to raise special loans for Krakatau Steel. President Soeharto also gave presidential authorisation for Pertamina to withhold US$800 million in oil taxes from Bank Indonesia to sustain the momentum of its special projects. Those not happy with the president's decision considered this policy a sign of President Soeharto's lack of enthusiasm for privatisation. By retaining full control of major state enterprises, President Soeharto could secure the funding required for the foundations he patronised. Next, critics questioned the major contracts given to corporations belonging to his cronies: Pertamina, PLN (the state electricity company), Telkom (the state telecommunications company), Bulog (Logistic Affairs Agency), PT Timah (the state tin-mining company), Garuda Indonesia (the national carrier), Jasa Marga (the state road agency) and others under the supervision of the Ministries of Transportation and Forestry became targets. Indeed, these giants among corporations employed thousands of bureaucrats. Could President Soeharto have been held accountable for this? From a political standpoint, he had been smart. The bureaucrats had secured jobs and income for a lifetime. It was rare for the government to lay off its employees. The same principles were used in the technocrat's concept of having to "bake the cake first" before it could be ready for mass distribution. The bureaucrats felt that they were the team in the baking process. President Soeharto had always believed that development could only be achieved if there was political stability and for this reason, he needed political support from the bureaucrats together with the armed forces. They were the backbone of his rule and he needed to make them happy.

In 1972, Pertamina reduced its tax payments to the government. It started borrowing heavily for both short- and long-term periods, ranging from one to 15 years. It had circumvented the restrictions imposed for long-term lending. The government failed to figure out the extent of Pertamina's violation in this respect. Pertamina had become too powerful and no Cabinet member had the authority to stop it. As a state-owned corporation, Pertamina was to forward its income to the government; it was also responsible for collecting fees from foreign contractors under the production sharing policy. The first indication of trouble surfaced in 1974, when Pertamina withheld the quarterly income payment due to the government and the revenue from the foreign contractors. It started to borrow from the domestic market, where previously it had only borrowed from offshore entities. In October 1974, Pertamina completely stopped paying taxes and used the money for its own projects. In February 1975, Pertamina missed a payment on their US$40 million loan from the Republic National Bank of Dallas, which was a relatively small bank that no one in the government was familiar with. As with most sovereign commercial loans, there was a cross-default clause in this loan agreement. Pertamina's problems soon became public knowledge when it accumulated around US$10.5 billion in debts, with approximately US$1.5 billion on short-term loan.[8] In fact, Pertamina's rapid expansion posed a real threat to the fiscal viability of the country's economy as a whole. Furthermore, it would deplete the government's revenue and adversely affect its foreign exchange position. Many became worried about President Soeharto's clear support for Ibnu Sutowo's extremely ambitious expansion plans.

A power struggle emerged when ministers tried to stop Pertamina. The organisation's management had contravened rules and influential bureaucrats had come to rely on it as a major source of non-budgetary income. In 1975, Pertamina's accumulated US$10.5 billion debt was significantly higher than the debt inherited from President Soekarno and even exceeded the present government's total borrowing.

President Soeharto instructed a rescue operation which consisted of a combination of technocrats and the military. Widjojo and Rachmat Saleh were to review Pertamina's loan portfolio. Sumarlin was responsible for reviewing and renegotiating its contracts with all other parties. From the military, Hasan Habib, Piet Haryono and Ismail Saleh were responsible for reviewing its organisational structure. Radius Prawiro, who had initially worked with Sumarlin, took responsibility for resolving Pertamina's tanker deal.

Ibnu Sutowo and seven other directors were dismissed. Piet Haryono, former director of budget in the Ministry of Finance, became the new head of

Pertamina. Sumarlin and his team found evidence of persistent overcharging. The team proposed reduction of charges to Pertamina's contractors, an extension of payment date and revised the agreements to enable Pertamina to reduce its burden.

A famous case was Pertamina's dealings with tanker magnate, Bruce Rappaport. At the peak of oil prices when there had been strong indications of oversupply in the tanker market, Ibnu Sutowo had committed Pertamina to leasing a tanker to the value of about US$1.55 billion. Rappaport had 1,600 promissory notes signed by Ibnu Sutowo on flagrantly bad terms, which reflected the country's naivety. The court battle shook the confidence of the banks with whom the government was attempting to reach an agreement on settling the outstanding debts. Pressure mounted for a quick settlement of loans and the country's future was very bleak. The case remained deadlocked with expensive lawyers engaged in battle, leading to large losses for both parties in the dispute. The international financial world lost confidence in Indonesia, while Rappaport tankers involved in the dispute could not be leased out. The government decided to stand firm. In the end, Ibnu Sutowo agreed to file an affidavit which implicated Rappaport of fraud. For both parties, the legal fees were extraordinarily high. In August 1977, after two years of battle, an agreement was reached: the Indonesian government paid US$150 million to cover the US$1.55 billion in contracts. Although the Pertamina debacle had, in theory, been brought to an end, the scandal had a long-lasting impact for the country's economy and economic policies.

Pertamina's outstanding loans were reduced from US$10.5 billion to US$6.2 billion, more than triple that of the whole country's international debts. The cost of Pertamina's scandal was not only immense in economic terms, but the country's reputation also emerged as one riddled with corruption.

The financial irregularities that abounded in Ibnu Sutowo's management of Pertamina mirrored the fraud in small fiefdoms to the massive corruption pyramid in the government.

Radius Prawiro referred to the Pertamina affair as "an accident waiting to happen". Pertamina had lacked good systems, controls, management and experience. In 1975 and 1976, Pertamina's debt grew due to the decline in oil revenue and international recession. This was the time when economic nationalism confronted crises. The second surge in oil prices took place in 1979 to 1980 and managed to push the government's revenue to US$13.4 billion. However, the country was dangerously dependent on one single commodity. In the fiscal year 1981, exports of oil and gas made up more than 80 per cent of total merchandise exported and created a revenue of 71 per cent for the government. Meanwhile, Indonesia's preference for foreign capital started to cool off.

FOREIGN INVESTORS

Two big mineral deposits in Indonesia lie in the copper mountain in Ertsberg, West Irian, and nickel in Central Sulawesi. When the country started to invite foreign investors in 1967, it welcomed everyone and did not have the courage to check the accuracy of their credentials. The first mining company virtually wrote its own ticket as the country had no concept of what a mining contract was all about. Freeport, from USA, set up to mine a rich copper outcrop which was 11,500 feet above sea level and located in one of the least accessible parts of West Irian. The cost quickly rose to US$175 million, some US$55 million above the original estimated cost. The company had to build an aerial tramway system spanning 4,800 feet to bring ore down to a mill in a town constructed 9,000 feet above sea level. A road and slurry pipeline was pushed across 116 km of mountainous terrain, jungles and coastal swamps. Freeport needed to provide further infrastructure in the form of a new port, an airstrip and a power plant. By then, the country realised how difficult it was to exploit the wealth that God had bestowed upon it. The technical and financial risks were great, but so were the rewards. In the first two years after production began in 1973, Freeport earned over US$60 million net of taxes. The hard work and danger then seemed distant.

Nevertheless, within a short period of time, the government started to learn quickly when other foreign mining companies followed in Freeport's wake. Within a year, the government tightened up tax and other concessions. International Nickel, a Canadian mining firm, started a project in the centre of Sulawesi and invested US$850 million. This was another daring move, as Islamic rebels had their stronghold there until 1965. In a few years, dozens of foreign companies took concessions in forestry within the deep jungles of Kalimantan to supply hardwood lumber to East Asian mills. Indonesia now stood fast at the top of the priority list for long-term foreign investments. During the early 1970s, investments in manufacturing were more sizeable than by the end of 1975. The total approved investments were close to US$200 million. The heaviest concentration of Japanese investors was in 65 textile projects worth US$440 million. In spite of all this, perhaps only one-third of foreign investment approvals materialised. Still, fast development and paramount capital opened another important door for the economy's recovery. Labour demand increased accordingly and companies had to take on local resources, including unskilled labour. Not only the blue-collared workers were in demand, but white-collared jobs were also widely available. Accountancy, administration and marketing and public relations positions and all secretarial jobs were available. The momentum did not stop there. With a higher demand for workforce, business opportunities opened for training in the new occupations. It created demand for trainers and teachers. To put into effect this new learning experience, classrooms were required. The heartbeat of these activities was capital. To supply capital, banks were needed. Banking knowledge, specifically in lending, was in high demand hence banking institutions had to be based there in order to give the necessary training. The overall impact of such fast economic growth was overwhelming. Job opportunities were now ample in almost every field and this was what President Soeharto had wanted to achieve.

President Soeharto now knew he was moving in the right direction with the right steps. The majority was happy to join the fast moving bandwagon into the nation's dreamland of prosperity. As we all know, however, dreams are not easy to attain; for some, dreams remain forever as dreams. The main obstacles soon surfaced and originated from the approving authority— the bureaucrats. The bureaucrats were jealous of the private sector for receiving higher salaries and seeming as if they had endless opportunities. The bureaucrats' wages were known to be low due to their large numbers, and promotions were very difficult to achieve. Their only retaliation was to ensure that the private sector's approval processes were delayed. If investors were not patient, there was a way out: payment to expedite things or "to grease the wheel". Businessmen from the Chinese community found an ingenious solution. They complied with the system to pay the fees and did so by borrowing from the banks. This was the start of the country's "social illness" which quickly became unstoppable. Unfortunately, few detected that it was the beginning of the end that would tarnish President Soeharto's legacy. Another method was to create unregistered foreign investments through loans obtained from families or friends in Hong Kong, Singapore, Taiwan and other overseas Chinese commercial centres. In this case, the loans were simply disbursed and repaid as remittances as there were no controls in the country's free foreign exchange system. The boom in the modern sectors of the economy rapidly transferred to other big cities in Java, and to a lesser degree to major cities in Sumatra, Sulawesi and Kalimantan.

Hundreds of construction works took place along Jakarta's main avenues. Jalan Thamrin and Jalan Sudirman were the main sites for new office blocks. Thirty years ago, these were the places where robbers stopped people who were travelling from the northern part of Jakarta to the southern districts. With the increasing population, many families had to move to the southern part of the city. Now named Kebayoran, it became the next prestigious residential area after Menteng. The streets were full of new cars which replaced the traditional public transport like the *becak* (pedicabs) and *delman* (horse carriages). These modes of transportation were pushed aside to the old small side streets.

The foreign capitalists wanted to manage the first stages of their operations closely. Consequently, there was a high demand for hotel rooms and residential housing. As assignments extended, the families of these foreigners stayed on for years. Schools for the children of expatriates boomed. A shortage of Western-style housing emerged. Housing rental fees climbed up in 1970, from a minimum of US$1,000 a month, payable three to five years in advance. To install a telephone line cost around US$1,500 on the black market and reached a peak of US$3,600 in mid-1976, before new capacity brought the illicit rates down to US$1,800. When expatriate families moved to the big cities, international schools were established, from playgroups to high schools. English teachers were in high demand and English courses were offered by private companies. A few schools started to work together with the American, British and Australian associations. There were 77 institutions of higher education administered by the government, with 31 universities and student numbers close to 500,000 in 1996. Schools managed by the private sector totalled 1,293, including 262 universities with student numbers up to 1,448,775. The privately managed institutions were three times larger than those run by the government. The increasing number of students in private education almost doubled from 1986 to 1996.

Foreign-operated schools also started in places where joint venture companies were located. One area was Bali, where the Australian International School now offers classes from preschool to secondary levels, with campuses also in Jakarta. There is also the Bali International School, Bali's oldest and most prestigious Western school started in 1986, which is co-educational and teaches preschool up to Grade 10. Such schools also developed in places where oil refineries or manufacturing companies operated as joint ventures, such as Balikpapan in Kalimantan. In Bandung, West Java, where many textiles factories existed, the Bandung Alliance International School stands as one of Indonesia's oldest international schools with a 40-year history and covers preschool for three-year-olds through to Grade 12, with American-style academic programmes. The Bandung Alliance International School provides a comprehensive, process-oriented, liberal arts education in the English language for children of expatriates temporarily residing in the country.

In Sulawesi, where there is mining exploration, Batu Hijau International School was specifically established to cater to the needs of PT Newmont Nusa Tenggara and PT Fluor Daniel expatriates. The same type of schools were established for expatriate families in Bogor, Cilegon, and many other cities, with classes ranging from preschool to baccalaureate degrees. Many foreign embassies also opened their own educational institutions such as, Gandhi Memorial International School, German International School, French International School, Dutch International School and British International School. Nevertheless, Indonesia is still unable to catch up with the developments that have taken place in other ASEAN nations such as Singapore and Thailand, where joint ventures with Western universities grow rapidly.

Once settled down, the expatriates wanted to see the natural beauty that the country was known for. In particular, they wanted to visit places like Bali, Yogya and Lake Toba, which they had only read about or seen in movies before they came to Indonesia. Indonesian and foreign entrepreneurs did not want to miss this new opportunity. They invested in three, four and five-star hotels in the tourist destination areas. Once again, the entrepreneurs with sharp foresight were the Chinese, and measures "to grease the wheel" were the only way to make things move. Transportation by air, rail and road were required to carry the increasing travellers who were hopping from one island to the next. The airline, hospitality and even construction industries tagged along in the development euphoria.

THE MALARI INCIDENT

On the other side of the technocrats was a different think tank. A few Chinese intellectuals had aligned themselves with Ali Moertopo since 1966. One of the best known was Liem Bian Kie, who became his assistant in 1967. Another ally was Harry Tjan. At that time, some referred to Ali Moertopo and Soedjono Hoemardhani as the "financial generals". They were alleged to have used the influx of foreign investments, combined with oil revenues, to form a sizeable pool of funds as their patronage machinery. A think tank, the Center for Strategic and International Studies (CSIS) was established in early 1970. Ali Moertopo and Soedjono Hoemardhani were among its creators. Liem Bian Kie and Harry Tjan had been active members from the start. CSIS was the academic incubator for the New Order's major policies. A coalition soon took place between Ali Moertopo, Soedjono Hoemardhani and Ibnu Sutowo. They were then the Head of Intelligence, Inspector General of Development and Head of Pertamina, respectively. President Soeharto did not budge on receiving arguments from the technocrats about Pertamina's style of entrepreneurship, which he persistently endorsed. A year later, Ali Moertopo was thrown on the defensive by the dramatic collapse of Ibnu Sutowo's oil empire.

In the early stages, the army was not intrinsically in opposition to the nationalist or modernist Islamic. The army looked at them as a valuable partner against the communists, although in the future, the nationalist party, PNI, and Islam were viewed as potential alternatives to military rule. Opponents accused Ali Moertopo and Soedjono Hoemardhani of advising the president on how to resolve potential threats by using various degrees of manipulation across the political spectrum. They claimed that the two took preventive measures and actions to weaken political parties while creating an effective state party for the first time in Indonesia's history. Critics viewed the approach of the two figures as being highly unconventional.

The economy was increasingly overwhelmed by mounting inflation and this sparked the 1972 rice crisis, which surfaced as proof of the growing imbalance in wealth distribution. The riot that took place in Bandung in August 1973, followed by protests in the universities, cast doubts on the achievements of the regime's economic programme. The actions crystallised the results of the discussion held by the Students' Council in the University of Indonesia on 24 October 1973, when several speakers questioned the military's dual functions (*Dwi Fungsi*) and the "theoretical approach" of the technocrats. Furthermore, the Muslims blamed the Catholics and mystics that were supposedly present in the army's Golkar camp. One of the Muslim groups attacked "sinful activities" such as the proliferation of massage parlours, casinos and gaming machines, and extended their animosity to the "immodest" Western-style dressing and behaviour which had infected the country's younger generation. More seriously, the Muslims felt that they had been ignored in favour of the Chinese and foreigners.

As a result of concern that the protests might get out of hand, two generals closely linked to security measures stepped in. They were General Sumitro, the Head of the Armed Forces Internal Security Command (Kopkamtib), and General Sutopo Yuwono, Head of Bakin, the Intelligence Agency. They initiated behind-the-scene discussions with the Muslim parties in October and reached a compromise after some weeks. The intervention of General Sumitro and General Sutopo signalled that another struggle had broken out, this time within the armed forces itself. General Sumitro, born in East Java in 1923, was one of the most skilled and politically astute officers in the Indonesian army. He had graduated from the West German Military Staff College. Immediately after the 1965 *coup* attempt, he had been given the delicate task of controlling East Java, the strongest bastion of Soekarnoism (manned by the loyalists of Bung Karno's ideologies). As Chief of Staff to the Defense Minister, he had supervised the reorganisation of the armed forces that took effect in 1969. He was a friendly general but could be tough when required, as shown in a statement he made about CIA involvement in the G30S affair. He defended President Soeharto's action to punish the PKI members involved in the affair and said it was the time "to kill or be killed".

General Sutopo Yuwono's reputation as a reformist was boosted when he was appointed as a member of the "Commission of Four" during the

Pertamina affair. Until 1973, these two generals were strong opponents to the political activities of Ali Moertopo and Soedjono Hoemardhani.

In late 1973, resentment surfaced again as anti-Chinese riots took place in Bandung. The riots damaged 1,500 shops and houses. The army seemed sluggish in taking action against the mob. Thus, many speculated on the military's sympathy for the demonstrators. General Sumitro, whom a month before had annoyed the students with a campaign against young men with long hair, took a surprisingly reconciliatory approach. He toured the campuses, received student delegations and held debates with the intellectuals. By the end of November 1973, General Sumitro declared that a new style of leadership was needed. Protests, initially focusing on the development strategy, had by the end of 1973 turned to accusations of mismanagement of the country's wealth. The main target was the group of presidential advisers, the *cukong*, the cronies and relatives of those in power. Ali Moertopo, Soedjono Hoemardhani, Lim Sioe Liong, Liem Bian Kie and even Ibu Tien herself came under direct attack.

Sharp criticisms came from the Muslims, the press and the modernist intellectuals. The students issued a list of "Three Demands", calling for the suspension of President Soeharto's *Aspri*, reduction of prices of commodities and eradication of corruption. While General Sumitro held on to his receptive approach, General Ali Moertopo issued instructions for the demonstration to stop. General Sumitro was accused of using the students' criticisms to further his own ambitions and change the leadership to his own interests. On 11 January 1974, President Soeharto agreed to hold a meeting with 35 students' councils. It was an awkward and formal gathering, at which the students raised concern on the role of *Aspri*, the business involvement of senior government figures and their wives and the government connection with the Chinese business community. By this time, President Soeharto was often dubbed as "the smiling general". Famously known to give noncommittal replies, the president pointed out that *Aspri*, in fact, held no executive powers, but this only served to further upset the students. It intensified when the then Japanese Prime Minister, Kakuei Tanaka, came for a state visit.

Tanaka arrived in Jakarta on the evening of 14 January. The next morning, thousands of students demonstrated in the streets of Jakarta, calling Japan an "economic animal". In front of Ali Moertopo's office they burnt an effigy of Soedjono Hoemardhani. General Sumitro was charged with giving the green light to the demonstrators as a way to pressure the president and to distance himself from his two most influential advisers. By the afternoon, the demonstration had turned into a riot in which hundreds of cars were burnt and shops looted. As the students converged at Merdeka Palace to press their demands, violence broke out in two nearby Chinese commercial areas. One of them was at the Pasar Senen shopping centre. When they attacked Astra, the Toyota dealership, schoolchildren and bystanders joined the rioting and burnt the Astra building to the ground. William Soeryadjaya, Astra's owner, was alleged to have had a close relationship with Ibnu Sutowo and Ibu Tien. The uprising continued as the burning of the Japanese-made vehicles took place. Shortly afterwards, the military declared a dusk curfew. They began to crack down on the aggressive crowd. Shots were fired and hundreds of arrests were made as the incident continued through the night. About a dozen people were reportedly killed before the military could bring the riots under control.

Tanaka left Merdeka Palace in a helicopter on 17 January 1974, by which time the city was tense but firmly under army control. During the two days of riots, 470 people were arrested and some 800 cars and 150 buildings were destroyed. The affair was called the Malari incident or the 15 January incident (Peristiwa Lima Belas Januari). It was considered to have been anti-Japanese in nature and marked a turning point for President Soeharto's presidency. The fact that the army was unable to maintain law and order during the state visit of an important foreign leader served as an early wake-up call to President Soeharto's government. Opsus publicly made a stand that General Sumitro's supporters were pro-US forces and that they had a plan to stop the country's attempt to build its national industries. This clearly shocked the government and the reaction was swift and effective. Yet, despite the political manipulation, the government became convinced that anti-Chinese sentiments would remain as long as their economic domination existed.

On 28 January 1974, *Aspri* was abolished and Sutopo Yuwono was appointed as the country's ambassador to the Netherlands. President Soeharto took over Kopkamtib and General Sumitro remained as Deputy Armed Forces Commander, but he soon decided to resign. The president also replaced two of his trusted comrades—Sumitro and Sutopo Yuwono. General Yoga Sugama was appointed the Head of Bakin and Admiral Sudomo the

Chief of Staff of Kopkamtib. The removal of General Sumitro and General Sutopo Yuwono was to divert the students' anger against the technocrats, IGGI and the World Bank, *Aspri* and other perceived "corruptors".

In times of crisis, as what President Soekarno did in former times, President Soeharto decided to take the single most important job into his own hands.

One of the students' leaders, Hariman Siregar, was imprisoned soon thereafter. On hindsight, Hariman said that the students' genuine protest had nothing to do with the political power struggle between General Sumitro and the president's personal assistants. The real motive had been the students' unhappiness and disagreement over the Japanese investors' choice of the Chinese as their partners and ignoring the *pribumi*. Meanwhile, the middle class intelligentsia was not able to build up a power base. Their powerlessness might have been due to their reluctance to set up alliances with the workers or the peasants or even to mobilise effective commitment from the urban middle class. This middle class had benefited from the New Order and they were not prepared to share the wealth or accept a redistribution of affluence with the workers or peasants. For the liberal intellectuals, the Malari incident was the beginning of a different era. From then on, President Soeharto effectively concentrated most of his energy on suppressing the universities, the press and the civil service, all demanding more freedom and that their criticisms against the government be heard. The president was perceived to have succeeded to some extent in this area.

One week after the Malari incident, the National Economic Stabilization Board made major changes to investment rules. Credit policy was designed to benefit those left behind in the country's development process. Changes of investment laws emerged to speed up the process of share divestment for foreign companies. It was modified to prevent 100 per cent foreign ownership. Foreign investors were required to form joint ventures. It also stipulated a higher level of a *pribumi*'s equity in domestic investments and this had to take place within a set period of time. Capital equity in joint ventures was to be progressively transferred to the Indonesian partners, so that within 10 years, the local partners would gradually achieve 51 per cent ownership. All foreign investment projects had to be in the form of joint ventures with indigenous partners. In addition, where the local partners were not indigenous, the 51 per cent national equity had to be effected within a shorter time through public stock offering. Fifty per cent of the shares had to be disbursed to the indigenous partners. State banks could only allocate investment credits to indigenous investors. In domestic investment projects, the indigenous partners were to have 75 per cent equity, and where the management was largely in indigenous hands, 50 per cent indigenous equity was required.

The Malari incident was a response against big businesses owned by Liem Sioe Liong and Bob Hasan—the first two Chinese businessmen whom Soeharto got to know while being an army officer in Central Java and who eventually became the richest persons in Indonesia—whose business groups were not particularly popular among the students. At that time, there were strong negative sentiments between the indigenous and non-indigenous. The root of the problem lay in the perception that the Chinese group had managed to get big businesses over the *pribumi*. The *pribumi* or the indigenous felt they received only small or insignificant projects. The government realised that there was a need to accelerate growth at a faster pace, but they argued that the Chinese were in a better position to get the ball rolling in this area due to their experience and skills.

OTHER DISCONTENTMENT

Another unhappy group arose on 17 July 1976, focusing on the way in which President Soeharto had carried out his duties and used his power. They felt that President Soeharto had abused his power to enrich his family and cronies. The religious circle which included Cardinal Darmoyuwono from the Catholic church, TB Simatupang, Chairman of Indonesian Council of Churches, and Prof Hamka, from Islam, had endorsed this movement as well. The document named "Towards Salvation" had originated from Sawito Kartowibowo, an unknown figure. Sawito was fired in 1968 from his job due to his left-wing orientation. Sawito proposed that the presidency should be transferred to Bung Hatta. Sawito might have had millions of fans but he did not have enough influential defenders. In June 1978, he was convicted of a wide range of charges and sentenced to eight years in prison.

The most popular and respected figure in this group was reportedly Bung Hatta, who had co-signed the country's proclamation of independence. Bung Hatta's full name was Mohammad Hatta. He was born on 12 August 1902 in Bukitinggi, Sumatra. He was raised by his maternal family and was the only son among his mother's brood of six daughters. He had been active in the Jong Sumatranen Bond (Association of Young Sumatra) since 1916. His specialisation was in economics but he had a large interest in politics. In 1926, to raise the profile of the name "Indonesia" in the international arena, he led a student delegation to a conference on international democracy and peace in Bierville, France. The name "Indonesia" was accepted even though the country was still part of the Dutch colony. During his student days abroad, he had come across young students who later became leaders in Asian and African countries, with Jawaharlal Nehru, India's first Prime Minister, being one of them and their friendship remained for years to come.

After he completed his study in the Netherlands, Bung Hatta returned to Indonesia in July 1932. In his writings, he countered Soekarno's imprisonment by the Dutch in Ende, Flores viciously. Later in 1935, he too was exiled to Boven Digul, Papua.[9] He had been Indonesia's first vice-president from 1950 to 1956, in fact, he had been the only vice-president that President Soekarno had ever appointed. He resigned from the government on 1 December 1956, in spite of President Soekarno's attempt at persuading him to stay on.

When President Soeharto came to power, Hatta distanced himself from the political arena and kept his status as a statesman. He passed away on 14 March 1980. Although they had never been close, President Soeharto referred to Bung Hatta with high esteem in his biography.[10] Bung Hatta was the complete opposite of Bung Karno. As my father described him, "Bung Karno is like the waves in the open ocean; Bung Hatta is like peaceful water in the river."

In 1976, a student from the University of Indonesia was arrested for allegedly preparing Molotov cocktails to harm the president's family. At the same time, he wanted to destroy the prostitution centres and gambling casinos. On the surface, this incident appeared to be a re-emergence of Islamic fanaticism. However, it might have reflected a deeper issue—the declining moral values of the nation. The military looked on it as a threat to destabilise the country's development and failed to analyse it deeper to reveal the real source of discontent. The restlessness continued and on Christmas day in 1976, grenades went off in nightspots in Medan, North Sumatra.

In January 1977, the entire board of the largest government commercial bank, Bank Bumi Daya, resigned after revelations of massive irregularities, which were later revealed as Astra's loan defaults to the amount of US$984 million. *The New York Times* printed allegations of a US$40 million payoff in connection with the Palapa domestic satellite system. Bambang Trihatmodjo, President Soeharto's second son, was one of the owners of this project. In February 1977, the United States authorities announced possible legal proceedings over funding of a Pertamina owned restaurant in New York City. In March that year, Ibnu Sutowo was placed under arrest. In April 1977, a provincial chief of Bulog was put on trial for embezzling US$4.5 million. Similar notorious scandals were to surface again in the early 1990s.

PETISI 50

On 13 May 1980, 50 well-known national figures signed what was later named *Petisi 50*. This petition, called "Statement of Concern", was sent to Parliament and raised the issue of whether President Soeharto had enhanced his power in excess of Pancasila. The petition signatories were respected leaders like General Nasution and Ali Sadikin, the popular former governor of Jakarta. Also included were figures such as Syafruddin Prawiranegara, Moh Natsir and Burhanuddin Harahap, three former prime ministers of the early Republic. The petition originator was Ali Sadikin or Bang Ali, as he is popularly known. Born in Sumedang on 7 July 1926, Bang Ali, one of President Soeharto's vocal opponents, was extremely popular with the students when he was governor of Jakarta from 1966 to 1977. He built Jakarta into the metropolitan city that it is today. Museums, historical sites, parks, and the like, had all been preserved under his instructions. To obtain funding for the upkeep of the city, he allowed gambling to take place, but restricted it to only certain places. In addition, gambling was intended only for the business circles but not for government officials or the military. These two latter groups were not allowed to enter gambling places where identity cards had to be produced at the entrance. It was a daring move as many criticised him for it, but he chose to ignore them. Bang Ali was also a pragmatic leader and the protests became subdued when the results were seen.

Very outspoken in a refined manner, he was, not surprisingly, the students' choice for president. He was the staunchest opponent of President Soeharto to date. He still argues for the thousands of communists who were killed during the G30S affair. He has always claimed that the country had killed millions, like the situation during the Vietnam War. My father tried to calm him down during the several visits he made to our house and pleaded with him to consider what would have happened if the communists had won and how many of the Muslim population would have been killed. Recently, on Lebaran, he went to Jalan Cendana to visit Pak Harto and with a naughty glint in his eyes, he told me that he and Pak Harto had hugged each other. I often went to see him for discussions during my preparations for this book. He is a likeable person, straight, honest and stands firm on issues which he strongly believes in. Indonesians need leaders like him who are willing to let bygones be bygones. We may have different opinions on politics, but there is a need to treat each other in a decent manner. This is what leadership is about and this is what Indonesians should aspire towards.

Another one of President Soeharto's prominent opponents was General M Jasin. Years ago, he had been President Soeharto's ardent supporter. Born and raised by a father from Surabaya and a mother from Minang, his career included being a military attaché in Moscow. He was a deputy in KASAD when his rank was raised to Lieutenant General. M Jasin recalled a meeting in mid-October 1967, where the generals had given full support to General Soeharto in order to govern under the New Order. M Jasin claimed that President Soeharto made changes and exerted pressure on the country's social institutions. By streamlining political parties down to only three, President Soeharto could easily control and manoeuvre power. In the end, Parliament would also have been contrived and the presidential election would be manipulated. He further criticised the way the 1971 elections were handled. He questioned the motives behind the cloves monopoly given to President Soeharto's cronies and the method President Soeharto had used in acquiring Tapos.[11]

On 13 March 1974, M Jasin attended a meeting for discussion about Presidential Rule Nos 6 and 10. The chairman was Sumarlin, then the Minister of Planning, and Sudharmono, then the Minister of State Secretariat. The discussion was about rulings on business involvement of officials and other restrictions. M Jasin claimed the spirit of PP Nos 6 and 10 was for a clean and honest state apparatus, in order to gain respectability. The state apparatus should stay away from the commercialisation of its vocation. Involvement of government employees in private businesses should be restricted. Since then, most of the signers of *Petisi 50* have been cast out from their positions or businesses.

If only the clock could be turned back, such scandals involving Bulog and Pertamina could have been avoided, or at the very least, the detractors could have been imprisoned. The way President Soeharto had handled the two cases of extreme corruption was lacking in the elements of law enforcement, which was a great disappointment to the public. Ibnu Sutowo went on to hold the chairmanship of the Red Cross, instead of being sent to jail; his family also became untouchable. This did not aid President Soeharto's cause as the public had demanded from the start the reasons behind his leniency on this issue. Unfortunately, a few people have pointed to a business link between the families of President Soeharto and Ibnu Sutowo. When there is no law in place, the whole pillar of the nation's progress is fractured.

It had been those amongst his former strong supporters who had spearheaded the Malari incident, and the Sawito and *Petisi 50* incidents, including the students and army generals. In the Malari incident, it had been the students and a few army personnel such as General Sumitro. In the Sawito incident, it had been Bung Hattta, one of the cleanest leaders the country has ever had.

As for *Petisi 50*, General Nasution was among those involved, not to mention Bang Ali, who even now claims he does not regret the "punishment" he received from Pak Harto. He was not allowed to go overseas for many years, but Bang Ali, with his great sense of humour, said it was a blessing in disguise—in being prohibited to go abroad, he was able to save money. When speculation persisted that Pak Harto was faking his illness, Bang Ali told the newspapers that when he had gone to Jalan Cendana and met Ali Alatas, the former Minister of Foreign Affairs, he and Ali Alatas had done all the talking, as Pak Harto had been too ill to speak. For whatever reason, President Soeharto did not ask his detractors to engage in an earnest discussion with him. It would have been commendable if he had been willing to meet them half the way. Instead, he seemed to use a distant and cold approach. This might well have been one of his faults. Indeed, it must be distressing for him to know that the successes he achieved in rice sufficiency, family planning and healthcare have been overshadowed by the Bulog and Pertamina scandals.

ENDNOTES

1 *Tempo* magazine, 24 June 1989. Here, Bung Karno was referring to an irrational form of nationalism based on the traditional Javanese practice of burning incense in prayer.

2 After the Round Table Conference or Konperensi Meja Bundar (KMB) in Den Haag, the Dutch had finally agreed to recognise the country's independence in December 1949, almost five years after it had been declared, but they imposed a federation of states, hence the drafting of a Federal Constitution.

3 In May 1980, 50 national figures signed and sent a petition to Dewan Perwakilan Rakyat (DPR) or the People's Representative Council and named it "Statement of Concern": it raised the issue of whether President Soeharto had enhanced his power in excess of Pancasila.

4 G Dwipayana and Ramadhan KH, *Soeharto, Pikiran, Ucapan dan Tindakan Saya* (PT Citra Lamtoro Gung Persada, 1988). This biography was written from President Soeharto's own account as dictated to the two authors.

5 Radius Prawiro, *Indonesia's Struggle for Economic Development—Pragmatism in Action* (Oxford University Press, 1998).

6 Radius Prawiro, *Indonesia's Struggle for Economic Development—Pragmatism in Action* (Oxford University Press, 1998), p 135.

7 Richard Robison, *Indonesia, The Rise of Capital* (Asia Studies Association of Australia, Southeast Asia Publication Series (No 13), 1986), p 232.

8 Radius Prawiro, *Indonesia's Struggle for Economic Development—Pragmatism in Action* (Oxford University Press, 1998), p 108.

9 Papua is the old name (under the Dutch) of West Irian.

10 G Dwipayana and Ramadhan KH, *Soeharto, Pikiran, Ucapan dan Tindakan Saya* (PT Citra Lamtoro Gung Persada, 1988), pp 344–345.

11 Tapos was President Soeharto's famous farm located in Ciawi, Bogor (60 km from Jakarta), where research was undertaken for crossbreeding of livestock.

1950s.
Soeharto as a young soldier.

1964.
As a paratrooper in West Irian.

October 1965.
Attending the state funeral of the six slain generals during the G30S event at the
Kalibatan Heroes' Cemetery.

1966.
President Soekarno signing papers for the promotion of Soeharto (standing) to General.

*March 1967.
Soeharto signing papers after being appointed as Acting President.*

*27 March 1968.
Being sworn in as President.*

1969.
Mingling with farmers and their families.

21 June 1970.
Addressing the nation during the state funeral of Bung Karno.

January 1970.
With President Tito
(second from right) of
Yugoslavia during a state
visit to Yugoslavia.

September 1971, Merdeka
Palace, Jakarta.
With Prince Bernhard
and Queen Juliana of the
Netherlands during their
state visit to Indonesia.

1976.
With fellow ASEAN
leaders (from left): Prime
Minister Datuk Hussein
Onn of Malaysia, Prime
Minister Lee Kuan Yew
of Singapore, President
Ferdinand Marcos of the
Philippines and Prime
Minister Krukit Pramoj
of Thailand.

October 1977.
With Egypt's President Anwar
Sadat (left) during a state visit
to Egypt.

May 1978.
With Malaysia's Prime Minister
Datuk Hussein Onn (centre).

June 1978.
With Singapore's Prime
Minister Lee Kuan Yew in
Bali.

July 1979.
With Philippine President
Ferdinand Marcos and
First Lady Imelda Marcos
in Manila.

December 1980.
With India's Prime
Minister Indira Gandhi
during a state visit to
India.

November 1983.
With German Chancellor
Helmut Kohl (second
from left) and Mrs Kohl
(extreme right) at the
Merdeka Palace.

1985.
Celebrating with the farmers
after Indonesia achieves self-
sufficiency in rice.

April 1985.
Welcoming Britain's Prime
Minister Margaret Thatcher
during her state visit to
Indonesia.

August 1985.
(L-R) Sihwati Nawangwulan,
President Soeharto, the author,
Hubert Knapp, Ibu Tien and
Roeslan Abdulgani in Cendana.

1986. US President Ronald Reagan giving a speech during a state visit to Indonesia. (Seated L-R): Ibu Tien, President Soeharto and Mrs Nancy Reagan.

*May 1989.
With Japan's Prime
Minister Noboru Takeshita
at the Merdeka Palace.*

*June 1989.
Receiving the UN Population
Award in New York City.*

September 1989.
With Soviet Union's President and Mrs Mikhail Gorbachev during a state visit to Moscow.

November 1989, Merdeka Palace.
With the Prince and Princess of Wales, Charles and Diana, during their state visit
to Indonesia.

July 1990.
With HM King
Bhumibol Adulyadej of
Thailand (right) during a
state visit to Thailand.

June 1991.
Hajj pilgrimage in Mecca.

With US President George
Bush in Washington DC.

December 1991.
Visiting one of the housing
complexes for low income
residents in Kemayoran,
Jakarta.

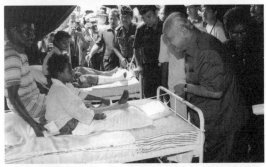

December 1992.
Visiting victims of natural
disasters in Maumere, Nusa
Tenggara Province.

1992.
Officiating at the
construction of a dam
to stop the flooding in
Sumbawa.

June 1993.
With Malaysian Prime
Minister Mahathir
Mohamad during a state
visit to Malaysia.

November 1993.
With Iranian President
Hashemi Rafsanjani during a
state visit to Iran.

November 1993.
With the President of Tunisia
Zine al-Abidine Ben Ali and
his wife during a state visit
to Tunisia.

November 1993.
Participating in a world leaders' meeting in Seattle, Washington, USA.

November 1993.
A handshake with US President
Bill Clinton during the celebration
of the agreement between the
Municipal Area of Jakarta and
the Federal State of Arkansas, US,
becoming sister states.

July 1994, Merdeka Palace.
Greeting Palestinian President
Yasser Arafat during his state visit to
Indonesia.

April 1996.
Visiting Indonesian boy scouts in Pulau Tunda. Deserving members of the Boy Scouts Movement receive scholarships from one of the president's foundations.

1996.
A visit to Tapos, West Java, where cross-breeding of Australian cows take place.

August 1996.
Inspecting the vegetables grown on his farm in Mekarsari, West Java.

August 1996.
Witnessing the success of a fish breeding project in Matoa, Jakarta.

October 1997.
With (L-R) Ibu Nasution, General Nasution, General Try Sutrisno and others during
the promotion ceremony of General Nasution to a five-star rank.

January 1998.
Signing the Memorandum of Agreement between Indonesia and the
International Monetary Fund (IMF) as witnessed by IMF Director
Michael Camdessus (standing).

May 1998.
Announcing his resignation at the Merdeka Palace.

May 1998.
Congratulating BJ Habibie on his presidency.

2000.
Family photo in Cendana.(Standing L-R) Indra Rukmana, Sigit, Tata, Mamiek, Bambang, Tommy; (seated L-R) Elsye, Titiek, Pak Harto, Tutut and Halimah.

September 2005, Kalitan, Solo. Health check with Dr Hari (standing behind) and Dr Yuniarti while the author looks on.

September 2005.
With Tutut and Dwidjo family in Klaten.

September 2006.
With Hubert Knapp and the author in Cendana.

Chapter 3

SAILING INTO THE SUNSET

All men want,
not something to do with,
but something to do,
or rather something to be.
— Henry David Thoreau

In her book *The Downing Street Years*, Margaret Thatcher described Indonesia as:

> A state created out of some 17,000 islands, a mix of races and religions, based on an artificially created philosophy—the Five Principles of "Pancasila"—it is a marvel that Indonesia has been kept together at all. Yet, it has an economy which is growing fast, more or less sound public finances, and though there have been serious human rights abuses, particularly in East Timor, this is a society which by most criteria "works". At the top, President Suharto is an immensely hardworking and effective ruler. I was struck by the detailed interest he took in agriculture—something which is all too rare in oil-rich countries like Indonesia. He spent hours on his own farm where experiments in cross-breeding livestock to maximise nutrition were the order of the day.[1]

Margaret Thatcher clearly understood the difficulties that President Soeharto had to face in ruling a nation spread across thousands of islands, where the inhabitants have different traditions and religious beliefs. From Sabang in the west to Merauke in the eastern part of the archipelago, the topography ranges from mountains, swampland and jungles to plantations and cultivated rice terraces. The geographical, ethnic and cultural aspects from one region to another are so diverse that the people do not necessarily understand each other's languages and dialects. Yet, President Soeharto managed to keep the country united by using Pancasila as the bond that kept the people together. Although Pancasila was thought of as an artificially created philosophy, for the Indonesian people, Pancasila had been in existence for centuries, long before Indoneisa's founding fathers were born.

President Soeharto admitted that President Soekarno was the one who "compiled" the set of ideals as outlined in the five principles of Pancasila: belief in God, humanitarianism, nationalism through unity of the country, consultative democracy and social justice. My father said that Pancasila was the result of one of President Soekarno's many moments of ingenuity and that only a leader of Bung Karno's calibre could have successfully formulated the idea with such clarity. It was mainly through Bung Karno's exceptional talent that Pancasila became meaningful even to the uneducated masses. President Soeharto knew how well my father understood his predecessor's concept of Pancasila. Hence, he appointed my father to head his advisory council on Pancasila. This decision was, in my father's view, proof that President Soeharto had every intention to continue the policies of his predecessor if he thought that they were good for the country. Therefore, for those who have the impression that President Soeharto had wanted to totally disregard President Soekarno's role in Indonesia's history, this would serve to prove otherwise. His appointment of a team to focus on Pancasila reflected his pragmatism, his intentions to continue the policies started by Bung Karno and the fact that the most important thing on his mind was to keep the country afloat and to move forward.

At the most basic level, President Soeharto's success in governing the country was due to his understanding of the farmers' mentality, coupled with military discipline, which he favoured, and the Javanese way of thinking. That this understanding enabled him to hold power for three decades is indeed inspiring. However, the issue on East Timor and human rights abuses were completely different matters. Indonesia's argument when President Soekarno wanted West Irian back as part of Indonesia's lawful territory was the same argument President Soeharto has used, that East Timor belonged to Indonesia.

President Soeharto's major achievement was the nation's self-sufficiency in rice in 1984, taking into consideration that the population had almost tripled at that stage. This sufficiency in rice was not only the number one criterion or yardstick used to measure the success of Repelita, but the way in which it was achieved also deserves credit. Various integrated policies have been viewed as the reasons for this success, including the establishment of Bulog to monitor supply and demand, family planning to control population growth, the transmigration policy to reduce the dense population in Java, the opening of fertiliser plants and the improvement of highways, harbours, shipping and so forth. These have been brought together in an overall strategy and not dealt with in a piecemeal fashion. Transmigration was not easy to carry out as it needed a mind-set change and was costly. To change a closed mentality required persuasion and the incoming families needed housing, schools and new sources of income in the new places. Transmigration was as complex as the implementation of the family planning programme. In addition, areas where transmigration was targeted included Sumatra, Kalimantan and Sulawesi; this not only posed problems such as adjustment to a new environment, but more importantly, the local people had a different language, traditions and faith. Newcomers were usually looked upon with suspicion and this was where the ideals of Pancasila came as a solid and supportive foundation.

MODERATE MUSLIMS

As good Muslims, President Soekarno and President Soeharto learnt that Prophet Muhammad had perceived the great problems confronting his people at a deeper level than most of his contemporaries. The Prophet had to delve deeply and painfully into his own inner being to find a solution that was not only politically viable but also spiritually illuminating. Islam is a religion that teaches its followers about life and what follows after death.

Both presidents were moderate Muslims as they followed the Qur'an's teaching that "there shall be no coercion in matters of faith". It commands Muslims to respect the beliefs of Jews and Christians, whom the Qur'an calls *ahl al-kitab* or "People of the Book". Muslim scholars also reason that had Prophet Muhammad known about Buddhism or Hinduism, the Qur'an would also have endorsed their sages, as it is believed that all rightly guided religions that submitted to God and not to man-made deities and preached justice and equality came from the same divine source. More importantly, the crucial virtue of Islam is social justice. Muslims were commanded as their first duty to build a community (*ummah*) characterised by practical compassion, in which there was a fair distribution of wealth. In fact, social concern is always an essential part of the vision of the world as perceived through the eyes of the world's major religions.

This is what Pancasila's first point, "belief in God", meant, that is to respect all faiths. A Muslim leader had to concentrate on social, political and military matters in life, while religion prepared him for the time beyond life. Both presidents viewed women not as second-class citizens; the Qur'an gave women rights of inheritance and divorce centuries before Western women were accorded such status. Under President Soekarno and President Soeharto, there was never a requirement for women to be veiled. They knew that certain apparel were adopted some three or four generations after the Prophet's death. Muslims at that time were copying the Greek Christians of Byzantium, who were veiled. Hence, women were never forced to wear veils but were left to decide based on their own personal choice.

When faced with a crisis or dilemma, the Prophet entered deeply into himself and tried to get close to God in finding a divinely inspired solution. Similarly, President Soekarno remained alone and sought God's guidance on the eve of the declaration of Indonesia's independence. President Soeharto used to wake up very early to find peace and seek spiritual guidance as well. Both presidents were not against Jewish people but Zionism. In fact, in September 1979, Indonesia reportedly signed an agreement to purchase 28 Skyhawks and 11 helicopters from Israel. In September 1982, the country publicly admitted for the first time that it had ties with the state of Israel through a third party. On 15 October 1993, President Soeharto met wth visiting Prime Minister Yitzhak Rabin not as president of Indonesia, but as Chairman of the Non-Aligned Movement, a position he had been selected for in September 1991. Taking into consideration the sensitive religious issues at stake, the meeting had been kept secret and the media only knew about it four hours after Prime Minister Yitzhak Rabin had left Indonesia. At the same time, General Feisal Tanjung, Commander of the Army, had denied the assertion that Indonesia had bought arms from Israel. However, during the first half of the 1990s, commercial ties between the two countries reportedly grew considerably. The local newspapers reported that in 1991, Indonesia exported a little over US$31,000 worth of goods but the figure went beyond US$1.7 million over the following years. In October 1994, a large delegation of the Israel Chamber of Commerce visited Jakarta. All this shows that President Soeharto maintained his pragmatism when it came to business and he was prepared to face any challenge.

FATHER OF DEVELOPMENT

On 10 March 1982, as a result of the influx of foreign investors, the awakening of domestic entrepreneurship and the fast growth of development, President Soeharto was named *Bapak Pembangunan* or "Father of Development" by the MPR. Nevertheless, discontentment abounded as he approached the third term of his presidency, with riots taking place during a Golkar rally in Lapangan Banteng. Yet, Golkar managed to attain 64.2 per cent of votes on 4 May 1982. That was when public apprehension came to light and the way that Golkar had tried to manoeuvre vote-gathering was revealed. State employees claimed to have received their wages in an envelope with the Golkar logo, which many considered as a warning on whom to choose during the general elections. Another practice involved placing ballot boxes in office buildings, with each box printed with a party's name and logo. This was how the government monitored which company in which building had supported Golkar or the opposition. This was perceived as a direct threat and the beginning of abuse of the citizens' privacy. Whether the president knew about this or whether it had been shielded from his knowledge is difficult to ascertain. Unfortunately, only very few had the courage to complain, especially amongst the bureaucrats who made up the voting majority. State employees wanted to play it safe and protect their positions. The private sector too were motivated by their own self-interest in preserving the status quo, since any change of a ruler might jeopardise their positions. This practice made the country's sail to prosperity for all harder and rougher.

The fourth Development Cabinet formed on 16 March 1983, which lasted until 1988, consisted of 32 ministers and 5 junior ministers. President Soeharto chose General Umar Wirahadikusumah as vice-president of the country. In economic affairs, Radius Prawiro replaced Ali Wardhana as the Minister of Finance. Ali Wardhana moved to the position of the Coordinating Minister for Economy and Finance/Chairman of the National Development Supervision. JB Sumarlin was appointed the State Minister of National Development Planning/Chairman of Bappenas.

General Umar was a low-key figure, not ambitious but a hard worker and a loyal subordinate. He was born in Sumedang, West Java, on 10 October 1924. Unlike the Sultan, General Umar attended a local university in Bandung.

Like President Soeharto, he received military training during the Japanese occupation. He joined PETA, TKR and after various military stints in West Java, was appointed Commander of Jakarta in the late 1950s. He then took over General Soeharto's position as Chief of Kostrad. In 1967, he became Deputy Commander of the Army. He was involved in combat against the communist rebellion in 1948, DI/TII in West Java and PRRI in North Sumatra. As with the two previous vice-presidents, there were no doubts about General Umar's loyalty. He played an important role during the G30S event. Even though he was a military man, the public did not perceive his appointment as a change towards a military government.

A few days before President Soeharto entered his fourth term in office, the country's security deteriorated significantly. The big cities became unsafe. Serious crimes like robberies and killings were being regularly committed. Intelligence sources identified the felons as those with tattoos and prisoners who had escaped from jails. The government decided to take harsh measures. Perpetrators were shot on the spot and their dead bodies left for public viewing. The shootings were referred to by the media as *Petrus*: *pembunuhan misterius* or "mysterious killings". Those against such callous acts claimed that shooting persons with tattoos was too simplistic, just as it was to accuse any man on the street with a tattoo as being against social stability. However, for the victims and their families, the act was justified. President Soeharto was aware that his critics were from all sectors, including the international forum. He stood fast on his beliefs and explained that "shock therapy" was necessary for those who violated law and order, and committed crimes beyond human decency. He argued against the application of human rights for those who had behaved in an inhumane way. Every human being had rights, but, at the same time, every individual was expected to preserve order and peace. Otherwise, rapists and murderers would make use of human rights as an excuse to commit offences. Indeed, the "mysterious killings" led to an instant decline in the high level of crime. President Soeharto also believed in the death penalty, and he would not have stopped an execution if the Supreme Court had decided to proceed. On the other hand, if there were strong reasons to grant a pardon, he would not hesitate to grant it, like in the case of Soebandrio and Omar Dhani—who were sentenced for life due to their involvement in the G30S event. After spending 30 years in prison and as both of them were more than 80 years old, they were pardoned by President Soeharto after the Ramadan in 1996.

More than a year down the road on 12 September 1984, unrest erupted and gunshots were fired in the harbour of Jakarta, Tanjung Priok. The unrest came from the extremist Muslims, who questioned the validity of Pancasila as the only lawful basis for all political parties. President Soeharto said that he had no objection to this stand, but there were other ways of presenting their case. In his view, gripes against the government should not lead to a call for rebellion, or to demands for the freedom of prisoners; or even worse, the use of bombs to destroy the nation's precious heritage sites such as Borobudur, which the extremists had actually succeeded in doing. He had no reservations about resorting to strict punishment for such an act. He maintained that this type of violence would create political instability. Time and time again, he had emphasised the necessity of maintaining security and political stability in order to enable the country to progress. Only under such conditions could Indonesians improve their standard of living. As a result, Pancasila was considered the best tool and it was therefore imposed upon all organisations to adopt Pancasila as their sole foundation in May 1985.

His critics maintained that through Pancasila, President Soeharto intended to strengthen and legitimise his political stand. On 9 November 1986, feeling that political stability had been established, President Soeharto decided that the time had come to honour the legacy of the country's two great leaders by naming President Soekarno and Bung Hatta as the nation's independence proclamation heroes.

It was in his fifth Development Cabinet formed on 21 March 1988, which lasted until 1993, that Sudharmono became his vice-president. That cabinet had 32 ministers and six junior ministers. JB Sumarlin now moved to the new position of Minister of Finance, while Radius Prawiro became the Coordinating Minister for Economy and Finance/Chairman of the National Development Planning Board. Saleh Afiff was State Minister of National Development Planning/Chairman of Bappenas. Born in Gresik, East Java, Sudharmono was a retired Lieutenant General and had obtained a law degree, when he became the fourth vice-president. From 1978 to 1988, he was the Minister of State Secretariat and the coordinator of the foundations that President Soeharto built. His role in leading Golkar was significant, as

Golkar became the absolute winner during the elections in 1987. Tall, slim and energetic but quiet, he was called a loner by the foreign press who felt he was aloof.

During the vice presidency elections, there was a split in Golkar as a few wanted Try Sutrisno as the vice-president. Golkar's civilians preferred Sudharmono, while the military faction opted for Try Sutrisno. General LB Moerdani was often named as the prime mover for support of Try Sutrisno. Politics is often filled with self-interest and those against Sudharmono alleged that he had been involved in PKI. However, the allegation could not be proven. In fact, similar accusations were levelled against Adam Malik, whose Murba party was considered to have had a close link with PKI. Sudharmono's death on 25 January 2006, proved to be a great loss for Pak Harto—aside from his position in the Yayasan, he had been very close to Pak Harto.

The fourth Repelita from April 1984 to March 1989 focused on raising the level of the country's current achievements. The government acknowledged that meeting basic needs was still a major concern for many of the people. One of the outstanding issues was the improvement of wealth distribution, as well as increasing job opportunities without discrimination (that is, opportunities for people of different races and backgrounds). Developments were needed all over the country. If economic development could be accelerated, then stability could be maintained.

The fifth Repelita from April 1989 to March 1994 aimed at yet another phase of upgrading Indonesia's standards of living and education, in order to enable the country to take off as an industrialised nation. The process was estimated to require 25 years. In 1990, President Soeharto decided that 25 years after G30S, there had been sufficient time to heal the wound. He had met the Chinese Foreign Minister, Qian Qichen, a year earlier. In September 1989, he had visited the Soviet Union. Communism was still in existence there but the Cold War had ended. China, the sleeping giant, was stirring from its long sleep. President Soeharto, with his keen eye on business, saw this as an opportunity to establish trade relations with China. As a result, Indonesia normalised its relations with China on 8 August 1990.

The sixth Development Cabinet formed on 17 March 1993 lasted until 1998. Try Sutrisno replaced Sudharmono. In the Cabinet sat 38 ministers and new faces held key economic posts: Mar'ie Muhammad—Minister of Finance;

Ginandjar Kartasasmita—State Minister of National Development Planning, Chairman of Bappenas and the Coordinating Minister for Economy and Finance; Saleh Afiff—Chairman of the National Development Planning Board. Not only were they new players, they were also Muslims. The "RMS" (Radius, Mooy and Sumarlin team) was no longer in the picture. This was how President Soeharto stopped the protest against the alleged "Christianisation" in his Cabinet. This proved that, at times, the president did listen to criticisms.

Born in Surabaya on 15 November 1935, Try Sutrisno was the youngest vice-president and he represented the change of a generation. Good looking, personable and humble, his education had been entirely military-based. He was the adjutant of President Soeharto from 1974 to 1978. After various postings, he was appointed Commander of the Armed Forces. He was loyal, principled and not ambitious. I was particularly touched when he provided me with a 20-page document containing his opinion of President Soeharto when I asked for an interview whilst undertaking research for this book. In his writing, he displayed a clear and unshakeable loyalty to his former boss. He followed the principle *mikul dhuwur, mendhem jero*. He was not involved in any of President Soeharto's foundations and has a reputation for distancing himself from the conglomerates. Many wanted him to stay as vice-president in 1998, but as the Ikatan Cendekiawan Muslim Indonesia (ICMI) gained more control in Golkar, the votes went to BJ Habibie.

This led the way to the critical years, when President Soeharto himself deliberated over whether he should remain in power. In 1988, he gave some indication that it was perhaps time for him to step down. He was also aware that old age could impair a person's ability to focus on matters of importance. Try Sutrisno stated, in his 20-page document, that in 1993, President Soeharto had come to his own conclusion that his presidency from 1988 to 1993 could well have been his final term. He had once said of himself that he was already *tua, ompong, peyot, pikun* (TOPP) or old, toothless, dented and forgetful, which was reason enough for many to wonder why he was still willing to be re-elected for the next period from 1998 to 2003. He should have followed his instincts instead of believing his cronies who begged him to stay on under the pretext of national interest, when in fact it was for their own self-interest.

FAST DEVELOPMENT AND THE NEGATIVE EFFECTS

Not only had Indonesia failed to learn from what corruption had brought to Bulog and Pertamina, it had even allowed corruption to spread quickly like a disease. Banking was amongst the contaminated sectors. As corruption was so widespread, it became a national joke that if one stayed honest, one was stupid. Bung Hatta declared openly that corruption had become a way of life. President Soeharto, unfortunately, never paid close attention to this issue, even though he had been recorded as having said in his biography that nobody should tolerate corruption.[2] He referred to the establishment of the Badan Pemeriksa Keuangan (BPK), the country's Audit Board, which was responsible for examining the accountability of state finance. He said that in 1967, Attorney General Sugiharto had led an anti-corruption campaign, and a few people were punished. He pointed out that in January 1970, he had formed Komisi Empat, a team which consisted of Wilopo from the Indonesian National Party, IJ Kasimo from the Catholic Party, Professor Dr Ir Herman Johannes, Dean of Gadjah Mada University from 1962 to 1966 and Anwar Tjokroaminoto from the Muslim Party PSII. Bung Hatta was appointed the advisor and General Sutopo Yuwono the secretary. These two figures were generally accepted by the community which had faith in them as clean leaders and politicians. However, the public remained skeptical, as the ones who were sentenced to jail in this campaign were the "small fish" rather than the "big fish".

There is no question that banks are the life-support machines in the development of a nation. In the early 1970s, when opportunities to do business were in full swing, the number of credit requests—from speculators to the consumer industry to the construction industry for financing of major projects—escalated. The government was so enthusiastic and caught up with the beat of progress that it lulled itself into believing that there was no danger of lending to non-productive operations or interests. The rich borrowed from the banks to buy cars, jewellery, houses and even to speculate in land. In the meantime, the technocrats convinced the *wong cilik* or the masses to save.

A banker in New York City once told me that a banker should not think only about how to give credit; more crucial is the question of how to get the money back. Good judgment dictates that a banker should understand the client's state of mind before a loan is disbursed. One of the critical factors is to investigate the client's past performance. One must undertake to do bank and trade checking. Due to rigorous competition and a shortage of experienced bankers, this is often neglected or deliberately dispensed with. Due diligence is often abandoned. The Pertamina failure receded into the history of a distant era as the country approached the 1980s and the faults and deficiencies became merely a legend.

The reason for this is clear: temptation to make money fast. Law-breakers usually learn quickly and each time a new law is introduced, they would find a way around it. The more experienced the criminal, the more sophisticated his schemes and devices. Unfortunately, bankers often pay more attention to what they see than to their other instincts when assessing the character of the borrower. They forget that appearances can be deceiving. It is, indeed, not always easy to detect whether the assets that the clients present to the banks are really theirs or whether they are derived from borrowing from other banks. There are times when factories and lands provided as collateral are also pledged to other banks.

It is common knowledge in the Indonesian banking circle that their clients keep three sets of books: one is for tax purposes, one is for their banks and one for themselves. It is almost impossible to get hold of the last one. When a banker goes on a factory visit, often the sign of ownership displayed on the premises would have just been changed, possibly only an hour earlier when another banker was present, and the other name may even still be displayed somewhere on the same premises. This ruse is not difficult for clients to employ, as stock inspections cannot be carried out on a random or unannounced basis. A bank must advise its client when a stock inspection is due, as factories are usually well-guarded. The inspection itself is yet another ballgame: stockpiles are often heaped up to the ceiling and as there is usually only one entrance, it is difficult to ascertain if the stocks really fill the entire warehouse. The banker's rule of thumb of the 4 Cs of capital, capability, character and capacity is often overlooked.

Whether due to declining moral values or drastic changes to the country's value system, the fast jump to riches has created an unstoppable desire to make money in quick and easy ways, and the ends seem to justify the means. Cheating is no longer considered a shameful act but a technique for doing business. This is, in fact, the worst illness that has taken place in Indonesian society, and it creeps into and within various institutions from day to day. As the country faced a moral crisis, the reminder from President Soeharto in the beginning that material accomplishment was to go hand in hand with spiritual advancement seemed to be long forgotten. So where did the country go wrong? Perhaps President Soeharto was too trusting and abdicated control although he had written about how crucial control was and that it should be maintained at all times. Perhaps he had assumed that his subordinates would carry out their jobs in the manner in which he had specified. There is no doubt that shared responsibility was missing, instead, shared benefits materialised.

It was the corrupt practices in state-led institutions that became the major cause for state losses. The term is nicknamed *kebocoran* or "leakage". It was compounded by another bad practice: entrepreneurs managed to obtain easier access to the state banks through a combination of bribery and trickery. They bribed officials to expedite state banks' approval for their projects. The state banks were the biggest custodian of the *wong cilik*'s life savings. The bureaucrats, including the state banks' officers, accepted pay-offs as an easy way to make money. President Soeharto's original intention was to bring the *wong cilik* up to be on par with the rich, but the result was the reverse: the *wong cilik* became the "milking cow" of the rich. It was then that the public became increasingly frustrated with the foul play going on and the big groups of entrepreneurs and conglomerates that set the rules of the game.

THE *PRIBUMI* ENTREPRENEURS

Despite the concerted effort to build a *pribumi* bourgeoisie, growth had not been impressive. As early as 1956, it was clear that the indigenous capitalists had not made inroads into Chinese economic dominance. At the same time, a large percentage of government financing given to indigenous enterprises did not bear fruit. Credit was misused on a large scale. Unfortunately, the same situation was to recur in the late 1980s. Back then, in spite of strong support for the national banks, the 42 indigenous national banks accounted for only 11 per cent of domestic credit. By 1953, in the agricultural sector, 70 per cent of the estates in Java and Sumatra were back in foreign hands.

Political pressure to end state subsidy for indigenous capital came from the socialist party, the Muslims and the moderate nationalists. They argued that the government should move towards a more market-oriented economy, but the left-leaning nationalists and PKI preferred, and had more faith in, the country's own people. Hence, the state had to assume the burden of creating a national economy.

The political and social consequences of state protection and subsidy for *pribumi* capital did not help the situation. It became clear that Chinese capital was integral to the structure of Indonesian capitalism. This was carried over from the time of the Dutch, whose economic policy was to leave minority-held key positions in Indonesia's economic life, so much so that it continued to constitute the dominant element of domestic investment. Indigenous capital was unable to expand beyond petty trade and small commodity production. The combined domestic capital of the Chinese and indigenous people was not enough to replace foreign capital, particularly in the mining and other large-scale industries. As a result, the state was forced to play a central role in owning, financing and managing its investments in those sectors. Furthermore, there was keen competition among officials for the responsibility of allocating credits, licences, monopolies, contracts and other concessions as they could use their authority to supplement their meagre wages on the side. This secured them an additional source of income, for political or personal needs.

The bureaucrats leaning towards narrow nationalism were operating from two major bases: one was within the political and bureaucratic apparatus that was Pertamina, and the second was within Opsus. The bureaucrat nationalists were represented mostly by intellectuals associated with the Center for Strategic and International Studies (CSIS). CSIS was the only coordinated policy body in opposition to Bappenas.

J Panglaykim, a Chinese academic and businessman, was one of the most important economic theorists who believed in economic nationalism. In his view, the absence of a coordinated economic strategy linked with the state and business circles made the penetration of foreign capital explosive and destructive. In 1974, J Panglaykim argued that the Bappenas policy—guided by western free-market, private enterprise and open-door economic policies—was a repetition of errors from the past. In addition, it only dealt with the multinationals in a fragmented fashion. J Panglaykim believed that Indonesia should follow the Japanese and Singapore governments' example of playing a central role in their economies. He believed that the state should play a key role in choosing the appropriate type of infrastructure, and to mobilise finance and induce investments. State participation in private business could provide cohesion and protection, hence preventing the domination of foreign capital. A crucial component for success would be a state-led and nationally integrated financial sector. This had to incorporate state and private banks, merchant banks, financial institutions and the capital market. Tension between the Chinese and the *pribumi* would be reduced if both enjoyed guaranteed and defined areas within an integrated economy. At the same time, the participation of foreign capital should be restricted to sectors where foreign capital and technology were necessary. However, the Pertamina and Bulog crises were clear evidence that Indonesia's installation of state enterprises in positions of control on nationalist principles failed due to corruption, mismanagement and unchecked power by the top management.

THE BANKING SYSTEM—A BRIEF SUMMARY

From 1949 until 1957, President Soekarno had focused on four sectors of the country's economy. The most important action was to secure control of the Central Bank by taking over the previously Dutch-managed Java Bank and restructuring it as Bank of Indonesia. Next was to take control of a range of public utilities, as well as pawnshops, agricultural estates, postal/telegraph and telephone services, electricity, ports, coalmines and railways. This was followed by the formation of state-owned corporations in areas such as cement production, textile manufacturing, automobile assembly, and glass, bottle and hardboard manufacturing. The final measure was to break Dutch control in the import-export trade by establishing the Central Trading Company (CTC) to export agricultural products. An auto assembly plant, the Indonesian Service Company (ISC), and a shipping company, PT Pelni, were also set up.

In the old days before banks were established, people used barter to trade. However, the economy could not depend on bartering or trading alone: it was necessary to buy raw materials and process the materials into final products, then package the products so that they appealed to buyers.

In order to buy raw materials and machinery, pack materials and undertake marketing, capital was needed. To meet capital requirements, the government had to balance the money supply from the state budget and from the public at large.

The key financial organisation in Indonesia is the People's Bank, the Volksbank or Bank Rakyat. Bank Rakyat has branches in the remotest areas. As the country is a huge archipelago, with a population that is spread across thousands of islands, having only a few big banks in major towns would not have made practical sense. Bank Rakyat's offices are not extravagant and each one is manned by a small number of staff members. Everything remains simple to mirror the simplicity of a village. The bank's operations are also very simple: saving and borrowing of money—a simple solution for a society that is still simple-minded. President Soeharto was a simple person who looked upon things in simple ways and he created a solution to a problem in a simple manner. This was his biggest success.

Bank Rakyat or the Volksbank was started by the Dutch. Bank Rakyat Indonesia (BRI) was created in Purwokerto, Central Java, by Raden Aria Wirjaatmadja. In the Dutch language, the name of the bank is Hulpen Spaarbank der Inlandsche Bestuurs Ambtenaren, loosely translated as "the bank for helping and saving". Owned by the *priyayi* for the indigenous people, it was first established on 16 December 1895. It later changed its name to Bank Rakyat Indonesia. In 1946, the republic named BNI as the first state-owned bank. The bank stopped operations temporarily in 1948, but was reactivated after the Renville Agreement was signed in 1949. The name was changed once more to Bank Rakyat Indonesia Serikat. In 1960, Bank Koperasi Tani dan Nelayan (BKTN), a bank for farmers and fishermen, was formed. After mergers with two other banks in 1965, the bank was integrated into the Central Bank (Bank Indonesia). A month later, the government announced the formation of a single government bank, Bank Negara Indonesia or the State Bank of Indonesia.

In 1967, yet another change took place and Bank Negara Indonesia reverted to its original role as the Central Bank. The other units were hived off according to their function. One, Bank Rakyat Indonesia, was active in rural areas; another, Bank Ekspor Impor Indonesia, was in export-import activities. On 1 August 1992, Bank Rakyat Indonesia's status was changed to PT Bank Rakyat Indonesia (Persero), with 100 per cent of its shares in the hands of the government. At the time of writing this book, Bank Rakyat Indonesia has 4,447 operating offices, including its Head Office, 12 regional offices, 170 domestic branches and others, including two foreign offices in New York and the Cayman Islands. There had been other major banks: Bank Bumi Daya, Bank Dagang Negara and Bank Pembangunan Indonesia. None of these survived the end of the economic boom, however. Like a house of cards, the banks in the system fell one by one because of the same reasons that caused Pertamina's downfall: an outdated organisational and management system, lack of control, lack of experienced staff and over-expansion.

Another bank whose role was important was Bank Tabungan Negara (BTN), the state savings bank. BTN's history dates back to 1897 when it was formed under the Dutch as Postspaarbank in Batavia (the old name of Jakarta). Postspaarbank introduced the banking institution to the public and encouraged people to save. Up to 1931, the role of Postspaarbank in collecting public funds was highly successful. From 1928 until the end of 1934, branches were maintained in Makassar, Surabaya and Medan and in 1939, the funds reached Rp54 million. In 1942, when Japan occupied Indonesia, Postspaarbank became inactive. The Japanese introduced Tyokin Kyoku, a savings bank whose concept was to encourage people to save money in the bank. However, Tyokin Kyoku was a failure. At that time, a branch was opened in Yogya. The Japanese occupation did not last long and after the country attained independence, Tyokin Kyoku was taken over and the name was changed to Kantor Tabungan Pos (KTP). KTP played a crucial role in converting the Japanese currency, which was then called Oeang Republik Indonesia (ORI). In June 1949, the government opened and at the same time changed KTP to Bank Tabungan Pos RI . That was the beginning of BTN. Originally, BTN operated mainly as a savings bank for the public. On 1 August 1992, BTN expanded into general banking. In 1994, it operated as a foreign exchange licensed bank. After the economic crisis in 1997, BTN increased its capitalisation and in 2002, it concentrated on its in-house financing with no subsidies.

The New Order created a banking system to support stable growth. The Central Bank relinquished its three principal duties: preserving the local currency's value, maintaining stability in the banking system and serving as a lender of last resort. The Central Bank's function was taken over by Bank Negara Indonesia, which was a consolidation of several units of state-owned commercial banks and the Central Bank. In 1966, the banks took a radical frontline role in the battle against inflation. In essence, the strategy employed was designed to reduce inflation, stop spending and instead, encourage savings. In the mid-1960s, there were 14 private savings banks all over the country. The banks, both private and state-owned, had their focus on commercial banking activities rather than on savings.

In 1974, the government announced the development of public housing and BTN was to extend credit for home buying under the scheme Kredit Pemilikan Rumah (KPR). It was to comply with Repelita to provide the people with *sandang, pangan, papan*: "clothing, food and housing". The first housing loan was extended in Semarang in 1976 and it reached its peak in 1982 to 1983. Bank Indonesia published annual reports as well as monthly publications of its financial position. The governor of Bank Indonesia, together with the Ministry of Finance and Ministry of Trade, formed a monetary council that determined the interest rate charged for government lending. The banking law of 1968 deliberately built a system that favoured the state banks. The state banks gave selective credits, applied differential lending rates and offered various savings schemes. State banks set differential rates applicable to various sectors. Furthermore, state-owned corporations were required to keep their funds with the state banks. State banks in turn received preferential rates from Bank Indonesia and the government would not let a state bank go bankrupt. This was meant to induce the people to deal with state banks. Consequently, the state banks maintained dominance in the country's banking sector.

In the past, ordinary people had little access to banks. Typically, people used to keep what was left from their disposable income in tradable goods such as rice or livestock. It was a common practice in the past for farmers to keep their money under their pillows or in compartments under their beds as a safeguard against having their money stolen. Those who had more money purchased plots of land for long-term investment. They knew that land prices would rise as the population grew; at the same time, they also intended their plots of land to be handed down to their children as inheritance. Additionally, landowners were also looked upon as having a higher social status in the community. For the government, however, when the people held their wealth in the form of goods or land, the barter system would still be firmly anchored, and it also encouraged hoarding. Most importantly, it slowed down the development of a modern economy.

To encourage the public to save in banks, enticement and rewards in the form of high returns were needed. In the effort to change old established habits, the banks had to give strong incentives. Hence, the government allowed the banks to set the interest rate at 6 per cent per month, tax free. The banks' first step was to explain the benefits of saving, which provided a regular fixed income on a monthly basis to depositors. Furthermore, they pointed out that if extra money was used to buy land, rice or livestock as a form of savings, these commodities would not provide a monthly income. The banks had to assure the public that it was safe to deposit their money with them. In addition, they would not ask for the source of the money as money laundering was not known at that time.

The bank's efforts in marketing the new concept met with big success. As time went by, the poor and the rich started to move the holding of cash into saving deposits. In record numbers, urban workers and small farmers started to open bank accounts, which for most of them was the first time they had done so in their lives. The people started to grasp the concept of saving as the idea of getting an interest of 72 per cent per annum, taken on a monthly basis, was hard to resist. Furthermore, the wealthy Indonesians who used to protect their investments in foreign currencies by keeping them in banks overseas soon transferred their investments to the local banks. It was difficult to resist the temptation of a high interest rate which the overseas banks could not compete with.

Seventeen years down the road, the New Order took a big step into deregulation and economic reform by announcing a series of regulations on 2 June 1983. In addition to Bank Indonesia, the government controlled five state-owned commercial banks, including a development bank (Bapindo) and a savings bank (BTN). There were also 27 provincial development banks (BPD). At the end of 2003, BNI had 41 subsidiary companies, of which 28 were Bank Perkreditan Rakyat (BPR) and 13 others were in financial institutions such as insurance, securities, venture capital and finance companies.

On 2 October 1998, Bank Mandiri was formed as a part of the Indonesian government's banking reforms. In July 1999, soon after the Asian financial crisis hit the country, four of the state-owned banks, BBD, BDN, Bank Exim and Bapindo, were amalgamated into Bank Mandiri.

The Private Banks
In the private sector, there were 72 local banks, which were mostly controlled by the Chinese. The oldest Indonesian private bank was Bank Windu Kencana, established in 1954 by Liem Sioe Liong. In 1957, Bank Central Asia (BCA) became the flagship institution in Liem's banking and finance group. After 1965, Bank Windu Kencana was taken over by a foundation related to Kostrad, hence it became a military-owned bank. Amongst the directors were Soedjono Hoemardhani and the president's older children, Tutut and Sigit. BCA became one of the largest private banks in the country with a string of subsidiaries including the insurance company PT Asuransi Central Asia. All privately owned banks, including foreign banks, were given a credit ceiling. The government also set the maximum lending and deposit rates. Depending on each bank's performance, the lending limit could be increased or decreased, at the end of the fiscal year. Priority for lending was given to the manufacturing sector, which could absorb a larger workforce, and also to exports that would create foreign exchange earnings. The fundamental change that took place on 2 June 1983 was the removal of credit ceilings. The banks could now determine their own loan and deposit rates. Taxes derived from interest payments, dividends and royalties on foreign currency deposits in state banks were abolished.

The government continued to provide subsidised loans to farmers and small businesses through Bimbingan Massal (Bimas) or Kredit Invetasi Kecil (KIK, or small credit investment). Apart from these, the banks were free to decide their rates and their own acceptable risks. In February 1984, Bank Indonesia introduced two new instruments to manage their money supply. Similar to the United States Treasury Bill, it was named Sertifikat Bank Indonesia (SBI) or Bank Indonesia certificates. It was meant to be a discount window where an SBI holder could receive the principal plus accrued interests. The main objective was to establish an intermediate money market through buying and selling. Bank Indonesia acted as a lender of last resort by taking the role of discount window. At the same time, Bank Indonesia could exert indirect control over the country's money supply by deciding on the rates of the discount window. By doing this, the government could either increase or drain the liquidity in the banking system.

Due to an excess of liquidity, on 1 February 1985, the government announced another instrument, the Surat Berharga Pasar Uang (SBPU). It was a promissory note used to pay off obligations or to overcome liquidity problems. This reform was a giant step for Indonesian banking and in the management of the economy. Prior to the commencement of banking reform in 1983, the state banks' market share was close to 80 per cent, but it was the result of regulations and not fair competition. One downside risk was the lack of innovation, as a protectionist approach could not lead to initiative and competitiveness. The state banks became oligopolies and more bureaucratic. Under the new system, they were now competing directly with the private sector, especially the foreign banks. The private and foreign banks were, in most cases, more energetic, efficient, innovative, or simply worked harder. As predicted, the private and foreign banks became the winning horse. In the 15 months ahead, the local banks' lending activities increased by 90 per cent. The state banks soon realised that they could not stay on their pedestals and they adopted a new approach of becoming more professional, more effective and less bureaucratic in making decisions as well as learning more about market orientation. By the 1990s, they had regained their dominant position.

The Foreign Banks

As early as 1968, many of the foreign banks had a keen interest to start doing business in Indonesia. At that time, only 10 foreign banks had licenses to open a single branch each in Jakarta. Four were from the United States, three from Europe and three from Asia. From the United States: Chase Manhattan Bank, Bank of America, American Express and First National City Bank of New York (later renamed Citibank). From the United Kingdom: Chartered Bank of London. From Holland: Pierson & Heldring and Algemene Bank Nederland. From Hong Kong: Hongkong and Shanghai Banking Corporation. From Japan: Bank of Tokyo. From Thailand: Bangkok Bank. The presence of these new players posed a threat to both the state and private local banks. Not only did they have stronger capitalisation with unlimited support from their headquarters, they could afford to pay more for recruitment of experienced staff. Their deep pockets also meant that they could provide their staff with training and therefore be able to achieve higher work efficiency.

Another banking reform was introduced five years later in 1988. The regulation was named the October 1988 package or Pakto (Paket Oktober). It allowed foreign banks to set up branches outside Jakarta in any of Indonesia's six major cities: Bandung, Surabaya, Semarang, Medan, Ujung Pandang and Denpasar. However, the foreign banks were required to direct 50 per cent of their loan portfolio to export-oriented business. Foreign banks were also allowed to start joint ventures with Indonesian banks, private or state-owned. For the local banks, the opening of additional branches was made easier. State-owned corporations were allowed to keep only 50 per cent of their funds in state banks, while a maximum of 20 per cent could be held in one private bank. The government now taxed interest from savings and time deposits at a rate of 15 per cent per annum, whereas before Pakto, interest was tax free. By this time, the government had decided to discontinue Bimas and Inmas, the subsidies given to the farmers.

THE FATE OF THE RUPIAH

At the end of 1967, the exchange rate between the rupiah and the US dollar was Rp235 to US$1. Four years later, on 23 August 1971, the government devalued the rupiah by around 10 per cent, bringing down the exchange rate to Rp415 to US$1. Six years later, on 15 November 1978, the rupiah was further devalued by 50.6 per cent, resulting in a value of Rp625 to US$1.

The target of the 15 November 1978 devaluation was to enhance the country's exports. In fact, due to a 100 per cent increase in oil prices in the world market, Bank Indonesia, Pertamina and the Ministry of Finance were able to hold on to a substantial quantity of US dollars to hedge against currency fluctuations. From then on, the government no longer fixed the local currency to a rate and allowed it to float to a certain level against the US dollar. On 30 March 1983, when world oil prices went down drastically, the government once again devalued the rupiah by 38 per cent. The rupiah then stood at Rp970 to US$1. The government tried hard to push exports of non-oil products while at the same time encouraging consumption of local products. However, the rupiah fell continuously under heavy pressure. On 12 September 1986, for the fourth time, the government devalued the currency by 21 per cent, making a value of Rp1,644 to US$1.

In reality, the rupiah had depreciated by 40 per cent before the devaluation was announced. From then until October 1997, the rupiah continued to lose its worth by 124 per cent. To avoid further decline, from mid-1977, the government decided to announce foreign exchange savings by not interfering with the purchase of US dollars by Bank Indonesia. This way, the currency could be stabilised. They postponed major projects where many components were priced in US dollars. The government increased the issue of Sertifikat Bank Indonesia-Certificate Bank Indonesia (SBI) by 30 per cent in addition to the quantity sold to attract more depositors. It was intended that the public should sell their US dollar holdings and buy SBI instead. On 8 October 1997, the government asked the International Monetary Fund (IMF) for help to disburse fresh capital so that the rupiah could be stabilised. In short, after 30 years under the New Order, the Indonesian currency had depreciated by 1,466 per cent.

Deregulations

Since the introduction of PMA (Foreign Investment Law) No 1 of 1967, the government had closed certain sectors in the economy to new investments. At the same time, it offered taxation and other incentives for investments in specific targeted sectors. The law restricted foreign investments in transport, communications and public utilities. The banking industry was also affected: foreign banks were restricted to maintaining a maximum of two branches in Jakarta. A ruling was introduced for the formation of financial institutions as joint ventures between local private or state banks and foreign banks. The New Order's economic policy in 1970 had focused on the countryside. The subsidised credit programmes introduced after the Malari affair was another attempt to support indigenous businesses. Unfortunately, a great deal of the credit never reached the intended group. Much of it was grabbed by the middlemen and kept in time deposits, which earned high interest.

The domestic and foreign capital development from 1975 to 1982 indicated a significant growth. Foreign corporations were compelled to provide local investors with a degree of equity under the new joint venture regulations. Foreign investors could no longer operate in import-substitution industries that required a high level of capital or technology which could not be found locally. As banks and financial institutions expanded, there was a shortage of qualified staff. For the foreign banks, the situation was more complex because they needed staff with fluency in a foreign language, which was English in most cases. The high demand for experienced bankers created a tough competitive environment, as those with good skills demanded high salaries. The biggest challenge was faced by Bank Indonesia. With the development of more branches, the supervisory task became more complex. There was a shortage of experienced staff too. The problem was compounded by factors such as quick hiring, lack of training and staff resorting to short cuts instead of being thorough in their work. There were cases of former messengers becoming debt collectors, security guards becoming cashiers and drivers assuming the role of marketing people. These were the early signs that the banking system had dipped into serious problems.

Furthermore, as deposits increased, the funding position went up accordingly and this forced banks to extend more loans. Amateurish businessmen and new bogus companies began to take advantage of the situation. Loans for the consruction of new hotels, for example, were approved even though there was an over-supply of hotels. Credit was extended for unproductive consumption purposes like credit card use, car financing and others. Banks also offered foreign currency trading indiscriminately, which was speculative in nature. The banks disregarded the rules of thumb to "know your client" and "how to get your money back". There was a proliferation of bad loans and fraud took place almost daily, followed by the banks' failures due to the lack of professional staff. The banks' self-indulgence was by now deep-rooted. As lending activities went ahead on full speed, the money supply increased, the economy overheated and the government faced difficulty in controlling the inflation that followed.

A presidential decree in 1980 imposed restrictions on access to contracts, closing all contracts with a value of less than Rp200 million to foreign contractors. The government gave the economically weak group preference by awarding contracts under Rp100 million to them. It created initiatives and provided a mechanism to facilitate access to local businesses for joint venture partnerships. The most important players were the state investment underwriter, PT Danareksa, and the state investment trust, PT Bahana. The capital market was not developed until 1988, and by then, these institutions were not able to make a significant impact on financing local equity.

By the mid-1980s, the country was ready for change and to move away from the government's intense involvement. The government realised as early as in 1983 that deregulation was a step in the right direction but it would have resulted in insufficient control. After over a decade, Indonesia's economic development was based on an inward-looking mode and it was sustained due to the huge income from oil revenue. After the Malari affair and Pertamina's downfall, fear and suspicion of foreign investment gradually disappeared. In addition, with the unexpected collapse of its backup support when the oil market broke down, the technocrats saw deregulation as the best prescription for the recovery of the economy, which would also enable the country to focus more on adopting an outward-looking approach.

The 1988 reforms changed the fundamental character of the economy. In the late 1980s, the success of the entrepreneurs made the government realise the enormous potential in the private sector. With the opening of bank branches and financial services in the rural areas, the government found a huge untapped market. With this new financial system, remote villages now became integrated into the country's formal economy. Opening a bank account was no longer an act of vanity. Competition among banks was fierce. Many new tactics such as offering gifts and holding lotteries were developed to attract depositors. Promotional strategies were developed and they extended to the use of advertisements in the media as by this time, television, radio and the like were available in a few remote areas. However, like everything else in life, these advancements came with a different set of problems.

In 1990, the subsidised credit programmes were replaced by a new regulation. All banks had to allocate 20 per cent of their total loan portfolio to small businesses in yet another effort by the government to improve wealth distribution. Again this was circumvented; fictitious borrowers were created. As supervision was weak, it was easy to create such companies. While President Soeharto had a strong grip on security and political matters, he was too trusting and lacked control in economic matters.

Early Financial Crisis

The first major problems occurred in 1990. Among Bank Duta's major shareholders were the foundations established by President Soeharto. Bank Duta had lost some US$420 million in foreign exchange transactions. The three foundations—Yayasan Supersemar, Dakab and Dharmais—had to bail Bank Duta out with a cash injection to prevent it going bankrupt. This should have been seen as an early sign of how dangerous the banking world had become. Firstly, there had been lack of supervision, especially if the director was related to people in the government. Secondly, the Central Bank lacked a good operating system prompting President Soeharto to fire the Board of Directors, amongst whom was a son-in-law of Vice-President Sudharmono. President Soeharto immediately replaced the Board with a team of professionals headed by Winarto Soemarto.

Low-key, polite and personable, Winarto was the former President Director of Bank Negara Indonesia and Bank Rakyat Indonesia. His entire career had been in banking, hence he was the right choice. Winarto confirmed with me that President Soeharto had given him a free hand and left the rescue of Bank Duta to his team. After Bank Duta's failure, the three foundations that were the brainchild of President Soeharto, became exposed to the public. People started to notice the foundations because they held majority shareholdings in Bank Duta, each with about 27.5 per cent. The rest of the shares were held by the public, employees of the bank and staff cooperatives. Debates went on about whether Bank Duta's failures had caused losses for the state. This allegation was rejected as the foundations had never received any assistance from the state budget. Instead, these foundations relied on donations from the private sector. Bank Duta's failure became a sore point for the foundations' charitable activities.

Amongst the rescue team members chosen by Winarto were non-Muslims. Soon thereafter, those not happy with the president claimed that the non-Muslim professionals were taking over the key role in economic affairs. An accusation of "Christianisation" soon came about. There were three monetary functions headed by non-Muslims: JB Sumarlin, Radius Prawiro and Andrianus Mooy. They held the position of Minister of Finance, the Coordinating Minister for Economy and Finance/Chairman of the National Development Planning Board and the Governor of Bank

Indonesia, respectively. (As mentioned earlier, they were nicknamed RMS, as a pun on Republik Maluku Selatan, a past rebellion that had wanted to separate South Maluku from the Republic.) This signified a move towards religious issues in the political arena. To counter such an issue, the formation of an association of intellectual Muslims was put in motion.

On 5 December 1990, the Ikatan Cendekiawan Muslim Indonesia (ICMI) or the Association of Intellectual Muslim Indonesia was established. The main goal was to prove that among Muslims, many had the same knowledge that was previously within the monopoly of the West and non-Muslims. This idea arose before Indonesia attained freedom as Islam had penetrated at the grassroots level because of the Dutch segregation policy in education. Only the minority non-Muslims obtained higher learning at that time. Thus, to the people who lived in *kampongs*, being a Christian was seen as merely being Dutch. Six months later in June 1991, President Soeharto and his whole family embarked on a pilgrimage to Mecca. This move was seen as a strong signal that he leaned more towards conservative Islam.

The next major catastrophe in the banking sector occurred in 1992 when Bank Summa, one of the top local banks, became a victim of bad loans linked to property market speculation. Bank Summa's main shareholder was Astra, then a leading conglomerate, the same group that had been the target of riots during the Malari affair. This episode was not a good example for portraying the success of President Soeharto in government. Astra should have been more wary after it was badly burnt in 1974, and should have kept away from the risk of being embroiled in another scandal. This was an example of the conglomerates' greed and their appetite to make money in the absence of moral values.

At that time, the public were becoming aware of the government's lack of control over the fast-paced developments that were taking place in the country. The *pribumi* raised their eyebrows at the conglomerates, which were mostly of Chinese origin. Jealousy became more transparent. The tension between the *pribumi* and the conglomerates soon heightened. Students began to compile a list of the imminent links between the big conglomerates and high-ranking government officials all the way up to President Soeharto's family. By then, unfortunately, President Soeharto's family's business relations with the conglomerates had increased to a substantial level. If they had only amounted to a few links, it might not have been so critical, but his family's involvement in major public projects, like road tolls and oil distribution, was too much and too noticeable for the public to disregard.

Bang Ali and my father had also been very critical of this issue, as were many of us. Lee Kuan Yew pointed this out in his book.[3] He admired President Soeharto's achievements and was deeply regretful of his flaws when it came to the business involvements of Soeharto's children. President Soeharto's children were too naïve and failed to realise the conglomerates' real motives in making them business partners. President Soeharto was focused on his job and Ibu Tien was deeply involved in her charitable activities. It was the view of some that this was the situation which the conglomerates exploited to brainwash Soeharto's children. In reality, these were partnerships of convenience because the main element in any true business partnership was missing: there was no intention to conduct the business at hand as partners as each "partner" had different interests. To be fair, the conglomerates were not alone, as foreign multinational corporations were also using the same tactic. Sadly, President Soeharto's good intentions were freely taken advantage of by many. The situation became increasingly worse until direct contact with him and his family was difficult to achieve, as his cronies had by that time encircled the family like parasites.

My personal experience did not give me a good picture of what was happening during that period. My consultancy company, PT Immacon, represented a major German trading company, Metallgesellschaft. When the company's representatives came to Jakarta, we planned to pay a courtesy call to Siemens, which had a very close business relationship with Metallgesellschaft. The secretary of Siemens' top man kept us waiting for 15 minutes before he finally came out. When he found out that the local partner had nothing to do with Jalan Cendana, we were asked to leave their office in less than five minutes, his excuse being that he had another important engagement.

The "cluster of crooks" included Westerners as well. For example, a former general manager of an American bank in Jakarta who had joined a client's business later embezzled another party's money. The party managed to win the case against him in Singapore but it was of no help, as Indonesia did not have an extradition agreement with Singapore. To make matters worse, the offender moved to Surabaya and worked in the local dealership of Mercedes Benz. When the case was reported to the company owner, the protest was completely ignored. How could a foreigner found guilty in Singapore work in

Indonesia? The local law firm hired to work on the case was not above board either: they took the legal fees but did not bother to pursue the matter. This is just one example of how shaky the legal situation was in Indonesia at that time. This was perpetuated many times over as the country became a safe haven for felons. It illustrated the communication breakdown in President Soeharto's government as he had lost touch with what was really going on under the veneer of progress.

THE CAPITAL MARKET

President Soeharto felt that the development of a capital market was necessary so that the community at large could share in the economic progress achieved by the big businesses. The capital market had existed since 1912 in Batavia (the old name of Jakarta). Trading on the exchange ceased in 1956 when the foreign firms were nationalised. In 1976, the government formed PT Danareksa to buy and sell shares of publicly listed companies and price fluctuation was kept within a 4 per cent band.

On 10 August 1977, the Jakarta Stock Exchange was launched with a single listing of PT Semen Cibinong. By 1984, the number of listed corporations was only 24. A second exchange was soon opened in Surabaya— the Surabaya Stock Exchange (SSX)— on 16 June 1989 with 36 new shareholders. After the October financial package (Paket Oktober or Pakto), a new set of deregulation measures was introduced on 22 December 1988. It was called Pakdes (Paket Desember) or "December Package", its main goal being to reactivate the capital market. The government decided to remove the 4 per cent fluctuation limit on listed shares and permitted the creation of new, privately operated stock exchanges in several provincial cities, although only two survive to date—Bursa Efek Jakarta (Jakarta Stock Exchange) and Bursa Efek Surabaya (Surabaya Stock Exchange). The December Package provided guidelines for other financial services: factoring, leasing, securities trading and credit cards, to name a few. The market's reaction to the 1988 deregulation measures was quick and intense. New banks and public offerings mushroomed.

Problems due to gross negligence on the part of the supervisory body and unchecked greed on the part of the entrepreneurs recurred repeatedly, however. Thus, the government privatised the Jakarta Stock Exchange in April 1992 and formed PT Bursa Efek Jakarta (BEJ) for greater management efficiency. The trading system was now computerised after comparison studies were made with the stock exchanges in Singapore, Manila and New York. In 2003, PT SSX shareholders increased to 123. On 22 July 1995, SSX merged with the Indonesian Parallel Stock Exchange (IPSX). At that time, hundreds of corporations in East Java had been identified to have the potential to float shares. However, up to 2003, only 40 companies were listed. From 1996, SSX systematically moved its operations to Jakarta. The government also introduced the Over The Counter institution for the trading of shares of small or start up companies that were not large enough to be traded on the regular stock exchange.

When Pakto and Pakdes were introduced in 1988, my consultancy company worked closely with the supervisory body of the Indonesian Stock Exchange (Bapepam) in conducting seminars for small, medium and large corporations. The government's intention was honourable. In launching public offerings, companies were encouraged to sell 15 per cent of their share offerings to their own employees. The government intended, with this policy in mind, that wealth should trickle down the corporate structure and be shared by both the management and the workers. The policy was geared towards two targets: firstly, to encourage workers to do a better job, and secondly, to afford the public the opportunity not only to participate in business they would otherwise not be able to do on their own but also to exercise some control over the operations. This sounded good in principle, but reality painted a different picture.

In the beginning, the entire nation was fixated by the stock exchange. Whenever a "good" business was about to launch a public offering, taxi drivers, housewives and domestic workers would join long queues to buy the shares offered. A few of them were genuine investors who used their life savings to speculate. Some buyers were front men paid by existing shareholders to buy their own shares to excite the market. The more shares were traded, the higher the price would rise; by this stage, it had become purely a game orchestrated by a few inside players. Such shareholders looked for loopholes to protect their own interests, and it was not unknown that they had, at times, misused their connection with Jalan Cendana—they faced no trepidation in claiming that it was the president who wished to have his children among the shareholders. In reality, the majority of the shares listed remained in the hands of the original owner. Therefore, the minority shareholders had hardly any influence in the organisation. Furthermore, the majority shareholders soon found ways to consolidate their own position. They asked friends or paid people to buy the shares during public offerings. Hence, the new shareholders were often just puppets on strings.

The government's intention to bring the have-nots up the ladder of wealth was easily undermined. Companies found countless ways to work around regulations requiring indigenous people as shareholders. People working as domestic help quickly became their newfound stooge. It was common to find in a corporation's articles of association, the names of domestic help, babysitters, guards and drivers. To keep them happy, financial compensation was of course arranged. These "shareholders" were given token shares of 1 per cent, 2 per cent or even up to 5 per cent of the required 51 per cent indigenous shares.[4] This was definitely not what the government had in mind. The minority shareholders were managers in name only and were told what to decide or say during shareholder meetings. The term "Ali Baba" was coined: "Ali" characterised the name of the indigenous people and "Baba" was commonly used to refer to the Chinese.

The multinational companies targeted a different level—the children of generals, high-ranking military officers and political figures. The financial payout in this case was higher. The more important the parents of these children were, the higher the price to recruit them, for the simple reason that these children were usually more educated than the domestic help.

The practice that was dominant in the 1980s created a shortage of indigenous people with skills. At the same time, only the rich, usually the Chinese, could send their children abroad for their education. Consequently, foreign companies recruited young Chinese individuals who had studied overseas (foreign banks' managements were often filled with the Chinese). Meanwhile, if the companies had indigenous partners, their main task was to gain access to government contracts, forestry concessions and monopolies. This situation worsened as President Soeharto's children grew up. Under such a scenario, the boom of the stock market did not last long as within the next two years, the bubble burst. In 1990, the "bulls turned into bears"—high prices in the stock market plummeted. Unfortunately, the bursting of the bubble affected only the small and genuine investors.

In retrospect, Pakto and Pakdes contained certain excesses and they went too far. For one, the banks' capital reserve requirement was brought down to 2 per cent from the previous 15 per cent. The government learnt valuable lessons from this and subsequently adopted a policy of gradual change. The government became more focused and took a drastic turn from the previous oppressive rules to complete freedom to enhance the banks' market stability. The regulator had to be alert and watchful for insider trading and other abuses as well.

THE DISTRIBUTION OF WEALTH

The key dilemma was the ongoing discrepancy between the "haves" and the "have-nots". There was no doubt that as a whole, the country's standard of living had improved remarkably from the 1970s to the mid-1980s. Unfortunately, equality was still an unreachable goal. The situation was aggravated by the rich flaunting their wealth shamelessly. More seriously, Chinese conglomerates still ruled the economy and this became a major issue of resentment, not only from the indigenous people, but also from the small Chinese entrepreneurs. A lack of sensitivity was another serious matter. Displays of wealth returned in 1990, some two decades after the Malari affair. The five-star hotels, which had increased in numbers, were often booked months in advance for weddings, anniversaries or birthday celebrations. Not only was the number of guests at these events overwhelming, the excesses of food and drink in these luxurious environments would have been sufficient reason to upset many. For example, there was a wedding party hosted by a conglomerate where the announcer proudly stated that guest number 5,000 had just arrived. The guests at these events were driven in chauffeured cars. The drivers discussed the lifestyles of their bosses while waiting in the car park. Smart reporters were able to figure out the costs of such celebrations and quickly linked it with the outstanding debts they had with the banks. In the end, this was the root cause of resentment. The people concluded that the New Order's economic system enriched only a selected few.

Many had warned President Soeharto about the situation; there were also ongoing criticisms from his half brother, Probosutedjo. However, the president believed that in the end, the conglomerates could be managed. This was similar to President Soekarno's train of thought when he felt he could rein in the PKI. Both men were convinced that they would not lose control. In both cases, the two presidents had misread their situations.

STOCKTAKING

Approaching the general elections in 1987 at the age of 66, President Soeharto himself was doubtful whether he should continue although many wanted him to take on another term. He admitted his misgivings and referred to his feelings in Javanese as *miris*: a feeling of apprehension when one was faced with uncertainty, knowing that there was a chance of failure. He had this anxiety as he knew only too well his own limitations. He knew that some still depended on his leadership, although in normal circumstances, he would be considered at the age of retirement.

President Soeharto felt it necessary to take stock of what he had done. He reflected on the fact that under the Constitution, the president was elected to carry out the state directives or Garis-garis Besar Haluan Negara (GBHN). The people chose their representation in Parliament (DPR) and Parliament had the control of the GBHN. The president was only accountable to the MPR and Parliament. If there was a conflict, the MPR was to resolve it through an extraordinary meeting. The MPR consisted of the Members of Parliament, the regional representatives and functional groups.

To illustrate, one could look at the situation that existed at the time when Islam had expanded its influence beyond Saudi Arabia. Caliph Muawiyyah (661–80) had managed to restore the unity of the empire. He had built an efficient administration in which Islam remained the religion of the conquering Arab elite. At first, the Arabs, who had no experience of imperial government, relied on the expertise of non-Muslims, who had served the previous Byzantine and Persian regimes. In the course of the next century, the Umayyad caliphs gradually transformed the disparate regions conquered by the Muslim armies into a unified empire with a common ideology. This was a great achievement, but through the course of time, the court began to develop a rich culture and luxurious lifestyle.

Therein lay a dilemma. It had been found, after centuries of experience, that an absolute monarchy was the only effective way of governing a pre-modern empire with an agrarian-based economy, and that it was far more satisfactory than a military oligarchy, where commanders usually competed with one another for power. The idea of making one man so privileged that both rich and poor alike are vulnerable before him would be distasteful in a modern democratic era, but it must be realised that democracy was a concept developed by an industrialised society which had the technology to replicate its resources for an indefinite period. This situation did not exist before the advent of Western modernity.

This illustration gives a clear picture as to why President Soeharto had taken the approach he had. Further, he needed the Indonesian-Chinese to be in the driving seat. He needed non-Muslim economists to lead the way but it had nothing to do with Christianisation as alleged earlier. His strategy was not wrong, but the real problems developed after his cronies started to develop a luxurious lifestyle through bribery or corruption and this became his real dilemma. On the one hand, he knew that he might have been taken for a ride; on the other hand, his government had also gained benefits from his cronies' successes.

As for democracy, Indonesia was still far away from becoming an industrialised nation, although that was President Soeharto's target for it in 25 years. The technocrats were opposed to measures that would impede Indonesia's progress and development. They would have opposed a liberal form of capitalism. They preferred to avoid "western democracy in our economy" and to apply "Pancasila in our economy". President Soeharto took the middle road; he avoided extreme nationalism and at the same time welcomed restricted capitalism. He stood between idealism and reality. However, he allowed a form of capitalism in which the forces of market elements were let loose to produce maximum growth. He stood fast and was unwilling to compromise when it came to the issue of which he was willing to sacrifice: nationalism or capitalism. An effective leader could not make everyone happy, but the important thing was to ensure that progress reached the majority of the people, which he managed to achieve during the first decade of his rule.

Growth was vital for a poor country like Indonesia. In 1966, the per capita income was US$60, while India, considered one of the poorest countries in the world, had US$90 or 50 per cent more than Indonesia. Social justice is also the key for sustainable stability and growth but it is easier said than done. The country's bitter experience in living under Dutch colonialism was a case in point of capitalism at its worst. The huge income disparities that existed among various groups under the Dutch were typically linked with free-fight capitalism or liberalism.

At the start, President Soeharto was very cautious and concerned that everyone should benefit from growth and that wealth was not only for a small number of the elite. Ironically, his move to prevent businesses from over-expansion was not fast enough. However, his biggest achievement in attaining self-sufficiency in rice for the country should not be forgotten. FAO Director General Edouard Saouma praised the hard work of the country's farmers which led to the success in rice self-sufficiency. This triumph could not be viewed in isolation from the strategies such as Bimas and the formation of village cooperatives.

During the first Repelita, farmers were able to irrigate a total of 3.6 million hectares of their farming land and during the second Repelita, cultivated land had increased by 1.3 million hectares, making a new total of 4.9 million cultivated hectares. President Soeharto was extremely pleased when FAO invited him to give a speech during their 40th anniversary. Among the developing countries, Indonesia was selected to represent the southern part of the hemisphere. On this occasion, President Soeharto was asked to explain Indonesia's achievements while President Francois Mitterand from France gave his views on behalf of the developed nations. President Soeharto was proud to stand up and deliver his speech in Rome on 14 November 1985, at a time when the world was full of disparities. More than half of the world's food production came from the developed countries and yet, at the same time, their lands were populated by only one-third of the world's total inhabitants. The productivity level of these developed countries was as high as 2.5 times the developing countries'.[5] He recalled how sad he had been when he realised that the rich nations had decided to destroy over-production of food supplies in order to maintain price stability, this being a preferred course of action when many human beings were still living in starvation. He knew that the job he had to do for equality and justice was far from over.

Yet, he was happy when he officiated at the opening of a new complex at the University of Indonesia in Depok, a suburb of Jakarta, on 5 September 1987. The new complex had a meeting hall, library, mosque, research and social centres. The faculties of medicine and economics were expanded, while faculties of dentistry, nursing and postgraduate studies were new additions in this new complex. Finally, he felt that he had managed to contribute to the country's higher learning, in spite of being deprived of the opportunity to further his own education when he was young. In September 1987, the Sultan of Brunei, Sultan Hassanal Bolkiah, visited Indonesia and gave an free-interest loan of US$100 million, which demonstrated confidence and support from a close neighbour in the government's efforts to build the nation.

President Soeharto recalled his relationship with his loyalists who were no longer alive. Two of his closet allies and former *Aspri* members, Ali Moertopo and Soedjono Hoemardhani, had passed away: Ali Moertopo in May 1984 and Soedjono Hoemardhani in 1986. His recollection of them, especially of Ali Moertopo, was rather critical. He wrote that CSIS was often likened to the "kitchen" where government policies were initiated. In a kitchen in the chef's absence, trouble would usually brew. In this case, he pointed out that he had managed to govern even after Ali Moertopo was no longer around. Further, he wrote that in 1967, Ali Moertopo had been worried when he decided to raise the oil price from Rp4 to Rp16 per litre. Ali Moertopo had cautioned him that the New Order would collapse if he went ahead with his decision. President Soeharto had ignored his words of caution; the government raised the oil price and the New Order survived.

In his 1988 biography, President Soeharto mentioned with great pleasure that the 1986 Indonesia Air Show had seen 237 corporations from 20 countries participating.[6] Industri Pesawat Terbang Nusantara (IPTN), one of BJ Habibie's pet projects, had organised that event. He genuinely believed it when BJ Habibie said that Indonesia's planes could be sold abroad and this would increase revenue from the exportation of non-oil and gas products. He was convinced that IPTN would be able to compete in the international aircraft industry. Despite many warnings from his economic team, he considered IPTN as one of the best national strategies. He emphasised the potential for IPTN to absorb the country's abundant labour force. He made a comparison with the textile factories, which could at most only employ 3,000 workers in each factory, so too Krakatau Steel (steel production), while IPTN could conservatively absorb 13,000 skilled labourers. This would be especially true if a company such as Boeing appointed IPTN as a sub-contractor in the future. If this happened, IPTN could create 40,000 jobs. To accomplish this dream, Indonesia had to start using IPTN planes, named CN-235, for its domestic flights. It was an ambitious programme, but as it turned out later, the CN-235 domestic flights experienced a few accidents.

President Soeharto reflected that 1986 was the year when the economy had not yet fully recovered from the international crisis. It was the year when oil prices dropped, resulting in the currency being devalued for the fourth time since he assumed power. The country was fortunate in that it had managed to attain self-sufficiency in rice and that much of what the people needed could be produced locally. President Soeharto categorically denied that Indonesia was under the shadow of the Americans. He protested against America's attack on Libya. Indonesia's stand on this was clearly announced prior to President Ronald Reagan's visit in May 1986. President Soeharto stood firm on this position within the Gerakan Non-Blok or Non-Block Movement.[7] He elaborated that non-alignment did not mean non-involvement. He reaffirmed the nation's stand on a free foreign policy, not only in terms of the military or politics, but also in ideology. He defended the ties the country tried to establish with the Eastern bloc countries. Indonesia would stand on its own ideology and not enforce its will on other nations. He referred to a Javanese philosophy: War without army, win without assault. He knew that the people had asked why Indonesia should maintain friendly ties with the communist nations after it defeated PKI. "Communism does not fit with our Pancasila, but communism might be good for other nations. We do not want to interfere," he said before he visited Moscow and China in 1989. He wrote that Malaysia and Singapore had demonstrated their positive impressions of what he had achieved so far. This was not untrue—Singapore's Lee Kuan Yew had written positive things about him and had visited him on 22 February 2006.

On the issue of monopoly, President Soeharto confirmed that under Article 33 of the Constitution, items relating to the country's basic needs like electricity were required to be brought under the government's control and, therefore, this was not a monopoly. However, monopoly in the private sector was not allowed. On the issue of corruption, he knew that there were serious issues at stake. He knew that some were pessimistic that the country could no longer get rid of its corrupt practices. He wrote that the younger generation could be more corrupt than the previous one. He quoted a Javanese proverb, "*Menangi jaman edan, yen ora edan ora keduman*": "In mad times, one had to be crazy or end up with nothing." He related it with something he had learnt from one of his ancestors, "*Sa begja-begjane sing lali isih begja sing eling lawan waspada*": "Much as one can obtain from temptation, those who watch their steps would be better off." In short, he asked that the people not resort to corruption. In this context, he admitted that control had to be widened but asked the top leaders to be watchful and not to consider control as merely looking for someone's faults. Control was the best tool for ensuring good management performance. He asked top managements not to be disheartened when it was necessary to take corrective or disciplinary action. Corrections were very important so that an offender was made aware of his mistake. Preventive actions were necessary and these could have ranged from bringing corrupt activities to a halt to outright suppression of those involved in corruption. In his biography, President had set out a challenge to his fellow officials to take action.[8] What went wrong and why was that challenge never met?

In order to pacify the "unhappy ones", the president had to create a balance of power. The "unhappy ones" were the small businessmen, mostly the indigenous people who were Muslims. Therefore, ICMI was formed to counter criticisms that only non-Muslims had gained more benefits under President Soeharto's rule. In fact, by having ICMI, there was a higher risk for a sectarian break-up. Soon, after the onset of sectarian clashes, a massacre took place in the Santa Cruz cemetery in Dili, East Timor, on 12 November 1991. The social and religious tensions did not stop as riots in Medan took place in 1994.

President Soeharto's first obvious mistake was to allow Soeryadi to oust Megawati Soekarnoputri as Partai Demokrasi Indonesia (PDI) leader during a congress in Medan. In July 1996, riots started in Jakarta: mobs burnt buildings, many people were killed, injured and a few even disappeared. Megawati, President Soekarno's eldest daughter, became the symbol of reform.

All of a sudden, nostalgia for the Old Order resurfaced. Megawati took on the image of her father and became a "goddess" for the *wong cilik*, the deprived group. By then, most had forgotten that her father, too, had once been named a dictator and autocrat. However, nobody dared to say anything at that time, when world attention had turned to Bishop Carlos Belo and Jose Ramos Horta from East Timor, who were awarded the prestigious Nobel Peace Prize. There were accusations of human rights abuses in the state's dealings with East Timor. East Timor was plainly a tiny part of the nation; compared to West Irian, it was comparatively insignificant. Further, the Portuguese had been there and there was no justification for treating East Timor as an independent state. Geographically, East Timor was clearly part of Indonesia.

The anti-Chinese riot that took place in Tasikmalaya on 26 December 1996 felt like a deep stab in President Soeharto's heart. It would have been his 49th wedding anniversary that day. A few weeks later, on 30 January 1997, another anti-Chinese riot took place in Rengasdengklok. It was not only between the Chinese and the indigenous people but also amongst the tribes: the Dayaks were killing the Madurese immigrants in West Kalimantan earlier that year.

PILLAR OF STRENGTH

In 1987, President Soeharto was pleased when General Benny Moerdani awarded Ibu Tien the *bintang gerilya* (guerrilla medal). President Soeharto had awarded the same medal to my mother, and my father and the family had been very pleased with the award. From this, it was clear that they—both Pak Harto and my father—valued their spouses greatly and were proud of their wives' contribution during the nation's war for independence. Pak Harto recalled how his family had celebrated his 66th birthday when his mother-in-law, then in her 88th year, was present. He had given the top of the *nasi tumpeng* to Ibu Hatmanti whom he had grown to love dearly and respect highly; it could have been because he had already lost both his own father and mother. He remembered how afraid he had been when he had asked Ibu Hatmanti for her daughter's hand in marriage back in 1947.

President Soeharto had been in good spirits when Ibu Tien opened Taman Mini Indonesia, which had a scaled-down miniature model of Indonesia, in 1975 and when he officiated the opening of the Purna Bhakti Pertiwi museum in July 1987. Within the next few years, however, President Soeharto faced the saddest part of his life with the untimely death of Ibu Tien on 26 April 1996. Theirs was an arranged marriage 49 years ago which turned out to be a blessed, secure and happy union. Ibu Tien was not only a good wife and mother, but she had also become President Soeharto's strongest pillar of strength. There was no doubt about Ibu Tien's dedication to her husband and family. She had given him her full support to enable him to fulfill his dreams of helping the needy through charitable foundations. The early rumours about her asking for commission from private businesses for personal enrichment soon faded away after it had been proven that the donations she had collected were used for her charitable foundations.

With Ibu Tien's death, President Soeharto had lost the greatest ally in his life. Stories also surfaced that it had been Ibu Tien who could control her children to mind the sensitivity of their business dealings. It was also Ibu Tien who had a premonition that Pak Harto should not seek re-election in the early 1990s. As she was of minor aristocracy, the Javanese believed that she had been the one given the *wahyu* or special gift. It was her *wahyu* that made President Soeharto one of the greatest leaders in Asia. With her passing, the *wahyu* was gone and many thought that President Soeharto's days in power were numbered. Whatever the Javanese believed in, the fact remains that President Soeharto stepped down just two years after her death. As if her demise had not been a sufficient cross for him to bear, political developments also became increasingly unsettled. By that time, more people were calling him a dictator and autocrat.

BENCHMARKING

When General Soeharto took over from President Soekarno, he knew of the strong emotional attachment the people had for their first president. President Soeharto had rarely confronted the then President Soekarno and had tried to approach him in an indirect way, the Javanese way. President Soekarno was a skilled statesman and an infallible penman. Through him, Indonesia had regained its previous glory. He had inspired great pride amongst the people through his high level of oratorical skills, which he used to illustrate the glorious achievements of the Sriwijaya and Majapahit empires. He spoke brilliantly of Prambanan and Borobudur, so that the people's souls were rekindled with a strong sense of patriotism. To him, culture was the most noble need of mankind.

However, it was President Soeharto who asked the Angkatan Bersenjata Republik Indonesia (ABRI) or the Armed Forces of the Republic of Indonesia to work harder and sacrifice what had been their privileges for the sake of development and the masses. The top priority was the improvement of the economy by reducing the defence budget and removing various army privileges. This decision was accepted as a whole by ABRI. ABRI did not get salary increases in the early 1970s, compared to the ten, five and threefold increases of the various government offices. The improvement of the soldiers' lot only commenced during the second Repelita, from 1974 to 1978. In his speech of 9 June 1971 in Pasar Klewer, President Soeharto said, "All our borrowing is to be used for development. None will be utilised for routine budget, less so to buy weapons for our armed forces."

President Soeharto also placed more importance on national interest. At times, this created a contradiction. In July 1982, President Soeharto reiterated that ABRI's role should be in line with the Javanese proverb "tut wuri handayani", to be the dominant set in maintaining national stability. ABRI did not want to create a military dictator, because if this was what they had intended to do, they could have done it right at the beginning of the country's freedom or at least on 1 October 1965. President Soeharto recalled that it was during that critical period that ABRI did not want to take over the government in unconstitutional ways. ABRI's role was to safeguard the existence of Pancasila and the 1945 Constitution.

President Soeharto made the right move as during his long rule, the key positions in economic affairs were filled with civilians, although ABRI did have a key regional position. There had been a regeneration process amongst the military personnel, as many from the 1945 generation had left the stage and were replaced by the younger ones. Perhaps President Soeharto had been wrong in depending too much on ABRI, but that had not been due to favouritism, merely pragmatism. In some cases, perhaps ABRI had used too much power or had perpetuated abuses toward civilians and President Soeharto had not paid close attention to this. This had been one of his weaknesses.

The cost of living in Jakarta before G30S had risen close to 500 per cent in 1965 and there had been a further sharp decline in exports. The decline in earnings, coupled with growing foreign loans to support manufacturing, created a severe balance of payment crisis. Export earnings had declined from US$750 million in 1961 to US$450 million in 1965, while import obligations reached US$560 million (these related mainly to rice, raw materials and spare parts). The government was forced to implement increasingly inflationary policies to finance the country's development projects and to support the military budget. At the same time, there were huge government expenditures, mostly to fund state enterprises, and inadequate skills for collection of taxes. There was no foreign exchange left and the country owed US$230 million in debts in 1965.

Following G30S, the ministries made desperate attempts to bring the economy under control, with new taxes being amongst other measures introduced and attempts were made to remove the heavy subsidies from public enterprises. The currency depreciated and reform was initiated by the issuance of a new rupiah, which was worth 1,000 of the old currency. Subsidies were removed from staple commodities. President Soeharto knew that a bitter pill was needed for recovery. It would be a painful process as it required austerity and contraction in economic growth. The government's economic team took unorthodox and radical steps in their efforts to pressure supply and demand in a forceful way. In the first place, the government had to reduce inflation, while at the same time stimulating production that would run in parallel. To bring the high inflation under control, the government initially had to watch its own overall spending. The government stopped undisciplined spending habits and focused on living within its means. The existing black market and barter practices were replaced by official trade and commerce.

The government had played a crucial role in the economy of post-colonial Indonesia. It had pushed for the ownership of capital when the expropriation of Dutch enterprises in 1957 to 1958 took place. In December 1957, this process began suddenly, and there were takeovers of a number of Dutch firms by workers and unions. Soon thereafter, all Dutch properties were placed under military supervision, such action having been endorsed by Parliament. Understandably, these proceedings were a major blow to foreign capital investments. The events evolved around the transfer of ownership of 90 per cent of plantation output, 60 per cent of foreign trade, some 246 factories and mining enterprises, plus banks, shipping concerns and a range of service industries. This signified a starting point of the military's involvement in businesses. For the military, state ownership was attractive and a good prospect for direct military power in the economy. In political terms, neither the Chinese, the national bourgeoisie nor the petty indigenous bourgeoisie could have challenged the verdict. Hence, the role of the military in the country's economic life was present from the beginning. As President Soeharto needed their support, he chose not to rock the boat.

One of Indonesia's major successes over the last few decades was being able to persuade many of the working poor to become more nationalistic. President Soeharto was very effective on bread and butter issues like healthcare, nevertheless, he came across as being more on the side of the conglomerates. This was comparable to the notion that President Soekarno had been leaning towards PKI. President Soeharto was considered to be out of touch whenever a discussion shifted to reformed values and democracy. Sadly, under both presidents, many substituted "greed" for "need" and "power" for "culture".

Born among farmers, President Soeharto understood that at the heart of all problems was hunger. The people had simple minds and simple wishes, but once their patience was tested, that simplicity could turn into extreme complexity. After the euphoria of surviving G30S had faded away, the people wanted more. They wanted more opportunities and a better lifestyle. Once in power, President Soeharto had immediately decided to tackle the three basic human needs: food, clothing and housing. The new demands that surfaced could not fall on deaf ears. As a military man, General Soeharto did not want to fight a losing battle nor did he intend to be a friend of lost causes. An early political move had been to ban PKI while at the same time maintaining the integrity of former President Soekarno. An initial economic measure was to discontinue unproductive projects. Soon thereafter, the government had to concentrate on creating revenue-generating projects. This had to be done together with the reorganisation of the antiquated and inefficient taxation system that had been operating for years. There was also an increased tightening of credit except for selected types of investments such as the rehabilitation of existing production facilities or projects with great potential to expand. Indonesia's balance of payment position gradually improved through the accumulation of foreign reserves and the move to a unified exchange rate. To manage the debt position, the government needed a new infusion of foreign resources, which was accomplished through the assistance of a consortium of creditors, the Inter-Governmental Group on Indonesia (IGGI).

Foreign aid that poured into the country was largely divided into two kinds: those relating to planned actions and those connected with projects. Aid within the planned programme not directly aimed at special projects could avoid the rules on foreign exchange funding. The donor countries usually demanded that the loan be used for purchasing goods and services from the originating donor. These tasks required detailed analysis and technical expertise across a wide spectrum of the economy. Throughout the stabilisation period, the advisory groups and ministers were guided by a sense of crisis.

This sense of crisis led the way towards success. Sadly, this sense of crisis has now diminished and the prime focus has shifted to personal interest and not that of the public.

Since the technocrats were fresh from the academic world, they were inexperienced in politics. They were very young, mostly in their 30s, but full of confidence that they would be able to resolve the problems and restore the country's economic well-being. They thought of their assignment as a political apprenticeship, but faced it with the thought that millions of lives depended on them. This made them work hard. The team also had a high degree of *esprit de corps*. They shared similar experiences and spoke the same language. There were almost no instances of irreconcilable differences hence they could focus on formulating the best strategies and tactics, as they knew that time was of the essence. A sense of crisis achieved magic at times like this. Under such conditions, President Soeharto's team of technocrats set its course from 1969 with the modest Five-Year Development Plan.

There was a lesson to be learnt here. Consensus and mutual cooperation could work well together when there was a sense of urgency. Their similar experiences while studying abroad overrode the differences in their backgrounds. In the past, one would have been cautious about talking about anything that originated from the West. This included western political ideology, social behaviour and economic points of view. However, the technocrats were able to use an analytical and flexible approach which was common amongst those who were educated in the West. President Soeharto, in spite of the vast differences in his educational background with those of the technocrats, knew that he could depend on them. Like in the Bank Duta crisis, he had left them alone, given them a free hand and had been far from being autocratic.

It is indeed an odd blessing that the style of Indonesia's modern-day economic policymaking was created in a time of emergency. The country's survival as an independent nation was no doubt dependent on economic recovery. Crisis is the mother of pragmatism. Pragmatism meant that in formulating an economic policy, there was limited room for mistakes. Two criteria were essential: one is that the new policy should support development and the other was that it had to be politically justifiable. Wisdom taught the technocrats that to be successful was to be pragmatic. The art of finding the middle ground was of utmost importance. Instead of making use of economic reasoning to support political belief, it was political belief that was used to support the country's growth. Therefore, free market and open door ideologies flourished during the early years of the New Order. There were only a few political options available to the debt-ridden economy in a state of chaos. In such an environment, where collapse was imminent, there were few choices.

Over the years, Bappenas was invaluable in directing Indonesia's development, which benefited the whole country. In later years, the benefits increased faster for a few selected groups. Two developments in the mid-1970s undermined the influence of the technocrats and ushered in the second phase of rivalry between the technocrats and the nationalists. The first was the Arab-influenced boost in oil prices in 1973, which put massive resources at the disposal of the government. When the Malari riot took place in January 1974, it mirrored what had been boiling underneath the surface. The Malari affair had been a reflection of the political discontent due to the rising dominance of foreign investors and ethnic Chinese businesses. Meanwhile, the majority, the indigenous people, felt that there had not been enough improvement in their living standards. Nevertheless, the wealth derived from higher oil prices enabled President Soeharto to try a new approach in dealing with public restlessness. For President Soeharto, it had been a period of great risk and difficult choices whether to "stop the running horse or to try to steer it slowly back to the right path".

President Soeharto knew that corrective measures could not be delayed. He knew that to safeguard political stability, it was necessary to move fast to achieve economic recovery. From the start, there was a close relationship between the top executive and the technocrats who served as policy advisers. The only way to move forward quickly was to allow his technocrats a high degree of freedom and flexibility, although the same approach could not be applied in defence and political matters. For this, he had to support unpopular actions, such as during the Petrus incident. Consensus and cooperation had to exist if the revised economic policy was to be a success. In addition, it required collective effort and close co-ordination in its implementation. The technocrats trusted the market to determine how capital should be allocated. By the end of 1969, the government had approved foreign investments outside the oil sector totaling US$1,226 million. The largest shares were held by mining, forestry and manufacturing.

The degree of change experienced by the country from its very bleak situation has given rise to various discussions and seminars on Indonesia's "economic miracle". It is comparable with the economic boom that is currently taking place in China. With a high level of foreign business interest and the oil windfall profit, the country has met its Five-Year Plan targets very quickly. The hyperinflation has almost been completely brought under control. Indonesia has been compared to Brazil and is now able to write its own ticket for aid from the IGGI donor countries. After several devaluations and uncertainties due to multiple exchange rates, the rupiah, was fixed to the US dollar from August 1971. From pessimism of revenue earned from exports, the country suddenly gained abundant foreign exchange income.

For the first time since its independence, Indonesia has enough money to spend. One of the continuing worries is the high deficit on current account as a result of the government's deliberate choice to be heavily dependent on foreign capital inflows, almost in disregard of the wisdom of not being overly dependent on one source of revenue. There was a cautious optimism over whether Indonesia could be steered to a more sustainable base. The poor harvest in 1972 and the multiplication of the world oil prices in 1973 completely destroyed any optimism in this regard.

In the early days of President Soeharto's New Order, the vision of development was based on the three major fundamentals of stability, growth and equity, otherwise known as Indonesia's "Development Trilogy". This had been a great idea and it expressed a pragmatism against which ideological concept and economic policies could be benchmarked and measured. The country's experience in overcoming hyperinflation and ongoing political unrest had taught the people a valuable lesson: stability was an absolute must if they wanted to move ahead. President Soeharto felt that unstable political conditions made the economy stagnant and would endanger the country's unity. This would then develop into a vicious cycle. Therefore, the government used the phrase "dynamic stability", which meant the country would proceed to cultivate conditions suitable for economic growth. This also meant that it would have been impossible to keep everyone happy. The sacrificial lamb was chosen: the country would have less freedom.

LESSONS TO BE LEARNT

During President Soeharto's later years in power, the free market concept intensified into a "survival of the fittest" situation. It had turned controversial and became a hot topic for public debate. Critics claim that the period from 1965 to 1974 marked a definite stage in the development of economic policies; yet, even within this time-span, it was hard to find examples of success to illustrate the strength of the policies effected by Bappenas. There were allegations not only that Bappenas policies were contradictory, but there had also been incompatible explanations on the whole outcome of their courses of action. It followed then that Bappenas must have provided a protective framework for the inflow of local capital dominated by state corporations which were owned by the military and its Chinese connections, even though the government had planned to give fair and equitable treatment for private businesses and a guarantee of freedom of management to all. In theory, the labour law should have observed the balance between capital requirements and appropriate protection for workers. However, the labour force was very restricted, as labour was considered the easiest channel for PKI to penetrate.

President Soeharto knew that the Dutch economic practices where foreign business smothered the growth of indigenous business should be shunned at all cost. The crucial aspect of the trickle down effect of wealth from the rich to the poor would determine the invasion of foreign capital instinctively and generate a process of growth and ensure a healthy climate in domestic business. Unfortunately, in its economic philosophy and in its political stance, the technocrats no longer spoke as a unified group in the early 1980s. That was the first sign of trouble. Another lesson to be learnt from the past Malari affair was the danger of having factional disputes within the nation's leadership spilling over into various groups, namely, civilians, the press, Muslims and students. The Malari affair marked a decisive shift from the relatively open, pluralistic phase of political life under the New Order. After a few months, five of the most critical newspapers were closed down and hundreds of people were put on trial for their role in the disturbances. Campus life became submissive and the press became more controlled. President Soeharto had meant what he said: stability was of prime importance above all else and the time was not ripe for Western-style democracy in Indonesia.

As mentioned in the previous chapter, the changes that the National Economic Stabilization Board made to investment and credit rules after the Malari incident signalled an important change to the existing free market and open door policies. It was also a fundamental shift in the balance between domestic and international capital. The latter faced increasingly stringent rules as they were required to take on more equity participation. More importantly, government control over areas in which international capital could be invested was increased. Ironically, with all the best intentions behind the revised regulations, in the second half of the 1970s, it became clear that it was not the indigenous petty capitalists who benefited the most, but the larger Chinese and state-owned entities, which had moved into a much stronger position than that of international capital.

Obviously, the president became aware of the unpleasant rifts. He was wise enough to give in to a few demands which he thought were reasonable and sensible, but at the same time, he put his foot down firmly on too much freedom. He pleaded with the elite to restrain themselves from excessive displays of wealth by practising a simple lifestyle. Officials were asked not to organise lavish parties or to visit places such as nightclubs and steam baths. The importation of assembled cars was banned. However, President Soeharto was caught off-guard by the "Ali Baba" schemes, where the "Ali" or front men positions in large businesses were hotly contested over by the sons and daughters of government officials. The "Baba" or Chinese businessmen who did the real work behind the scenes started to expand their operations, including into areas which were not related to their main businesses. Instead of steering clear of Ibnu Sutowo's style of business expansion, this method became a national disease and an epidemic.

By this time, it was clear that progress was not reaching the masses as quickly as had been anticipated by them. Those who were rich soon became uncaring and ignored the dangers that lay ahead. Across the road from Bappenas, there was a small park called Taman Suropati, where small vendors sold gaudy paintings and simple snacks and drinks. These people had different dreams which were much simpler than the dreams of the rich. While the wealthy wanted more luxury, the concerns of the poor remained rooted to basic ones such as having enough money to feed their families, send their children to school and have roofs over their heads. The paintings exhibited in Taman Suropati gave a clear picture of the type of prosperity they had in mind. It was obvious that the garish paintings did not whet the appetite of the rich. The rich had already acquired a sophisticated taste for refined art from international artists.

Despite the tremendous growth of the country's towns and industries, the underlying fact remained that Indonesia was a predominantly agrarian nation with some 85 per cent of its people still living in rural areas. The realities of life in the villages were far from the harmonious ideal the government had in mind. The inner islands remained caught in an ecological trap, placing a question mark over the true extent of the achievements of the technocrats and entrepreneurs like Ibnu Sutowo. President Soeharto realised the critical twofold conditions that remained: the existence of the very rich and the very poor, and the big difference between Java and the remote islands. These were two critical conditions which created jealousy amongst the people, but there was no easy and immediate solution.

When Probosutedjo denied that his business success was due to favours from the president or special treatment from the government, the press had a field day. Probosutedjo claimed that if government officials gave him special treatment, it was because he was just lucky and not because he was a relative of the president. He had been a good businessman from the beginning. The operation of Mercu Buana started in 1960, a few years before his brother became president. However, many of the government officials extended favours to President Soeharto's family, especially those who wanted to be acknowledged for "facilitation". The practice became excessively worse, paving the way for the attitude known as "ABS" (*Asal Bapak Senang* or "As long as it pleases Father"). When asked, President Soeharto's children said that hundreds if not thousands of people—all with business proposals—had approached them. Their naivety and the fact that President Soeharto and Ibu Tien had been very busy with their work at that time contributed to their being manipulated by various people with vested interests.

The technocrats realised that the nation's core problem lay in human resources development. President Soeharto knew only too well that education was the necessary pillar of support for development and to improve the standard of living. Indonesia's founding fathers wrote into the 1945 Constitution the right to an education for all. He was aware that at the end of the day, final judgment on his governing of the country would be based on his ability to achieve this noble goal. Education had been more complex under Dutch colonial rule, where there had been a discriminative policy in learning methods and types of schools. As a result, only a limited few in urban areas were able to get sufficient academic instruction. Until the 1970s, the usual education accessible to children was in trading, customs and knowledge imparted through parents' wisdom. A few youths might also have learnt special skills such as carpentry, dancing, midwifery and others. In the mid-1960s, the educational system was in disarray as nothing could be done while a flurry of hostile rebellions were taking place in various parts of the country. Schools were in bad condition and there were shortages in basic school supplies such as chalk, paper, blackboards and, most of all, books. Appeals for teachers met with little success due to the low wages. It was common that teachers would hold two or three jobs at any one time. These conditions are still very much in place today and the teaching profession is still an unpopular choice of career.

By virtue of the country's tight financial situation, the technocrats had to choose two basic areas in education to focus on: firstly, the main purpose of education, and secondly, the most effective way of ensuring that equitable education could reach the masses. From a broad perspective and taking into account the vast geography of the country, the diversity of its culture, faiths and even languages and dialects, the education system had to cater to the wide and varied needs of the Indonesian people. Not only was education intended to impart intellectual skills, it was also to instil a sense of civic duty in the people.

For President Soeharto, it was clear that education had to be part of the country's development plan if Indonesia was to become a modern state. The people needed the basic skills in reading, writing and mathematics. These skills were necessary for jobs in industry as well as in agriculture. In the field of agriculture, a lack of education would, for example, result in illiterate farmers not being able to read instructions for the proper use of pesticides or fertilisers. In the presence of illiteracy, it would be difficult to modernise the country's farming techniques. Another example of the effects of a lack of education is the problem of illiterate mothers not being able to administer accurate dosages of medicine to their children. The ability to read instructions properly was important if the population's standard of health was to be upgraded.

The next crucial stage for consideration was whether the construction of new schools should start in the urban areas and gradually spread to the rural areas or vice versa. In 1973, the government decided to embark on an ambitious goal that would serve as one of the cornerstones of its national development policy: to make six years of primary school education available to every child. With help from the country's oil revenue, the government launched a programme of building schools and training teachers in 1974. The government promised to build schools if the villages were willing to give up some of their land. By the end of 1979, 25,000 schools had been built. Correspondingly, the number of students rose from 16.8 million in 1969 to 33.2 million in 1984. With the increased training, the salary of teachers also increased and teachers in public schools automatically became government employees. Even so, the salary of teachers was still way below earnings in the private sector. The Ministry of Education became the largest employer and in 1986, it represented 48 per cent of the country's civil servants. This was an extra burden for the government, which was already working with a limited budget.

However, despite the budgetary restrictions, in May 1984, President Soeharto declared that it was compulsory for every child to attend primary school and collections of school entrance fees were stopped. Three years down the road, the government announced its plan to lengthen primary school education from six to nine years. One of the things President Soeharto had promised himself when he came to power was that he would improve the country's living conditions from that which he had experienced in his early life. There were those in the minority who believed that the president wanted to keep the people simple and ignorant, but this view is in total contrast to the number of schools he had given instructions to build and the thousands of students who have received scholarships from his foundations.

A QUESTION OF VALUES

The biggest impact of globalisation was that it created an awareness of what life was like in the West. Most Indonesians thought that all Americans and Europeans lived in big houses with large swimming pools, saunas and tennis courts as portrayed in Hollywood movies. Years ago, my father warned about the dangers of abruptly crossing over from poverty into middle class existence instead of through a slow and gradual transition: an abrupt change from one to the other would have the most revolutionary but negative impact on Indonesian society. He said, "When masses cross the poverty line and become consumers, almost everything about them will change, their physical appearance as well as their mentality." The worst result was that moral values became distorted. Money became the pinnacle of many people's dreams and the only measurement for social standing. Consequently, many ways of making money became justifiable, whether through hard work, by using a *cukong* or an "Ali Baba" arrangement, by cheating or through plain corruption. Those who held fat purses could pull the strings of others.

While Bung Karno and Bung Hatta had been intellectually occupied with Socrates, Plato, Marx and Revere, Shakespeare, Mozart and imagining the world of Utopia, the new generation had different dreams: that of driving Lamborghini sports cars accompanied by the music of Michael Jackson with their spirit more often than not boosted by the Ecstasy drug. This younger generation dreamt of being footballers, tennis players, golfers or becoming film stars where they could make much more money than by being historians, teachers or professors. Young Indonesian girls wanted to be "artistes" and young men wanted to be like Donald Trump. President Soeharto's concept of developing Indonesia in terms of material success accompanied by higher morals did not seem to work.

The core of public discontent centred on the fact that President Soeharto's extended family and 50 other families were seen to control most of the country's economic successes. His children's involvement with Golkar did not help his political standing; his family's close relationship with the conglomerates affected public opinion about his impartiality. Among the well-known figures in Golkar that came under public scrutiny were Akbar Tanjung, Abdul Gafur and Harmoko. Among the conglomerates that people were not happy with were those of Liem Sioe Liong, Eka Tjipta Widjaya, Sukanto Tanoko, Soeryadjaya, Nursalim, amongst others. Those in the military that were distrusted by many were Wiranto, Prabowo and Hartono. However, among those within his inner circle who were outspoken about the conglomerates was Probosutedjo, who wrote:[9]

> If the conglomerates really love Indonesia and not their original place of birth, they should be thankful for the wealth they could accumulate because of Indonesia with our 1945 Constitution and Pancasila. They have attained prosperity not from their place of origin or where their ancestors lived. It is because the conglomerates are spoiled by the government that the New Order has fallen.

Probosutedjo was indeed an unusual figure who paid close attention to the fate of the country's elderly leaders like Ibu Trimurti. Ibu Trimurti had been with Bung Karno when he proclaimed Indonesia's independence and her contributions to the country's freedom were significant. At the time of writing this book, Ibu Trimurti is in her early 90s and still lives modestly, far from the style of the new rich. The same applies to Abdul Madjid, a freedom fighter who still lives humbly. Thus, it is easy to understand why Probosutedjo becomes emotional when he compares the living conditions of these two individuals with the lifestyle of the conglomerates. In his eyes, these two figures were present when Indonesia fought for its freedom with blood, sweat and tears; but where were the conglomerates then? His patriotic sentiment rebelled against the government's apparently unfair treatment of the country's freedom fighters; it was for this same reason that he decided to distance himself from the Chinese conglomerates, of which a few have taken on board the president's children. There were certainly indications of friction within the president's family and it appeared that the president did not want to be caught in his family's conflicts.

It is not difficult to be impressed by and admire Probosutedjo's dedication to his brother's legacy. He collected news clippings from 1965 until 1998 as he believed that it was his duty to put his brother's role in the country's history on record. Probosutedjo was a teacher early in his career and after he became successful in his business, he did not want to forget his past, so he opened University Mercu Buana. He also decided to open museums and improve the roads and preserve his family grave around Kemusuk. He was bitter and very critical of the 14 ministers who decided, at the last minute, not to join the reshuffled Cabinet that President Soeharto had in mind before his resignation, especially since a few of them had gained benefits during his presidency. Probosutedjo wrote about the final stages of his brother's presidency in a straightforward fashion as he quoted what the president had said the night before his fateful meeting on 19 May 1998 with the 14 ministers who declined to be in the reformed cabinet: "*Saya kapok, nggak jadi Presiden nggak patheken*" or "I don't give a damn about not being a president."[10]

Probosutedjo stood with President Soeharto through thick and thin, an admirable trait, regardless of the faults he may have had. Unlike his brother, Probosutedjo is more vocal and shows his feelings openly. At the time of writing this book, he is in jail. After Tommy and Bob Hasan, Probosutedjo is the last one from within President Soeharto's inner circle to have been put on trial and sent to prison.

PRELUDE TO THE FINAL HOURS

The end of President Soeharto's rule was fast approaching, partly triggered by the economic collapse of the so-called Asian Miracle. However, the economic crisis was not the only cause, as it was a combination of factors, including his advanced age, betrayal from those whose businesses he had helped to develop, exposure of the family's business interests and having remained too long in power. The Asian Miracle that had impressed the world took a sudden turn into disaster, which started when the Thai baht was hard hit by speculators in May 1997. However, some observers had foreseen the fall of the Asian economic boom.

ASEAN economic growth had lured speculators from Europe and the United States, while the ASEAN countries, lulled by glory, had expanded wildly without restraint. As a matter of fact, the government should have known how the big groups such as Liem Sioe Liong, Eka Tjipta Widjaya, Sukanto Tanoko, Soeryadjaya, Nursalim and the like were able to manipulate the capital market. By then, the public at large realised that President Soeharto had lost his grip on the conglomerates due to globalisation. Globalisation brings in a flutter of new concepts, new ways to think and act. The development of technology, in particular communications, has shaken the very ground we stand on: what happens in the North Pole can be heard on the radio or seen on television within minutes. The rupiah managed to hold its own ground, until July 1997, and soon the Malaysian ringgit, Philippine peso and the rupiah started to slide. This contributed to the weakening of President Soeharto's position.

As with President Soekarno before him, President Soeharto's detractors took advantage of the wobbling economy to prepare themselves for the next set of key players in Indonesia. In addition, the public knew that his old age and physical condition meant that it would be a matter of time before the changing of the guard took place. For example, on 25 September that year, Amien Rais, the leader of Muhammadiyah,[11] in response to a question, declared that he was willing to be nominated for the presidency. On 31 October, the IMF package was revealed and it provided US$23 billion with an additional assistance of US$20 billion in stand-by loan. On 1 November, 16 banks—a few of which are owned by President Soeharto's children and family—were closed in line with the terms of the IMF package but it was painful as depositors moved their investments overseas. IMF later admitted it was a mistake to take such drastic action.

On 6 January, President Soeharto unveiled an expansionary budget contrary to the IMF demands for budget surplus. Megawati's popularity went up and on 10 January 1998, she announced that she was ready to become the president. On 15 January, the IMF Director stood over President Soeharto with his arms folded while the president signed a Letter of Intent

(LOI) . The pictures were splashed on the front pages of all the newspapers, creating a furore. Many Indonesians thought it was very condescending that the Head of State was treated in such a manner. On the same day, a group of retired military officers and national figures called for Vice-President Try Sutrisno to take over from President Soeharto at the end of his term in March.

The demand for a change of ruler got stronger as the rupiah kept plummeting. On 20 January 1998, in one day's trading, the rupiah plunged 23 per cent, resulting in an exchange rate of Rp17,000 to the US dollar. Critics became more vocal about President Soeharto's militaristic style of government and the KKN (*korupsi, kolusi, nepotisme*) or corruption, collusion and nepotism that had taken place for a few years and the public demanded a total reform. On 27 January, the government announced a moratorium on repayment of debts and interests and promised to guarantee all obligations entered into by the commercial banks. This indicated that the state had hit rock bottom, as there was no other reason why the government would have been willing to be responsible for the commercial banks, which were mostly owned by the conglomerates, a few with his children as shareholders.

On 2 February, Steve Hanke[12] introduced the "currency board system" which he claimed could fix the rupiah's fate without pain to the IMF. A week later, President Soeharto foreshadowed the government by instituting a "currency board" system to peg the rupiah to the US dollar. The IMF World Bank and then US President Bill Clinton thought it would not work and threatened to cut off aid. On 19 February, following food riots that took place all over the country, University of Indonesia students carried out their first demonstration, demanding lower prices and more democracy. On 3 March, Bill Clinton sent a special envoy, Walter Mondale, to meet the president and urged him to act on the agreed IMF programme. In relation to this, Lee Kuan Yew wrote in his book, *From Third World to First*:[13]

> Two months later, in March 1998, former US Vice-President Walter Mondale carried a message from Clinton to Suharto. He then met Prime Minister Goh and me in Singapore on his way home. After comparing notes on Suharto's likely course of action on reforms, Mondale tossed this question at me: "You knew Marcos. Was he a hero or a crook? How does Suharto compare to Marcos? Is Suharto a patriot or a crook?" I felt Mondale was making up his mind on Suharto's motivations before submitting his

recommendations to his president. I answered that Marcos might have started off as a hero but ended up as a crook. Suharto was different. His heroes were not Washington or Jefferson or Madison, but the sultans of Solo in Central Java. Suharto's wife had been a minor princess of that royal family. As the president of Indonesia, he was a mega-sultan of a mega-country. Suharto believed his children were entitled to be as privileged as the princes and princesses of the sultans of Solo. He did not feel any embarrassment at giving them these privileges, because it was his right as a mega-sultan. He saw himself as a patriot. I would not classify Suharto as a crook.

On 4 March, two magazines depicted the president as the King of Spades, which many considered to be an insult.

Yet, in spite of the strong protests to end his leadership, President Soeharto was persuaded to stay on when leaders from the representatives of the MPR came to Jalan Cendana and asked him to stand for re-election. As he was re-elected on 10 March for another five-year term, the students' protests spilled out of the campuses. The rest, as they say, is history.

THE FINAL JOURNEY

The real crisis occurred when President Soeharto formed the seventh Cabinet in 1998. The Cabinet formed on 14 March 1998 was quickly dissolved on 22 May 1998. The vice-president then was BJ Habibie and the Cabinet consisted of 34 ministers. All the old guards in economic affairs had not been around since 1993. The president appointed his eldest daughter, Tutut, as the Minister of Social Affairs and Bob Hasan as the Trade Minister. Many wondered why he had taken such a step when public criticism of nepotism was increasingly being voiced. What he had in mind might have been far from wanting to practice nepotism. He might have believed that someone like Bob Hasan would do well as the Minister of Trade, as Bob had been a businessman for years. As for Tutut, from the beginning, President Soeharto had wanted to have his children involved in helping the underprivileged, hence their involvement in the Yayasan (foundations) that he built. Whether these ideas had been discussed among his inner circle was not easy to find out. Whether his close friends had failed to warn him of the political risks and dangers remains unknown. The temperature of the political climate was comparable to that of President Soekarno's final days. One comes to the inevitable conclusion that in both cases, power had overstayed, and combined with advanced age, it made both leaders blind to reality and deaf to unpleasant news.

On Saturday, 9 May 1998, President Soeharto left for Cairo, Egypt, to attend the 15 Islamic Nations Conference. As usual, the president tried to combine two or three different overseas trips into one, in order to keep the costs of overseas travel low. He planned to visit Saudi Arabia after Cairo. Widjojo Nitisastro, economic advisor, was one of the team members, as was Foreign Minister, Ali Alatas, and Minister of State Secretariat, Saadillah Mursjid. His return had been scheduled for 16 May, but they arrived home one day earlier.

On Wednesday, 13 May 1998, the riots and demonstrations that had taken place during the last few weeks reached their peak. Four students had been shot dead a day before during a confrontation with security forces outside the campus of Trisakti University. Ironically, a few students were from University of Indonesia, the institution that had endorsed President Soeharto's rise to power 32 year ago. It was like a *wayang* performance with the common underlying theme of "one day everything must end". President Soeharto, too, once wrote that life was like a rotating wheel, what went up had to come down. However, no matter how philosophical one might have been, it was still very hard to accept such dramatic and drastic changes. Within 48 hours, another student would die as the demonstrators quickly declared the students heroes of the reform movement. Many of the students and masses had been injured or had gone missing. Before long, the students claimed that the dead were shot inside their campus by President Soeharto's security forces.

Something similar had taken place in 1966, but in 1998, controversy centred on the shootings. In 1966, the communists had been the culprits, but in 1998 it was the reformists. There was an allegation that the police firing from the overpass were actually soldiers disguised in borrowed uniforms. During the funeral of the students, who were deemed fighting for justice, thousands rallied to pay their last respects. It was a national tragedy and many condemned the brutality. In 1966, it had been the army that was called brutal by the communists; in 1998, it was the army being called brutal by the students. A few questioned whether the students' demonstration was a plot to bring President Soeharto down. One of the favourite targets of suspicion was the Central Intelligence Agency (CIA). The students did not respond to calls for revenge, but the mob, including the ubiquitous high school students, certainly did.

The number of rioters grew quickly from hundreds to thousands and spread like a forest fire to the north and western parts of Jakarta, where there were concentrations of ethnic Chinese shop houses and shopping malls. In Jakarta's urban *kampongs*, the poor were simmering. That time around, jealousy over the minority Chinese went out of control. The Chinese packed whatever they could and rushed to the neighbouring country of Singapore. Those who were lucky flew out immediately but those stranded moved into hotels. The situation did not apply to all Chinese people, as many of them were still poor as well. It was this group that had to pay. Not only were their shops looted and their houses ransacked, but there were also reports of rape and other brutalities.

A mob situation is extremely dangerous in a country like Indonesia. For some unknown reason, Indonesia's peaceful character is capable of changing very quickly to one of uncontrolled anger. The rupiah slumped to Rp11,000 to the US dollar and stock market prices dipped. The economy was in a mess and the government was blamed. President Soeharto was held responsible for corruption, collusion and nepotism instead of safeguarding the people's welfare. In a few days, the fury of the mob broke out again, this time in Tanggerang, West Java, an area of regular worker unrest over low wages and where there were Muslim protests against the presence of bars and discotheques.

As riots erupted in several places, Armed Forces Commander, General Wiranto, announced that the Trisakti University accident should never have happened, adding that ABRI did not intend to stand as the students' opposing group. General Wiranto and ABRI commanders were photographed smiling and shaking hands with the students. President Soeharto had been left alone by the military and the only forces he could rely on was to be found at the Army's Strategic Reserves (Kostrad), which was led by Lieutenant General Prabowo Subianto. Kostrad had become prestigious under General Soeharto's leadership and since then, he had used Kostrad, with its unique and discrete network of links to other units, as the headquarters from which he restored security and order in the wake of the alleged communist coup attempt in 1965.

There was talk of a silent and discreet power struggle between the army and the Muslim-oriented group under BJ Habibie. The army also lost its confidence in President Soeharto's ability to lift Indonesia from its economic crisis. However, BJ Habibie was certainly not the army's favoured choice of leader. The mass media, especially television, revealed widespread anarchy characterised by burning and looting. Mindless mobs, not students, brought a reign of terror to the city streets.

In 1966, a similar mob situation had taken place after President Soekarno became very strong. President Soekarno's power base had been Nasakom, but the communists had betrayed him. As the political machinery of President Soeharto's for 32 years, Golkar gave the impression that their power base was financial gain. The inclination of Golkar towards materialism and arrogance did not go down well with the people. In July 1982, President Soeharto had said that Golkar was a functional group based wholly on Pancasila and it would seek the balance between material and spiritual achievements. However, Golkar leaders were so eager to win over the suburban professionals that they lost touch with the blue-collared Indonesians or Bung Karno's *wong cilik* group. To put it another way, as perceived by some, President Soeharto peddled issues, and President Soekarno sold values.

Kosgoro, a mass organisation affiliated with Golkar, called for the president and vice-president to return the mandate they were given in March 1998 and backed the calls for an extraordinary session of the MPR. Also, a statement signed by officers of the Armed Forces Generation 1945, several of whom were members of the Petition of 50, encouraged President Soeharto to resign. The unity began to break up and stability was endangered.

There were also mobs and riots in places such as Surabaya, Solo and Bandar Lampung. President Soeharto returned on 15 May and many wondered how his close inner circle felt at that time and whether they would stand by him or allow him to step down. The president's plane landed before sunrise. Arriving back at Jalan Cendana, he immediately summoned the minister in charge of security and head of intelligence, Bakin, to meet at Jalan Cendana five hours later. After hearing reports on the latest developments, specifically in Jakarta, he decided to wait for two days to see if the situation could be brought back under control. A President's decision to restore Security and Order (Kopkamtib) was prepared in case the riots went out of control. The

Armed Forces Commander with the Chief of Army as deputy would lead Kopkamtib. A few alternatives were prepared as well.

On Saturday, 16 May 1998, President Soeharto received a nine-member delegation from the University of Indonesia, whose students had promised to march into Parliament within a few days. During the session, the president voiced his appreciation for their suggestions and asked if other universities would follow. That same evening, President Soeharto announced the impending Cabinet reshuffles. There had been mixed feelings about this; some thought it was a positive step, but it was insufficient to meet the people's aspirations for political reform.

On 17 May, Saadillah Mursjid, the Minister of State Secretariat, was asked to amend the planned Keppres. The next day, Saadillah was called again and instead of Keppres, it had been amended to Inpres—Komando Operasi Kewaspadaan dan Keselamatan Nasional, with the Commander of Armed Forces as the head and the Chief of Army as the deputy. Keppres was prepared for a reformed Cabinet.

Soon after, a few people suggested that the president should resign. The discussion that evening on Monday, 18 May 1998, concluded that the president should meet with the Muslim leaders, including Indonesia's later fourth president, Abdurrahman Wahid (Gus Dur). As 20 May approached, massive protests were planned for the day. Indonesia was poised on the brink of political change. A deep sense of threat was felt by the New Order regime as a whole. The speaker of the House of Representatives, Harmoko, a former loyalist to President Soeharto, made a bombshell statement. He claimed all factions of the House of Representatives, including the Armed Forces, had agreed to ask the President to resign. This was a definite breach of respect for a Javanese leader. The media could hardly believe Harmoko's statement was serious as only two weeks earlier he had flatly rejected calls for a special session of the MPR to ask the president to be accountable. Many were astounded by this latest development. The mice had now jumped off the sinking ship.

The next day, 19 May 1998, the rupiah went down to Rp17,000 against the US dollar. President Soeharto sounded out the opinion of nine members of the public, mainly Muslim leaders, at Merdeka Palace. Following the meeting, President Soeharto told a press conference that he was quite willing to step down. As President Soeharto outlined his willingness to step down at some point "soon" and unveiled his plan for reform, the situation did not change. On the contrary, the security forces dramatically left their on-campus watch. This allowed more than 30,000 students to storm the Parliament building and take up positions on the roof. There were signs with the words "Hang Soeharto" along the streets. Three decades ago, it had been "Hang Durno", Soebandrio's nickname in 1966. Pictures which were published showed campuses with troops exchanging smiles and giving the students the thumbs up. What did all these indicate? No more and no less than the fact that the president was slowly losing the grip on his power. In the Parliament building, over 1,000 labour activists from the Federation of All Indonesian Workers Union soon joined the students. The newspapers carried endless quotes from all walks of life calling for President Soeharto to resign. From overseas, he found little encouragement, including from President Bill Clinton of the United States.

Like President Soekarno, President Soeharto did not want to use force to cling onto power, which would have made civil war a real possibility. After he came up with a proposal to reform the Cabinet, 14 of the candidates he had chosen refused to stand by him on 20 May 1998. Among them were Akbar Tanjung and Ginandjar, two of his former loyal supporters. Like President Soekarno, President Soeharto's dedication to the country would not allow him to destroy a united Indonesia. On 20 May, there were once again demonstrations in Yogya, Surabaya, Purwokerto, Medan, Semarang, Bandung, Bogor and Ujung Pandang. It was too little, too late done on the part of the government by then. Like President Soekarno in 1966, President Soeharto cut a lonely figure by himself; indeed, it must have been lonely at the top. In Jalan Cendana, President Soeharto came to realise that he had run out of options as the forces were marshaled against him. His wisdom told him to agree. At 9 am on Thursday, 21 May 1998, he handed over power to BJ Habibie.

There is real irony if we consider his view of BJ Habibie as written in his 1988 biography. In his biography, President Soeharto said that he had given BJ Habibie a note on his 50th birthday in 1986.[14] He was happy that this message was included in BJ Habibie's book. It said in Javanese: "*Wong sing eling, percaya mituhu marang kang murbeng dumadi, iku dadi oboring urip kang becik, sejatining becik*" ("Man is to always remember and believe in the Almighty; to live in decency and wholesomeness") In short, President Soeharto concluded, "We have to bear in mind, believe in the Almighty; do not ever use science with no wisdom." He was happy that BJ Habibie had chosen a picture of him in Javanese clothes for display in his office and inserting in his book. He claimed that he had never treated BJ Habibie out of the ordinary. He had given BJ Habibie the same opportunity as the others, such as Sudharmono, Moerdiono and Ginandjar.

President Soeharto was aware that some were suspicious of BJ Habibie as the latter was educated in Germany. Many were worried that BJ Habibie would influence him because he was intelligent. However, many did not know that BJ Habibie was the one who was always asking for his guidance and that BJ Habibie was still a Javanese at heart. BJ Habibie would stay for hours listening to him whenever he visited Jalan Cendana as he wanted to know what the president really had in mind. The president's children confirmed that BJ Habibie used to visit for hours, while other ministers would stay for only 15 minutes. The children were also surprised as to why their father was so impressed by him, but President Soeharto was convinced that after BJ Habibie had digested and understood his philosophy, he would use it in his capacity as a trained engineer.

President Soeharto was also proud of BJ Habibie's willingness to give up his personal interests. When the president asked BJ Habibie to return from Germany in 1974 and join Pertamina, BJ Habibie's salary in Germany was US$10,000 per month. It was equivalent to Rp25 million at that time. He received only Rp250,000 when he came back to work in Indonesia. President Soeharto had referred to this in his speech in Pasar Klewer, where he explained his strategies for the short-term and long-term. He needed a person with BJ Habibie's qualifications in order for the country to be able to join the industrialised nations. He wrote that BJ Habibie always thought of him as his own father. However, things changed completely after BJ Habibie became president. It was under BJ Habibie's rule that Pak Harto was dragged to court. It was under BJ Habibie's government that Indonesia gave up East Timor. It was during BJ Habibie's reign that donations to his charitable foundations were discontinued. During the brief ceremony when he handed the presidency to BJ Habibie in Merdeka Palace on 21 May 1998, he only shook the hand of BJ Habibie (there was no hug considering their close relationship), once his staunch and most loyal supporter. Pak Harto felt betrayed and he has never forgiven BJ Habibie; every approach by the latter to see him has been incessantly rebuffed.

In 1998, young students, probably not yet born when he came to power, pushed President Soeharto out. In 1965, President Soekarno tried to balance the power of three major existing forces: the army, the communists and himself. In 1998, President Soeharto tried to balance the power between the army, the Muslims and himself. In both instances, they failed. President Soekarno and President Soeharto fell out of power when the country faced a critical economic period: President Soekarno when inflation reached 600 per cent and President Soeharto when the rupiah fell to Rp17,000 to the US dollar. President Soekarno lost his grip on power at the age of 64, after over 20 years in power. It took President Soeharto over 30 years in power to lose it at the age of 77.

THE DAYS AFTER DEPARTING FROM OFFICE

Thousands of letters sent to Pak Harto after his departure from office were consolidated and published in a book by his daughter, Tutut. All of these were sympathetic notes which were read and replied to. The senders came from all over: from children to the elderly; from playgroup to elementary and high school students, university graduates to doctorate degree holders, from farmers, labourers, fishermen, small businessmen to government officials, former officials, national leaders and foreign heads of state, university lecturers, lawyers and members of the clergy. These notes and letters expressed empathy, sympathy and feelings of sadness. They relayed their appreciation because they considered President Soeharto to have been a dedicated leader who had contributed good things to Indonesia. All letters started and ended with prayers for Pak Harto to have courage to accept the tribunal's judgement and for God to bless him. On the issue of making President Soekarno and President Soeharto face trial, the reasons are not only for the "sins of governing" but corruption as well: President Soekarno for his "revolution funds" and President Soeharto for his "foundations". President Soeharto stopped President Soekarno's court case due to a lack of evidence, while Gus Dur promised to forgive President Soeharto. History seems to have repeated itself.

President Soeharto knew that restraint was crucial. He had treated President Soekarno and his family with fairness as he placed President Soekarno's legacy in the right perspective. He ordered the building of President Soekarno's tomb in Blitar. He reinforced President Soekarno and Vice-President Hatta's legacy as *Pahlawan Proklamator* and built a monument for them. He immortalised their names by changing the name of Indonesia's international airport from Cengkareng to Soekarno-Hatta.

In this regard, President Soeharto followed the strict rule of respecting one's elders and leaders. The national heritage and culture would not have tolerated a bad exposure of their weaknesses. For him, it was important to remember the proverb "*Menepuk air didulang, terpercik ke muka sendiri*": if one splashes water in a bowl, it will rebound and splash back into one's face. In other words, one should refrain from washing dirty laundry in public. The rural, working class areas were where most people benefited from President Soeharto's early policies on farming and healthcare. Nevertheless, many disdained his political machine, Golkar. The *wong cilik* now called Golkar members elitists who empathised with spotted owls rather than loggers. After 32 turbulent and tumultuous years, President Soeharto had managed to expand his support base but the country was still divided along many of the same lines. Some strongly believed that the electoral map during his seven general elections was starkly separated into real counting and made-up votes, with Golkar dominating the civil service and major businesses. The PDIP remained the most contested party with President Soekarno's loyalists clinging to a narrow lead in East Java. The race underscored the strength of the regional and cultural divisions shaping modern Indonesian politics.

In fact, one has to look for the positive in both leaders. President Soekarno and President Soeharto chose the path of living with the enemy, rather than destroying them, and by doing so, they also laid the basis for a multiracial but very controlled democracy. It was a brave choice and a hard one. Having made it their solution, they stuck with it. The legacy of President Soekarno and President Soeharto is a painful one that will not be forgotten quickly.

ENDNOTES
1   Margaret Thatcher, *The Downing Street Years* (HarperCollins, 1993), p 503.
2   G Dwipayana and Ramadhan KH, *Soeharto, Pikiran, Ucapan, dan Tindakan Saya* (PT Citra Lamtoro Gung Persada, 1988).
3   Lee Kuan Yew, *From Third World to First, The Singapore Story 1965–2000* (Singapore Press Holdings and Times Editions, 2000), pp 311–319.
4   After 10 years from 1985, the indigenous Indonesian shares were to amount to 51 per cent (Radius Prawiro, *Indonesia's Struggle for Economic Development — Pragmatism in Action* (Oxford University Press, 1998), p 272).
5   G Dwipayana and Ramadhan KH, *Soeharto, Pikiran, Ucapan, dan Tindakan Saya* (PT Citra Lamtoro Gung Persada, 1988), p 2.
6   G Dwipayana and Ramadhan KH, *Soeharto, Pikiran, Ucapan, dan Tindakan Saya* (PT Citra Lamtoro Gung Persada, 1988), p 452.
7   G Dwipayana and Ramadhan KH, *Soeharto, Pikiran, Ucapan, dan Tindakan Saya* (PT Citra Lamtoro Gung Persada, 1988), p 480.
8   G Dwipayana and Ramadhan KH, *Soeharto, Pikiran, Ucapan, dan Tindakan Saya* (PT Citra Lamtoro Gung Persada, 1988), pp 538–539.
9   Translated from a book by Probosutedjo, *Kesaksian Sejarah H Probosutedjo Runtuhnya Pemerintahan Bung Karno — Pak Harto — BJ Habibie — Gus Dur* (Gemah Ripah, Jakarta, August 2001), p 102.
10 Translated from a book by Probosutedjo, *Kesaksian Sejarah H Probosutedjo-Runtuhnya Pemerintahan Bung Karno — Pak Harto — BJ Habibie — Gus Dur* (Gemah Ripah, Jakarta, August 2001), p 106.
11 The second biggest Muslim organisation after Nahdatul Ulama (NU) which was chaired by Gus Dur.
12 Professor of Applied Economics at the John Hopkins University, Baltimore, USA.
13 Lee Kuan Yew, *From Third World to First, The Singapore Story 1965–2000* (Singapore Press Holdings and Times Editions, 2000), p 314.
14 G Dwipayana and Ramadhan KH, *Soeharto, Pikiran, Ucapan, dan Tindakan Saya* (PT Citra Lamtoro Gung Persada, 1988), p 455.

Chapter 4

THE FOUNDATIONS

Truth is the trial of itself
And needs to other touch
And purer than the purest gold
Refine it ne'er so much
— Ben Jonson

It was impossible for my father and me not to feel compassion for the fallen president. It is not denied that he might have misused certain parts of his power and trampled on a few of the people's rights, suppressed his opponents' voice and, to a certain degree, deprived the people of a chance to do business in the way that his children and cronies had been able to. His stay in power was generally felt to have extended for far too long and it was time for change. Yet, many people were also aware that he had done much good for Indonesia. President Soeharto had restored order and constructed roads and factories, built Indonesia into a more modern state, and even managed to obtain a fair share of the oil revenue. Millions of Indonesian children are now studying in schools that he had built. However, the moment he fell from office, all these efforts counted for nothing.

Public opinion at this stage focused only on President Soeharto's faults and weaknesses. They held him fully responsible for BJ Habibie's insatiable appetite for embarking on fancy development projects, many of which the country did not need, such as IPTN and the like. He was blamed for starting the practice of not distinguishing between the public purse and his family's private wealth, and that he had treated the national income as though it was his own to spend as he wished, with virtually everyone in the government following suit. Hundreds of people used connections in high places, especially connections with Jalan Cendana, to swing "commissions" of hundreds of thousands of dollars for brokering government contracts for Western corporations, not to mention the Chinese conglomerates that rushed to take advantage of the spending spree.

The public pointed to the millions that were made overnight on rake-offs from loans from his family to build factories, luxury hotels and offices, including the opening of new banks when deregulation took place in 1988. They blamed him for the creation of a new class of Indonesian *nouveau riche* and shopping malls that were swarmed with Daimler Benz and BMW cars which blocked the traffic while the passengers they ferried splurged from deep pockets on Louis Vuitton, Charles Jourdan and Versace goods. Indeed, the *wong cilik* were dazzled by the sight of five-star hotels, shopping malls and the conspicuous, new consumption trends, in which it was obvious that the big spenders had not come by their money selling magazines at newsstands. The public now voiced out that if the government could make these people rich overnight just because they had the right connections, why did it not do the same for everyone else? This preoccupation with material wealth became wedded to the simmering discontent of the last 15 years.

Did President Soeharto try, as it was claimed, to cling to power by using his plan for the reform of the Cabinet as an excuse to drag out his time in office? I believe President Soeharto's intention was to put in place a smooth transition so that the country's unity would not be fractured because he was concerned that BJ Habibie would not have sufficient time to learn the full scope of what the presidency entailed. Bung Karno, too, had at that stage in his presidency doubts over whom to choose as a protégé to succeed him. In both instances, the presidents finally bowed out in order to maintain the country's unity and to avoid civil war and bloodshed, and took the risk of facing public outrage in the courts of law.

On 20 May 1998, at 10.15pm on the eve of President Soeharto's descent from office, he said in the presence of Saadillah Mursjid: "We have done all we can do to save our people and the nation. However, God has something different in mind. Therefore, I have decided to resign in line with clause 8 of our 1945 Constitution."

It must have been painful for him to see that the few who had begged him to stay on in power had deserted him. It must have hurt him to watch those who used to bow at his feet suddenly make public statements about his wrongdoings. As a Javanese, he did not show his emotions in public.

COURT HEARING

The public demanded that Soeharto be brought to trial. This call also came from the Chairman of Partai Amanat Nasional (PAN), Amien Rais and Yusril Ihza Mahendra, Chairman of Partai Bulan Bintang (PBB), amongst others. Yusril Ihza Mahendra asked for transparency in the Tanjung Priok shooting incident in September 1984, while Amien Rais rejected the idea of letting this incident go, although it took place 14 years ago. They wanted to reopen the investigation into this incident. Another hot issue was the mass killing of civilians in Aceh and East Timor. Those who had been previously mute on the matter now publicly came up with figures and data on how many had been killed from 1989 to 1998 in Aceh and East Timor.

Demonstrations continued until November 1998 as pressure mounted to look for President Soeharto's secret bank accounts, which were supposedly holding funds of billions of US dollars. When the bank accounts could not be found, public reaction was that the money must have been hidden in other ways, in a well or a bunker. A few even suggested that the government should dig a tunnel from Jalan Cendana all the way to Merdeka Palace to look for the "treasure chests". A criminal investigation into President Soeharto's corrupt practices through the misuse of his presidential power was demanded. The Attorney General's office was to inspect the foundations which he and his family had built with the state enterprises (BUMN). An examination was required to determine whether the foundations which he chaired had collected funds through monopolies or privileges using his presidential power, which might have been against the law in causing losses to the state.

The main features of the criminal allegation were corruption and the missing Supersemar document that had allegedly gone astray, civil suits related to the performance of the state administration and, last but not least, human rights abuses. Above all, it was alleged that through KKN, President Soeharto had enriched his family and cronies while leading the economy into disarray through the government's huge borrowing in US dollars from overseas.

President BJ Habibie formed the Kabinet Reformasi Pembangunan, or the reformed development Cabinet, which consisted of 36 ministers. In his speech, the new president declared that there were three major issues which his Cabinet had to manage or resolve. Firstly, an improvement of the rules for the general elections; secondly, an assessment of the rules relating to subversive activities and detention thereunder; and thirdly, to expedite the rules for fair competition and monopolies. Those who knew that President Soeharto had given all of BJ Habibie's multi-million dollar pet projects favourable treatment reacted with cynicism to the latter's approach. It was ironical as BJ Habibie had been the one that Pak Harto had been so supportive and proud of. Pak Harto had supported BJ Habibie in his career in spite of harsh criticisms and, most importantly, had considered him as his own son. The students had thought that BJ Habibie would protect his former mentor. However, this was not the case; in fact, his mentor was saddened by his action and took it as a direct betrayal.

In protecting his new position, President BJ Habibie bowed to pressure to drag his predecessor to court. It was not incorrect for President BJ Habibie to agree that former President Soeharto should be investigated, but in view of their close relationship, he could have been present as a witness at the trial and requested all the former ministers that were involved in President Soeharto's government when he issued the Keppres or Presidential Instruction in question to stand trial as well. However, this was not the case and all blame was laid solely on the shoulders of the former president.

Less than a year after Pak Harto had stepped down, the Attorney General, in his letter dated 4 December 1998, announced that an interrogation had been deemed necessary, based on the MPR decision dated 13 November 1998 and the Instruction of the President dated 2 December 1998.[1] For the Soeharto family, this came as a harsh slap, as they felt that there were other ways to resolve the crucial issues and in a more diplomatic manner. Three members of the Attorney General's office conducted the inquiry in the High Court in Jalan Rasuna Said on 9 December 1998. It was also ironical as the building where the interrogation took place was not far from the headquarters of a few of his foundations. He was asked to explain three main issues:

1   The reason for the issuance of Presidential Instructions No 2/1996 and the Presidential Decision No 42/1996 with the objective of developing the national car industry. What was the link between the Presidential Instructions and the Presidential Decision, in which credit was exempted from taxes and granted to a private company, PT Timor Putra Nasional? The crucial link was Tommy Soeharto, who was one of the main shareholders in PT Timor Putra Nasional.

2   The misappropriation of state resources for the benefit of the foundations he had created.
3   The financial irregularities, if any, during the course of the interrogation.

In December 1998, Pak Harto, who was still in good health, gave his answers. In his defence, he affirmed that in line with the country's 1945 Constitution, the president, as the mandatory of the MPR, held the highest power with the help of a vice-president and ministers. The president was to perform his duties as outlined in the Constitution through the GBHN. Thus, both the Presidential Instructions—Keppres and Inpres— were within the president's authority as mandatory of the MPR. Further, he explained that stages were needed in the country's development as outlined in each Repelita and the country's long term planning was for a period of 25 years, with the plan mapping out the establishment of Indonesia as a strong industrial nation with a modernised system of agriculture at the end of the 25-year period. It was important for the country to become an industrial nation and the first step related to manufacturing activity that could sustain its agriculture; the next step was to process its raw materials for final products; and there was also a need to make components for the country's machinery.

These stages, as he explained, were related to the national car industry. In 2003, there would be free trade in the ASEAN Free Trade Area (AFTA), which would be extended to the Asia-Pacific Economic Cooperation (APEC) members by 2010. The country needed national cars not only for domestic requirements, but also for export. For this purpose, the people of Indonesia should learn from more experienced countries like Korea, which has two national cars: KIA and Daewoo. The two Korean companies were ready to cooperate with the Indonesian private sector. KIA was also willing to transfer the technology and to produce the components locally by using local raw materials. If this was to take place, there would be many opportunities for workers to find jobs. Hence, in the end, the country's labour force would learn new skills in producing quality products that would be acceptable in international markets. When the project became bigger, more of the abundant workforce would be able to find jobs and more of the country's raw materials would be used.

It had been a very good concept in theory. The main flaws were that the project was not taken through open tender and, most critically, the winner was a company led by Tommy, his own son. He argued that Keppres and the like had to go through a long process involving various departments. At the end, the State Secretariat undertook the final checking. Only after it was proven not to be against the law did the president sign to seal the ruling. Within their respective jurisdictions, many ministers were involved in the process: the Minister of Industry and Trade together with the Minister of Finance and the Minister of Investment/Chairman of Board Coordinating Capital Investment had to agree on the issuance of Inpres No 2/1996. He was entirely right about this process, but the increasing number of "yes men" in the final years of his rule had made it difficult to have a system of checks and balances in place. Asked whether Inpres No 2/1996 and Keppres No 42/1996 were meant to facilitate PT Timor Putra Nasional's development, he rejected this assertion and said that it was not the government's intention to give favours to any individual or corporation. He said it was pure coincidence that PT Timor was owned and led by his youngest son and that PT Timor's proposal was in line with the government's programme.

President Soeharto should have known that even if what he said were true, it would have been very difficult to prove to the public that PT Timor had won on merit, more so when there was a tax exemption involved. President Soeharto should have drawn a strict boundary between his action as the Head of State in issuing the ruling and the benefits it gave his son in business. His greatest weakness was failure to draw a strict line and prevent public perception of nepotism and collusion. He should have discouraged his children from participating in major state projects. At the same time, the ministers were also accountable as they had the responsibility of alerting him to the dangers of such a policy but no one was willing to risk his position.

At the hearing, Pak Harto tried to clarify the issues surrounding his seven foundations. He explained that building his foundations, he believed, would expedite the eradication of poverty. He saw the need for the private sector to share the government's burden in the area of social welfare. The core of his development programme was to develop the human being as a whole, in terms of material wealth and spiritual well-being. The foundations he built were an integral part of his responsibility, as the mandate of the MPR, to achieve a prosperous society. His accountability to the MPR had always been accepted in the past. He questioned why, after 32 years, there was so much protest at this point in time? There had been ample time for dissenters to voice their disagreement.

He reiterated that he had no regrets in setting up Yayasan Trikora, Yayasan Supersemar, Yayasan Dharmais, Yayasan Amalbakti Muslim Pancasila, Yayasan Dana Abadi Karya Bakti (Dakab), Yayasan Dana Gotong Royong Kemanusiaan and Yayasan Dana Sejahtera Mandiri (Damandiri). He said that he was behind the establishment of these foundations and had guided them to where they were at the present time.

Yayasan Trikora was formed when he was the Commander sent to liberate West Irian back in 1962. Close to 200 combatants had fallen as war casualties and as the Commander, he felt responsible for the fate of their children, who had lost their fathers during the battle. He said it had always been his intention to adopt the role of being the children's father by taking care of their needs when they grew up. I, for one, will always remember his benign face and smile as he said, "I believe the children are proud that their fathers' substitute is a president."

After he became the president, he thought it was a good move to use the same concept to help bright students whose parents were unable to send them for further education. At the same time, it was also his policy that his development programme should create a new class of wealthy citizens. Subsequently, he invited the new cluster of wealthy Indonesians to participate in or contribute to his charitable foundations to speed up the process of distributing wealth from the rich to the poor. Yayasan Supersemar was created to provide scholarships to students selected from the Dean's List. As Head of State, he knew that the government could not, on its own, carry out the task of providing education for all, as inscribed in clause 33 of the 1945 Constitution. To achieve that, the government had to build more than 136,000 elementary schools to meet the needs of the compulsory primary education rule which he had introduced in 1988, in addition to the secondary and high schools that had to be established. Yayasan Supersemar also provided financial assistance for training to produce skilled labour, so that an intermediate level workforce could be created. Proficiency in farming, fishery, husbandry and the like was as important as having university graduates in a large and diverse society like Indonesia.

Yayasan Dharmais was set up to help the orphanages and shelter the homeless. It provided training to the Javanese community who, when they moved to the other islands, were expected to transfer their new skills. Teaching or training was not only given to the heads of the families but also to their wives and children in cities like Bogor, Yogya, Kulon Progo, Magetan and Magelang. Yayasan Dharmais also provided financial assistance to the physically and mentally disabled and built houses for war veterans. Every year, 10,000 people benefited from cataract operations paid for by Yayasan Dharmais.

Yayasan Amalbakti Muslim Pancasila was formed to provide for the spiritual needs of the people. Funds came from the contributions of Muslim state employees and the military corps. Similar donations from non-Muslims were forwarded to Yayasan Dharmais.

Yayasan Damandiri obtained donations from individuals and corporations with a net annual income of over Rp100 million for its initial funding; the organisation's main activity was to help the people to start their own businesses.

As for Yayasan Dakab, Pak Harto cited the common practice in which party cadres were often asked for contributions and if they failed to contribute, they would be indicted or punished. In his opinion, the responsibility to get donations lay with the party itself and that was why he founded Yayasan Dakab. It was to help the "big family" of Golkar, but not Golkar as a purely political party. However, because of the benefits, many voted for Golkar during the general elections. In 1998, the practice was discontinued and Yayasan Dakab activities were no longer for Golkar as its activities were steered towards reducing poverty.

Pak Harto reiterated that the foundations were his pet project to help causes that remained dear to his heart and he intended to continue the charitable works until his last breath. He was upset that the investigators posed so many questions and he asked whether the interrogators thought that he had built the foundations because, as president, he had spare time to fill. He expressed irritation as he said he had intended the foundations to help in resolving the government's deficiencies, but aspersions were being cast that that was his way of accumulating personal wealth. He argued that his foundations were established with proper Notary's Deeds approved by the Department of Justice. This included the targets of those to be helped and the type of operation. The initial funding was in line with the existing rules in the banking system as banks and other financial institutions were required to give 5 per cent of their profits after taxes for social welfare purposes. Once his foundations were established on the Minister of Finance's instructions, the financial institutions were instructed to forward their mandatory contributions directly to them. Of the 5 per cent funds collected, 2.5 per cent were for Yayasan Supersemar and 2.5 per cent for Yayasan Dharmais (half for students' scholarships and the remaining half for orphanages and the like). None went to political or religious purposes, such as to Yayasan Dakab or Yayasan Amalbakti Muslim Pancasila. Most importantly, the funds collected were deposited into the state banks and were still there today.

On 11 October 1999, the Attorney General issued instructions to end the investigations as no proof could be found that, in his capacity as the chairman of the foundations, Pak Harto had been involved in corrupt practices. Yet a few weeks later on 6 December 1999, there was another set of instructions to investigate HM Soeharto that as president, he had issued Keppres and Peraturan Pemerintah (PP or government regulation) as mechanisms to collect funds for the foundations chaired by himself and his families and cronies, which resulted in losses to the state and economy. This time, the Attorney General no longer pressed the issue of Keppres because the PP and Keppres were deemed valid and within his power as president.

On 6 December 1999, the court case was reopened. The Attorney General's office handed the case over to the South Jakarta State Court because of public pressure. The hearing took place from 31 August to 28 September 2000. On 2 September 2000, the Attorney General's office requested a team of doctors to examine Pak Harto's state of health for investigations that could lead to court prosecution. On 28 September 2000, the South Jakarta Court decided that they were not able to accept the case. Pak Harto was released from city arrest and the case was returned and crossed out from its registration.

THE CONCEPT BEHIND THE YAYASAN

My father was among those who believed that in order for history to pass fair judgment on Pak Harto, the Yayasan that Pak Harto had built had to be explained and made known to the public, especially because most members of the public had the impression that these Yayasan were the source of Pak Harto's family fortune. It did not help that he had been considered to be very secretive when it came to the reasons why he had started the Yayasan. In his 1988 biography,[2] President Soeharto explained why he gave monopolies, why he allowed the conglomerates to grow and why he had started Yayasan.

"The development under President Soeharto's government was not only for the attainment of material welfare but it also relates to our progress within the context of spirituality, science and humanity," wrote my father back in January 2004, in the Yayasan Amalbakti Muslim Pancasila's 22nd anniversary commemorative publication. It had not been easy to convince someone like my father that the Yayasan had indeed provided contributions towards the people's welfare. It was only after familiarising himself with the foundations for years, whenever he was asked to write for their commemorative publications, that my father finally understood the concept that Pak Harto had for the Yayasan. To my father, there were four main issues to be analysed: the concept behind the foundations, the motivation behind their establishment, the policies behind their operations and the reasons why Pak Harto's family members were involved.

President Soeharto was aware that the majority of the people were farmers and the economy was highly dependent on agriculture. Not only was farming a traditional way of life but it was also an existence prone to natural disasters. His years among the poor farmers had made him conscious of the unpredictable power of nature. In such an environment, the spirit of *gotong royong* was a matter of necessity. This community spirit was ingrained in his soul and stayed with him for the rest of his life. He never forgot that in village life, one always tried to help the other, and for those who had helped him in the past, he wanted to return the good deeds. Subsequently, he became too forgiving of their mistakes. At the same time, he never forgave easily those who betrayed him.

As Head of State, President Soeharto realised that Indonesia's social welfare system was poorer than that of the Western world and even that of wealthier Asian nations. To address that, President Soeharto concluded that the best solution was to use his roles as a private citizen and as the Head of State: as Head of State, he asked for donations, and as a private citizen, he channelled funds through the Yayasan for the deprived. He created a welfare scheme for the non-governmental institutions, private sector and wealthy individuals to play a role as he knew how limited the government coffers were. Donations were also in line with the Muslim faith to give *zakat*. Muslims donate a percentage of their wealth to the needy. However, because substantial donations could not be collected from ordinary citizens, President Soeharto developed a class of "super rich" Indonesians. The country was rich with untapped natural resources. The missing link was capital and know-how, thus he had to find a way by targeting those with wide contacts and deep pockets.

President Soekarno's dreams had been for all of the people to attain a better life than they had experienced under colonialism. Not only did President Soeharto want to continue President Soekarno's dreams, but he also wanted to turn those dreams into reality. Building a nation was like building a house. President Soekarno was the architect and he had created the blueprint for the house; President Soeharto wanted to build it. His target was to build the country into a modern state. He knew that President Soekarno did not have the time to develop economic stability in Indonesia.

Economic development could only begin when national stability was achieved and, following that, the distribution of wealth could start. As the pillar of the country's economy lay in farming, President Soeharto tackled the main issues which related to agriculture. Once farming was modernised and the people were well-fed, clothed and had roofs over their heads, the move towards a modern state could proceed. In modernising the country, he began building new towns, ports, schools, universities, hospitals, factories, roads and power stations. He made every effort to see that the natural wealth of the country became the national wealth. With this concept in mind, President Soeharto felt that the establishment of his foundations was in line with his task as president/mandatory of the MPR, as well as to fulfill his duties as a private citizen. He wanted to make the most of the country's assets and those resources accessible in the public domain. The public at large had to be involved through participation by all citizens. While the government did not have a sufficient budget, he saw the opportunities from non-governmental resources to install social welfare into place. He needed to identify which groups in the social strata were well equipped to support his ideas.

THE CHOSEN POLICIES

The Chinese minority had been the partners of the Dutch as they posed no threat to the latter's power. Therefore, the minority Chinese were given more opportunities to trade than the *pribumis*, hence they managed to gain knowledge and expertise in business by the time the country obtained its freedom. President Soeharto, a pragmatist, accepted the fact that the potential in the minority Chinese was higher than in the majority *pribumi*. He felt that there were only two choices available. The minority Chinese had to be encouraged to do business so that their capital and expertise remained in the country and would not be moved abroad. Hence, the creation of an economic dynasty was meant to be a temporary measure, a stepping-stone to his next target. In his biography, President Soeharto clearly said that the government would steer the capital and wealth found in the local market for development, thus increasing prosperity for all.[3]

In the early 1970s, the overseas Chinese made up only 3 per cent of Indonesia's population. The Chinese bourgeoisie, with their strong capital base and organisational structure, had an inbuilt resilience. One of their strengths was their family set-up and kinship relations which provided access to distribution and solid networking. Many of the Indonesian Chinese maintained links with traders and industrialists in Singapore, Hong Kong and later Malaysia. For example, if a family in business had three sons, each son may live in a different neighbouring country and would establish close links with each other for trading. President Soeharto sought to capitalise on it. Why not allow them to do business in Indonesia, as long as their capital stayed within the country? Why not give them a certain degree of freedom and a few privileges as long as they created progress for the country? The incentives given could be in terms of lower taxation or easier access to credit. When they became richer, he could approach them to contribute part of the money they had made to his Yayasan. This way, the Yayasan would be able to take their wealth and ensure that it was given to the poor masses. The foundations he built would act as catalysts between the rich and the poor, a bridge between the wealthy and the deprived. It all made sense, as long as everyone played within the rules of the game. Indeed, as he introduced more freedom into the economy, the potency of their capital and the overseas organisational bases made the Chinese businesses more of an acceptable credit risk to the banks, even to banks based abroad. Hence, their businesses were able to grow at an amazing pace. Within just over 20 years, a few Indonesian Chinese businessmen joined the ranks of multi-billionaires, when the timeline for this would usually have been two to three generations.

President Soeharto had started the Yayasan for humanitarian, social welfare and religious purposes. The contributions from the conglomerates which he had helped to develop turned his charitable organisations into extraordinarily rich, complex and yet effective tools for the building of hospitals, health centres, orphanages, hospices and the like. However, he could not achieve the most important part of his development programme, that is prosperity for all, if there was no wealth to be distributed. His foundations became his main tool for sharing the wealth of the conglomerates with the poor, but he could not ask the conglomerates to contribute directly to the state as their contributions would have fallen within the state budget, which would then have made the disbursement of funds more complex. Not only would the process take much longer, but he also knew from experience that "greasing the wheel" would become part of the process of fund disbursements.

So far, the president's plan had been good. For the few new rich who forgot about the poor majority, he informed them that their time to "pay back" had arrived when he invited them to Jimbaran in Bali and Tapos. The conglomerates had no choice if he, as the president, or Ibu Tien as the first lady, asked for their contributions. There were philanthropists who did not want their names or the amounts they gave to be made known to the public. This was due to reasons of either personal safety or to keep similar appeals at bay (due to the fear that refusal to accede to other appeals would hurt their businesses). The negative impact of these "anonymous" donors to the Yayasan was that the sources of funding were shrouded in mystery and became an object of speculation.

FAMILY INVOLVEMENT

President Soeharto selected only those people whom he trusted to sit on the boards of his foundations. They were also people who understood his concept and shared his ideas. To that end, he relied on his family members and cronies. As a result, people pointed to the fact that his foundations were filled with his cronies and were a manifestation of nepotism. In his 1988 biography, President Soeharto mentioned his reason for wanting his children involved in the Yayasan: he wanted them to learn about taking care of the destitute, to help the weak and unwell and to show the terminally ill and the old a glimmer of hope. He wanted his children to get involved in the humanitarian foundations for the exposure and experience and through these foundations, he hoped they could make a difference to the lives of the less privileged. His children were only involved in the Yayasan which dealt with social welfare issues and not those which dealt with education and religion.

President Soeharto could have thought that it was better for his children to enter into business instead of becoming scholars, especially in Indonesia, where an academic's salary was nothing close to that of a businessman's. Therefore, he did not seem to mind his children's lack of enthusiasm in intellectual pursuits. Obviously, many businesses were keen to take them on, which is not an unusual practice even in the West today. There was one main difference though. In Western countries, the children of the privileged would have had a good education and so could contribute meaningfully to the organisations which trained them. In Indonesia's case, President Soeharto's children, who should have started at the bottom of the corporate ladder during their apprenticeship, were instead instantly appointed shareholders and sat on the management boards. Instead of learning the tricks of the trade, the children were used to open doors for the companies to win lucrative projects. The companies which the children joined saw the obvious way of reaping the benefits of making the president's cronies and family members partners in their organisations. The conglomerates soon found that this was a route to partially recoup the contributions they had to make to his Yayasan.

In having his children involved in the Yayasan, although only in management, President Soeharto thought they could learn and in turn help the foundations. Unfortunately, there were close links between the donors and government projects such as PT Timor Putra Nasional in which his children had interests.

The public eye now focused on the connection between his children and the winners of huge projects, and the luxurious lifestyles of donors to his Yayasan, whose activities remained ambiguous at that stage. President Soeharto failed to see the path that all that would lead to.

THE DILEMMA

The public soon started to question the extent to which the rich were willing to donate voluntarily. Was there a secret deal involving tax benefits or were privileges granted to the donors through presidential power? If the latter were the case, it was an abuse of presidential power. Pak Harto explained that the formation and management of the Yayasan and the collection and distribution of their funds were undertaken with the knowledge of the authorities. The establishment of each Yayasan had been through a Notary's Deed and properly registered with the Ministry of Justice. Furthermore, the recipients of the donations were within the boundaries of the law and within the criteria of the needy. Hence, if there were any doubts about the validity or operations of the Yayasan, it should have been addressed by the MPR during his annual accountability exercise.

In his defence, Pak Harto affirmed that the Yayasan did not belong to him, his cronies or his family, but it would take time for the majority of the public to believe it. The Yayasan in truth belonged to the government and he was ready to hand it over when he was no longer in power. His genuine intention was to form the Yayasan to help take care of the country's social welfare needs, which under the 1945 Constitution was to be handled by the government.

However, along the way, the genuine intention and purpose of the Yayasan was sidetracked in favour of the personal interests of some of the players involved. Perhaps the management of the Yayasan had hired too many of their direct family members or given too many jobs to their own relatives. For example, when the Yayasan renovated its buildings, the work would be given to contractors whose businesses belonged to the relatives of the management. By doing that, they had certainly stretched the concept of *gotong royong* just a bit too far. The village practice of lending a helping hand should not have been used for projects at a national level. That was what my father had in mind when he reminded Pak Harto not to confuse *azas keluarga* (family affairs) and *azas kekeluargaan* (family-style affairs).

It also did not help that President Soeharto believed that one should go about quietly when making contributions. He said that those who gave donations should inscribe their deeds in the sand, but those who received help should engrave it in stone (that is, one should not boast when giving help to others but should always remember when help is received from others). This was in line with the notion of humility that is taught in all Javanese families. Only when criticisms and misunderstandings over the foundations persisted did President Soeharto see the need to speak up. Although he had explained his concept of the foundations in his 1988 biography, the public was no longer listening.

The close connection between the contributions, cronyism and nepotism made his critics sceptical about his true intentions. The only route Pak Harto could take was to replace the management of the foundations with professionals or those not considered to be his cronies. He knew that times had changed and that in the 21st century, the axiom "silence is golden" no longer worked in his favour. In 2005, he told me that it was indeed time to expose the seven foundations he still chaired in response to the speculations and insinuations that were circulating.

THE QUESTION OF DONATIONS

President Soeharto explained that he felt that if the government imposed a higher level of taxation, the business circle would not be happy. Even if the businessmen were willing to pay higher taxes, the tax proceeds would have ended up as part of the state budget, from which the diversion of funds would require Parliament's approval, and because of the complex bureaucracy, the disbursement of funds to the poor would have been slow. Hence, the Yayasan was used as a way to get around the bureaucratic red tape.

The formation of the Yayasan was part of his overall strategy for national development and the organisations in the private sector which he had asked to contribute were those which he felt had clearly benefited from the economic policies instituted during his 32 years in power. This was also the principle of *gotong royong* that he believed to be necessary between the government and the private sector. From the beginning, he was aware that this had made him unpopular and many thought that this was one of his corrupt practices. He had weathered a few controversies in his life, which had started in the late 1950s, when General Nasution had ordered an investigation into his "smuggling" activities, at the time when he had given monopolies for the import of cloves, among others. Yet, back then, even President Soekarno had supported the establishment of Yayasan Trikora; in fact, it was stated in his biography that President Soekarno had given him a substantial amount for that foundation. Hence, he believed that many would support his ideas in forming charitable institutions.

The proceeds of the collected funds were used to support activities listed within the category of "non-budgetary" activities or those outside of the state budget. President Soeharto said that if the rich were asked to pay more taxes, they might move their businesses to countries where the taxation rate was low. Or they might pay a "service fee" to the tax authorities for a tax reduction as, in Indonesia, everything was negotiable. The tax could also be "misappropriated". Whichever the scenario, the country would lose out. Thus, President Soeharto opted for the "gentle" approach, so that businesses would stay in the country and for this to take place, he had to compromise. The wealthy were asked to give donations, the funds stayed with the state banks and the proceeds went to the less privileged.

These funds were deposited in the state banks and, as I was to find out, have remained there until the present. Thus, indirectly, the state banks have also enjoyed the benefits as well, more so since the Yayasan never touched the principal amounts. The Yayasan only used the interest received from the banks for their operations; therefore, when the interest went up, the activities of the Yayasan increased and vice versa. When the banks paid higher interest, the Yayasan could help more needy people. The local development banks also received their share of benefits, as they were the ones who disbursed the financial help from the Yayasan all over the region.

As for the donors, some operated their businesses through hard work and a few obtained privileges. Either way, as far as they were concerned, donating money to the Yayasan was just another form of taxation. However, this was a more flexible form as they could choose to contribute a smaller amount or not attend the charity events organised. It was common knowledge that when an invitation came from those in high places for a charitable lunch or dinner, businessmen would leave the country, so as to excuse themselves. (Once, I met a well-known businessman who always travelled economy class from Jakarta to Singapore. When I asked why he did not travel in business class, he said that he was afraid he might be seated next to an official who would then ask him to make a donation, as the country's government officials usually travelled in business class.)

To the public, the gifts of cash from the private sector appeared to be the result of President Soeharto and Ibu Tien having abused their position in soliciting donations or the money having come directly from the state budget. The public also questioned why the private sector had, instead of paying tax to the government, given donations to President Soeharto and Ibu Tien's charitable foundations, whose activities were shielded from their view. The uncertainty lay in whether the donations were really used for general welfare purposes or channelled towards his family's personal use.

When I reviewed the Yayasan activities, it became clear that they did manage to help in improving the people's well-being. Above all, they had taken the right strategy, as the Yayasan did not provide a "quick-fix" solution that would only make the recipient dependent on alms, without finding a solution for the real cause of the poverty. In giving financial help, the Yayasan also helped the recipients by informing them of how to get better income and hence achieve higher living standards through their own hard work. For those who lived in orphanages and shelters, the Yayasan would help them to be independent from just receiving gifts from donors. For instance, after the recipients finished their schooling or training, they were helped to find jobs or given capital to start businesses of their own.

The financial help from the Yayasan was meant to be a real and lasting social change and it was the result of careful planning. Changing the living conditions of the poor could not be achieved overnight. It should not take place through violence or revolution either, but through educating the people. Above all, it had to come from hard work and persistence. The Yayasan helped the poor to understand that the yearning for material goods should not just revolve around thinking about how the government's growing wealth could bring benefit to them. Further, they should not feel envious and resent those who could achieve success. The Yayasan gave inspiration to those who wanted to do something for themselves and the community and not just moan or complain about their situations. The people they helped had to be able to improve their standard of living through their own actions. Just smashing teacups was no answer at all to their problems; this was the philosophy of the Yayasan.

On the other hand, the rich were also warned that prosperity, standing and respect from the community was crucial for them to sustain their success. There would be a real danger if the rich lived in Western-style houses with showers and indoor bathrooms, carried Gucci bags and ate Kentucky Fried Chicken while the majority of their kinsmen still lived in huts, took their communal baths in the rivers and scrounged around in garbage bins for food. A friend of mine, Harjono Kartohadiprodjo, told me long ago as we drove from Jakarta to Cilegon, that if only the owners of the stalls along the road that we were travelling on could have enough money to eat in a restaurant in a five-star hotel, Indonesia would be paradise. He was right, it would lead to a win-win situation for all; the rich would have more customers and the stall owners would not feel jealous of them. In short, it was necessary to narrow the wide gap between the rich and the poor.

President Soeharto, together with the management of the Yayasan, had intended to do that. The government was to concentrate on making the economy conducive for businesses which President Soeharto felt would push the wheels of progress to move faster within the country. For example, Yayasan Supersemar required the students whom it had helped to undertake fieldwork and live with the villagers in the remote areas so as to train the inhabitants on matters such as the importance of hygiene. It was hoped that the graduates of Yayasan Supersemar would develop a bond with the community and gain sufficient experience to be able to embark on projects for shelters, orphanages, etc, on their own.

To prove that he had not reaped personal benefits from the Yayasan, Pak Harto suggested that the government take over the foundations, but the government decided to leave them as they were, with a few adjustments made. The concept of the Yayasan as a whole was worthy of praise. In spite of all their faults and weaknesses, the foundations did manage to help and benefit many of the poor. This was what Pancasila was, in fact, all about; this was the notion of *gotong royong* in action.

THE EARLY PERIOD

The first foundation was started in 1957, when General Soeharto was commander of the army in Semarang. In June of that year, he formed the Fourth Territory Foundation (YTE) to raise money for the improvement of the well-being of his troops and to support their widows and orphans. In July 1957, he created the Fourth Territory Development Foundation (YPTE) to help farmers and others as a token of his appreciation for their continuing support. He also encouraged Ibu Tien to get involved in the social welfare of the troops and she founded Persit, an association of military wives.

When he became president and continued with his foundations' activities, some considered the practice to be a patronage from the ruler to the ruled. Some went further and compared it with the traditional behaviour of a sultan towards his subjects. Needless to say, a charitable foundation needed patronage from a person with visibility, influence and fame. Sultan or otherwise, his actions illustrated the true paternalistic outlook of the country's feudalistic society. It is highly probable that he had kept his Yayasan activities within closed circles and in secrecy because the military had been the first to benefit from them.

In 1964, when General Soeharto became the Commander of Kostrad, he established Kostrad Dharma Putra Social Welfare Foundation. The foundation's interest expanded into ventures such as banking, film production, transport and food production. The investments became so large that the military was soon accused of accumulating wealth through unlawful means and abuse of power. General Soeharto did not pay too much attention to the negative criticisms as he was accomplishing too much.

However, in affairs of the state, those in leadership are expected to be free of engaging in profit-making activities. In retrospect, this could well have been the cause of his problems as, regrettably, the concept of the Yayasan was not clearly explained from the start—especially the reason for their formation. Pak Harto still chairs seven major foundations to date. Whether their formation was related to the political circumstances at the time of their establishment would be difficult to conclude definitively, but it is likely that there was a link between the prevailing situation and their formation. It all made sense at that time and the foundations provided a solution to the welfare issues of the people.

THE SEVEN FOUNDATIONS

Yayasan Trikora was formed as result of the fight for West Irian and the subsequent military conflicts. Yayasan Supersemar was formed on 16 May 1974 to grant scholarships to bright and talented students from deprived families. It took place a few months after the Malari riots. In 1975, Yayasan Dharmais was organised to help orphans and poor families. This was the year when the conflict with East Timor sharpened, after the movement Frente Revolucionária de Timor-Leste (Fretilin) or Revolutionary

Front of Independent East Timor declared East Timor independent on 28 November 1975. Within nine days, the military had arrived in East Timor, on 7 December.[4] Yayasan Amalbakti Muslim Pancasila was started on 17 February 1982 to build mosques. This was the year that the third New Order elections took place, in May 1982. Yayasan Dakab was formed to coincide with President Soeharto's 64th birthday on 8 June 1985. In the beginning, Yayasan Dakab was to support his political machine, Golkar. This was the year when all social organisations were asked to accept Pancasila as their sole basis. It was also the year when the country became self-sufficient in rice production. In 1986, Yayasan Gotong Royong was established to help in cases of fatalities resulting from natural disasters. The latest foundation was Yayasan Damandiri, established on 15 January 1996 for the main purpose of financing small businesses (ie micro finance). It was also meant to counter the rapid progress of the conglomerates as President Soeharto wanted to help the small businesses to grow as part of the country's economic development. It was the right move on his part, as the discontent and unhappiness over the conglomerates' avarice had become increasingly vocal. The year 1996 had been a volatile one. For President Soeharto personally, it was the worst year in his life as he lost Ibu Tien on 28 April. President Soeharto also made his first wrong move politically in allowing Indonesian Democratic Party (PDI) leader Soeryadi to oust Bung Karno's daughter Megawati during a tussle for the party's leadership. She later became a strong opponent of his government.

In addition to the non-budgetary programme, President Soeharto also took steps to raise education standards through Inpres (Presidential Instructions). Elementary schools, junior and senior high schools were built in every corner of the country through Inpres. In 1974, 6,000 new elementary schools were built and 1,000 out of the existing 1,427 junior high schools were rebuilt. In addition, 200 out of 421 senior high schools were renovated. The number of universities was increased from the existing 29 to the hundreds. Sadly, though thousands of schools were built, there were families who could not afford to send their children to school. President Soeharto also set up Bantuan Presiden (Banpres) or Presidential Assistance for those who were interested in the arts, for example dance.

Prosperity, like beauty, is in the eye of the beholder. What is considered to be prosperity in the West may be a luxury in the East, and something which is considered to be sufficient in the East may be minimal in the West. The criteria for prosperity should be taken within the context and framework of each society. President Soeharto argued that in the past, the Indonesian people could only afford to eat once a day, but after his third term in office, they had three meals a day. However, the more one has, the more one continues to want even more. It is not easy to fulfill the people's demands, as not only does the nature of demand change constantly, people continue to want more.

On 8 June 2005, Pak Harto's 84th birthday, my father and I visited Pak Harto to wish him a happy birthday. It was during that visit that Pak Harto agreed that I should write this book, especially to clarify the concept underlying the foundations he had built. He appeared to have been convinced by my father's last words: "Mas Harto, let her write the book for Indonesia's younger generation, so that they may understand our history from our perspective."

As a result, I was authorised to meet the Yayasan management, which would not have been easy otherwise. While we were in Kalitan, Solo, on 23 and 24 September 2005, Pak Harto decided that it would be best for me to meet each of them and to hear about their operations directly from them. The first meeting was with Yayasan Dakab and Dr Rusmono, Pak Harto's former doctor (now working with Dakab) who helped to coordinate my meetings with each of the seven Yayasan. The meetings started with Dr Rusmono, Subono, Soewarno and Sulaeman, who were superb in making the arrangements for all of my subsequent meetings. Not only did they assist in making the arrangements, they also helped to check my notes and conclusions after each meeting to ensure that I had captured accurate data.

Lively and straightforward, Dr Rusmono had a great sense of humour and I ended my research wishing that I could have spent more time with him in order to find out more about what Pak Harto was like when he was still in good health and was the president of the nation. Dr Rusmono told fascinating stories which I thought worked well in presenting an alternative image of Indonesia's second president from that which has been widely paraded in the public eye. After all, every coin has two sides with a different picture on each side.

YAYASAN TRIKORA

This was the Yayasan which Pak Harto had formed when President Soekarno was still in power. This was also the Yayasan which Bung Karno had supported financially, although those funds were disbursed in 1962, one year before its official formation. Therefore, those funds, although mentioned in President Soeharto's 1988 biography, are not stated as being part of Yayasan Trikora's present principal. My visit on the early morning of Monday, 3 October 2005, was hosted by Syaukat Banjaransari and Syahfrudin. As we walked through the building, I noted that there was nothing in view which indicated any sign of luxury in the office; in fact, the place was very simple and rather subdued. Located in the same street as the Bank Duta building (which is now empty), the other offices also looked rather deserted. There was not much activity going on that day. Syaukat and Syahfrudin were very personable and humble in their interactions with me. I was made to feel welcome and at ease as they were helpful and explained very patiently and at length about Yayasan Trikora's activities. They showed me all the supporting documents as well as the brochures explaining how people could apply for Yayasan Trikora's help. Yayasan Trikora's full name is Yayasan Bantuan Beasiswa Yatim Piatu Tri Komando Rakyat, translated as Scholarship for Orphans of the Three Commands of the People. The foundation was established on 2 May 1963.

After the Round Table Conference in 1949, there remained one unsettled issue, the question of West Irian (Papua). On 19 December 1961, President Soekarno had declared his intention to take the region back as Indonesia's lawful territory from Dutch occupancy. President Soekarno had named the action the Three Commands of the People, namely, to defeat the Dutch intention to create Papua or West Irian as their puppet state, to raise the Indonesian flag there before 17 August 1962 and to create national mobilisation for this purpose. By then, General Soeharto was appointed the commander to lead the troops in this military action, called Mandala. This war must have left a lasting impression on Pak Harto, as he named his youngest son Hutomo Mandala Putra or Tommy. Soon thereafter, General Soeharto became alarmed with the potential extent of war fatalities that would arise from this military action and in anticipation of providing help to the widows and orphans who would result from this war, he formed Yayasan Trikora.

Yayasan Trikora was to provide initial capital for widows to start small businesses, such as catering, to support their ongoing needs when their spouses were no longer able to fulfill the role of the breadwinner. The intention of Yayasan Trikora was not to give the people fish to eat, but to give them fishing rods so that they could fish for themselves. In fact, this was the basic guiding principle behind most of the foundations established, that the people should not just be receivers of donations all the time, but should instead create or develop skills that could be used to earn a living. The application of this concept would bring dignity to recipients of financial help and, more importantly, their new skills would also contribute towards the improvement of their self-esteem. Furthermore, if the cash donations were used merely to buy food, clothing and the like, the money would run out in time. However, if contributions were given as capital to start businesses, there would be unlimited prospects for the future of the beneficiary.

The same rule was applied to the donations received by the Yayasan. The contributions received were deposited into state banks to earn interest. Cash disbursements were made only from the interest earned and the principal stayed intact in the banks. At times, the principal was able to grow when the disbursed amounts were less than the interest earned. This was the way in which the foundations' capital was maintained for such a long time. They called it *dana abadi* or eternal funds. Yayasan Trikora's permanent capital amounts to a total of Rp32.5 billion and it is deposited in the three state-controlled banks. In reality, this is the lesson we have learnt from our ancestors, to ensure that we are frugal with our money. My grandfather taught his children an even tougher lesson. My grandfather taught my father to live only on the interest earned from the interest on capital.

Yayasan Trikora gave scholarships to the children of soldiers who were killed during the Mandala war and the grant was given to cover their education, from elementary school until they finished their higher education or were able to find jobs. Yayasan Trikora's initial capital was Rp25,000; the capital had risen to Rp5,800,000 in June 1968 due to the donations received from the private sector. As of 2005, 325 students, the children from 121 widows, were given scholarships. None were in elementary school because the fight in West Irian had taken place some 42 years ago, so most of the children were now adults with only 256 still in high school and the rest in universities. Those in elementary school received the equivalent of US$6.00 per student per month, while those in junior high schools received US$8.00; for senior high schools, it was US$10.00 per month and for university, it was US$15.00 per month, all paid up three months in advance. Considering the average per capita income in the lower class and the living standard at that time, this sum was more than adequate. At the time of writing, the amount of each endowment given depended on the area where the family lived. The funds disbursed also fluctuated every year, as it depended on the prevailing interest being earned. As of December 2004, the donations granted from Yayasan Trikora had reached a total of over Rp17 billion.

Yayasan Trikora's funds were disseminated to the public through coordination with the regional military commanders. Candidates had to fill in application forms providing their personal data, including a statement from their schools and their parent's death certificate. For widows, it included the monthly pension. One hundred and twenty-one widows, whose husbands were war casualties, were recipients of financial aid from Yayasan Trikora. The financial assistance to widows was meant as start-up capital to start small businesses like catering and others. In the starting phase of the new businesses, if necessary, Yayasan Trikora was prepared to be the buyer of their products. Once the businesses were operating properly, Yayasan Trikora would help them with the marketing as well. When this was accomplished, the foundation would stop its financial help and move on to help others with its funds.

As the Cold War continued into the early 1960s and while President Soekarno was still feeling the traumatic effects of Dutch colonialism, he viewed the Federation of Malaya as a British attempt to return under a new form of colonialism. Thus, at the end of 1962, the government decided to take military action against the new Federation of Malaya. At that time, President Soekarno had appointed General Soeharto as the vice commander of this action. It took two years, from 1964 to 1966, for the country to carry out its action, named "Dwikora". Once again, General Soeharto felt that he had to be responsible for those whose lives were affected by this military action. As a result, Yayasan Trikora expanded its operations to help the Dwikora war fatalities. The Dwikora casualties resulted in a total of 56 widows and 177 orphans. Up to 1998, the combined number of orphans resulting from Trikora and Dwikora totalled 500 children and 177 widows.

Military operations started in East Timor in 1975. Obviously, there were victims. Even though by this time General Soeharto had become the president, and was therefore not directly involved in the combat operations, he was nonetheless the highest commander of the country's armed forces. Thus, Yayasan Seroja was founded to take care of the East Timor fatalities. Soon, it was decided that Yayasan Trikora would also be responsible for the

Yayasan Seroja operation. The number of victims in the East Timor military action was much higher compared to Trikora and Dwikora. This was reflected in the data collected from 1973 to 1977: a total of 2,538 children became orphans and 830 wives became widows. In addition to the war victims, Yayasan Trikora also helped casualties like when the Hercules air force plane crashed during a flight in 1991. Furthermore, there were also occasions when it helped out in non-war related operations which involved members of the military and police forces. In such events, Yayasan Trikora gave scholarships to a total of 294 orphans and 135 widows. To date, Yayasan Trikora has also helped victims of conflicts where the military were involved, such as in places like Aceh, Ambon, Papua and Poso. It is worthy of note that these clashes took place in 2003, five years after President Soeharto was out of power. In this, Yayasan Trikora has granted 126 scholarships and helped 77 widows. Yayasan Trikora also gave financial assistance to civilians who died while performing their duties in connection with military operations. In such cases, they have given 80 scholarships to the children and 38 widows have received help. Yayasan Trikora's activities continue to date for the causes it has supported from its early formation, even after the conflicts themselves have been over a long time. Yayasan Trikora also offers financial contributions to those who do not have enough money to celebrate auspicious occasions such as Lebaran, Christmas and other religious holidays. Yayasan Trikora have maintained a detailed breakdown of their activities up to 31 August 2005, including the amount of interest earned, which at that time ranged from 6.5 to 7.5 per cent per annum.

I left Syaukat and Syahfrudin that day with a sense of accomplishment and gratitude. From both of them, I discovered a different perception of the Yayasan while previously, my impressions were that they were a goldmine for Pak Harto and his family. My discussions with my hosts were very open and rewarding, and had been a real revelation of the extent of the financial assistance that Yayasan Trikora has given to the families of war casualties, while the country had been caught up in military conflicts in attempting to preserve its freedom. Discussing those times of war in the country made me feel rather poignant; much more so after Syaukat, Mayor General by then, told me that he was the one who had given my late mother the *bintang gerilya* in appreciation from the government for her role during the country's war for freedom. At times like these, I am filled with admiration for the many who have sacrificed their lives or have been left with permanent injuries and disabilities in serving their country.

As I left, I imagined how the orphans and widows who had lost their loved ones in war must have felt. I thought not only of the dead but also of those who had been wounded, as the wounds had prevented them from taking on normal jobs after the war. All of a sudden, the image of my father's right hand with only two and a half fingers flashed in my mind—that injury had made it impossible for him to write, and that injury, too, had been a casualty of war. That day, as I drove in to see the management of Yayasan Trikora, I had felt like a hawk but two hours later when I left, I felt like a dove.

YAYASAN SUPERSEMAR

While I was engrossed in conversation at Yayasan Trikora, the telephone had rung several times. Syaukat's benign face had a big smile as he told us that Yayasan Supersemar had been on the line and was waiting for my arrival to see them that day. The traffic was on my side as I arrived almost on time and was met by more people than at the previous meeting. The anxiety on the faces of the management was obvious as I walked in like a long-awaited guest. Arjodarmoko, Soebagyo, Abdul Rahman, Herno Sasongko and Guritno soon showed signs of relief as I explained that I was a little late and blamed it on the traffic. Their office was in Kuningan, where the four other foundations were also located and was in a much better environment than the previous place. Not only was it larger in terms of space but it also appeared to have more activity than Yayasan Trikora. Again, everyone was helpful and friendly and my mood became progressively more peaceful that day. The books they provided gave a good illustration of the experiences of the students who had worked on Inpres Desa Tertinggal (IDT). Yayasan Supersemar recipients were required to work in rural villages to improve the living conditions in those areas in support of this Presidential Instruction, which they have been doing so for the last 30 years.

Yayasan Supersemar was founded on 16 May 1974. It was the second foundation to be set up after Yayasan Trikora, but it was the first to be established after Pak Harto became the president. Its main purpose was to help the government to overcome the country's education problems, especially in relation to students who had the intellectual ability but were unable to further their education due to financial problems.

Semar is the name of a respected *wayang* figure: ugly and fat with a protruding stomach, he is the personification of a deity on earth. Surat Perintah Sebelas Maret, the document which contained the information regarding President Soekarno's instructions of power, is abbreviated as Supersemar. Pak Harto's critics have claimed that he wanted to show that this important document was, in fact, a Super Semar, that is, something bigger than Semar. When the original document went astray, Supersemar became a hot subject of speculation among historians, a popular innuendo for his opponents and a definite headache for the government. Hence, because of its name, Yayasan Supersemar became something of a mystery and was often looked upon as an instrument to support Pak Harto's political ambition. However, I found out on the day of my visit that the foundation's only purpose was to award scholarships. Perhaps due to its work in providing financial help to students and students being the future of the nation, Yayasan Supersemar became an object of varied interpretations.

President Soeharto's pillars of development were, firstly, to provide material comfort which the people were entitled to have. Secondly, and simultaneously, it was the government's duty to preserve and strengthen the people's spiritual and moral ideals. To this end, Yayasan Supersemar's aim was to make the dream of the country's founding fathers a reality, as under the 1945 Constitution, it is stated that the government is "committed to improve knowledge and education for all".

When the Malari affair took place on 15 January 1974, the students were disenchanted about the way the government had been performing. The government realised that corrective measures were needed. The government was aware that higher education was still far too expensive for most of the people. Yet, it is well known that brainpower is not the privilege of the rich and, to the contrary, young men from poor families in Indonesian society usually tended to perform better than the rich, spoilt students. Many of the country's young men and women have academic abilities, but it is their limited financial resources that prevent them from developing the potential that they have. This is where Yayasan Supersemar comes into picture, as the foundation grants scholarships to talented students with good aptitude. Students who are granted financial support may attend any state or private institution, or technical schools. There are no strings attached and the scholarship is also extended to those who want to study in the Institute of Islamic Religion (IAIN).

The basic criteria for financial help is that a recipient has to be a young "Pancasila-ist", in addition to possessing intelligence, diligence, talent and good behaviour. A recipient is also expected to maintain an agreed level of achievement at all times. The scholarships are offered through the Deans of each university and are disbursed on an annual basis until the students graduate. The amount awarded is related to the local living standards in the area where the students study, with Jakarta having the highest standard. In some cases, the number of students awarded financial support may increase based on the recommendation of the Dean in the respective university. Yayasan Supersemar granted scholarships to only 3,135 university students in 1975 but in 2006, the number increased to 37,067. The foundation also grants scholarships to those who excel in sports. Yayasan Supersemar also provides financial assistance to institutions engaged in the fostering of children and family planning, in order to support the government's programmes in these areas.

A few high schools have received financial help from Yayasan Supersemar, although its main targets are students. Yayasan Supersemar has donated computers and printers to universities, including well known ones like University Gadjah Mada in Yogya, University Diponegoro in Semarang and University Brawijaya in Malang; universities located in Sumatra and East Indonesia have also been included. Students assisted by Yayasan Supersemar play an important role in helping to improve the living standards in remote villages as they are asked to train the rural communities and teach the villagers how to dig wells, install water pumps, purify canals and springs, channel water, install baths and so forth. When Pak Harto was in power, besides recipients of financial support from Yayasan Supersemar, all university students were also required to perform Kuliah Kerja Nyata (KKN) or practical community work while attending university. Medical students were to give training on how to prevent epidemics, the treatment of illness and the promotion of hygiene. Up to 2006, close to 427,789 university students, 889,961 high school students, over 13,060 sportsmen, over 832,500 foster children, 5,972 masters degree holders and over 1,160 doctoral degree holders have obtained financial support from Yayasan Supersemar. The total funds that have been distributed are close to Rp455,261,962,000.

Yayasan Supersemar raised its initial funds through voluntary donations from wealthy individuals, corporations and businessmen. The initial funds have remained as permanent deposits in the state banks. Yayasan Supersemar grants are distributed from the interest earned on the deposits only. In the beginning, the 10 founding members each contributed Rp10 million; they then approached companies in the private sector for donations and soon accumulated Rp1 billion. The foundation then needed to raise substantial capital to meet their objectives, so they gave donors the opportunity to become honorary members by contributing funds, which many did so for reasons of prestige. With the funds deposited in the state banks earning an interest of 0.75 per cent per month (9 per cent per year), they obtained Rp3,369 billion per month (Rp40,432 billion per year), which was a substantial amount to support thousands of students.

Yayasan Supersemar was one of the shareholders in Bank Duta, which faced financial crisis in 1990, hence the foundation had to swallow losses from this investment, although there were reports that new funds had been injected into Yayasan Supersemar by donors. Many of President Soeharto's opponents did not want to believe in the voluntary nature of the donations, because in the business world, there are no such things as free lunches. They alleged that there had to be deals made behind close doors. The foundation's early members were, amongst others, Ibnu Sutowo, Widjojo Nitisastro and Sudharmono. Ibnu Sutowo was one of the richest persons in Indonesia at that time and perhaps that was why Pak Harto was lenient with him when he caused the Pertamina crisis. It made sense for Pak Harto to ask Ibnu Sutowo to join the foundation because he was highly educated and he had helped Pertamina to make a lot of money. Widjojo Nitisastro was also an intellectual and he had the right image; in addition, he was Chairman of Bappenas. Most importantly, none of his children were involved with Yayasan Supersermar.

The graduates formed an association in 1979 with membership reaching a total of 796,489 in 1999. The association was to function as a networking opportunity and a few graduates started to donate part of their salary to help the next generation of deprived students. These graduates knew what the foundation had done to help them achieve success in their lives. In fact, a few of the graduates became Cabinet ministers, governors and deans of universities. Unfortunately, I could not find out why they did not come forward to explain to the public what Yayasan Supersemar had done for them.

I have not come across a book written by the graduates based on their own experiences to illustrate the positive aspects of Yayasan Supersemar, except a book on IDT. Whether the reasons were based on concern for their personal safety, protection of their present positions or a lack of opportunity to write, one would never know. It makes me unhappy whenever I think about this silence shrouding the positive work the foundation has done. Pak Harto, too, became subdued when I asked him why the graduates did not come forward to tell the truth about Yayasan Supersemar's work. The graduates are intelligent and should have the courage to voice their opinions even if a storm was blowing their way. As academically inclined individuals, they would be able to set the record straight, not necessarily by defending Pak Harto, but by painting the true picture of Yayasan Supersemar. Having an alumni association with over 790,000 members, they are in the position to write about their experiences, or at the very least distribute their book about IDT to the media for public consumption. The graduates are in the best position to explain the inside story of Pak Harto's concept of the foundations and how their work was carried out. Perhaps this book will encourage and prompt some of them to share the story of their success and the role that Yayasan Supersemar had played in supporting their rise to success.

YAYASAN DHARMAIS

We met with Yayasan Dharmais on 5 October 2005. Indra Kartasasmita, previously a director with Pertamina, was the secretary and he was accompanied by Zarlons Zaghlul, the treasurer. Indra Kartasasmita is good looking, small in stature but a very lively person and hospitable, while Zarlons, full of wisdom, was always ready to provide us with data, magazines, brochures and handicrafts produced by those who have been given assistance. An impressive team, as was each management team we met from all the Yayasan. Their office was in the same building as Yayasan Supersemar and I noticed Pak Harto and Ibu Tien's picture hanging prominently on the wall. They had published a book in 2003 to commemorate the three decades of their dedication to the community. In the book, there are pictures of the founders of Yayasan Dharmais who are no longer alive. Pak Harto gave his keynote speech as chairman and simply signed his name as HM Soeharto, H for "Hajji", and M for "Muhammad". Several national figures contributed their messages as well, one of them being my father. "It is time for us to reflect on what had been the ideas and motivation when the foundation was founded," wrote my father.

Yayasan Dharmais stands for Dharma Bhakti Sosial and it was established on 8 August 1975. It was just a little over one year after the formation of Yayasan Supersemar. The wording in the 2003 book expressed the founding father's feelings. The heading read "*Tak surut oleh waktu*" ("not affected by the changing times"); the Preface said "*Seuntai melati*" ("a string of jasmine flowers"). To me, this said it all, as Pak Harto and the management had wanted to show that Yayasan Dharmais was able to do tangible deeds for the needy, while the management was caught in the eye of the storm.

Years after President Soeharto was out of power, while the misunderstanding about the foundations lingered on, Yayasan Dharmais' contributions needed a sound footing in terms of proper and accurate records. This was also applicable to his remaining charitable institutions. In 1988, President Soeharto wrote[5] that the Indonesian people should feel fortunate to have their freedom and realise that they were not alone as there were many others like them. However, a few of the developing nations were not yet able to have realistic and pragmatic plans for development. Even though small compared to the developed countries, in time to come, the developing nations would be able to voice substantial opinion in the world forum. The success of the developed nations gave an indication that progress could be achieved through a country's own strength. For this, self-reliance and self-determination were important. Accordingly, Pak Harto saw the need for establishing the foundations. The people had to work together, and also amongst nations as demonstrated during the Asia-Africa Conference in Bandung. That conference gave birth to the 10 principles, the spirit of which is relevant even within a changing international situation, the most important being peaceful co-existence and mutual respect for individual countries. He said that political differences were common and should be tolerated, provided that each nation honoured the others' supremacy and stayed away from each other's internal problems.

The history of modern Indonesia cannot be alienated from what President Soeharto had achieved. His rule was enduring in spite of the adversities experienced during those years. His greatest strength was his extraordinary instinct to meet the expectations of the common man from a ruler's point of view. Clause 34 of the 1945 Constitution declared that the "government is responsible for the poor and orphans". As a child, one of President Soeharto's dreams was to make the lives of the peasants happier. Although fairness dictated that all men should have equal opportunities, he was practical enough to know that one would face difficulty in meeting this objective. However, he also knew that if the people were desperate as a result of not being able to meet their basic needs, the extremists would have an opportunity to step in and take over and this would endanger the nation's stability. Social upheaval would provide a good opening for the return of communism. Therefore, social welfare needs had to be addressed properly.

Yayasan Dharmais was born in this spirit and its main aim was to help the orphanages, the homeless, the hospices, the disabled and the like. The foundation's paid up capital was Rp10 million. The start-up capital came from the contributions of the founder, the donors and the banks. As with Yayasan Supersemar, the initial funds remained as deposits in the state banks. To support its philanthropic activities, the foundation merely used the interest earned on the deposits. However, unlike Yayasan Trikora and Supersemar, President Soeharto had placed one of his sons and a son-in-law on the management of Yayasan Dharmais. He considered Yayasan Dharmais to be the best place for them to learn about and understand the hard life of those less privileged. Thousands received cash contributions from Yayasan Dharmais on a monthly basis. Yayasan Dharmais collaborated with the local administration or social organisations to disburse financial assistance. To help the very poor with medical treatment, Yayasan Dharmais joined forces with the eye specialists, plastic surgeons and other medical personnel and associations.

From 1976 until the time of writing, the foundation gave financial assistance to 1,424 orphanages, homes for the aged and disabled and hospices. About 58,000 people lived in these homes. The donations averaged Rp31 million per annum. In 2005, the foundation gave Rp40,000 for food and Rp5,000 for health check-ups for children in orphanages. The regular health check-up ensures that the food they are given has sufficient nutrition. On religious holidays such as the end of Ramadhan or Christmas, a sum of Rp50,000 (US$5) is given to each child to buy clothes. The orphanages themselves receive money to buy new equipment and for building maintenance and repairs. This is important as the buildings where the needy live must be in good condition at all times. For this, they require regular maintenance. The total financial support disbursed from 1976 to 2004 amounted to Rp474 billion.

Yayasan Dharmais also provides contributions for the disabled, so that they can be trained to make handicrafts. These handicrafts are for export to Korea and other countries. I was impressed when Indra Kartasasmita and Zarlons showed me a few bags and tissues boxes made from leaves. Not only were the designs up to date, they were also meticulously woven. A few weeks later, while in Cirebon, I noticed the products displayed in an exhibition organised by Pertamina to raise funds for charity. From 1976 to the present, Yayasan Dharmais has disbursed Rp2 billion for such activities. Indra and Zarlons have a right to be proud of their achievements. They have helped those with severe disabilities to aspire further and not stop them from having ambitions just like anyone else. The skills they have gained through the help of Yayasan Dharmais have made it possible for them to move out and live a normal life in the community. The social welfare centres that Yayasan Dharmais has helped can show them how to become more independent and to make the most of their abilities and their lives. Without the vital support from Yayasan Dharmais, much of this work could not have been carried out.

In 1985, the government decided that the benchmark of poverty (or the poverty line) in the country would be the consumption of 320kg of rice per person per annum. This was a model devised by the country's economists. To rise above the poverty line, one had to consume more than 320kg of rice per year. Calculating on the basis of each family having two children, this meant a demand for 1.3 tonnes of rice per year in the country. To meet this demand, each farmer would have to cultivate ½ hectare of land. The census conducted in 1980 revealed that 11 million families in the country have less than ½ hectare of land, with 6 million among them having less than ¼ hectare of land for farming. Up to 1985, the average land cultivation was only ¼ hectare. Therefore, transmigration became an important issue and the government embarked on the transmigration programme very quickly.

Indonesia has many outer islands with fewer inhabitants than Java. Useful and attractive benefits were given to those who were willing to move. The island of Sumatra was the main target due to its large size and richness in untapped natural resources. In line with the government's transmigration programme, starting from 1987, Yayasan Dharmais provided training to the labour force to enable the people to gain new skills. Preparation for the migrants focused on how to adjust to a new environment. It would not be easy as not only were the local customs and religions different, but the natural and physical environment were also poles apart. There were still wild animals roaming the undeveloped and forested areas and tigers were known to have attacked humans in remote parts of Sumatra. With the help rendered by Yayasan Dharmais in providing training and support activities, the foundation proved its worth in standing side by side, supporting and supplementing the new government programme in order to make it successful. From 1987 until 1998, 26,573 families or 94,769 persons were trained at a cost of Rp30 billion. The training proved valuable in reducing clashes between locals and migrants that would usually take place in such an exercise.

President Soeharto realised how modest a retirement his compatriots would get, based on the funds available for this purpose. Things were made worse when they were wounded in war. To help the veterans, Yayasan Dharmais built 2,810 units of simple houses for war veterans. The total cost was over Rp16 billion. President Soeharto decided to enforce education for the homeless and problematic youths. Approaching the 40th anniversary of the country's independence, there was an exhibition of the nation's domestic products in Monas, where he was happy to see the achievements of the younger generation. The younger generation could now aspire to be architects, engineers, doctors, researchers, etc. In relation to this, he recalled that many years ago, there were grave doubts over whether the country could keep its freedom and develop as a modern nation. History proved those doubts unfounded. The nation was able to stand on its own feet. Nevertheless, this satisfaction should not blind the people to the many other things left to be accomplished. Bung Karno used to say that there was no end to a revolution. Bung Karno did not mean this in the physical sense but in terms of the human spirit. President Soeharto agreed with this as he wanted Yayasan Dharmais to help the homeless and young people with family problems. In this context, he encouraged the wealthy to become foster parents. Foster parenthood was introduced as a government programme wherein Yayasan Dharmais would provide scholarships to these children through their foster parents.

From 1985 until 2001, 50,000 children received scholarships from Yayasan Dharmais at a cost of Rp23 billion. In 2000, together with the regional governments, the foundation trained the homeless and those unable to finish school to learn practical skills. With skills in areas such as carpentry, plumbing and electrical works, they could earn a good living. This was precisely what the country needed and still needs. The intellectuals were needed to design the development strategies, but practical skills were also necessary to implement them. Even in developed countries like England, skilled labour is in high demand, backed up with ever increasing hourly fees. I remember viewing a BBC programme once, which showed that blue-collared workers in England earned much more than professors and researchers, so much so that an assistant researcher in the country decided to change his profession to become a plumber!

Yayasan Dharmais owned several mobile libraries. These mobile libraries went from school to school in poor areas where pupils were not able to buy books. This was also to encourage a reading habit in the young. This is a point worth noting, as many thought that President Soeharto's interest in reading was minimal. This might have been true of him personally, but it did not mean that he did not try to encourage reading amongst the young. Reading was a sore point in my father's mind. He was disappointed to see that those from the wealthy strata in Indonesian society rarely read. Instead of having a library, they would have five expensive cars in their garages. Instead of visiting libraries or museums, the rich went shopping and gambling when they were abroad. Subsequently, my father asked me to obtain secondhand children's books from the charity shops in England for the mobile libraries operated by Yayasan Dharmais.

The reputation of Indonesian hospitals is nowhere near that of its neighbour, Singapore. The rich and famous usually go to Singapore for medical treatment, but not President Soeharto, who had only been to Germany for a medical check-up once, on the advice of BJ Habibie. For the very poor, medical treatment is a major financial burden. This is another area which Yayasan Dharmais focuses on. Yayasan Dharmais has helped those in need of cataract, kidney and cleft lip operations. Yayasan Dharmais offers a helping hand to those condemned to a life of malnutrition, shame and isolation. Nowadays, virtually all of these problems can be treated, but for the poor, it all comes down to the issue of cost, and this is where Yayasan Dharmais steps in to offer assistance. There are also special illnesses which the local hospitals are not able to treat, such as cancer. For the rich, it does not pose any problem as Singapore is only a one-hour flight away, but for the lower middle class and the poor, it is a very serious issue. They have to obtain local treatment and care. As a result, Yayasan Dharmais built a cancer hospital at a cost of Rp112 billion and named it RS Kanker Dharmais. In November 1994, the hospital was handed over to the new government. Yayasan Dharmais cooperates with eye specialists (Perdami), plastic surgeons (Perapi) and eye banks to help those who have no money for treatment which they badly need. The foundation had helped to fund cataract operations to the amount of Rp210 million. Yayasan Dharmais also contributes towards the cure of osteoporosis, for which they have donated Rp375 million for the purchase of a Dexa Bone Densitometry, for the measurement of bone density. The machine is now located in RS Cipto Mangunkusumo, a government-run hospital. The foundation has also helped to pay for liver patients' operations and to purchase equipment for blood transfusions, eye operations, laser skin treatments and many more. The hospitals which have received financial support include those located beyond Java.

The activities of Yayasan Dharmais are indeed impressive, as supported by the information which surfaced during my research. An unexpected cold call was made to a Muslim orphanage, Panti Asuhan Muslimin in Kramat Raya, Jakarta. The secretary, Masbukin, whom I met later that day, was very candid and helpful. According to his account, after Pak Harto's resignation, he had immediately sent out questionnaires to all orphanages that received contributions from Yayasan Dharmais. The responses which he managed to collect was a good reflection of the situation at the grassroots level at that time. All the orphanages that received help from Yayasan Dharmais raised objections over the possibility of the succeeding government taking over the management of Yayasan Dharmais. They were concerned if it was transferred to the Ministry of Social Welfare, the donations would eventually stop. Alternatively, in the best possible scenario, the donations would be delayed for months due to bureaucracy, not to mention corruption. "Ironic" is the word I would use to describe the situation, considering that the succeeding government wanted President Soeharto out of office because of corruption.

As an organisation, Yayasan Dharmais made tax payments, for instance in 2001, they settled a tax payment of Rp262,483,100.[6] At the same time, all financial assistance rendered were given completely free of obligations. However, one cannot help but wonder: is money given to charity not supposed to be free of taxes?

If my mood had been sombre when I thought of Yayasan Supersemar graduates, my spirit was certainly lifted sky-high after the cold call to Panti Asuhan Muslimin. In fact, Masbukin encouraged me to visit another two Catholic-run orphanages located on the same street. It was only due to the tight deadline for the submission of my manuscript that I was prevented from doing further research on this area. Indra and Zarlons had also suggested attendance at the Halal Bihalal (social meeting after our fasting month), which was intended to take place in November 2005 in Surabaya and attended by hundreds of *panti asuhan* that Yayasan Dharmais has helped. I was sad that I was not to be able to attend, nevertheless, from what I had seen of Yayasan Dharmais, it gave me confidence and hope that there is always a light at the end of every tunnel. As I left the meeting that day, I could hardly forget the enthusiasm shown by all of the gentlemen I had met; they are brave men who stand ready to weather any incoming storm.

YAYASAN AMALBAKTI MUSLIM PANCASILA

I met Sulastomo on Monday, 10 October 2005. He is the most familiar face to me from amongst those involved in the management of the Yayasan. He was the Chairman of Himpunan Mahasiswa Islam (HMI) or the Islamic Students' Organisation when G30S occurred. He has written books which are useful for gaining an insight into what really happened during that time. As he was the leader of HMI, he knew both Bung Karno and Pak Harto personally. Sulastomo's personality is such that it is difficult not to like him: calm and composed but keeping a strong stand on his principles, this is how he is perceived by most. A medical doctor by profession, he once admitted that he did not know why he liked to write books on subjects such as history and politics. Pak Harto seemed to like him too: whenever I mentioned his name, Pak Harto's eyes would twinkle with happiness. Sulastomo was also welcome to our house at any time; my father would not have been irritated even if he had been ready for bed when this particular guest arrived. I think his saintly look and calm personality certainly go a long way towards making him so likeable. Needless to say, I hold him in high esteem.

Yayasan Amalbakti Muslim Pancasila (YAMP) was established on 17 February 1982 and this foundation derived its funds from voluntary collections from civil servants and military personnel. Their main goal was to improve the people's religious well-being, in particular for that of Islam.

My father used to say that a strong nation was a nation whose people loved God and had empathy and sympathy towards each other. The evidence of this belief can be seen in the fact that when our country had a little money to spend, President Soekarno decided to build the Syuhada Mosque in Yogya. Opened on 20 September 1952, it serves as a memorial to those who died during the country's fight for freedom. Next, President Soekarno gave instructions for the construction of Mosque Baitul Rahim, located in the presidential complex, which was followed by Istiqlal Mosque, which was intended to be the largest mosque in Southeast Asia at that point in time. Istiqlal Mosque commenced construction on 7 December 1954, although the first stone was laid only three years later. It took seven years to complete and was officially opened on 22 December 1978 by President Soeharto, as Bung Karno had died eight years earlier. The country's tradition of building mosques continued under President Soeharto.

YAMP, like Yayasan Dharmais, has published an inspiring book. The book portrays how the principle of *gotong royong* was implemented within its true spirit as YAMP constructed mosques all over the country. Although many were cynical about Indonesian ideals and believed that *gotong royong* existed in name only, in the construction of mosques it was proven to be alive and working effectively. YAMP's book, published in 2004, contains a foreword from its chairman, Pak Harto. The accompanying photograph with his smiling face belies the criticisms he received as he initiated voluntary contributions when he started YAMP. He should feel happy that in spite of the hurdles, YAMP has survived for over two decades and has constructed over 950 mosques to date.

As with the book published by Yayasan Dharmais, national figures were also asked to give their remarks, including my father, who emphasised in his message that President Soeharto's development of the nation included government efforts to upgrade not only knowledge and science but, most importantly, to strive towards a society with moral values that would think charitably to assist widows, orphans and other destitute members of society. Further, he wrote that YAMP was a representation of mutual concerns and was the product of hard work and joint effort by the country's civilians and armed forces working together for a worthy cause. My father further quoted Einstein's famous words: "Science without religion is lame, religion without science is blind". He also pointed to the fact that YAMP should accept the public's suggestions, corrections and criticisms for its future growth. In fact, this should be applicable to all of Pak Harto's foundations. Obviously, they could all do with improvements, but in fairness, it is hoped that the public will come to realise and acknowledge that the intention behind the creation of the Yayasan was not for the accumulation of Pak Harto's personal wealth.

YAMP's initial capital was collected from gifts from devout Muslims. On the formation of YAMP, President Soeharto reminded the people that as Muslims, they were encouraged to contribute 2.5 per cent of their disposable income to help the poor. For Muslims, the collection of alms is called *zakat*. Using this religious concept, President Soeharto pleaded with civil servants to make donations to YAMP ranging from Rp50, Rp100, and Rp500 to Rp1,000, depending on their positions and wages; this was not enforced but done on a voluntary basis. This was supported by his letter dated 8 November 1982, addressed to the Chairman of Korpri (Corps of Civil Servant). In his capacity as a private citizen and not as president, Soeharto informed them about the establishment of YAMP and pleaded for their support on a voluntary basis. He signed the letter on behalf of YAMP. Korpri, in their reply of 27 November 1982, stated that they had no objections to making contributions, a decision which had been made after a formal meeting of its management. A similar letter was sent to the armed forces, to which Pak Harto received a similar reply. Hence, nothing was dubious about the way the funds were raised. However, his critics argued that even though the contributions were voluntary in nature, the implementation looked like coercion. They alleged that no one would have dared refuse, as even if Pak Harto had signed as a private citizen, everyone knew he was the president at that point in time. This was a clear example of a situation where he was blamed for doing something, yet at the same time, he would also have been cursed if he had not done anything.

To show solidarity, the non-Muslims were also asked to make contributions. Contributions from non-Muslims were forwarded to Yayasan Dharmais, as churches and temples were generally more affluent and they did not require financial help from the Yayasan. Yayasan Dharmais channelled the donations to help orphanages, whether organised by Muslims, Christians or other faiths. The contributions from the civil servants started in January 1983 and the armed force's donations started from the beginning of October 1983. The highest contribution from the military was Rp2,000, while the maximum from the civil servants was Rp1,000.

YAMP was unique in the sense that all the mosques they financed had a similar design. Each consisted of three levels but there were three different types, the smallest being 15m x 15m, the middle sized being 17m x 17m and the largest 19m x 19m. The sizes depended on the area of location. A few were built within hospital or office complexes to accommodate employees's daily and Friday prayers. In some remote regions, it had not been easy to find building materials and local labour. Often, building materials and construction workers had to be transported from Jakarta. In Wamena, West Irian, steel had to be transported by Hercules aircraft. YAMP also provided help for the maintenance and repairs of a number of mosques. Up to 2004, YAMP had spent Rp168 billion to build 940 mosques. At the time of writing, the total number of mosques built was over 953. To date, YAMP has built mosques in 30 provinces in 216 regions and 52 small cities. Mosques symbolise the importance of the Indonesian people's spiritual life as the majority are Muslims.

When BJ Habibie became president, he announced, by Inpres dated 16 July 1998, his decision to discontinue the practice of receiving donations from civil servants and the armed forces. Not many of us understood the real reason behind this decision. It was especially strange in view of the fact that BJ Habibie was the prime mover of ICMI, which used Muslim academics for his political base. An immediate result was that YAMP encountered difficulties in building new mosques, compared to the early years of its formation. Many felt sad about that decision because such drastic action was not necessary. A middle path could have been taken by stressing the voluntary nature of the contributions and moving away from the perception that the contributions were the result of coercion. I believe this was the solution Pak Harto would have liked BJ Habibie to choose. YAMP confirmed that without the voluntary contributions, they faced financial difficulties in building the number of mosques that Pak Harto had in mind. Pak Harto wanted to build a total number of 999 mosques. It is not clear why the number was not 1,000.

Like the other foundations, the original donations had remained as deposits in the state banks, but the interest earned had decreased drastically over the last few years. In 2005, the foundation managed to build only 12 mosques as the cost of building materials, especially steel, had increased.

YAMP also built hospitals and training places for Muslims before they embarked on the *hajj* to the holy cities of Mecca and Medina. YAMP also contributed to the building of four hajj hospitals, which cost a total of Rp2 billion. These were crucial projects, as most would-be *hajj* travellers have never been abroad. This would, in all probability, be their first and only time going overseas. Not only would they experience a different climate on their pilgrimage, but there would also be millions of pilgrims during the *hajj* season. It is, therefore, important that they are instructed on the basics, like what to do if they got lost or fell sick. Similar to Yayasan Dharmais, YAMP was also involved in training transmigrants by working with Majelis Ulama Indonesia (MUI), which provided training for Imams who wanted to move to the outer islands. To date, they have trained 2,777 migrants, and amongst them 968 are Imams. YAMP also gave subsidies to religious publications which encountered financial difficulties.

There is little accusation, almost none, against President Soeharto when it came to YAMP. Blamed for almost everything that went wrong, YAMP is considered to be President Soeharto's best side. Ibu Tien's foundation also built mosques. At Tin, within the Taman Mini Indonesia Indah complex, is a model built on a futuristic concept of how a mosque should be. A mosque should be a place where spiritual and intellectual activities convene. Thus, at At Tin, there were regular discussions and lectures on Islam. In 1995, the Indonesian Muslim Community in New York built Mosque Al Hikmah and asked YAMP to contribute. YAMP agreed and paid US$150,000. In 1996, YAMP, donated US$100,000 for the construction of a mosque in Port Moresby in Papua New Guinea, upon their request. The two cases fell within the spirit of *dasa sila Bandung*, peaceful co-existence and mutual cooperation.

YAYASAN DANA ABADI KARYA BAKTI (Dakab)

I first met with Dakab on 29 September 2005 before going to see the rest of the Yayasan and again on 13 October to wrap up my findings. The first meeting took place just before the fasting month began. I had to prepare myself mentally at that point in time. I was more apprehensive about meeting the Yayasan for the first time than I had been before I met Pak Harto himself. The Yayasan, in particular Dakab, was considered to be *angker* in Javanese, meaning frightening. In the eyes of the public, Dakab was full of tough military men and members of Golkar. That day, the four gentlemen whom I met were Dr Rusmono, Subono, Soewarno and Sulaeman, and fortunately, none of them looked as tough or as scary as I had anticipated. They were relaxed and jovial, with a great sense of humour, and I soon felt at ease among them.

Dakab was another one of the three Yayasan that had experienced bad luck in its Bank Duta shareholding. Indeed, if the public had looked upon YAMP as the "saint" among the seven of Pak Harto's foundations, then the "sinner" was Dakab. Dakab, established on 8 June 1985, stands for Yayasan Dana Abadi Karya Bakti. The "sin" of Dakab was due to the fact that it was looked upon as a money-printing machine to support President Soeharto's power base, especially in the beginning due to its close link with Golkar. The word "karya" used in Golkar (Golongan Karya) and Dakab were often associated together.

Golkar was the Functional Group. In 1964, Sekber Golkar or the Joint Secretariat of the Functional Group was an entity which the army was meant to counter and prevent the rise of communism. Golkar became a powerful engine in the electoral arena for years to come. It was one blade with two edges: one was to contain the communists and the other to secure the 1945 Constitution and Pancasila. One side was for civilians to take active part in and the other was where the military played a key role. Golkar needed to safeguard against penetration by the communists, especially during important events like the general elections. Dakab itself did not belong to Golkar. Golkar only received donations from Dakab, but so did the other political parties, although in lesser amounts. Dakab's main activity was also to help Golkar in economics and social/cultural matters which included the youth and student activities, including Muslim organisations like Muhammadiyah and HMI. The last two were moderate Muslim organisations.

Dakab's assets in 1985 reached a total of Rp43 billion. The funds were derived from donations and contributions from individuals and corporations. Dakab also engaged itself in long-term investments. Deposited in the banks and through investments, Dakab's working capital came from the interest earned and dividends received. As Golkar turned into the most powerful and important political party and as Dakab was closely associated with it, one could only imagine how many contributions Dakab received during the peak of President Soeharto's rule. The businesses that needed political stability for them to turn profits decided to support Dakab. Pak

Harto had been amused, during an interview which took place 48 days after his resignation, as he recalled a number of Golkar members who wanted to know the whereabouts of the contributions that Dakab had collected. They thought the funds should be transferred to them. President Soeharto's relationship with his old political machine, Golkar, changed dramatically after May 1998 as Golkar tried to detach itself and lay all blame on him. Now, Golkar refers to itself as a "reformed" or "new" Golkar.

Thus, Dakab steered away from its former close link to Golkar. Its prime goals were changed to the improvement of education and helping the underprivileged to overcome poverty. However, the prime task to safeguard and secure Pancasila and the 1945 Constitution was maintained. The annual programme is decided at the meeting of the management and after the chairman's approval, the programme is forwarded to the State Secretary. In 2005, Dakab worked together with Bank Pembangunan Daerah (BPD), the regional development banks, to disburse credit given to small businesses or micro credits. There were 20 provinces where Dakab's micro credits were disbursed in cooperation with BPD. The credits were meant for productive business. It was paid out to small cooperatives (*koperasi pasar*) and the civil servant's cooperatives with interest rates of 6 per cent per annum. Loans were also given to the farmers' association, Himpunan Kerukunan Tani Indonesia (HKTI) to enable them to process land ownership; this was important as land titles or land ownership was always a major problem in Indonesia as from the time of the Dutch, farmers usually worked on land that was not theirs.

Cooperating with the Indonesian Medical Doctors Associations (IDI), Dakab upgraded the health of the *santri* (Muslim scholars), which was spread out over 150 *pesantren*. The *pesantren* was a religious boarding school. We were surprised as Dr Rusmono, in his typically entertaining ways, told us how stubborn the orthodox Muslims who lived in the *pesantren* could be. They refused to sleep on mattresses and chose to slumber on floors. As a result of the dust and dirt, they often developed skin rashes or serious skin diseases. Only after long and firm persuasion were the orthodox Muslims willing to change the habit of sleeping on dusty floors. Apparently, they considered the customary practice to be in compliance with Islamic teaching, when in reality the opposite is true as Islam teaches its followers to be clean at all times. That is the reason Muslims have to wash their faces, arms and feet before each prayer session, which takes place five times a day.

Dakab gave financial support for medical treatment of eyes, nose, hearing, skin and mouth diseases. In collaboration with the Central Civil Servants Women Associations (Persatuan Dharma Wanita Pusat), Dakab printed writing books for school children from poverty-stricken remote and backward places. The book covers were printed with educational objects and a few were also meant to test their eyesight. When I was given a few samples of the writing books, I was indeed impressed with the innovation.

RSCM hospital and RSPAD Gatot Subroto in Jakarta and RSUP Dr Jamil in Padang were able to acquire a Dexa Bone Densitometry machine through Dakab's financial help. The public accountant now audits its financial statement, as with the other foundations. It appears that the Dakab that was once envied, misunderstood and struck fear in people's hearts is now changing its image into a benevolent organisation. Dakab's new image deserves better understanding, and public relations for all the Yayasan seems to be focused one way or another on resolving their image problems. Under the lead of someone like Dr Rusmono, who has a practical mind and a straightforward approach, it is just a matter of time before their deeds are known. His team of Subono, Soewarno and Sulaeman reminded me of unsung heroes who did their jobs and moved on. Not only that, but their dedication to the causes they believe in is touching. In addition, they have stood firmly by Pak Harto's side during his sunset years.

YAYASAN DANA GOTONG ROYONG KEMANUSIAAN

While the other Yayasan were located in the middle of the city, this one was in the outskirts of Jakarta. I met with M Yarman, Djaeni, Ali Wathon and Istikomah. The office was within the complex of a TV station, TPI, and it was where Tutut had signed the opening monument that was placed at the entrance to the building. This was no doubt a family foundation. It seemed that Pak Harto had stayed with his concept and when it came to welfare matters, the family was involved. The meeting was friendly as usual, not to mention relaxed and open. They provided me with their publication, the commemoration of its 19th year of formation. I pointed out that after Ibu Tien's passing, her pictures should have been removed along with those of the other deceased members, as was done in the book published by Yayasan Dharmais. They were pleased with my suggestions. The best pictures were taken in the aftermath of the tsunami in Aceh in late 2004, when Titiek had flown there to give donations on behalf of Yayasan Gotong Royong.

Ibu Tien had accompanied President Soeharto during his visit to Rome when he received the award from the FAO in 1985. It was during this trip that Ibu Tien was alerted to the issue of starvation in Africa caused by natural disasters. Upon her return, she made plans to form Yayasan Dana Gotong Royong Kemanusiaan, as a precautionary measure in case such calamities occurred in Indonesia. Thus, on 30 March 1986, she invited businessmen to Bogor Palace for a charity event. On 23 August 1986, on the occasion of her 63rd birthday, the foundation was formalised. As Ibu Tien was the patron, many businesses were willing to donate. As in many other countries, those who are famous are sometimes motivated to use their fame to establish or support charitable foundations. The farmers are naturally the ones to feel the impact of drought and they are also the ones prone to suffer the impact of other natural catastrophes. On behalf of the farmers, President Soeharto contributed Rp17.5 billion. Not only the rich donated their money, but those less wealthy, including high school pupils, also chipped in. Indeed, when natural catastrophes strike, the principle of *gotong royong* is implemented at its finest.

Yayasan Dana Gotong Royong clearly defined what was considered a natural disaster. It consisted of calamity caused by floods, volcanic eruptions, lava flows, earthquakes, landslides, hurricanes, storms, long drought and fires. However, it did not include accidents like electrical faults or any other calamity caused by human error. As usual, the contributions were deposited as permanent funds in the state banks. From May 1986 to October 1998, they have disbursed over Rp34 billion for 454 natural disasters in 714 locations in the country's 27 provinces. This included assistance to the victims in the 1990 Mina Tunnel collapse during the *hajj* pilgrimage. Like Yayasan Trikora, they also helped sufferers of the Hercules aircraft that went down in 1991. Up to July 2005, the total amount paid out had gone up to Rp48 billion spread over 665 disasters in 855 locations in 32 provinces. The biggest amount was given to floods and earthquake victims, and for the 2004 horrific tsunami catastrophe. Those who were helped were the wounded and the families of the dead, including those who had lost their homes and lands for farming, and also the survivors who had to live in temporarily accommodation.

The method by which the funds were granted was through requests from the head of the affected region, and a copy of the request was then sent to the Minister Coordinator of Social Welfare and the Department of Social Welfare and the Department of Domestic Affairs. The applicant had to describe the type of disaster, the place and date and the type of wounds suffered. In the case of a house, the level of damage had to be elaborated. Photographs, if any, could be submitted and they could be helpful in expediting the process. It was not unlike filling in an insurance claim. The donations were in the form of cheque, cash or in kind like foodstuffs, medicines, school uniforms, etc. They were handed over directly in the local sites of the office of the local government where the disaster took place. When the situation made the journey to the locality of the disaster impossible, it was handed over in the representative office in Jakarta. Lately, the foundation has started to work closely with the government. Sending aid, especially to places beyond Java, is usually difficult in this vast country. Some never reach the intended parties due to bureaucracy or corruption. In this respect, international organisations, too, have set bad examples: one year after the tsunami in 2004, many victims were still living in tents in Aceh, while staff of international organisations that were there to help were often spotted staying in hotels and drinking beer.

As of September 2005, the deposits of Yayasan Gotong Royong had exceeded Rp65 billion, almost double that deposited in 1998. This was mainly due to undistributed interest that had been ploughed back into the principal.

As this foundation had been the brainchild of the late Ibu Tien and considering the very nature of its aims, almost all of Pak Harto's children and their spouses are members. As a result, this was the main reason for the accusation that the foundations Pak Harto had built were there to enrich his family. This was where the line between the donations from the conglomerates and his children's involvement in the conglomerates' businesses became blurred to many observers. Looking back, it would perhaps have been best if his children had formed their own foundations, raised funds from their own friends and stayed away from the foundations linked to Pak Harto as the president. The public would inevitably be critical of the involvement of his family members, regardless of the number of times Pak Harto had declared that in the seven Yayasan he had formed, his role was that of a private citizen.

After Ibu Tien passed away on 26 April 1996, the management asked for the family's consent to rename the Yayasan "Yayasan Dana Gotong Royong Kemanusiaan Siti Hartinah Soeharto".

YAYASAN DANA SEJAHTERA MANDIRI (Damandiri)

This was the last foundation I visited as I completed my research. I met Prof (Dr) Haryono Suyono and Subiakto Tjakrawerdaja on 11 October 2005. Haryono Suyono was the State Minister of Population/Chairman of the National Family Planning Board from 1993 to 1998 and became State Minister of People's Welfare and Poverty Eradication/Chairman of National Family Planning Board from 1998, that was dissolved on 22 May 1998. Subiakto Tjakrawerdaja was the Minister of Cooperatives and Small Enterprises from 1993 to 1998. Haryono Suyono is good looking, very energetic and charming, with the skills of a star performer. His picture is often in the newspapers as he goes about on Yayasan Damandiri's work. Subiakto is quieter by nature, but he was also very informative and helpful during my visit. Rumour has it that this is the richest of all the Yayasan and this was where Pak Harto had to "put the gun" to the conglomerates when he asked them to meet in Tapos and Jimbaran, Bali, to give contributions. This was also the last Yayasan he managed to form before his resignation There is a close association between Yayasan Damandiri and the government, in terms of the former's role in the area of social welfare.

Yayasan Damandiri was formed on 15 January 1996. The name stands for Yayasan Dana Sejahtera Mandiri, which refers to self-reliance. The success of President Soeharto's presidency should not be separated from the reduction of poverty in the country. In 1993 to 1994, the level of poverty was 12 to 13 per cent, down from 60 to 70 per cent in the 1970s. It went down further to 11 per cent in 1996. Nevertheless, the government noted that the downward trend had been slower since the early 1990s. The government soon identified the reason: the very poor were still there in the remote rural areas. As a result, the president issued Inpres for Desa Tertinggal or the villages left behind in the nation's development due to their remote locations. The international community had highly praised Indonesia's success in the field of family planning, whereby families were encouraged to have no more than two children, referred to as Keluarga Sejahtera. Yet, this was not enough to reduce poverty at all levels. The question was how to improve the standard of living in remote places. In 1993, Inpres Desa Tertinggal (IDT) identified families within the classification of being "extremely poor", where they were only able to eat once a day. Within this classification, there were 22,000 villages. To resolve this problem, the government needed a budget of Rp20 million per annum. The funds were meant to be paid up capital for them to start businesses. Considering that a minimum of three years would be needed for a business to take off, more capital was needed to make it a success.

At the same time, there was potential in the rural areas, as rural areas usually have more in terms of natural resources. However, the big cities have lured people away from the villages, in the belief that job opportunities were more plentiful in the cities. Those who went to the big cities were more often than not unskilled. The situation reminded President Soeharto of his own decision to leave Kemusuk years ago to look for a better life in Yogya. He asked his team to come up with a solution for resolving this issue. They had to consider what resources were present and to devise a method or approach to manage the resources which could be combined with a strategy for growth and to link it with the village or rural population. In a nutshell, to convince the people to remain in the villages with good jobs and be happy with their lives in the villages.

The sudden influx of people into the big cities had resulted in abundant workers, which the government had to absorb by employing them as municipal administrative workers. However, the consequence of this was that it made the bureaucracy worse. Although this approach was the easiest way for the government to create employment, President Soeharto felt it was a shortsighted solution. In the long run, it would not be effective. Another negative effect was that property speculation started to emerge in the big cities. This made the economy over-heated. Traffic congestion over the last 20 years has also damaged the quality of life in major cities. The worst impact has probably been the erosion of the people's sense of identity and moral values. With more people cramped into each city, life becomes competitive and the rules of the jungle take over, where survival of the fittest becomes the ultimate prize. The hospitality that the Indonesian people were known for descended into aggression and selfishness. Therefore, encouraging the rural population to remain in their villages became vital in the national development plan.

Therefore, from 1995, the spirit of being proud of one's village, *Bangga Suka Desa*, was introduced. Its focal point was to encourage the people to be self-reliant by increasing productivity through entrepreneurship. A village should be able to create job opportunities and absorb the existing workforce. Agriculture-based businesses were obviously one of the best options. The government came up with the model "*Pelaju, petik, olah, jual dan untung*" or to pick, to process, to sell and make profits. Each village was to consider what were the best resources they had. The next step was to process the assets so that they could be turned into saleable products. The final product was, firstly, for their own consumption, and secondly, if there was any surplus, they could be sold to make a profit. This would be the ideal way for a village to be self-reliant. The government also came up with another model, "*Pemaju, proses, kemas, jual dan untung*" or processing, packaging, selling and making profit. It was a chain action situation, where one stage was linked to another. This would also mean that the village inhabitants would have a chance to participate in each step of the process in accordance with their abilities. This way, the government could stop the ongoing exodus into the big cities.

The success of the family planning programme enabled the government to focus on improving the standard of living of the very poor. The village family units were grouped into "*Pra-Sejahtera*", the very poor, and "*Sejahtera*", the poor. It rating system went further into "*Sejahtera I, II, III*" and "*Sejahtera-Plus*". In ascending order, it ranged from extremely poor, very poor, poor, minimal income to those with an acceptable living standard. Surprisingly, the extremely poor and very poor were found in non-IDT villages as well. Thus, the number of extremely poor and very poor had increased from a total of 22,000 to 38,000 villages, or 17.8 million people, from 1990 to 1995. Those were the figures as of 1995, with a breakdown of the numbers into 6.3 million in IDT and 11.5 million in non-IDT villages.

The government realised that their objective to improve the living conditions of the very poor would not be possible without the participation of the private sector. This was in line with President Soeharto's policy to encourage private groups to make use of his economic plan to gain benefits, and to ask them for "payback" in the form of welfare contributions when their businesses reaped millions of US dollars in profit. This had been his strategy from the beginning.

Liem Sioe Liong, the richest man in the country, was asked to join Yayasan Damandiri. Liem was one of the founders and he sat on the management board as well. It was a brilliant move, as Liem would undoubtedly bring in members of the other conglomerates, such as Eka Widjaya, Prayogo Pangestu and Sudwikatmono. Less than a week after he had invited the conglomerates to meet in Jimbaran and Tapos, Yayasan Damandiri managed to collect Rp23 billion. However, it had not been smooth sailing all along. In the beginning, the conglomerates tried to drag their feet. As a result, President Soeharto saw the need to press organisations and individuals with a net income of over Rp100 million to donate 2 per cent of their annual takings. In 1995, he issued Keppres. First, he used a soft approach and used words to the effect of "persuaded to give donation". This Keppres was soon amended in 1996 and more pressure was used: "obliged to donate". This was sadly the result of the conglomerates' own fault and selfishness as their sense of patriotism came under question by the public at large. At that stage, the conglomerates had expanded their businesses not only in terms of numbers but also in terms of branches located in foreign countries. A few had subsidiaries or had invested in Singapore, Hong Kong, Australia and America. The public knew that their initial capital for expansion had been from the profits of doing business in Indonesia. It was at this time that the president had trouble trying to rein them in—it was like trying to slow down horses in a race.

In addition to pressing the conglomerates for contributions, the government commenced its campaign of "Gerakan Sadar Menabung" to promote awareness of the importance to save. Pak Harto was so personally involved in this issue that in October 1995, he wrote a poem about the benefits of saving for old age. This was, in fact, his approach and belief in handling matters, that personal involvement was the best way to promote a new concept. For months, he and Ibu Tien had travelled to every corner of the country to promote immunisation. Their pictures were found everywhere, even hanging in major streets to endorse family planning. He spent hours meeting the farmers and pictures showed his face beaming with happiness. President Soeharto has been aptly called "Anak Desa", the village boy. I saw how happy he was amongst the people at the grassroots level when we visited Kemusuk before the fasting month on 23 September 2005. He seemed very much at home, relaxed and happy among the villagers, the same feeling which I am sure my father had whenever he visited a *kampong*. Many of the country's leaders try to be "Westernised" and behave proud to be "city" men. They seem to want so much to portray themselves as being modernised and behave as if they feel embarrassed of their roots. Ironically, these are usually the intellectuals who have obtained higher education.

The awareness to save campaign was implemented by providing each person with a savings book with an opening balance of Rp2,000 which the government had deposited on their behalf. Eleven and a half million people received this savings book. It had not been easy to print 11 million savings books and had taken months at considerable cost. The savings was called *Tabungan Keluarga Sejahtera* (Takesra) or savings for prosperity. By producing the savings book, the holder could borrow from Bank BNI and PT Pos Indonesia. They could borrow 10 times of the given amount or Rp20,000. The loan was called *Kredit Keluarga Sejahtera* (Kukesra) and it was for the savings book holder to start a productive business, but it was not credit for consumption. Once the business makes a profit, 10 per cent is to be placed back as additional savings. Hence, the savings would increase to say Rp4,000. The savings book holder could then borrow 10 times or Rp40,000 for the next stage of developing his business. With this formula, in the next five stages, he would be able to borrow up to Rp320,000, a substantial amount for a business located within a village environment. This was the method by which the government had trained them to do business. Up to 2005, a total number of 11.5 million families in non-IDT villages have participated in the savings scheme and 8.3 million have taken the loan. While for IDT villages, over 79,000 joined the savings scheme and over 23,000 took part in the loan scheme.

My discussions with Yayasan Damandiri highlighted Try Sutrisno's comments about Pak Harto that he was a person who would always seek a solution by looking at the roots of a problem and then arrive at the solution in one complete strategy which enclosed everything related to it. He always found solutions in a single grand strategy and never on a piecemeal basis. Yayasan Damandiri had spent a total of Rp22.9 billion for Takesra in non-IDT villages and Rp12.6 billion in IDT villages as well as Rp396.7 billion in Kukesra in non-IDT villages and Rp63 billion in Kukesra in IDT villages; and, finally, the foundation had also extended credit for micro businesses to the tune of Rp250 billion. Thus, there was a trickle down from the rich to the poor, although a strong hand was needed to effect it. I left the meeting in satisfaction and with relief. I hope that those whose lives had been helped by one of Pak Harto's Yayasan would one day have the courage to publicly acknowledge the help received.

My meetings with the management of the Yayasan have expanded my horizon on how complicated it is to rule a country like Indonesia. Most importantly, the original concept of the Yayasan was a commendable one and provided valuable lessons to be learned. With improvements and more transparency, the Yayasan could serve as a bridge between the government and the private sector in a joint effort to move Indonesia towards becoming a prosperous nation, as had been envisioned by the nation's founding fathers. It is necessary for others to step forward and explain in writing about the strengths of the Yayasan instead of their focusing on their weaknesses. Nothing is perfect in life and it is only within this perspective that we can hope, one day, that the nation's founding fathers' dream will come true.

BANPRES (PRESIDENTIAL ASSISTANCE)

The private sector was also asked to help Banpres (Bantuan Presiden) or the Presidential Assistance scheme. Banpres funds initially came from the monopoly of cloves importation. President Soeharto had decided to give the monopoly to two companies. The public immediately jumped to conclusion that it was a lucrative undertaking as cloves are used in huge quantities in the local cigarette factories. The local cigarettes *kretek* are smoked by close to 75 per cent of Indonesian male adults. It is a big business with skyrocketing profits. One of the groups designated to import cloves was PT Mercubuana, headed by Probosutedjo. The other was PT Mega, led by Liem Sioe Liong. Probosutedjo was President Soeharto's half-brother and Liem Sioe Liong was a close friend. The two companies each received only 2 per cent of the profits, while the rest of the profits went to Banpres. From each company, Banpres received Rp128 billion. Pak Harto admitted this was an ample amount. The funds were deposited in the state banks and only the interest was used by Banpres. The public was outraged when President Soeharto chose PT Mercubuana and PT Mega. In his biography, the president had stated that if only the public knew that the proportion of the profits which the two companies were allowed to retain was a mere 2 per cent, their reaction would have been different. At the same time, PT Mercubuana and PT Mega had to borrow from the banks to import the cloves. Thus, the 2 per cent fees had to cover the interest that the bank charged for lending them money. The people grumbled, but no ministers dared to challenge this policy publicly. President Soeharto admitted that he had been blamed for the monopoly but it did not bother him considering that Banpres was able to get hold of Rp250 billion.[7]

The biggest Banpres recipient was the military hospital, RSPAD Gatot Subroto, which received an amount of Rp40 billion. Banpres gave assistance to farmers, those involved in other husbandry work, etc, for instance, those who wanted to grow the Hibrida coconut, an African coconut. Indonesia was already over-populated, with the majority of the poor among the lower class. They still subscribed to the belief that the more children they had, the better off they would be. This might have beeen true when the society was still at the stage of traditional farming, when the land was ploughed by water buffaloes pushed by men. However, this was not the situation and the associated hardship was what President Soeharto wanted to change. He had learnt from his ancestors about planting a coconut tree when a child was born. The coconut tree would grow and bear fruit as the child grew. By the time the child was ready to go to school, the coconut could be harvested for sale. It served as additional earnings to cover the child's education. In the family planning programme, a coconut seed for planting was given to each couple as a reward. That was the link between Banpres, family planning and the cultivation of the Hibrida coconut. Under Banpres, financial support was given to growers of Hibrida in Nusa Tenggara Barat, Aceh, Sulawesi and many other regions.

The same applied with regards to the improvement of farming in Nusa Tenggara Barat by using a method called *gogo rancah* (GORA). GORA was used for cultivating the land so that it became more suitable for farming. Banpres also helped the farmers in East and Central Java with the initial costs of increasing rice cultivation. Once the land issue was dealt with, it was easier for the farmers to do their farming under an improved infrastructure. In Aceh, each farmer was given Rp300 million to improve their growing of nuts. The land had been nurtured such that the farmers did not need to encroach into the forests. This helped to avoid soil erosion and maintained the greenery of *terra firma*. Banpres also helped to improve the process of clove budding. President Soeharto did not want to kill the cow that gave life to his project. By providing seeds to the farmers where the soil was suitable for clove growing, such as in Central Sulawesi, it soon enriched the local farmers. Banpres also helped hospitals to buy medical equipment for their Intensive Care Units (ICU). It also financed those who needed medical treatment abroad. Political parties other than Golkar received assistance under Banpres, too. President Soeharto stood firm on his view that through the role of Banpres, the government could be aided in developing the country faster. He had repeatedly said that the people could not depend solely on the government and that the principle of *gotong royong* should be used to push the wheel of development.

The ministers seemed to have no objections, a pattern that was followed for the rest time of his time in power. His ministers believed that he had excellent instincts for making things move in the right direction. His policies to help students through Yayasan Supersemar seemed to work well. His strategy to help those left behind in the country's development drive through the use of his foundations like Trikora, Dharmais, YAMP and others seemed to function well. His direct involvement in raising capital for his pet foundations symbolised his desire to have the dreams of the nation's founding fathers come true. More importantly, it gave legitimacy to his government.

IBU TIEN'S FOUNDATIONS

As far as Ibu Tien was concerned, she had supported her husband's strategy for managing the country's social welfare issues wholeheartedly as she had faith in it. The most notable foundation she built was Taman Mini Indonesia Indah, the Miniature Indonesia complex.

Her initial idea came about on 13 March 1970 and construction started on 30 June 1972. It was formally opened on 20 April 1975 and contained a model of Indonesia on a miniature scale. Located on 150 hectares of land, it illustrated the natural wealth and the diverse and rich culture of the archipelago. Ibu Tien felt that until the end of the 1960s, President Soeharto's plan to develop Indonesia spiritually had not been properly taken care of. The nation's development could not focus on the economic aspect alone but had to take into account the people's spiritual development as well, which encompassed elements such as education and culture. Only then, together with technology, would the country be able to achieve prosperity for all.

The president had said, "Economic development could not be taken without the growth of mental, spiritual, intellectual and social values." In education, he wanted the younger generation to learn organisational skills as well, in order to be responsible citizens. He believed that the people could and should learn from the outside world while maintaining their own Indonesian identity. Thus, Taman Mini was built, mainly for the younger Indonesians to understand and learn about their country's rich cultural diversities and natural resources. At that point in time, Indonesia had 27 provinces and the buildings depicted the architecture of each region and served as a museum with exhibitions of the local costumes, dances and music. Typical tools, ceremonies, sports, fauna and flora were shown in each pavilion. Performances and special exhibitions of local foods and handicrafts were held from time to time. The message was to understand and love one's own country.

A museum stood nearby, named Purna Bhakti Pertiwi. It had taken five years to build, from 1987 and to 1992. It stood on an area of 19,73 hectares and was formally opened on 23 August 1993 on Ibu Tien's 70th birthday. The building covered 25,095 square metres and included a library. Titiek, Pak Harto's second daughter, said her mother had come up with the original idea for this museum as her parents had received so many souvenirs and could not keep them all in Jalan Cendana; in addition, Ibu Tien felt that these gifts should be shared with the public. Some were state gifts from foreign heads of state and other national leaders.

Whilst undertaking the research for this book, I visited the museum in December 2004. The museum was well kept and clean, with a huge car park (we were driven in a cart to the main entrance). The exhibits were well recorded, with each cabinet holding a collection of gifts such as gold or silver. Not too many visitors were present on the day of my visit as it was a weekday. I was told that on weekends, there would be more guests, especially students. There was also a library, but, regretfully, it did not have many books.

Strolling through the cold place, it gave the impression that the museum was barely on the brink of survival. It was a poignant experience and invoked a similar sadness if one was to assess Pak Harto's legacy. I felt that it was necessary to consider how much money would be needed to maintain the museum, as the air-conditioning alone would cost a fortune. My guess was not wrong as I was informed that the museum faced financial problems in 2005. Yayasan Purna Bhakti Pertiwi also owned Taman Buah Mekarsari, a fruit and horticulture garden which was now under the charge of Pak Harto's youngest daughter, Mamiek. Mamiek is a graduate from Bogor Institute of Farming. Like Tapos for animal breeding, Mekarsari is intended for the development of research for improving fruit products for domestic consumption and export. Another of Ibu Tien's foundations,

Yayasan Harapan Kita, helped to build a maternity and children's hospital: RS Anak dan Bersalin Harapan Kita is now one of the best places for women's treatments. Pak Harto's six children started Yayasan Mangadeg to build a mausoleum for their ancestors, including Ibu Tien's final resting place.

FINAL THOUGHTS

Very few people know the facts to fully understand the complexity of how the Yayasan is run. In the face of the huge allegation of corruption against Pak Harto, the fate of the Yayasan hangs in the balance. To me, it feels like the foundations are being robbed progressively of all the good intentions they were established upon. The original intention and good concept of the Yayasan should not be neglected and should be forwarded to the younger generation, but they would have to detach themselves from the sense of self-interest which seems to consume their thoughts and behaviour.

Personally, I feel that it is necessary to press home the point that if President Soeharto had indeed accumulated billions of dollars as alleged, where would all of this money be? So far, there has been no proof that this money exists. Pak Harto has refused to go abroad even for his medical treatments, when most of the country's leaders would have done so as a first choice even for minor illnesses. Pak Harto has renounced all speculations that he would leave Indonesia to live abroad. Like Bung Karno, he has said that he would choose to die in his own country. If both Bung Karno and Pak Harto have been as corrupt as alleged, they could and would have easily moved out of Indonesia to enjoy their wealth in peace.

Lee Kuan Yew wrote:[8]

> The fortunes he and his family had were invested in Indonesia. The American journalist who had reported in *Forbes* magazine that the Suharto family had US$42 billion of assets, told me in New York in October 1998 that the bulk of it was in Indonesia. After the Indonesian meltdown, he estimated them to be worth a mere US$4 billion.

When I asked him, Pak Harto replied, "Yes, it is the foundation money," with a twinkle in his eye. A sense of satisfaction lingered behind his benign smile. He looked physically old and weak, but I could see that his spirit to defend the foundations he had built had not faded away.

The establishment of President Soeharto's foundations embraced President Soeharto's views on the status of the minority Chinese in the country. President Soeharto stated his stand on this issue firmly. To enable his development plan to succeed, the underlying jealousy towards the Chinese could not continue. A clear distinction had to be drawn between the Chinese and the Chinese who were Indonesian citizens. All Indonesian citizens, irrespective of origins, were equal in law, both in their rights and obligations. Those of Chinese origins were encouraged to integrate and assimilate with the *pribumi*. A few even went so far as to change their names; Liem Sioe Liong, for instance, became Sudono Salim.

During the G30S incident, the main suspect behind the communist *coup* had been China. The very sensitive issue of racism was heightened by the fact that although they were the minority group, the Chinese controlled close to 70 per cent of the economy. President Soeharto needed the business expertise of the Chinese to be the engine of the country's development growth. President Soekarno allowed the Chinese to be active in politics and government, but President Soeharto steered and contained them in economic matters only. His opponents laid blame on this policy as, in their view, as a result of this policy, the Chinese had applied all their energy purely to business. Many felt that this policy boomeranged in 1998, when he was unable to stop their self-indulgence. As businessmen, the Chinese bowed to his wishes, including donating to his foundations when asked. Business and politics exist together like in a marriage; one has to act in concert with the other. Business requires political and social stability to turn in profits. Businessmen have to be alert and take opportunities as and when they arise. This is the very nature of businessmen. The businessmen did not mind contributing to President Soeharto's foundations as long as it ensured political and social stability. They considered the donations a cost of doing business. When the time came and the opportunity presented itself, they would ensure that they were able to recover this cost.

Any writer broaching the subject of President Soeharto's successes and failures cannot avoid the relationship between his children and the Chinese businessmen. Probosutedjo, a businessman and Soeharto's half brother, had written openly about it in his book.

When President Soeharto was in power, many trailed his path for self-serving reasons, including the Chinese businessmen and his officials who spotted the opportunity to exploit his children. President Soeharto's children were tempted with easy businesses that required minimal work. In most cases, the children were treated as "door openers" to lucrative business deals. Some people believe that President Soeharto himself was corrupt from the beginning, a notion which my father and I have never agreed with. In the case of his children, I believe that in their naivety and away from the guidance of their parents who were busy with affairs of the country, the children were persuaded to enter into business.

A few people I know have admitted that in the beginning, the children were meant to undertake apprenticeships in these organisations. However, instead of being taught to run a business, they were used as shortcuts to make quick profits. Regrettably, the children did not pursue academic achievements.

President Soeharto was not fully aware as to what had gone wrong. The children may not have realised that they were being exploited. This is the tragedy.

When he came to power, President Soeharto's plan to govern was relatively simple: to improve the country's standard of living and to continue President Soekarno's policy of avoiding foreign interference in the country. He established and developed concepts and notions close to his heart, like the foundations, through a mixture of gifts and donations, voluntary or forced, from those he felt should rightly be called upon to contribute. This could well have been the practice in a Javanese court. When asked if he was "a mega sultan in a mega country", his reply was that Indonesia was a mega country but not all sultans were bad. There is certainly some truth in his words.

President Soeharto is often described as a simple man with simple tastes, that he ruled more with intuition rather than polished intelligence. He is not highly literate, but he admires those who are and has referred to and used their advice and wisdom. He has an extraordinary talent in being able to identify the right person for the right job at the right time. Timing appears to have been of utmost importance in all the major decisions he has made. He formed his foundations in stages. He used each opportunity to consider the country's needs and the reason for the formation of each foundation; most significantly, whom to target as donors and why it would be difficult for them to refuse. He did not ask for the businessmen's participation before their businesses took off, he approached them to donate only after their businesses had flourished. He made the benefits of their contributions very clear to them. He relied more on common sense and intuition, and less on theoretical principles.

This was the same approach he had used in defending why he had allowed the conglomerates to grow. He felt that citizens who had grown rich should, in turn, contribute towards his development programme and their contribution would function as a sample of the success that could be achieved and hence be an inspiration for others.

Through his foundations, President Soeharto had hoped that the rich would have an opportunity to show the poor that there was no cause for envy, by demonstrating that they were caring and willing to share their wealth with the poor and the destitute. This was a fundamental part of his development plan and what he had meant when he said that the country's development had to include the moral and spiritual aspects of life. Problems arose when his policies were looked upon as a way of selling favours and nepotism. He might well have respected those who had the courage to refuse when faced with a request or demand for favours.

Soepardjo Roestam, while he was governor in Semarang, once informed President Soeharto that one of his sons was trying to get a government project in Central Java. President Soeharto had replied that it was for Soepardjo Roestam to make his own judgment on the matter, as being the governor, he would know best what was required in the situation. Soepardjo Roestam declined the project. My father believed that if only most officials had dared to say "no" like Soepardjo Roestam, things would have been different. However, there are always two sides to a coin. When Benny Moerdani advised him to slow down on his children's involvement in business, the advice reportedly cost him his job, but Benny Moerdani had taken a stand and accepted the consequences.

President Soeharto is known to be a person who loathed contradiction in public. My father always said that he had to approach him in the Javanese way: politely and indirectly, with gestures instead of spoken words. A student once related to me that my father had given President Soeharto a book on *wayang* called *Dosomuko*. This was not exactly a complimentary gesture, as the book referred to a person with ten faces. The student understood that President Soeharto had been upset and had thrown the book away. When I asked my father for confirmation of this incident, he had laughed and replied, "Maybe." The fact remains that they stayed on speaking terms and it did not cost my father his job. It was clearly important to seek out the right method and the right moment to forward any constructive criticism to the president.

An interesting point to note of the foundations that President Soeharto's children were involved in is that none of them included Yayasan Trikora, Yayasan Supersemar and YAMP. In the remaining four foundations, they participated in the activities that revolved around poverty eradication.

Each foundation has two levels of management: the day-to-day management and the supervisory board. The day-to-day executives handle the administrative work, while the supervisory board provided policy guidelines. The end of the financial year for bookkeeping falls on 31 of March. Three months after the end of each financial year, each board would meet to discuss the past year's operations and the next year's plan. Up to 1998, examination and verification of the figures were assigned to the State Secretariat to ensure that the disbursements of funds were fully accountable. Unfortunately, in the past, there had been no transparency and the public did not have access to information and the foundations therefore became the target of gossip and speculation. This was a major mistake on the part of the foundations.

On the other hand, contributors often did not want the public to know about their contributions as there was a fear that the publicity would result in many direct appeals from the public for financial help and if they refused, their businesses might be jeopardised. At the same time, the Yayasan probably preferred to do good deeds quietly. For whatever it is worth, Pak Harto genuinely believed that the foundations which he chaired were run in a professional manner.

The allegation of misuse and abuse of power against President Soeharto in relation to the foundations is also the result of his decision to use Inpres and Keppres as legal forms of executing his decisions. There might be some truth to this allegation. However, his counter-argument that the ministers and the legislative and judicial bodies were aware of the situation also made sense. During the euphoria of the early days of reformation, BJ Habibie had issued Keppres No 98/1998, the grounds used being to "support reformation" and the restructuring of the national economy. The decision was issued on 7 July 1998, less than two months after Pak Harto's termination of power. It was soon followed by Keppres 195/1998, relating to the new status of the seven foundations built by President Soeharto. After 1998, to enhance transparency, the Public Accountant took over the auditing of the foundations' financial statements. The lists of their assets were also forwarded to the Attorney General's Office. The managements had acted accordingly as required and to date, there have been no proof of misappropriation of funds. Pak Harto had been willing to hand over the foundations to his successor, if this was what the government wanted. At the same time, he warned them of the consequences: funds handed to the government would be automatically included into the state budget and any disbursements out of the state budget would require parliamentary approval. In short, the foundations' activities would be severely delayed, if not terminated for good. What would then happen to the orphanages, the students, and the small businesses?

When Megawati became the president, the law relating to the establishment of foundations was enhanced. She issued Keppres No 16/2001 on 6 August 2001, stating that the formation of the foundations had been based on tradition only and there had been no lawful ruling or basis to their formation. Yet, the foundations have been growing fast. Therefore, transparency and accountability were necessary to assure the public that the foundations were functioning as intended by the founders. The new Keppres set a strict ruling on the separation between the advisors, the supervisory board and the day-to-day management. None of them could sit in one and the other at the same time. Investments by the foundations were also set at a maximum of 20 per cent of their total assets. As in the case of regular corporations, the foundations needed a notary public to process the applications for their establishment, followed by approval from the Ministry of Justice and registration in the State Bulletin. In the beginning, none of the officials could receive a salary, but it was amended through Keppres No 28/2004 to allow full time workers to be compensated for their jobs. Their salaries would be in line with the financial standing of the foundations. The seven foundations have complied with the new law. A couple of very important aspects are the streamlining of the foundations' managements and the audited financial statement by the Public Accountant, a copy of which is sent to the State Secretariat.

The foundations' operations are now more transparent and the inflow and outflow of funds are properly recorded. The Public Accountant audits them on a yearly basis and if there is any indication of unusual transactions in the past, the data would be handed to the Attorney General's Office for review.

Each foundation's management may be asked for accountability as and when it is deemed necessary. To date, the foundations still run their businesses as usual and the original funds are still deposited with the state banks.

ENDNOTES

1 The MPR is the People's Consultative Assembly. It is the highest institution where te president has to give accountability for hir/her performance in carrying out the mandate that has been entrusted to him/her. For this reason, the president is also referred to as the "mandatory" of the MPR, that is, one who has been given the mandate by the MPR. The MPR has the right to accept or reject the accountability given by the president.

2 G Dwipayana and Ramadhan KH, *Soeharto, Pikiran, Ucapan, dan Tindakan Saya* (PT Citra Lamtoro Gung Persada, 1988), pp 283–293.

3 G Dwipayana and Ramadhan KH, *Soeharto, Pikiran, Ucapan, dan Tindakan Saya* (PT Citra Lamtoro Gung Persada, 1988), pp 525–529.

4 President BJ Habibie offered East Timor autonomy and independence in January 1999; following a referendum on 30 August 1999, East Timor was declared an independent state on 4 September 1999.

5 G Dwipayana and Ramadhan KH, *Soeharto, Pikiran, Ucapan, dan Tindakan Saya* (PT Citra Lamtoro Gung Persada, 1988), p 418.

6 This figure is based on information provided in a report by the Yayasan, signed and dated 21 October 2005.

7 G Dwipayana and Ramadhan KH, *Soeharto, Pikiran, Ucapan, dan Tindakan Saya* (PT Citra Lamtoro Gung Persada, 1988), p 292.

8 Lee Kuan Yew, *From Third World to First, The Singapore Story: 1965–2000* (Singapore Press Holdings and Times Editions, Singapore, 2000), p 318.

Chapter 5

REFLECTIONS

Many a friendship,
long, loyal and self-sacrificing,
rested at first on no thicker a foundation
than a kind word.
— Frederick Faber

It is no exaggeration to say that only a super-human would be able to keep his or her health unaffected by the drastic turn of events in life. It is said that it is easier to ascend to than descend from power. This is especially so if the twists of fate include deceit and betrayal from those whom one has trusted and placed great faith in. There is no doubt that the accusations and the court hearings were a huge burden on Pak Harto and they affected his health badly. There are two very important issues which must have hurt Pak Harto deeply. Firstly, the challenge to his honesty and, secondly, the legacy that he wanted to leave. There should be no question of whether President Soeharto was a liar or a crook. His departure from office in such ill repute was no doubt related to his overindulgence towards his children and family. Alternatively, could the public perception have arisen from the impression that President Soeharto was not unlike a sultan who thought that his children were entitled to live as princes and princesses? If this was true, why did President Soeharto feel more at ease among the farmers and why was the behaviour of his children so down to earth? Those who supported him defended him and blamed it on the fact that he had over-trusted his cronies and his children had not been smart enough to realise that they were being used by a number of businessmen.

There is some truth to this: President Soeharto had lost control and his children were unable to see that their business interests would cost their father and his legacy dearly. Nevertheless, it is pointless to cry over spilt milk. All they can do now is to brace themselves, face the accusations and accept them as very costly lessons. They can talk openly now about the harsh treatment they received after Pak Harto had stepped down. They faced the trials with inner strength and are now focusing on Pak Harto's state of health. They have continued practising Javanese traditions at home, having *selamatan* and *tumpeng* on Pak Harto's birthdays, and continue to behave *alus* and *rukun* in public. They still have *sesajen* during *ruwah* and they, Pak Harto included, have kept their sense of humour intact.

Nevertheless, after the interrogation on 9 December 1998, Pak Harto's health started to deteriorate steadily. Still, it is astounding that someone who had been so powerful was, within a short period of time, dragged through so much dirt by his closest protégé, and yet was able to weather it with dignity. Not many people would have been able to remain as composed as he had, if they did not have as sound a conviction in their destiny as Pak Harto had in his, but the pressure took a huge toll on his health. The medical reports from his own team of doctors and the team appointed by the government on how the mounting stress was affecting the health of this ageing man from day to day made for poignant reading. As a private citizen, Pak Harto is a decent person with a gentle soul and, as the president, he has done so much for the country, even though along the way he had made big mistakes.

In this context, the performance of Indonesia's leaders should be considered based equally upon *das sollen*, or what it should have been, and *das sein*, or what it is. The two notions viewed together remind us not to be naive, whether in considering myth (*das sollen*) or reality (*das sein*). The myth refers to what Indonesia should be in comparison with the more developed nations. However, it should be borne in mind that the developed countries look upon other less developed countries from their own perspective and their own interests. President Soekarno and President Soeharto felt that what was best for the developed nations would also be good for Indonesia, but this was not entirely true. The same applies to the views and opinions of foreign observers about the country's two leaders: they theorise about what the two Indonesian presidents could have done differently during their respective rules, but the question remains as to whether their theories would have worked as anticipated if they had been applied in reality. On the other hand, Indonesia's intellectuals must tread with care and caution as well. President Soeharto had admired BJ Habibie because President Soeharto himself had received limited schooling while BJ Habibie had a good education. Pak Harto thought Indonesia would be better off with an intellectual like him at the helm. However, Pak Harto had managed to govern the country for over 30 years with a record of impressive developments, while BJ Habibie's biggest achievement was the loss of East Timor during a short tenure of less than two years as the president. Thus, it is important for the younger generation to realise that Indonesia should not blindly follow the standards set by other developed nations or believe without question what foreign observers and commentators have said about the country's leaders; everything should be taken with a pinch of salt.

More importantly, my father and I believe that President Soekarno and President Soeharto were equal in terms of their patriotism. President Soekarno had said, "Big nations should honour and respect their big leaders," while President Soeharto had abided by the philosophy "*mikul dhuwur, mendhem jero*". There is no obstacle in the path of the Indonesian people learning the best from both the East and the West. Why should we look only at things on the outside, when there is wisdom within sight in our own country, people and culture? Let us not forget that while the grass appears greener on the other side of the fence, there is also much greenery that grows within that should not be overlooked.

PAK HARTO'S STATE OF HEALTH

Since the beginning of 1999, Pak Harto has been in and out of hospital. A cardiovascular disorder affected him in July 1999 and he was hospitalised for 10 days. In September of the same year, he suffered a massive gastrointestinal bleeding. In addition to malaria which he had suffered during his younger days, Pak Harto has also been diagnosed with minor chronic diseases since 1949. Early one morning in September 2000, a black car left Jalan Cendana and drove Pak Harto, accompanied by his eldest daughter Tutut, to Rumah Sakit Pusat Pertamina (RSPP). He had to have his health checked in compliance with the initial court proceedings. In the beginning, the Attorney General's Office had wanted him to go to Rumah Sakit Umum Pusat Nasional Dr Cipto Mangunkusumo (RSUP). For security reasons, that decision was changed. This was just one of the many medical trips which Pak Harto had to undertake to check the state of his health to comply with the court proceedings.

Pak Harto was 79 years old by that time. That morning, he was examined by no less than a combination of five medical teams (!), whose members were chosen from amongst the best doctors and professors from the country's famous universities and organisations such as University Indonesia, University Gadjah Mada, University Airlangga, the Association of Indonesian Medical Doctors and the Indonesian Ministry of Health. The national team of doctors presented the results on 27 September to the State Court of South Jakarta. The tests revealed that he had had heart problems since 1949, a kidney operation in 1978, a prostate operation in 1982, and high blood pressure since 1990 which was likely to worsen. Most importantly, he had already suffered three strokes by that time. He was cooperative during the examination, but found it difficult to communicate. His ability to absorb information was poor and he could express only very simple views. Thus, when faced with long or complex sentences, he was unable to reply appropriately. His speech did not necessarily reveal what he intended to say. His thought processes were slow. The tests showed that he was experiencing difficulty in making comparisons and could understand simple ideas only. His sense of reasoning stayed within the boundaries of short words. His learning ability also decreased as he could not receive, execute or respond to new information.

During the physical examination, Pak Harto was cooperative and tried to do his best as instructed. In the past, his ability to grasp the economic team's concepts on new policies quickly was one of his strengths, but when the medical team gave him a "General Comprehension Test", his score was only 8 out of 20. Tests relating to problem solving, comprehension and mathematics gave similar results. His "cognitive flexibility" and "abstract reasoning" ability was also further weakened by his advanced age. When his blood pressure rose during the tests, especially during the "General Comprehension Test", the doctors gave him easier and less stressful tests. A comprehensive course of treatments that he had undergone for over six months concluded that there had been no improvement or progress. He was given a test and he scored 65 out of 100. It meant that he was moderately dependent. Using the test and scoring system Hachinski modified by Eisdover (1986), his average result was between 1 and 2 out of 10; this indicated "multi infarct dementia". His psychiatric test also reinforced the presence of "multi infarct dementia" and showed disguised depression. The dementia was the outcome of repeated strokes. When he was asked why he was taken to the hospital, he replied: "Because the Attorney General wants it." When he was asked why the Attorney General had wanted him to have a check-up, he replied, "I do not know." When his family asked him to go for the check-up, he replied in Javanese, "*Ana apa maneh?*" ("What else?"), when in fact the family had already shown him the letter from the Attorney General. Consequently, his children, especially his daughters, have stayed on guard by his side, restricting the newscasts that he watched on television and approving only selected people to visit him. It is not difficult to understand and sympathise with Pak Harto's children. In his daily routine, Pak Harto is still able to eat by himself, move from his wheelchair to his bed and take a shower on his own. He is able to get dressed, walk and go up and down short flights of stairs by himself. However, he rarely has the energy to indulge in his former hobbies and has given up golf and tennis, and rarely goes fishing.

Pak Harto's appearance did not manifest the true extent of his condition but the result of the "Moral Impairment Test" and the "Geriatric Depression Scale" said it all. The questionnaires which related to self-esteem indicated his true feelings of being useless and isolated. The tests had to be discontinued due to a life threatening surge in his heart rate and blood pressure. In short, the medical team's analysis found that he was unfit to stand trial, with his incompetent state being permanent in nature. Some people may think that it was an opportune time for him to have this medical finding, as the interrogation stage in the trial had just begun. On the other hand, it could also be considered bad timing as he had wanted to clear his name and this would have been his opportunity to do so once and for all. Some may consider it a blessing that the stroke made it difficult for him to communicate, while others may consider his condition to be God's will in preventing the interrogation from proceeding. Nonetheless, the prosecutor has asked that the case be assessed by the higher courts.

As a result of the skepticism surrounding the medical team's findings, the doctors involved felt offended, as they were reputed to be the country's best doctors. They believed they had been professional and had paid high regard to medical ethics, and had been disciplined under their oath to be impartial. In their report dated 27 September 2000, the doctors concluded that a person was incompetent to stand trial if he or she had lost the ability to comprehend the nature and objective of the court hearing and/or to consult his or her legal representative. Nineteen experts signed a report stating that he was emotionally depressed and concluded that Pak Harto was unfit and not competent to stand trial. They attached 21 sheets of medical literature as supporting evidence for their conclusion. These were the findings of the brightest doctors from the best medical institutions in the country. A few days later, the team gave a presentation to the judges on why Pak Harto was unable to stand trial. The reasons given were the high risk of cardiovascular problems, his memory loss and speech difficulty. The nature of his condition was permanent. Subsequently, the judges decided that trial would not be possible. Through their decision delivered on 28 September 2000, the case was considered closed and removed from the State Court of South Jakarta and sent back to the Attorney General's Office. Pak Harto was also released from city arrest.

Nevertheless, the prosecutor appealed to the High Court on 3 October 2000, on the basis that under section 23 of Law No 3, 1971, a court hearing could proceed without the presence of the accused in a corruption case. The appeal was forwarded to Pak Harto on 6 October 2000. In its decision on 8 November 2000, the High Court in Jakarta decided to allow the appeal and revoked the State Court of South Jakarta's verdict delivered on 28 September 2000 and instructed the State Court of South Jakarta to reopen and review the case, and to detain HM Soeharto under city arrest. His team of lawyers appealed to the Supreme Court on 23 November 2000. In February 2001, Pak Harto underwent an appendectomy. On 2 February 2001, the Indonesian Supreme Court stated that the prosecutor was to ensure that Pak Harto received proper treatment until he was fit to stand trial. This meant that Pak Harto's court case could be reopened at any time.

In real terms, this meant that the Supreme Court had ignored the opinion of the medical experts. The Supreme Court stated on 21 February 2001 that they could not accept the prosecutor's appeal to proceed with the hearing without the presence of the accused and that the state was to bear the cost of all medical treatments until HM Soeharto was fully recovered, after which he should be brought back to trial. Pak Harto's condition worsened after he was fitted with a permanent pacemaker on 13 June 2001. A team of doctors from RSUP Cipto Mangunkusumo stated, in a report dated 27 August 2001, that since 1990, Pak Harto has been suffering from hypertension and "diabetes mellitus". The report also mentioned that his previous check-up had revealed "chronic atrial fibrillation", "hypertension", "prostate hyperthrophy", "nephrolithiation", "hypercoagulation and hypoagregation", "multi infarct bihemispheric", "hemiparese duplex", "mixed non fluens aphasia" and "multi infarct dementia". Due to his advanced age, the "multiple infarct" was expanding to his brain. Combined with his incurable heart problems, the prognosis could not improve under the present ongoing treatment. On 11 December 2001, the Supreme Court decided that Pak Harto could not stand trial. Only the Attorney General's Office could decide whether his case could still proceed on the basis of criminal law. Meanwhile, from 17 to 23 December 2001, Pak Harto was once again hospitalised due to "bronchopneumonia duplex".

On 8 March 2002 the State Court of South Jakarta declared that they were unable to reopen the case of HM Soeharto. They would only accept the case after the defendant had recovered. In March 2002, Pak Harto suffered a second bout of massive gastrointestinal bleeding but on 23 May 2002, he attended his grandchild's wedding. The next day, in a local newspaper's headline "Who said President Soeharto is ill?", the article reported that he could walk without any help and was not in a wheelchair. Consequently, on 10 June 2002, another medical team was appointed to check the status of his health, this time from RSUP hospital, on the request of the Attorney General's Office. On 15 July 2002, the doctors published their findings that Pak Harto was still unable to explain his thoughts in more than four words and he was unable to understand long sentences or absorb complex verbal or non-verbal information. On 12 August 2002, the medical team forwarded the latest information on HM Soeharto's condition. Not only did the findings reinforce the previous one, but they also found new illnesses: he had irreversible "dementia vascular", problems in his speech and very limited ability in understanding things. His ability to understand what was said to him was very poor, there was an acute deterioration in his ability to express himself and in reaching conclusions. His fluctuating blood pressure would endanger his life if he was emotionally disturbed or put under pressure.

Ismail Saleh, the former Attorney General, said that as Pak Harto could not stand trial, the case should be discontinued once and for all. Pak Harto's family issued a statement, signed by Tutut, stating that they had no objections to Pak Harto's state of health being made public. They also wanted the government to respect Pak Harto's wishes that this would be the last examination that he would have to go through. They stated that there had already been many physical examinations conducted by teams of national or government doctors with the same results. In addition, his family asked the public to understand that Pak Harto had the right to continue his religious and humanitarian activities. They also pleaded for understanding that he still had family affairs to take care of, such as visiting Tommy who was in jail. More importantly, the doctors were of the opinion that such activities were therapeutic in nature and good for his health. The prohibition against his departure from the country based on the decision of the Attorney General's Office dated 12 April 2002 expired on 12 April 2003. From 27 May 2002 to 8 March 2004, the team of doctors explained his declining health to his personal doctor, Dr Hari Sabardi, that a "multi infarct" in his brain had broadened due to Pak Harto's age and heart problems; their entire prognosis indicated that it was impossible for him to recover.

The misery of undergoing continuous treatment did not abate. In April 2004, Pak Harto had a third massive gastrointestinal bleeding. In May 2005, he had a fourth massive bleeding in his gastrointestinal tract and a fifth occurred a few months later in November. That year, he stayed in hospital quite a few times. In February 2006, he suffered diarrhoea accompanied by bronchopneumonia, but was treated at home in Jalan Cendana.

Today, Pak Harto's appearance is indeed rather deceiving as he looks healthier in photographs than he really is in person. This could have been the result of his tough military training which has enabled him to carry himself well. However, on closer scrutiny, there is no question that his health has deteriorated. He is still able to respond with his usual benign smile, nod his head and shake hands, although more slowly than a normal person. It takes him a while before he is able to speak and respond to questions. He is able to absorb no more than a simple sentence and even so, one has to speak slowly to him. His verbal communication skills have become poor; he has difficulty finding the right words, has trouble speaking clearly and is unable to reply to direct questions.

Of late, my conversations with him have been limited to simple sentences. If I wanted to speak to him about an event from his past, I would have to create a story of when and where it happened, and only after such recounting and revival of the event in his mind would Pak Harto be able to give his recollection. If he failed to do so, his expression would change and he would get irritated and show his irritation and frustration through non-verbal gestures. Sometimes, he would slap his hand repeatedly on his knee to protest against my wrong interpretation or conclusion of what he had tried to convey. Hence, it was important that Suweden, Pak Harto's closest personal aide and retired Lieutenant Colonel, or Maliki, Pak Harto's personal aide in charge of administration and retired from the Military Police, were always near by. In such situations, they were the ones who could clarify what Pak Harto wanted to say or correct my mistaken conclusions. Only when Suweden or Maliki reached the correct conclusion would Pak Harto's face show his satisfaction. However, he looked happier if I was able to reach the right conclusion on my own.

In a relaxed environment, Pak Harto's responses were better and clearer as compared to when he was tired or after a long conversation. Tutut had asked me to stop when we were deep in conversation in Yogya in September 2005, because we had been on the road for a long time that morning. A few hours later, when Dr Hari Sabardi, Pak Harto's private doctor, took his blood pressure, it had indeed gone higher. Although these encounters have been sad experiences for me, I feel fortunate to have been able to visit him on those occasions, so that I could see with my own eyes how Pak Harto's health has really deteriorated and thus be in a better position to refute the allegations of those who do not believe the true state of his health and are quick to accuse him of faking it.

His ability to read has also deteriorated. It is best to read to him slowly and repeat words and phrases often. There were times when I felt exhausted (physically and mentally) after our talks, although they were rewarding experiences. After one of my conversations with him, I remembered an encounter I had with one of my former clients. The client had said loudly in public that Pak Harto enjoyed faking his ill health and he was sure that when Pak Harto was alone, he was having a good laugh at being able to fool everyone. As a person whose business had boomed under Pak Harto's term, his speaking in such a manner so loudly in public would undoubtedly provoke annoyance in any decent human being. I was lucky that my parents had taught me to retain my composure even in the most difficult of situations, as it provided me with the necessary restraint on hearing those dreadful comments. I responded with a few quiet words and reminded him that he had achieved success during Pak Harto's time in power. I am sure that this former client of mine is not the only person with such a view and behaviour; there must be tens if not hundreds of people who have spoken ill of Pak Harto after having made a fortune while he was still in power.

In his day to day life now, Pak Harto continues to practise military discipline: he is always punctual and never shows up late for appointments. During the Attorney General's hearing, he had arrived half an hour earlier while the investigators were late. Pak Harto's sense of punctuality is another of his qualities which my father had great admiration for, as it not only represented discipline but, more importantly, it also showed respect for others.

There are people who think that Pak Harto's court case could proceed *in absentia*. Ismail Saleh pointed out, however, that a trial *in absentia* was intended for the situation when an accused person could not be found, that is, for those who have disappeared from or flown the country, and in Pak Harto's case, he was present most of the time in Jalan Cendana. He had never disappeared nor run from Indonesia; in fact, he would refuse to leave even if he was forced to do so. Like his predecessor, President Soekarno, he intends to live in Indonesia until he draws his last breath. In spite of all the humiliation and misery faced by both presidents, neither are cowards; they have faced all allegations with their heads held high. In this regard, both presidents have, in common, true courage.

During Pak Harto's many stays in hospitals, a few loyal friends, my father included, visited him. My father had stood by President Soekarno when the latter became the object of hatred. My father had also stood by Pak Harto when the latter was brought to trial. No matter what their weaknesses and faults were, they were leaders whom my father had respected highly.

Dr Hari Sabardi highlighted an important issue, which echoed a sentiment held by my father: why were there still so many people in Indonesia who did not want to trust the expertise of the country's medical professionals? This was particularly glaring after the medical team which had examined Pak Harto had concluded that his illness was terminal. Or was there some truth in the question that Ismail Saleh had raised: "Is the Soeharto trial real law enforcement or is it just a political commodity?"[1] Ismail Saleh, who had been an Attorney General and Minister of Justice under President Soeharto, was not unlike my father. He had not been particularly close to Pak Harto when the latter was the president. He, too, had on a few occasions criticised President Soeharto. In 1982, my father was quoted as having said that "Everywhere, there seemed to be opposition to the military establishment, to the dictatorship of the bureaucracy, and to the manipulation of so many things."[2] However, after Pak Harto was out of office and his cronies had deserted him, Ismail Saleh offered his friendship. Indonesia's leaders, the highest if possible, have to garner sufficient courage to decide on Pak Harto's trial. My father had also believed that the time had arrived to decide that President Soeharto's obvious contributions to the country outweighed his faults, because no matter what mistakes we, as human beings, have made and will make, we want to be forgiven and long for kindness and understanding, which is a universal longing, and in reaching this understanding, we should rely on honour, respect and decency. Any reckoning should be undertaken on the basis of his deteriorating health brought about in part by his advanced age. President Soeharto had pardoned Soebandrio and Omar Dhani when they reached the age of 80. President Soeharto had rejected the demand to bring President Soekarno to court on the basis of lack of evidence. Furthermore, the responsibility for his faults should be shared amongst those who have been mute, afraid to tell the truth and to take the consequences of doing so, in the three decades when he was in power. At the time of writing, Pak Harto's health has not improved but continues to deteriorate.

FRIENDSHIPS

My father had been very close to Indonesia's first president and he had been considered one of Bung Karno's cronies and strong loyalists. For this reason, it was not surprising that Pak Harto and my father were never politically close, even when my father was the Chairman of the President's Advisory Team for Pancasila. Certainly, my father had met with Pak Harto as the president on a regular basis, but the meetings had been official and formal. Even though my father was appointed his advisor, their relationship had been lukewarm during that period of time. To this extent, my father and Pak Harto had another area in common: being practical in their political stand and realistic in their approach. Both were Javanese but from different parts of Java: Pak Harto was from Yogya, considered the centre of Javanese culture and the site of the monarchs, while my father was from Surabaya. The people from Yogya are considered to be more refined and sophisticated, while those from the eastern part of Java are often considered to be crude. People from Central Java tend to hide their true feelings behind an exterior of calmness, while those from the eastern part tend to show their true feelings in an upfront manner and are very outspoken.

The Indonesian indigenous people typically lived in *kampongs* within towns during the time of Dutch rule. They made their living mostly from small trading businesses. Only the Dutch lived in upmarket, Western-styled houses. Pak Harto was born, raised and educated in a typical village where the inhabitants depended on rice cultivation. As *kampongs* are in an urban setting and villages are in a rural setting, the thinking and behaviour of the people from these two different environments are often dissimilar.

Islam had a strong base in the *kampongs* when it first arrived in the country and it symbolised hope for the oppressed. Christianity was the religion of the Dutch, the oppressors. The Islamic faith, as with Hinduism and Buddhism, had a big impact on *kampong* life, but its influence was not as strong in the villages. Opportunities and access to education were also not the same in the two different settings. It has always been easier to find schools in cities than in villages, and not only were there more schools in the cities, it was also easier to find good teachers there. Communication with the outside world was also often easier in the towns than in the villages. Therefore, Pak Harto, with his village background, was often perceived to be inward-looking. His horizon, especially in terms of Western thinking, was restricted. An awareness of or belief in supernatural forces, in the roles of fate and destiny, exists in the consciousness of most Indonesians, but it is more pronounced in those living in the villages. In a country like Indonesia, where agriculture remains the backbone of the economy, an understanding of the roles of farming and the farmers is very important.

This had been the key to success in Pak Harto's presidency, as his strongest point had been his understanding of the village mentality. He was also aware, however, that Indonesia had to move towards industrialisation if progress was desired. That was why he had promoted industries related to agriculture, as it would not have been suitable to embark on industries that were not related to land cultivation. It would not have fitted in with the country's environment. Furthermore, Pak Harto had never tried to be what he was not and from the beginning, he had stayed faithful to his origins as a village person. Pak Harto never hid the lack of his intellectual achievements. However, he relied on his common sense and was a good learner. He knew that the farmers did not want to hear promises made through speeches, but what they wanted to see were better living standards. The farmers' demands were simple: to have three meals a day, two to three sets of clothing and adequate shelter. Most of the villagers had no idea what foreign countries looked like. That knowledge only came much later when the country had progressed to the point where radio and television sets were found everywhere. Pak Harto's sense of simplicity was another of his qualities which my father admired, just as he had admired Bung Karno for his great vision for the nation's state ideology. From my father's point of view, Bung Karno had given Indonesia ideals, while Pak Harto had kept the nation's stomachs full. For him, the progress from the gaining of freedom to attaining sufficient food for consumption, clothes to wear and roofs over the people's heads, had been close to ideal. Thus, it is not true that the first two presidents had contradicted each other; they had, in truth, supplemented and complemented each other.

On 29 July 1999, a little over a year after he had stepped down, Pak Harto suffered his first stroke. At that time, the public's reactions to him were varied. A few reports in the media were, in my father's opinion, offensive. The tones were vulgar and showed disrespect to an elderly person who was no longer a leader. In my father's eyes, it mirrored not only the quality of the country's moral values but, more importantly, it was an indication of how the high ethics that our society once possessed had deteriorated. Such reports did not reflect any positive contribution on the part of the media; they were nothing more than nasty pieces of work. My father felt that it was totally inappropriate and irreverent to write in such a manner, especially when these people had been "yes men" when Pak Harto was in power. He felt one should be brave in voicing opposition in a polite form and be willing to accept the consequences. One should not come forward only when the opponent has been defeated. In Indonesia, such people are called *pahlawan kesiangan* or belated heroes. Sadly, many "opponents" did not surface until after Pak Harto was no longer in power. To make things worse, a few of these people had been part of his inner circle and had benefitted greatly under his rule. To my father, it was a matter of simple ethics to be present for a friend who was in need, a lesson he had learnt from his mother in his early childhood. This explained my father's closer friendship with Pak Harto after the latter's status reverted to that of an ordinary citizen.

From my father's point of view, most books on President Soeharto and President Soekarno written by scholars typically contained the impression of an outsider: a few were very critical and a handful very commendable.

Very few people knew these two men well. Unfortunately, for reasons unknown, those who knew them well hardly put their experiences on paper. My father was sure that this must have been a disappointment to Bung Karno and Pak Harto. For them, it would have been better if the people who had worked with them had written the truth about their experiences, not only to put the country's own history into perspective, but also to counter the negative aspects which people had written about the two ex-presidents, hence providing readers with the option to decide whom they chose to believe.

Once, I heard that Pak Harto had offered my father the opportunity to make use of forestry rights, just as he had reportedly given similar rights to his close friends. This had surprised my father as they were not close friends at that stage. Although they had gotten along well, my father had maintained a certain distance and allowed their relationship to remain professional. He did not want to aggravate the situation, as he knew that Pak Harto was fully aware of his close relationship with Bung Karno. On the other hand, the offer showed that Pak Harto did not give rewards only to his cronies, but also to those whom he thought deserved special attention as a result of their contributions to the nation's fight for freedom. My father refused the offer, as he knew that it could have been seen as an example of the misuse of power. Unfortunately, only a few took a similar stand as my father's. Many took the opposite stand and took advantage of Pak Harto's intention, which, although not a bad intention per se, could be viewed as an abuse of his power. From a royal monarch's point of view, these practices might have been considered acceptable. It was common practice for the rulers to reward people with land or titles, therefore, some have considered President Soeharto's style of governing as being similar to that of a Javanese sultan.

To my father, it did not matter that Bung Karno was more of an intellectual than Pak Harto. My father, who was pragmatic by nature, referred to the length of their stay in power as the real barometer of their capabilities. For better or for worse, President Soekarno had stayed in power for 22 years and President Soeharto for 32 years. No matter what academics and writers have penned, the fact remains that President Soeharto, just like Bung Karno, have shaped Indonesia's existence for about a quarter of a century. One should view Pak Harto within the context of the Indonesian value system, which is undoubtedly different from the Western value system. Our values have taught us to be respectful of our leaders and the elderly, even if there is a difference in opinion or lifestyle between the assessor and the subject. Back in the 1920s, schoolchildren were taught *budi pekerti* (which literally means "good nature", but it has a broader meaning and refers to a high ethical standard) as an important aspect within the curriculum. In our daily lives, *budi pekerti* forms part of the very nucleus of our being. Everyone is considered highly civilised if they are able to show respect, courtesy and gratitude to his elders, in spite of their faults. A sense of forgiveness is always within reach for those who trespass, or those whose mistakes were not intentional. This should be the perspective from which President Soeharto is viewed and assessed, within the Indonesian context and value system.

SEPTEMBER 2004

"We can only learn history by comparing leaders," my father uttered one bright Thursday morning. It was 9 September 2004, a little before noon, as we left our house on the way to Jalan Cendana. In early 1998, Jalan Cendana was often the target of protesters, where soldiers and students stood face to face in confrontation. On our trip that September morning, Jalan Cendana was tranquil and deserted. The street that was frequently closed a few years ago was open to the public with unrestricted access. There were no more barricades to stop vehicles. Jalan Cendana is best described as a small lane lined with lush green trees, very much in contrast to Jalan Diponegoro, where public transport vehicles pass through day and night, creating agonising noise and pollution. The house we were visiting was very simple in appearance, with two or three men sitting quietly at the small terrace. There were only a few cars parked outside. More impressive houses stood nearby. Some of them belonged to Pak Harto's children. Another prominent family who lived close by was that of the late Ibnu Sutowo, Pertamina's former boss.

Pak Harto's house consists of three parts. The public entrance is through Number 6, a simple pale green building. This appears to be the oldest part, where regular guests wait before proceeding to the other rooms. The second part is Number 8, where Pak Harto meets official guests. The third, Number 10, is Pak Harto's private wing, where he meets informal visitors, and where he spends most of his time these days. Pak Harto has resided in Jalan Cendana since mid-1968 as he never moved to Merdeka Palace. He had refused to move to Merdeka Palace as Jalan Cendana was a better home for his children when they were growing up.

As our car approached the main entrance, I felt as if I was staring at a house with a great past but no present. In this house lived a decent person, who had suffered a decline from spectacular power in a tragic setting. In the small backyard, there were noisy birds in gilded cages. There was nothing new here, just a few cupboards filled with empty glasses kept for guests who visited during the end of Ramadan celebrations, when Pak Harto and his family would still offer an open house, although only for a few hours. There are still hundreds of guests who visit to pay their respect, but the numbers are far less than when he was president.

Since his downfall, I have accompanied my father on several occasions to visit Pak Harto. Our annual visit takes place on 8 June, which is Pak Harto's birthday. My father would also visit Pak Harto whenever he fell ill and was hospitalised. Pak Harto has also visited our home; he came to extend his good wishes to my father on his 89th and 90th birthday in 2003 and 2004, respectively. On Lebaran, 14 November 2004, my father asked my sister, Lia, and I to pay Pak Harto a courtesy call. He did not go himself, as it is the Javanese custom for the younger generation to visit their elders, but the elderly are not expected to visit those younger than them. As Pak Harto is seven years younger than my father, the latter never visited him on Lebaran, even when Pak Harto was president. However, my father visited President Soekarno on Lebaran, because Bung Karno was 13 years older than him.

Pak Harto's house is definitely simpler in comparison with those palatial houses built in Pondok Indah, Kemang, Permata Hijau and the like. Those houses belong to the wealthy businessmen who had built their wealth through their businesses during Pak Harto's time in power. It would not surprise one to know that the owners of these palatial properties are also the very same people who accused Pak Harto of corruption. Yet, many of these owners have undoubtedly bribed government officials in order to make their businesses a success. In discussing the issue of corruption in Indonesia, the state of Pak Harto's own fortunes should not be neglected. Most people who know Pak Harto agree that he is not a greedy man. Even when he was at the peak of his rule, he never showed an interest in foreign foods. He does not drink alcohol and he enjoys simple, traditional food and tea and coffee. He does not use gold plates or crystal glasses, which the Shah of Iran had been known to favour. The food he has served to guests from 1985 to date has remained the same: traditional Javanese snacks. He has never shopped in the hundreds of malls constructed during his time in power.

While we were in Pak Harto's house, his daughters Tutut and Titiek were present. Suddenly, the front door was flung open. We heard sounds of explosive blasts, but Pak Harto and my father did not seem to notice. Titiek ran over and whispered to Suweden. In the next room, they switched on the radio. Tutut and I pretended everything was normal, as we did not want to interrupt our parents' conversation. It was only after the two elderly men had finished talking that Titiek informed us the noise had been bomb explosions. As usual, the initial news was confusing. The only thing we knew was that it had taken place in the neighbourhood. Once again, it had been a bomb targeted against the Australians. First, there was the horrible Bali bombing on 12 October 2002, in two famous nightclubs in Kuta which had killed hundreds of tourists, mainly Australians. This time, it was in front of the Australian Embassy in Kuningan which was merely a few minutes' drive from where we were. Innocent people were killed and a helpless three-year-old girl was left badly wounded while her mother lost her life. The victims were Indonesians; none of them were from the Australian Embassy home staff. This was another tragedy in the country's history, another black spot that has left the people astounded and mortified. Up to that point in time, that is, the last six years after Pak Harto's presidency, the military was blamed for any catastrophe and acts of violence that took place. Many speculated that Pak Harto's loyalists had been the *dalang*, the master puppeteer behind these riots. Only after September 11 did the people start to think differently and looked upon the extremist Muslim movement as an alternative instigator of strife.

In 2004, Pak Harto was 83 years old and six years beyond his *lengser keprabon* or descent from power. His face still reflected wisdom and ease, which was remarkable for one who had gone through so much. He looked as if he was in a much better condition than those who had suffered multiple strokes. After the strokes, his ability to speak deteriorated, as did his mind. What struck me most about him were his expressions; it mirrored his acknowledgement of his fate with dignity. It is amazing how he has had the strength to prevail over his critics, including the harassment from those who were once his close friends. During the interviews with the management of his foundations, I was reminded to read what his cronies said about him on his 70th birthday. The compilation of these articles would serve as an excellent textbook on the subject of betrayal and deceit.

When he was the most powerful man in the nation, Pak Harto had smiled all the time. It was said that his smile could mean "yes", "no", "maybe" or "never". This is a true Javanese trait: to not show one's real sentiments and to keep the opponent guessing. Another of his characteristics is his benign expression. His gestures are more relaxed now, as he is no longer under heavy pressure as president. The one major difference in his life then and now is the environment around him. Before, hundreds if not thousands would be clamouring to meet him, if only for a brief handshake. If one had a photograph of President Soeharto shaking one's hand, one would display it prominently in one's office. Such a photograph guaranteed admiration, but it would be an even greater achievement if the picture had been taken with one standing next to President Soeharto and a few other people. Of course, the best is to have one's photograph taken with just him alone. Photographers made millions just by taking such photographs. This is, of course, no longer the case and people have now moved to Merdeka Palace to pose with other presidents. Psychologists would have a wonderful time analysing such swift changes in human behaviour.

Fortunately, Pak Harto still has a small number of loyal friends, a few of whom had worked in his administration. By now, Pak Harto has realised who the rats that jumped off the sinking ship were. In the end, he was able to identify who his true friends were and those who were not, that is, those who remained faithful and those who betrayed him. The worst are those who condemned him and pretended as if they had been against him all along. This is a sad state of affairs as we have been taught that true friends stay together in good and bad times. There is an axiom, *Habis manis, sepah dibuang*, which means to throw away the sugar cane after one has chewed and consumed the sweetness. In spite of all this, his children and most of his family members have continued to stand by him.

IN SEARCH OF A LEGACY

Early in the morning of 24 November 2004, the bell at our gate kept ringing. Deliveries of flowers and cakes came streaming in. We felt that we were the luckiest people in the world that day. It was my father's 90th birthday, which turned out to be his final one. The night before, we had received a call from Jalan Cendana informing us that Pak Harto would be coming over for a visit but the exact time was yet to be confirmed. It could be that day or the next day. Since 1998, Pak Harto has been very careful to choose the right time to be seen in public. He tries to avoid crowds so as to avoid speculations about his health. We fully understood the situation, because if he were to come that day, he would be seen by many other visitors and some would speculate that he was well.

At 3pm, the Blue Bird taxi that we had booked arrived. The driver had come an hour earlier. When asked to wait, he said that he did not mind. To the contrary, with his eyes gleaming, he seemed to enjoy himself watching the ins and outs of the non-stop stream of visitors. Luthfi, my assistant, and I left the house at 5pm to catch Garuda Indonesian Airways' last flight to Yogya. Gadjah Mada University was launching my book on my father's life story the next morning. Yogya is now a famous university town. In fact, we could have left on the earliest flight the next day as it was only a 50-minute flight. However, Garuda's reputation of being late ruled out this option. As a result of our departure that day, we missed the big celebration for my father's birthday that evening. I have never regretted this decision as launching the book on my father's life story in this famous university would have brought my father great delight and been a source of pride for him. Gadjah Mada was the first university to be opened after the country gained its independence under President Soekarno, unlike the University of Indonesia, which had been in existence since the time of the Dutch. The name "Gadjah Mada" was derived from the prime minister of the powerful Majapahit Empire.

The drive to Soekarno-Hatta International Airport was very slow due to heavy traffic. This often made visitors wonder: "Where is the economic crisis?" There is always a traffic jam at rush hour when office workers are trying to get home for dinner. From the centre of the city, it could take as short as 30 minutes or as long as 2 hours to reach the airport. Luck has a lot to do with it. The highrise buildings along the way stood as they had in 1998. Nearly all the buildings had been constructed during President Soeharto's 32 year-rule. He was also the one who had renamed the airport "Soekarno-Hatta" as a tribute to the two leaders who had proclaimed the nation's independence. Moreover, by renaming it from the old name of Cengkareng, President Soeharto had proven that he was loyal and grateful to the proclamators. Nevertheless, during the drive, my mind wandered and concluded that President Soeharto's success in the development of the country had not been free of scandals. Tutut, his eldest daughter, had been blamed for having the monopoly of the toll road that we were travelling on that evening. Bambang and Tommy had been accused of getting government privileges for their automobile businesses; many of their vehicles were seen on the road that evening.

What is the main difference in the situation between then and now? Most of the five-star hotels and office buildings are now experiencing a decline in occupancy rates. The average occupancy rate went as high as 80 per cent before 1998, but now, hotel operators count their blessings to have an occupancy rate of 50 per cent. Many tenants of the office buildings have closed their businesses. This was due to the inability of local companies to repay bank loans, because their businesses have been performing very poorly. Meanwhile, the multinational corporations have reduced their operations or have moved to one of the neigbouring countries.

Our friendly driver, who was in his late 30s, asked inquisitively why we were leaving when a big event seemed to be taking place. He asked whether one of the bouquets of flowers had been from Pak Harto. When asked the reason for his question, he replied: "I like Pak Harto and miss him as our leader. Under his rule, I had no problems sending my children to school. I had enough money to buy food, clothes and other necessities, but since Pak Harto has gone, I have difficulties in making ends meet." Comments like these are common among the *wong cilik* such as bus drivers, taxi drivers and peddlers. President Soeharto's successors have all promised to help in improving the standard of living at the grassroots level, but since his departure from office, expenditure on education and healthcare from the national state budget has been reduced. President Susilo Bambang Yudhoyono has said that since the 1997 economic crisis and following years of neglect, the country is now facing serious problems, including power shortages and bottlenecks at seaports, all of which would no doubt hamper economic growth and increase the cost of doing business in the country. Almost US$145 billion is required for infrastructure development, in addition to the US$4 billion required for rebuilding Aceh after the tsunami in December 2004.

As we rushed to the check-in counter after being dropped off by the taxi, our mood changed from light frustration to profound disappointment: Garuda Indonesian Airways had once again kept its reputation for delayed flights and we had a two-hour wait. The waiting lounge was crowded with passengers waiting for their flights as Ramadan had just ended. I thought of the same setting during President Soeharto's era. There was clearly a considerable change, especially in the appearance of the travellers. At the time when Pak Harto was in power, air commuters were comprised largely of foreign executives, sometimes more than 50 per cent of them, but now less than 1 per cent are expatriates. One of the main reasons is the threat from the terrorists. Furthermore, in the business arena, Indonesia is facing steep competition from giants such as China and India. These countries have successfully lured the Western corporations as well as Asian investors like the Koreans to invest in their growing economies. A few Korean companies, typically those in light industries, have left Indonesia due to the uncompetitive labour cost, which had increased when the labour union came into force.

Under President Soeharto, the labour force had been strictly controlled and their movement restricted. Demonstrations or strikes were almost unheard of. Nowadays, labour strikes and demonstrations by factory workers and hotel employees have become routine. The fountain in front of where Hotel Indonesia was located is the gathering point for members of the labour force, who demand more vacation time, better working conditions and salary increases. Even for local companies, the increasing labour demands have created problems; along with the increase in other costs such as electricity, it has become difficult to make their products competitive. Hotels are hardly able to attract enough guests and, in turn, they are unable to increase their employees' wages. In short, doing business has become more difficult, although there have been small improvements since Susilo Bambang Yudhoyono became the country's sixth president.

Less than an hour after our flight took off, we landed at Adisucipto Airport in Yogya. In stark contrast to the traffic in Jakarta, the streets in this town seemed to be deserted. However, there was one thing in common. Driving to the university guesthouse, our driver complained about how bad business has been since 1998. I started thinking that perhaps all drivers belonged to the same union and tended to complain a lot. He said that the decreasing number of tourists has been the result of the recent "sweepings", mostly against the Americans, by extremist Muslims from Solo, which was a mere 60 km away, where Ibu Tien hailed from. In 1745, the sultan of Mataram moved his court to Solo or Surakarta, as it was formally known. The sultan took with him musicians, artists, dancers, painters and silversmiths. It is a pity, because Central Java could have supplemented Bali as a tourist destination. Similar to Bali, the people here also celebrate everything from harvests to weddings with *gamelan* music and dancing. Located on the slopes of Indonesia's most active volcano, Mount Merapi, the area is indeed breathtaking, especially for nature lovers, trekkers, hikers and the like. Nearly 3,000 m in height, Mount Merapi is one of the many volcanoes which create a dramatic backdrop to the island of Java.

Unlike Britain, Indonesia is not a nation with a powerful literary tradition where the people are accustomed to finding answers in books. However, during my book launch in Yogya, I was happy to see that the situation was changing. The students at the university have a reading club and they were enthusiastic about my new book. When asked what my next book was about and I replied that it was about Pak Harto, they encouraged me to meet Suwito, the *lurah* or head of the village of Kemusuk. Suwito was Pak Harto's younger brother and the son of Ibu Sukirah by a different husband. Suwito passed away in 2006, at the time of writing.

After the book launch, we moved to Batik Palace, a hotel located behind Malioboro, the main street of Yogya. The rows of empty hotels and restaurants were a living proof of what has changed. As compared to a few years ago, Malioboro looked like an ailing old man, whose life would come to an end soon if his health was not taken care of quickly. Malioboro used to be a virtual street fair that was every shopper's delight. There were no fixed prices and bargaining was an art in itself, just like at Pasar Klewer in Solo. One could get better bargains if he or she spoke in Javanese. There were very few Western tourists in sight that night. The shopkeepers looked desperate while trying to keep their merchandise free of the dust. Many restaurants, bars and hotels that were buzzing in the mid-1980s were now having a hard time trying to survive. A feeling of emptiness, frustration and lost hope was evident. Consisting of individual villas built under shady trees and a swimming pool located in the middle amongst the villas, Batik Palace Hotel was another evidence of past glory. Owned by a well known *batik* factory, the hotel gave one the impression that it was succumbing to old age. Everything looked run down and worn out, no doubt due to the fact that it now had fewer guests and the consequent lack of funds for regular maintenance.

The rain that started to fall added to my gloomy mood. At around 2 pm, we decided to make our first journey to Kemusuk, located in the larger village of Godean in the region of Argomulyo, approximately 15 km west of Yogya. Kemusuk is an insignificant village which lies in the shadow of Borobudur, the largest Buddhist monument on earth. The monument, located between Yogya and Solo, once rival dynasties, was founded in the 18th century. Kemusuk has become a focus for writers, scholars and researchers who are looking to find out more about the country's history because it was the birthplace of Indonesia's second and longest reigning president.

Suratin, our taxi driver, was a sturdy looking man in his late 40s. He was very happy when he was asked to drive us to our destination. During our trip which lasted 25 minutes, he also started to complain about how difficult life had become. The road was in good condition, with rice fields stretching along the left and right, with some ready to harvest. There were also mango trees with fruits ripe for picking. We noticed many women working in the rice fields that day. Women play key roles in this traditional agrarian society. As the farmers started to use more mechanical tools, the women ventured abroad for better employment. In spite of criticisms over the issue of Indonesian women working abroad as domestic helpers because of the incidents of abuse suffered by these women, those who have worked overseas have managed to send millions of dollars home. In the final analysis, it has helped the expansion of the economy. The situation is comparable to that of Korean nurses in the 1960s and 1970s, who made a major contribution to the growth of Korea's economy. Nurses in the Philippines from the mid-1980s onwards were also in a similar situation, but the female labour force in Indonesia has not been able to get training like in nursing, hence their employment as housekeepers and babysitters.

A few minutes after we passed the sign for Borobudur, we approached the tranquil village of Kemusuk. Suratin pointed to an impressive structure that was built on a set of steps. It was Makam Gunung Puloreho, the resting place of Sukirah, Pak Harto's mother. She was born in 1903, the second of nine children. In 1946, after two marriages and eight children, Sukirah died at the age of 43 and did not live to see her first-born son become the president. Pak Harto was her eldest and only child from her first marriage to Kertoredjo, who later changed his name to Kertosudiro. Sukirah, known for her beauty and *joie de vivre*, was only 16 years old when she married a widower who already had two children. There was always a twinkle of joy and a radiance in Pak Harto's face whenever I referred to Ibu Sukirah. Pak Harto must have been proud of her and must have loved her dearly.

Along the main lane, there was a sizeable graveyard for the founder of Kemusuk, Wongsomenggolo, whose bloodline Pak Harto came from. The *kelurahan* office was already closed when we arrived, but Suratin did not give up easily. He took a chance and drove us to the private house of the *lurah* in the eastern part of Kemusuk. A stocky man wearing plain clothing who looked like a professional bodyguard stopped us at the small entrance to the property. Just metres away from where we were stopped, a statue of a man in a long white robe and a turban stood near yet another graveyard, Makam Si Sepuh (grave for the elderly). It was the statue of Pangeran Diponegoro, the country's hero, who in 1825 had bravely fought against the Dutch. This was a hero whom my father had admired and who had stirred his youthful soul. Pangeran Diponegoro is immortalised in the names of main streets in major cities. Diponegoro is also the name of the Military Division that Pak Harto had led in Central Java.

On the right of the statue stood a house that in the simple village looked luxurious. We felt the stillness and eeriness of the surroundings as we watched the rain trickling down the windscreen. My mind drifted back to young Soeharto's exploits with the water buffalo that had fallen into the river and I felt sorry at the thought of the young and helpless boy crying in frustration. I was quickly jolted back to the real world when Suratin, who had stepped out to speak to the man who had stopped our vehicle, rapped frantically on the window of the car. It was only at that point that Suratin finally found the courage to ask for my name and the purpose of my visit.

Jumping out of the taxi, we dashed towards a man who sat on a bench surrounded by four stern-looking and muscular men. There was no time to waste as it was getting late. Sitting cross-legged in typical village style while smoking a hand-rolled cigarette was Suwito. He gave us a piercing look and we could see that this was a no nonsense man. I felt as if he was assessing every single bone in my body. Satisfied with his assessment, he told his visitors to leave so that we could have our discussion in private. He smoked his cigarettes continuously over the next two hours of our meeting. Hot tea was served after we showed him photographs on my digital camera of our audience with Pak Harto taken just a few days earlier. The atmosphere became more relaxed as Suwito told us about the childhood years of one of the most remarkable persons in Indonesia. That rainy day in Kemusuk on

25 November 2004 opened a whole new chapter in my understanding of Pak Harto as it painted a rare but undoubtedly true picture of the person that he is.

That night, in a dilapidated bedroom of Batik Palace, a curious sense of apprehension came over me. I felt that I needed to return to Kemusuk if I wanted to understand Pak Harto's outlook on life. My feelings were right. I went back in September 2005 and the second visit was a total contrast from the first. On the second visit, I was a guest of the family and Pak Harto was present as well. His family had invited me to join them in visiting their family graves just a few days before the start of Ramadan. Then, I had lunch at the same table with Pak Harto and his family in Suwito's house. I was invited to stay overnight in their family home in Kalitan, Solo. It was during that visit that he gave his full consent for me to write this book. In 2004, however, it was still drizzling when we left. Daylight had turned to dusk as the lights in the small houses and street were switched on. My mood changed from one of excitement to serenity and peace. On our way back, Suratin, in an obviously pleased and happy mood, took a different route to our hotel. That night, I was happy I did not move to a more luxurious hotel, a thought which had occurred to me as we had checked into Batik Palace. It was a "palace" in name only, as there was nothing palatial about the establishment. However, I believed then that one could obtain a clear understanding of the country's second president only within a simple setting. Many who had learnt that I had managed to meet Suwito with no prior appointment were astounded.

We visited Borobudur the next day, with Suratin driving us again. The sanctuary consisted of a million cut-stone blocks and 1,460 stone relief panels, as well as 504 life-size Buddha statues, each sculpted from a single stone. A few were headless; some of the heads have surfaced in museums such as in the Netherlands. There were not too many visitors that day, and almost none were foreign tourists. We left our bags in the car with Suratin for safekeeping. Slowly, we climbed the steep steps to the top. A photographer offered to take our photograph. Instead of accepting the offer, I started my interviews to gather information. Similar to other members of the working class, he told us how he could barely manage nowadays. Unexpectedly, a guard who stood nearby joined our discussion. He, too, was frustrated with his life. He then pointed to an inspiring complex in the distance: Amanjiwo, one of the most luxurious hotels in the world. The name "Amanjiwo" means "peaceful soul" and the hotel was opened in 1997. It was built from *paras Yogya*, the local limestone. Fifteen of its rooms have private pools. The hotel has a library, an art gallery, a 40 m swimming pool lined with green tiles, two tennis courts and it offers a range of Javanese spa treatments and massages.

The guard begged us to visit Amanjiwo as his son worked there. Obviously, he was concerned that the lack of hotel guests would lead to his son being unemployed. We decided to listen to his request. As our taxi wound its way there slowly, we could not keep our eyes away from the rustic *kampongs* that were set into the jungle, along streams and across rice terraces while the people worked in the frontyard of their modest dwellings.

Suratin had been flabbergasted when we told him to go to Amanjiwo and from his expression, we knew he was wondering whether the hotel would admit us. We were in jeans and simple T-shirts. Suratin's car was an old rambling taxi, while guests of Amanjiwo were driven in BMW and Mercedes Benz limousines. Suratin was right, even though the hotel allowed us in, the foreign manager gave us a dirty look and completely ignored us. We received a few stares from the local staff who served us lunch. The room rates ranged from US$650 to US$2,600 plus per night. The rates would stun regular workers, as it did us. Our luncheon fare of one pizza, a fruit juice and a cocktail came to the same amount for a two-night stay in two rooms plus breakfast in Batik Palace.

There are other "Aman" resorts built in Indonesia during President Soeharto's era and there are also a few in Bali. In fact, places like "Aman" was one of the *raison d'être* for President Soeharto's downfall: the widening gap between the super-haves and the have-nots.

WEDNESDAY, 8 JUNE 2005

My father's mood was rather unusual on 7 June 2005. First, when I had just arrived home from Bangkok, he said we should visit Pak Harto the next evening, as Jalan Cendana had called that morning to formally invite us over. A few minutes later, he changed his mind and asked me to call Jalan Cendana to ask if it would be acceptable for us to visit in the morning instead. As usual, Suweden said that the door was always open for my father to visit Pak Harto at anytime. This was to be the fourth time that my father had seen Pak Harto in 2005, including the hospital visits. Pak Harto had visited RSPAD when my father was hospitalised on 4 February and we had visited him when Pak Harto was hospitalised in Pertamina Hospital on 6 May that same year.

Although Pak Harto's house was comfortable, it was simple and not wealthy by Indonesian standards. By this time, everyone should have been convinced that Pak Harto would never leave Indonesia. He was not like the tyrant Charles Taylor, the former president of Liberia who began his third year of a comfortable exile in Nigeria in 2005. Nor was he like Ferdinand Marcos or the Shah of Iran, both of whom decided to live in exile abroad. For Pak Harto, staying in Indonesia is a duty and, at the same time, a challenge that features an ongoing threat. His duty is to keep to the values he believes in. Of his own free will, Pak Harto has chosen to stay in the country; if he has the alleged billions of dollars he could easily have moved abroad. Besides, how comfortably can one live if demonstrations or a court trial can take place at any time of the day? My father recalled that when General Soeharto took over power, the people's hopes were low and the journey ahead as a nation was uncertain, yet Pak Harto managed to keep the flame of the nation's unity alight. He had stood proud and tall as he built hopes and dreams. The cynics now voice their long-suppressed criticisms against him and he is single-handedly blamed for the uncontrolled pursuit of material gains by his family members and cronies. "Do we want a society driven by the dollar sign?" asked his opponents. "Is that all we want after the noble vision of Soekarno?" asked his enemies.

A staff member had been waiting for our arrival and the gate was opened immediately. Soon after, we saw Pak Harto's smiling and happy face. He received us with open arms. He looked relaxed in a *sarong* and long sleeved shirt. For some unknown reason, Pak Harto seemed very pleased and contented as my father kept him posted of what had been happening since April that year. This was our second visit to Jalan Cendana in 2005; the previous one was on 28 April, after the 50th commemoration of the Asia Africa Conference. My father ensured that Pak Harto was kept abreast of what had taken place during the commemoration. On Friday, 22 April that year, we were surprised as we did not see any chair assigned to Pak Harto when we attended the ceremony at the Jakarta Convention Center in the Senayan complex. There had been chairs in the first row with seats allocated to all the former presidents, but none for Pak Harto. There was one for

BJ Habibie, Gus Dur and Megawati. BJ Habibie showed up but Gus Dur and Megawati's chairs remained empty. On Thursday, 28 April, as my father and I came to visit, Pak Harto, who was accompanied by his daughter Titiek, informed us that he did receive the invitation that was handed personally to him, but Pak Harto had declined due to health reasons. Not only did Pak Harto turn down the invitation immediately on receipt, he had also followed up his rejection in writing. Hence, there was no chair allocated to him.

As if he knew that his life was coming to an end, that evening, my father decided to visit Pak Harto again to attend his official birthday celebration. Usually, only close family and friends were invited for this occasion, but my father insisted that he wanted to be there. When Saadillah Mursjid saw us, he quipped, "Pak Roeslan, this is the second time you have come today." My father replied, "Why not?" Saadillah came to my father's funeral on 30 June. A few weeks after that, Saadillah fell ill and passed away as well. Pak Harto lost two of his best friends within weeks. At Pak Harto's birthday celebration, my father was seated at the main table with Pak Harto and Sudharmono. Although there were hundreds of guests, none dared to sit with them, a reflection of the practice in Javanese tradition whereby people kept their distance from those they respected. Eight years after stepping down from the presidency, it seemed Pak Harto still maintained his charisma among those loyal to him. Although we did not stay long, I could hardly miss the simplicity of the whole affair. It was nothing compared to the common perception of how billionaires celebrate their birthdays. *Nasi tumpeng* was on the menu. Pak Harto gave the first cut to his eldest daughter, Tutut, who gave a short speech to thank God for her father's life. We did not stay long, but a picture of my father as he bid his last farewell to his former boss will continue to evoke a strong and painful memory in me for the rest of my life.

On hindsight, I am now aware of why my father decided to see Pak Harto twice that day. It was as if he wanted so much to urge Pak Harto to be strong as he knew that he would not be able to stand by him for long. After our visit to Pak Harto's birthday celebration, Mamiek, another of his daughters, sent me a message via SMS: "Pak Roeslan is so kind to my father, my father is so happy that Pak Roeslan came that evening. My father keeps telling everybody that your father often visits Cendana." As I read that message to my father, he seemed very pleased. Yet, there was a light of concern on his astute face that we have not been able to reconcile

Pak Harto's place in the country's history. Perhaps it was the same feeling he had when he bid Bung Karno his last farewell. He probably felt pain for the national tragedy of how the people have treated Bung Karno and Pak Harto. My father would have had good reason to feel such pain, as he had come into public life filled with visions for his beloved country with all its possibilities. At the same time, he had wished that Indonesia would hold a place of substance in the world. Poignantly, I recall his words to Pak Harto that morning about my book: "Let her write and let her stand in the front to relay our feelings to the younger generation. Let us stand in the back and slowly fade away."

PAVILION KARTIKA, JUNE 2005

I was on two minds over whether to fly to Jakarta from Bangkok on 7 June 2005, the reason being that 8 June was Pak Harto's birthday. He would turn 84 years old that day. Knowing my father as well as I did, I knew that he would be happy if I accompanied him to wish Pak Harto well. Born on 24 November 1914, my father would have turned 91 years old in 2005, but God had decided otherwise. Nevertheless, his life had been blessed in so many ways.

As Javanese people, we are trained to take our intuition seriously, hence I decided to go to Jakarta. It soon proved to be the best decision I have ever made in my entire life. My beloved father passed away peacefully in the early morning of Wednesday, 29 June 2005, a mere three weeks after my arrival. In spite of his advanced age, my father had maintained a workplace, which was located within the compound of the Foreign Affairs Office. On 16 June, he experienced difficulty while trying to get up from his seat as he was getting ready to go home. The next morning, an ambulance rushed him to the military hospital, RSPAD, where Bung Karno's legendary life had come to an end on 21 June 1970. We followed the ambulance as it drove very quickly along Jalan Diponegoro in the elite part of Jakarta. At the end of the street, it turned left in the direction of Pasar Senen, where the traffic became congested. This area was the site of riots on 27 July 1996, when many of the office buildings were set on fire amidst strong protests against the removal of Megawati from her position as chairman of PDI. President Soeharto was named as the main player behind Megawati being cast out, as PDI was a main opponent to his government. That became the starting point of Megawati's ascent to the presidency a few years later. The ambulance soon entered the gates of Pavilion Kartika, an extension of the main hospital. In 1988, President Soeharto saw the need to expand RSPAD, and the new wing was constructed with an additional 99 beds, an intensive care unit, and maternity and specialist clinics. It had been formally opened on 16 September 1991 and it was where my father spent his final hours. He passed away on a beautiful bright morning on Wednesday, 29 June 2005. In their final hours, Bung Karno and my father had both bid farewell to their beloved motherland in a hospital that was close to Pak Harto's heart.

Two days after being admitted to Pavilion Kartika, my father's health worsened. We decided to inform Jalan Cendana and close friends. On Saturday, 18 June 2005, short messages were sent out. Early Sunday morning, while still half asleep, I received a text message from Mamiek informing me that Pak Harto wanted to visit my father in hospital. Half awake, I took a quick shower and, well aware that Pak Harto would be there on time, I jumped into a taxi. The driver gave me an uneasy look, wondering why a woman needed to put on her make up so early in the morning in the back of a taxi. As expected, Pak Harto arrived on the dot at RSPAD. I waited by the side entrance as Pak Harto used a walking stick to step down from his car. He looked very concerned, confused and distressed. We hugged each other and quickly took the elevator to Room 206.

By then, my father had descended into a coma. The doctors quickly decided to move him into the Intensive Care Unit (ICU). Pak Harto was stunned when informed of this, but he regained his composure almost immediately. He was upset when the ICU was not ready to make the transfer within the next 20 minutes. It was the first time I had observed how forceful Pak Harto could be. With difficulty in his speech but with firm authority, he asked us to check what was causing the delay. The ICU was immediately made ready when we informed the doctor in charge that Pak Harto had already been at the hospital since 8am. Pak Harto did not want to leave and decided to follow my father to the ICU. He also waited as the doctor and nurses installed the necessary equipment. At that moment, I perceived very clearly the depth of their friendship and how genuine it was.

"Dr Roeslan Abdulgani never spoke ill of anyone" was a statement from President Susilo Bambang Yudhoyono. Further, he has said that my father was usually critical, but in constructive ways. This is an accurate comment, as my father had been critical of Bung Karno and Pak Harto, but in a constructive manner. In his speeches, my father had often said that President Soekarno and President Soeharto had proven to be great leaders, regardless of what has been said or written about them. He had carefully studied speeches that President Soekarno and President Soeharto had made in their public engagements; he had recorded President Soeharto's speech in Pasar Klewer and made copies and sent it to Indonesia's leaders as he thought that President Soeharto's speech in Pasar Klewer was exceptional. Yet, at that stage, he was not close to President Soeharto and definitely did not belong to his inner circle. In fact, my father was Megawati's advisor in PDI and had guided her on how to watch her steps when President Soeharto was still very much against her. My father had said that big men made big mistakes and that President Soekarno and President Soeharto were equal in terms of being giants amongst the people, and both were icons that were larger than life. Since the era of reformation, he had hoped that, in the end, Indonesia would find a leader with the positive traits found in both President Soekarno and President Soeharto. The Indonesian people should not continue to bicker and find faults, so much so that they forget to move forward. Most importantly, they should close the chapter in Indonesian history which blames the two former presidents for what happened in the past. The people should read and study what scholars, historians and writers have written and their analyses and conclusions on the policies taken by these two leaders.

It should be borne in mind, however, that many of such published analyses and conclusions do not come from the voices of those whose lives have been directly affected by the two presidents, quite simply because the writers do not live in Indonesia. Figures like President Soekarno and President Soeharto were merely subjects of their academic studies. Therefore, it is necessary for Indonesians to view their history with a clear mind and within the context of the time, situation and conditions which affected the making or choosing of certain decisions or policies.

One should learn from the past with open eyes, with an open heart and with willingness to forgive the trespasses of others. In real life, there is *das sollen* and *das sein*, the "should be" and what is "real" in any given situation. Scholars usually observe history or the policies of a leader purely from the *das sollen* point of view and tend to have less empathy for the human factor. Perhaps that was how the term "ivory tower" came about, as scholars tend to live in a Utopian world. For members of the younger generation to be bright young things is one side of the story, but to be a worthy elder is another side of the whole equation. When we are young, we see things in black and white. As we mature and become older and wiser, we start to see things in shades of grey and brown.

As for President Soeharto's critics, my father had warned that they had "sensitivity chips … missing". It cannot be denied that Indonesia's economy had flourished in spite of corruption, human rights abuses and the "disappearance" of Supersemar. Majority of the people are well fed, sufficiently clothed and sheltered as compared to the situation in the early years of the country's freedom. Nevertheless, President Soeharto did not want to waste time arguing about the past but focused on fostering the spirit of unity while developing the country as best as he could. There are those amongst us now who long for a "return" of President Soeharto's era. On one occasion when I had mentioned this to him, Pak Harto had smiled and said, "*Saya sudah terlalu tua.*" ("I am too old already.") It was a similar situation which took place in 1998, when some were happy to have Megawati raised as the renaissance of President Soekarno era. As Pak Harto himself had written: "*Hidup seperti roda, apa yang naik akan turun.*" ("Life is like a rotating wheel, what goes up must come down.")

Just like Bung Karno, Pak Harto was also against total freedom. Freedom, as in a democracy, comprises an individual's rights, as well as the shouldering of responsibilities. Both presidents had doubts over whether the democracy known in the West was appropriate for Indonesia. President Soekarno and President Soeharto did believe in democracy, but the issue was which version would be suitable for Indonesia. President Soekarno introduced "Guided Democracy" while President Soeharto, "Democracy Pancasila"; both versions provided for a restricted form of liberalism as practised in the West. The restrictions were not imposed as a result of self-serving reasons, as many might have thought. The underlying factors which had led both presidents to a modified version of democracy as perpetuated by the West were Indonesia's culture, perspective of life and difference in lifestyle. In spite of being accused a lunatic and leftist-oriented, in reality, President Soekarno had leaned more towards Western ideas, while President Soeharto, despite his strong anti-communist stand and more pragmatic outlook, leaned inwards towards Indonesia's own heritage. Bung Karno was born in 1901. He had grown up and had been educated in an urban environment. Pak Harto was born in 1921. He had grown up and had been educated in a rural environment. They belonged to two distinctive generations. Nevertheless, the Javanese heritage was evident in both, but to a lesser extent in Bung Karno and more in Pak Harto. Both felt that free nations should take the firm position that no country in this world had the supreme right to use its power to dictate its concept of democracy and its views on human rights, much less to enforce them on others. The enforcement of a particular style of democracy is in itself a violation of its basic principles. It should be borne in mind and taken into consideration that each nation has it own value system different from other nations. Therefore, the concept of democracy needed adjustment to suit local conditions in order to be relevant to the place where it is applied.

Bung Karno's greatest achievements were freedom for the country and the unity of the people. Indonesia was one of the richest countries in the world, yet, most benefits had gone to the Dutch, its former colonial master. The people believed that after independence, social justice would be achieved. However, 21 years down the road, the government had a high deficit with rampant inflation. The share of the budget allocated to education and healthcare has steadily declined. The worst situation was in 1966, when the country was caught between two dangers. If General Soeharto had not done anything at that time, Indonesia could have become the second biggest communist country in the world. When General Soeharto stopped this, he was blamed for human rights abuses in killing thousands of communists. General Sumitro had said it was a matter of "kill, or be killed".

In the beginning, the Americans loved and fully supported President Soeharto, so much so that his opponents called him a CIA apparatus. The Japanese and Western investors put their money into heavy and light industries in the country because they trusted him. However, within a few years, President Soeharto's cronies and children came to be blamed for collusion and nepotism. In fact, foreign investors had also chosen his family members to be their business partners. When the honeymoon was over, President Soeharto became the sacrificial lamb. For now, writing about President Soeharto is like putting negative reviews of a book on its covers. For Pak Harto, it must feel like someone has broken into the house that he has spent a lot of time and faced great difficulty in building. The intruder has rearranged his furniture and made critical remarks on his taste, forgetting the limited resources that he had when he was building it. The West has also accused President Soeharto of having billions of dollars deposited abroad, including possibly in the United States. One wonders why the accusations have only arisen recently and the incidents were not dealt with at the time when they occurred, but that, as they say, is politics. My father had said, "In politics, there are no permanent friends and no permanent enemies; in politics, only self-interest is permanent."

The next day at 10.30 am, I called Suweden to inform him that my father had passed away. He asked me to advise him as to a suitable time that Pak Harto could come to our house as we had been told that President Susilo Bambang Yudhoyono was coming immediately to our house. Indeed, the president was there when my father was taken home. Soon, within half an hour after President Susilo Bambang Yudhoyono left, Pak Harto arrived with Tutut accompanying him. Try Sutrisno was there, as was Moerdiono and many more present and former ministers from the New Order and the Old Order. I could not help thinking that this must have been what my father had wanted: all the nation's leaders standing together and trying to continue what President Soekarno and President Soeharto had left unfinished. However, most of them kept their distance from Pak Harto as the latter looked blankly at my father's body. When he left, many photographers took shots of him but he did not show any emotion. The next day, Pak Harto's pictures were in almost all the newspapers. For the media, it seemed that Pak Harto remained a source of fascination and an enigma to them.

SEPTEMBER 2005

Those who have come to know Pak Harto all have one common impression of him: that he is a man from a simple background, and this was reinforced during our visit to Kemusuk, Yogya and Klaten in September 2005. Once a year, the ritual of visiting the graves of dead relatives takes place, usually a few days before the fasting month commences. For the Javanese, this is an almost sacred ritual. Mamiek had called me on 22 September to find out if I wanted to join her on her visit to Ibu Tien's grave. In fact, it had been my intention to visit Ibu Tien's grave before I finalised this book, and when I had once brought this subject up with Pak Harto, he had been happy with the idea and had agreed to it, advising me that it would be better if one of his daughters could accompany me. Thus, I jumped at Mamiek's invitation and immediately accepted it. Then, just a few hours before she came by to pick me up, she told me that Pak Harto was in Kemusuk as well and that I should prepare notes in case I needed to seek any clarifications for the book. I felt like I had won a million dollars in a lottery.

Mamiek and her son, Wira, picked me up and we flew to Yogya early in the morning of 23 September. By pure coincidence, we met one of Pak Harto's doctors, Dr Yuniarti Hatta and her husband, who were also on their way to Yogya. Unlike my trip in 2004, this time Garuda Indonesian Airways landed on time at Adisucipto Airport. A car was waiting for us and we were immediately whisked away to Gunung Pule in Kemusuk, as Pak Harto and the rest had already arrived there earlier that day. Mamiek's mobile phone kept ringing, almost every five minutes, for our exact location. One of those on the other end was Hardjo and his wife, Ibu Bress. Ibu Bress is Pak Harto's youngest stepsister, a sister of Probosutedjo and Suwito. All the children were there except for Titiek, who was still abroad, and Tommy, who was still in jail. Pak Harto, Tutut, Sigit, Bambang and others were waiting for our arrival; they had already visited Ibu Tien's grave in Mangadeg a day earlier.

Staring at the green rice fields and watching the humble houses along the way, I felt a sense of poignancy as the car sped along. It was all totally different from my trip in November 2004, when it had been raining and my spirit was gloomy. In September 2005, the sun was bright and my mood was upbeat, in anticipation of spending two full days with Pak Harto and his family. The people I saw along the way seemed to look happy and contented. It was still difficult for me to believe that my wish from the year before had come true as I was now returning to Kemusuk, but in such contrasting circumstances. There was no rain and there was no Suratin chatting non-stop while pointing out the important sites of Pak Harto's childhood.

It is common for the well-off to have their own family graveyard, thus when Ibu Sukirah died, she was buried amongst her own kin and her husband amongst his own, the Notosudiro family. Pak Harto's maternal family's burial place is on the same site as where Suratin had pointed out on that day in November 2004 when we were trying to locate Suwito. So, Suratin had been a good guide after all. Soon, our car arrived and there were many people standing at the bottom of the steps looking out for who would be coming next. Their faces showed curiosity, but they were respectful and kept themselves at a distance. There was no tight security as expected of a visit by a head of state. The cemetery was located on high ground, and as I put my feet on each step, I thought of how difficult it must have been for Suweden to help Pak Harto climb those stairs. We hurried to reach the top as we knew that everyone was waiting for us.

Once at the top, the first figure I saw was that of Pak Harto, with Tutut sitting next to him. Mamiek, Wira and I quickly kissed Pak Harto's cheek and we immediately took the flowers that had been left for us and laid them on several graves. There was a lovely smell as incense had been burnt in small decorative clay pots, which added to the serenity of the occasion. Meanwhile, Pak Harto waited and watched patiently as we moved from grave to grave, while Ibu Bress stood next to me, explaining which grave belonged to which person. Pak Harto's benign smile remained in place and his eyes showed contentment as he sat on the ground, his legs folded, looking pleased at what was going on. I reminded myself how lucky I was to have been there that day.

In the first row was the grave of Ibu Sukirah and this was the first grave we laid flowers on. The headstone simply read "Ny. Atmopawiro" as this was her married name when she died. Later, I suggested to Ibu Bress that perhaps "Ibu Sukirah" could be added on the tomb, so that it would be easier for historians to find, as this is how she is known as Pak Harto's mother.

Once we had finished, Pak Harto made the first move, followed by all of us. He walked very slowly when descending the steep steps accompanied by Suweden and Maliki holding each arm. We were all extremely concerned because it was not easy for him to walk down those steep steps. The people watched with anxiety and at the same time with gratitude, admiration and respect as a dignified elderly person stepped down slowly and with difficulty from the graveyard of his ancestors. There were no jubilant screams and no pushing and shoving to shake his hand. What was present at that moment was the expression of solidarity with the person who had been the pride of this village and appreciation for what he had done for their community. Their expressions painted the real picture of the common people, the genuine Indonesians, not the elite politicians who would have made use of such an occasion for their political benefit. These were the people for whom the government had in fact come into being. I was pleased to see that Pak Harto felt very relaxed and contented that day as he waved to hundreds of *wong cilik* as our cars left. Many of them managed to shake his hands but more were interested to take his photograph. Tutut and

Suweden politely apologised and told the crowd that Pak Harto had to go somewhere else.

Pak Harto sat in the same car with Tutut. At times like this, Tutut, being the eldest, was always by her father's side. With her veil, Tutut looked pretty and happy that day; she reminded me of Ibu Tien. She had taken over Ibu Tien's role after her mother's passing. I shared a car with Hardjo and Ibu Bress, as Tutut and Mamiek felt that Ibu Bress was the one who knew best about Pak Harto's family tree. Ibu Bress is an attractive lady, very friendly and down to earth. Her face is very much like the drawing of Ibu Sukirah (there being no photograph of Ibu Sukirah to be found anywhere). I was amused as she told me that she was a graduate of the "Ibu Tien School". What she meant was that she had been staying with Ibu Tien and Pak Harto since Tutut was a young child. I could clearly see how important Ibu Tien's role had been in Pak Harto and his family's lives. They adored Ibu Tien and she was the one who had managed to hold the family together.

Our drive took no more than 10 minutes to reach Suwito's domain. Pak Harto's father was laid to rest in the graveyard of the Kepoh family, which is located next to Suwito's house. It was there that I had noticed the statue of Pangeran Diponegoro back in November 2004. What a difference in my experience this time around as nobody stopped me and asked why I was there. Moreover, Suwito had been there with us from the start, but I did not think he remembered much of me. There were only two steps to climb to get to the site of the Kepoh graveyard; it was not as high as Gunung Pule and looked simpler. The names on the headstones were all written in Javanese script and there were more graves, making the graveyard more crowded. Flowers had been laid out, ready for us to spread and a different type of incense was being burnt. Again, I made a suggestion to Ibu Bress to add all the names, especially that of Pak Harto's father, in romanised letters, so that future researchers would not make mistakes.

It was almost one o'clock when we finished paying our respects to the dead. Lunch was served in Suwito's relatively large home and it consisted of a buffet set out on a long table with many local dishes that I had only seen for the first time in my life. This showed how diverse the country was; everything served were specialties from Kemusuk or the nearby vicinity. The glasses, utensils and plates were very simple. Pak Harto sat at the main table, again with Tutut beside him. I was asked to join them when Bambang came

over and knelt down to kiss his father's knee to bid him farewell as he had
to fly to Surabaya. Pak Harto gave him a fatherly peck on his forehead. This
is a very old Javanese custom that my siblings and I performed years ago on
our paternal grandmother, Mbah Plampitan, but not on my parents unless
it was during Lebaran. Soon thereafter, Dr Yuniarti and her husband turned
up unexpectedly and I could see how pleased Pak Harto was to see her as she
gave him a quick hug. They were comfortable and very friendly with each
other as they joined in and sat at our table. Pak Harto drank only water and
soon looked rather tired. Tutut encouraged him to take a short nap, and
he did but for no more than half an hour. After the afternoon prayer, we
proceeded with the next leg of our journey.

Pak Harto, 84 years old then, was attentive and looked very happy as
he visited each of the remaining families in Yogya and Klaten on the way
to Solo. Our first stop was at Hardjo and Ibu Bress' house. The house was
an old one and did not have much land, but the furniture looked nice and
fitted in well. There were several photographs of Pak Harto when he was the
president, just like in Suwito's house. It demonstrated the family's pride that
one of their close kin had become the Head of State. It was nicely decorated
but not extravagant. In this house, Pak Harto seemed very relaxed and this was
the place where Tutut asked me to sit with Pak Harto and speak to him about
what I was going to write in this book. Mamiek took a few photographs and
Pak Harto looked good in them as we shared a few laughs when I reminded
him of what had been written about him in his biography and other books. He
was mentally very sharp when we spoke about his childhood, how his marriage
had been arranged and his love for the farmer's life. However, he had difficulty
recollecting his last years in power. Less than an hour later, Tutut requested
that I end my conversation, as Pak Harto looked exhausted and too excited.

Soon thereafter, we continued with our trip, the next stops being the
homes of two women he had shared his tough adulthood with. They were
the sisters of Sudwikatmono or the children of Prawirowihardjo. The first
stop was the home of the elder of the two sisters. Mbah Hardjoso was in
her 90s and wheelchair bound. She was dressed in simple *kain kebaya* with
a tradition Javanese hairdo. There was no makeup, no gold nor diamond
jewellery that I could see on her. She looked like a middle class lady. There
was no air of snobbery about her; in fact, I did not detect any among
Pak Harto's close family. Pak Harto sat next to her and they held hands,

as they had not seen each other for years and this was the house they had grown up in together. I could see how close they were in the way they teased each other and the jokes that Pak Harto shared with her as they recalled the days gone by. Tutut asked Mbah Hardjoso whether her father had been a naughty boy when he was young; she gave a quick "yes" in reply and everyone had a good laugh.

We were served tea, coffee and cookies in very ordinary-looking cups and plates. There were no exquisite embroidered napkins, just plain paper serviettes. In observing the whole setting of his family and relatives in their home environment informally, I could not see any truth in the common perception that Pak Harto's family were all well-off with benefits received during his presidency; definitely not in the case of Mbah Hardjoso and Mbah Dwidjo Kartono, the next person whom we visited that day. The house was relatively big but with little and very simple furniture. There were no paintings on the wall. When we left, Tutut handed over a small envelope to Pak Harto, which he in turn handed over to Mbah Hardjoso. They bid farewell affectionately as she remained seated in her wheelchair with bare feet. Her face showed distress as she waved us goodbye.

On our way to Klaten, a police siren sounded and the police officers waved their hands for us to slow down so that another car could pass our entourage. It must have been an important or high-ranking official on his way to a meeting. Our cars drove with no escorts, so we slowed down and gave way. I wish I knew how Pak Harto felt at times like this as he must have gotten used to a police escort after over 30 years in office. I also wondered what the official with the police escort would have done if he knew that the car that had stopped for him had Pak Harto in it. Would he bow, step down and shake his hand or prefer to ignore him?

We soon reached Klaten and the house of Mbah Dwidjo Kartono, a younger sister of Mbah Hardjoso. She was in her late 80s and, unlike her elder sister, she could still walk, although she needed the help of a three-wheel push stick. While Mbah Hardjoso had only one child, Mbah Dwidjo managed to take care of 16 children, and yet her late husband had only been a teacher. Her house was smaller and simpler than Mbah Hardjoso's and it was also very close to her neigbours; there was no frontyard. Hence, all the cars were parked along the small street outside her house. The environment was more like a *kampong* as one house stood so close to another with hardly any garden in each property. The house quickly became very crowded as we entered and her family welcomed Pak Harto with obvious joy. They must have gone all out to welcome his visit. Again, we were served food and drinks in plain cups and plates, and with tin forks and spoons. Once again, there were plenty of food and drinks but the gold plated dishes and silver cutlery were missing. Mbah Dwidjo, like her elder sister, was dressed simply in *kain kebaya* with simple sandals, and no makeup and jewellery. The rest of the family were humble folks as well and many of their children stared at us with wide eyes, curious to see Pak Harto. Some of them had to stay in the kitchen or bedrooms, as the guest room was very small. The whole ambience was just like our small house in *kampong* Plampitan. Everybody wanted to take photographs with Pak Harto and Tutut. When we left, all of them stood in a row to shake our hands and it was such a touching sight to see how happy they were to receive Pak Harto that day. Pak Harto must have had a strong intuition, as Mbah Dwidjo passed away recently.

This visit in 2005 had been a rare occasion; Pak Harto had not done this in years even when he had been president. Therefore, I was extremely pleased to have been able to witness and to confirm his very traditional and very caring behaviour towards those who had done good things in his past. It also reaffirmed that what he has done for his family was to reciprocate their kindness as practised in the Javanese tradition. Their simple houses and the way in which ample food and drink were so graciously served prompted me to become nostalgic about my own childhood. The simplicity of their houses, the surroundings they lived in made me wonder what had happened to the alleged billions that Pak Harto was supposed to have amassed. Had Pak Harto been so stingy and unwilling to share it with those who had taken care of him when he was young? This is hard to believe knowing that no matter how poor or rich one is, one is expected to share accordingly: "*Ada sedikit dibagi sedikit, ada banyak dibagi banyak.*" ("If you have a little, share a little; if you have more, share more.") Being very traditional Javanese in character, if Pak Harto had indeed behaved contrary to what was expected of him, it would be completely out of character and in total contrast to the person that he is.

It must have been close to 4 pm when we reached the city of Solo and Ibu Bress asked where I would stay. My small luggage was in Mamiek's car, and she had not joined us in Yogya and Klaten as she had gone to visit other relatives who had taken care of her when she was young. Hardjo decided to call Mamiek and I was on cloud nine when he told me that I was to stay in Kalitan. Kalitan sounded like beautiful music to my ears as I had heard so much about the place that it made my imagination run wild. This small *kraton* was supposedly very lavish, with gold fixtures and silver cutlery for serving guests, just like the old European palaces. According to gossip, Kalitan was a palace with gold-framed doors and windows and chandeliers hanging from the ceiling, all imported from Prague. There were gold plates like those which the Shah of Iran used to have. In my imagination, Kalitan looked like a small version of Versailles, with a gallery of paintings costing millions of dollars; and why not, after all, Pak Harto was supposed to be a billionaire.

However, as we entered the courtyard of Kalitan, I was quickly disappointed. The main entrance was just a miniature version of an entrance to any *kraton* in Yogya or Solo. There was no sign of grandeur to be found so far; the *pendopo* (the front part) was tiny compared to the ones in Mangkunegaran and Kasuhunan Solo. Inside the building, there was a medium-sized living room and another larger family room close by, where Pak Harto often sat and watched the television. The dining area had a round table which seated no more than 12 people. There was a long hall or corridor with entrances to bedrooms on either side. Pak Harto's room was not located along this hall but it was close by. There was a picture of Ibu Tien and Pak Harto hanging prominently in the main living room. The furniture was similar to that found in Jalan Cendana. Overall, everything was very simple and ordinary compared to the houses belonging to the conglomerates in Jakarta and the palaces I have seen.

I stayed in Tommy's room, next to Tutut's while Mamiek's room was on the other side of the hall. Tommy's room has a picture of him with his wife and small son; in fact, there was still a crib in the room. Everything else was again far from luxurious. Pak Harto rested as I slept like a baby, feeling much relief that from what I had witnessed that day, everything had proven that Pak Harto was not a crook and was not living like a real sultan, at least not at Jalan Cendana and Kalitan. A sultan would have his *abdi dalem*, inner servants who were on call at all times and who would crawl on their knees whenever they served the sultan; the ladies would have to wear a *kemben*, a strapless dress made from *batik*, and the men had to wear the traditional sarong and shirt, with a *blangkon* to cover their heads. I looked around for such a scene, expecting that I would find one in Kalitan; instead, I saw men in ordinary trousers, short-sleeved shirts and no *blangkon* as they walked about in front of Pak Harto.

Although they all went back and forth to perform their routine jobs, no one serving him had to kneel like in a real *kraton*. There was no butler to be seen and I was advised to just get from the refrigerator if I wanted something cold and to pour my own tea and coffee. It was all self-service like in a modern cafeteria or school canteen. The food was there on a table and those who felt hungry could just take and eat whatever appealed to their palate. At 5 pm, I saw Pak Harto looking fresh in his sarong and long shirt while trying to zip his jacket. He had some difficulty with it until Mamiek went over to help him.

When Pak Harto asked whether I had slept well, I teasingly replied, "No, because I was busy looking for the gold hidden under Tommy's bed the whole night." We had a good laugh and I was, in fact, relieved that there was no proof of the gold and the situation had shown how rumours could spin out of control.

Kalitan was plain and very much like an average Indonesian middle-class household. It could certainly have done with better maintenance, as it looked rather run down. Ibu Tien had bought Kalitan from a princess who needed money, thus this property had a historical value. In any other country, places like Kalitan would have been taken over by the government if the owner was proven to have bought it with corrupt money. In the present case, the government had no money to take it over and, more importantly, there was no evidence that Pak Harto had bought it using corrupt funds. This same situation is in fact happening in Taman Mini, Museum Purna Bhakti Pertiwi, which the family has been willing to hand over to the government.

Not only did Pak Harto eat just rice and one dish at meal times, but his children also preferred to eat food that they bought from the local vendors. For the vendors, they must have considered it their lucky day whenever the family was there in Kalitan. The seller of *sate* (satay/kebabs), *soto* (soup) and other local goodies would come into the Kalitan compound and stay on the terrace. The offerings were delicious, with most of them being dishes from Solo and, best of all, they were very cheap. Some were just served on banana leaves; and no one had any qualms about eating the food directly from the very simple plates provided by the vendors. The bodyguards, drivers, Pak Harto's doctors and security personnel all ate the same food from these vendors. Pak Harto would pay for all the food. In fact, the glasses and crockery used in Kalitan were as simple as the ones used in Mbah Hardjoso and Mbah Dwidjo's homes.

At 7 am that morning and after taking a walk, I found Pak Harto already seated on the terrace and getting a little sun. Again, he wore a sarong and a long-sleeved black shirt. He looked so peaceful as he watched everybody going about their own business. Suweden said that this was the morning ritual he had to follow on the doctor's instructions. When it was time for us to have breakfast, once again the street vendors came into the compound as we moved into the dining room. Pak Harto again ate very little rice with one dish and drank some tea. The same routine was followed during lunch and dinner. The street vendors would return with different foods in the evenings. Most of the family preferred to eat food sold by the vendors and they spread out on the floor to eat their meal. Only Suweden, Sigit and I accompanied Pak Harto to have our food at the table. The whole atmosphere was very relaxed and informal; anyone could come and go as they pleased. In the living room, there were fruits, candies and snacks at all times and everyone was free to taste what was on offer.

After his meals, Pak Harto would take a short walk around the house slowly and in small steps. Dr Hari always stayed close by, as every few hours Pak Harto's blood pressure had to be checked. The first day when we had just arrived, Pak Harto's blood pressure was higher than normal. Apparently, the physical exertion of visiting the graveyards and families had made an impact on his health. In the early evening, Pak Harto watched television, especially the news. Suweden was never far from him. This was the best time to get his attention for my book; I had prepared the event on which I wanted Pak Harto's comments. I knew by that time that Pak Harto was not able to reply to direct questions. I had to reconstruct the incident in question and from there I would ask for his clarifications. If I made a mistake, he would get excited, as he wanted to correct it. Therefore, Suweden or Maliki had to be present nearby to lend a hand when necessary.

Pak Harto still maintains his sense of humour, but this is so only if he is in a relaxed atmosphere and with those he feels comfortable. On occasions like these, I would tell him things that made him laugh. One morning, after I had interviewed the gardener who had worked for years in Kalitan, I informed Pak Harto of my findings. When the riots occurred in May 1998, many buildings were burnt in Solo. The gardener told me that hundreds of people had marched with torches, ready to burn important sites. One of the houses that had been torched was the Harmoko family house. The mob had also passed Kalitan, but Kalitan was well guarded by the local residents. Hence, the mob stayed away. When I asked the gardener why the local residents had guarded Kalitan so well, he had replied that, firstly, the residents liked Pak Harto, and secondly, if Kalitan was burnt, their houses too might have caught fire. Pak Harto smiled upon hearing this, and commented slowly, "Of course, the second reason is more important." I was glad to see his happy face as he made this wise remark.

The gardener had recalled the times when Pak Harto was still president; he, too, confirmed that Pak Harto's lifestyle has never changed and has remained at the same modest standard through the years. The only difference when he came while he was president was that there had been more security personnel and guests. Even so, the food arrangements, the vendors and the way everybody dressed did not change. The gardener, too, felt sorry that Kalitan had not been properly maintained. He informed me that a few students still came to inspect Kalitan. They have the same intention as everyone else: to find the gold that is supposedly hidden somewhere out here. Of course, none has ever been found.

In the afternoon, Mamiek took us to Mangadeg to visit Ibu Tien's final resting place. Located on the slopes of Gunung Lawu, it is 38 km east of Solo. Dr Yuniarti, her husband Hatta, Wira, Mamiek and I went in one car. Pak Harto looked happy as he waved us off on a safe journey. It was a smooth drive and the scenery got better as we got closer to Mangadeg. The view from the site itself was breathtaking and the weather was much cooler in this locality. We noticed that there was fog as we looked down the side of the hill. At the top of Gunung Lawu is a cemetery called Astana Giri Bangun; it was built for the Mangkunegaran family and only direct members from this *kraton* were buried there. As Ibu Tien had only been a distant relative, she was not entitled to be buried there. Hence, Mangadeg was built in 1970 on a 2.5 hectare extension. Yayasan Bangun Mangadeg, established on 28 October 1969, was formed to build the new graveyard, Mangadeg, as well as to renovate Astana Giri Bangun. The foundation has 28 members; President Soeharto and Ibu Tien had sat on the board as the advisor and chairman, respectively. President Soeharto had officiated its opening in 1976 and since then, they have removed the remains of Ibu Tien's father from his previous burial ground and installed his remains in Mangadeg. In 1988, when Ibu Tien's mother passed away, she was buried in Mangadeg as well. On arrival, there was once again some disappointment as Dr Yuniarti and I were surprised that the graveyard was nowhere as lavish as what we had heard. The marble supposedly imported from Italy was only of a local variety and it was nothing like the graveyards of European royalty. It was more elaborate than an ordinary public burial ground, but not as elaborate as rumours had indicated. The wood was nicely carved, but no more than other elaborate carvings found elsewhere in the country.

As Mangadeg was built and managed by a foundation, members of the foundation would also be buried here even if they were not related to the Mangkunegaran family. The total site was able to accommodate 339 graves, therefore, it was not only a family graveyard but also for all the Yayasan members and their families. Mangadeg consisted of three levels with each one named in Javanese: *Argo Tuwuh*, *Argo Kembang* and *Argo Sari*. The steps leading up to the site were not as high as those at Imogiri, the burial ground for the Sultan of Yogya. Ibu Tien and her parents were located on the highest level, *Argo Sari*. Next to Ibu Tien is an empty plot reserved for Pak Harto. The second level, *Argo Kembang*, is reserved for Pak Harto's six children, amongst others. The third and lowest level is reserved for the foundation members and their children. A small pavilion had been built next to the site as a brief resting place for Ibu Tien and Pak Harto when they visited. The resting room was very simple and small, comprising only a small hall and a tiny washroom. As in Kemusuk, flowers had been prepared for our arrival and incense was being burnt. The ambience here was quieter due to its isolated location away from the main public road. After we had laid the flowers on the respective graves, a few people who had arrived before us started to pray. We managed to have a few small snacks that Mamiek had brought along. The people in Java like to eat at any time and any place, a custom not restricted only to the wealthy but also poor farmers, who carried food with them whenever they travelled, if they could afford it.

When we arrived back in Kalitan, Pak Harto was keen to hear about our trip. We had been given a local fruit, the Sawo Solo, a small brownish fruit that has to be peeled to reveal the edible interior, and it has a very sweet taste. Dr Yuniarti showed the package to Pak Harto as she made a lighthearted complaint that this was all we got instead of gold. Pak Harto's eyes beamed as we bantered, seemingly pleased that we had discovered the truth about Kalitan and Mangadeg ourselves.

My impression of Probosutedjo was completely changed as I got to know him during my research for this book. Probosutedjo is more open, direct and outspoken than his famous brother. Despite their difference in personality, they have something in common—not only their admiration for their mother, Ibu Sukirah, but, more importantly, the charities that they held close to their hearts. Sadly, however, just like his brother, very few people realise that Probosutedjo, in spite of all his mistakes and shortcomings, is also a philanthropist. Of course, his critics have claimed that the money spent on his charities was derived from corrupt practices. Probosutedjo has also opened schools, universities and given scholarships, amongst others, and when his brother was in power, he had often voiced strong criticisms against his policies which he felt benefited only the Chinese conglomerates. He often pointed to the different treatment which the government gave to the non-Chinese or small indigenous businessmen. President Soeharto's opponents considered this a cover-up to show that President Soeharto allowed criticisms. President Soeharto's opponents accused Probosutedjo's business ventures of being crony-capitalist. Among Pak Harto's cronies, Probosutedjo has remained loyal while others have detached themselves completely from him. Probosutedjo is often in the spotlight for his court cases. Unfortunately, at the time of writing, he has been sentenced to jail.

REFLECTIONS ON PAK HARTO'S LIFE

A tranquil environment still surrounds Kemusuk, which is proud that the family of its most prominent son has developed the village from every aspect, while retaining its essential cultural and historical characteristics. The road has been improved since the early 1970s, so have the houses, but the rice crops are still laid out on the asphalt to dry in the sun in preparation for milling, and when the harvest arrives, more space on the public road is taken for drying the crops. This symbolises the fact that even though there have been changes for the better, such as the asphalt road, some of the farmers' traditions have remained intact.

A long time ago, there was a rumour about Pak Harto's origins, that his father had been someone from the *kraton* of Yogya. To clarify this issue, a press conference was organised on 28 October 1974 at Bina Graha. At that event, his family tree was discussed with the local and foreign media, and his close relatives were invited as witnesses. President Soeharto firmly denied the rumour and quoted a Javanese saying: "A little bit of cough, an inch of land." In short, it meant that the rumour about his illegitimate origins would be detrimental not only to his standing and his family's but it would also be unsettling for the people and the nation. After all, he was the president and he did not want his mother's reputation to be tarnished as a woman without values. More importantly, a scandal like this could have been manipulated for political reasons and used to damage his position as the Head of State by referring to him as an illegitimate child. The incident showed that when it came to family matters, President Soeharto was able to stand upright and confront any hearsay in an open forum.

Yet, most of the time, Pak Harto's manner follows that of the Javanese: he behaves such that his speech does not show strong reactions or anger. He speaks with a serene tone devoid of emotions. Ambiguous phrases like *saya rasa* (I feel), *barangkali* (maybe) and *mbok menawi* (perhaps) amongst others, are considered by the Javanese to be terms of politeness. The Javanese do not make direct comments when asked but instead they believe in being non-confrontational. This behaviour was clearly evident in President Soeharto's style of governing.

As with any other Javanese person, Pak Harto's outlook on life was based on two factors: that fate plays a key role in every situation and human action and that it is impossible to change one's destiny. After he stepped down from power, Pak Harto wrote, "If God has decided for one to lead, nobody can make the leader step down from his/her rule. When God has determined for a leader to step down, nobody can put it off."[3] He had expressed this view to Saadillah Mursjid just hours before he gave the public statement of his decision to step down.

Some people have said that the Javanese in Indonesia are like the British in Europe, as the true Javanese are an extremely polite and refined people. Loud displays of emotions and flamboyant conduct are considered poor manners by the Javanese. This description paints an accurate picture of Pak Harto's manner and behaviour. However, his reserved approach and reluctance to make anyone feel uncomfortable or to embarrass anyone in public makes it hard to understand or guess what he is really thinking. Indeed, the last thing he would show is what he truly means. There are hints in his expression and gestures but they are not easy to decipher. He would only openly smile and joke with those whom he knows well and trusts, but getting to know him and earning his trust takes time and is not an easy task. Furthermore, he has very strong instincts and in most cases, except in a few rare cases, his judgment of people has always been very accurate.

Although fate brought him to the highest office in Indonesia, Pak Harto has been proven to be a person who is not easily impressed by those who are better qualified than he. He is not a person who can be easily challenged by intellectuals and academics, whether they have degrees in economics and/or the social and political sciences. He has not felt inferior in any way; on the contrary, he has managed to utilise their talents. He took on the academics as his advisors, especially in economic matters of which he knew the least. His ministers have affirmed that President Soeharto analysed economic issues in a simplistic way and applied common sense in working out problems. He would resolve issues brought to his attention based on his own judgment. As the Head of State, he never pushed for himself to be given any honorary degree or allowed himself to be intimidated by scholars. Pak Harto seems to be happy and contented and he took life in his stride and did not feel like a second-class citizen with his insignificant schooling. His self-confidence made him a successful person as he used his own limitations to improve education for the people whose fate had been like his. He used negative events in his early life as a benchmark for improving the living conditions of the people.

One of the key factors for President Soekarno's loss of control over his massive popular power was the economic issue, but Pak Harto never challenged the fact that Bung Karno and Bung Hatta had declared Indonesia independent and that Bung Karno and Bung Hatta had made Indonesia proud to be a free nation. He had been a faithful soldier in defending the country's achievements from the day it became a free state. He had obeyed President Soekarno's instructions to quash the rebellions and to take back the territory which had been legally Indonesia's, like West Irian. He was happy that the country has stayed united and that he has managed to keep it this way for over 30 years. Gone were the days of discrimination, when the people were servants or coolies in their own homeland. They are now masters in their own land. For this, he has a high regard for the nation's founding fathers and leaders like Bung Karno and Bung Hatta, although many doubted his sincerity.

A devout Muslim, just like Bung Karno, Pak Harto has respected the freedom of religious belief, which is a principle recognised by all modern nations. It is obvious that some Western countries have misunderstood and sometimes been skeptical about the wide appeal of President Soekarno and President Soeharto's strategy to keep Pancasila intact. However, when acts of extreme terrorism took place, these skeptics have kept silent. The West never criticised President Soekarno when he assailed DI/TII under Kartosuwiryo for years since 1950, neither did they make negative remarks when President Soeharto captured Abu Bakar Ba'asyir in 1983. During the Cold War, the West was happy when President Soekarno crushed the communist rebellion under Muso in 1948. When President Soeharto let the army kill hundreds of PKI members after G30S, only a few claimed that he had abused human rights.

For a diverse country like Indonesia, it was important to develop a national identity. President Soekarno introduced the national dress. President Soeharto continued his efforts by compiling the various traditions from each island, although, personally, he was more attuned to the Javanese culture and philosophy, the basic orientation of which was derived from the pre-Islamic era. However, both had managed to hold the country together by respecting other faiths and being moderate Muslims by relying on the five principles of Pancasila.

Pak Harto was considered to be an inward-looking individual with limited exposure to Western thinking. Hence, to compare Bung Karno, an urban product, with Pak Harto, who came from a rural setting, would be like comparing apples and oranges. Pak Harto himself had acknowledged this fact when he once wrote that Bung Karno and Bung Hatta were highly educated while he was not. His strength had been his reliance on common sense and his ability to be a fast learner. Bung Karno and Pak Harto have, in real terms, a similar view when it came to Western ideas. The West celebrated individuality and allowed people to make their own choices, including in the area of religion. Bung Karno and Pak Harto believed that the term "individuality" might have sounded too similar to the other American ideal of "individualism", the difference being that "individualism" referred to the principle of "I am for myself", while "individuality" related to the notion of being the person of one's own choice, that is, "I am myself, and my society should be able to benefit from my uniqueness".

President Soekarno introduced the concept of Guided Democracy in 1959. After his downfall, President Soekarno was bombarded with accusations and all kinds of names including "crooked", "corrupt", "power hungry", to name but a few. Alas, the observers and commentators had ignored the conditions surrounding the situation when President Soekarno made his decision to introduce Guided Democracy. He came to that decision at a time when the Cold War was being played out and communism was a force to be reckoned with. Many had conveniently ignored the fact that the communist rebellion under Muso in 1948 was an act against President Soekarno's policy of continuing negotiations with the Dutch for a peaceful solution. Muso had thought it was useless to prolong the discussions and President Soekarno decided to crush the Muso rebellion. Yet, in 1966, President Soekarno was accused of being too lenient and allegedly favouring PKI or the communist party. President Soekarno had argued that PKI had received six million votes in 1955, hence making it the fourth largest political party at that time. President Soeharto was obviously against the communist party from the start, but he did not join the Muslim radicals who were against the PKI. Like President Soekarno, President Soeharto wanted to stay neutral between the two opposing groups. The most significant early policy had been to devise an Indonesian brand of democracy and to name it "Democracy Pancasila". President Soeharto also declared that Pancasila was the only approved foundation for all political parties. This difference in terminology between "Guided" and "Pancasila" should not impede the crucial understanding that both leaders had assessed and concluded that Western-style democracy in its entirety would not have complemented the Indonesian ideals of governing.

President Soekarno's focus had been to keep the country's freedom intact. He felt that Indonesia would not be the same without Bali, Kalimantan, Sulawesi and the other islands. The dream of Indonesia's founding fathers would not be fulfilled if the vast archipelago was fractured due to differences in ideology, race and other beliefs. The Indonesian people's faith in the ideology of Pancasila had to be upheld at all cost. The price that President Soekarno paid for this was to be mocked as a dictator and an egoistical warmonger, and for causing the country's economic decline. There might well have been some truth in the allegations, but President Soekarno had to walk a very precarious tightrope between keeping Indonesia united and losing precious time for pursuing the country's economic development. President Soekarno had a firm answer to this issue: freedom and unity at all cost.

President Soekarno had tried hard to combine the three forces of nationalism, communism and religion (Nasakom), but that attempt failed with the abortive *coup* by the communists in 1965. President Soeharto had no intention of wasting time by allowing a repetition of history. President

Soeharto's main task then was to stop inflation, to avoid starvation and to spell out clearly what freedom meant in terms of the economy. His survival would depend on how quickly he could take remedial action on all vital fronts. Only a few were wise enough to note that President Soeharto had, in fact, continued the key and crucial policies taken by President Soekarno. His pragmatism dictated that he should learn from the lessons of his predecessor, hence he abolished the communist party immediately. For this, he was accused of murdering millions of communist party members and their families. President Soeharto, too, was termed as being autocratic and accused of having suppressed human rights.

Democracy is, without doubt, best for a society where the majority have achieved equality and equal access to education and where the welfare mechanisms are in place, in other words, where the majority fall within the middle class band. Western democracy may not necessarily be the right solution in a country where there is a wide gap amongst the people in terms of education, welfare and income. It is not right to accuse Indonesia of failing to implement democracy as practised in the Western world. President Soekarno had practised it during the early years of the country's freedom—it has been widely acknowledged that the 1955 general elections was the first truly democratic voting procedure in the country. However, soon thereafter, the number of political parties mushroomed and the euphoria of freedom for all led to the government's Cabinets surviving only less than an average of two years each. With such a constant fluctuation in the government, how could any country focus its efforts on development? It is perhaps also worth noting that Germany experienced a proliferation of political parties during the Weimar Republic, which subsequently led to the rise of Hitler. During their time in power, President Soekarno and President Soeharto believed that democracy was a precious but precarious set of values. In order to subscribe to the concept of democracy, it has to be demonstrated that the majority of the people have faith in the elections process and the virtues of responsibility and honour. Indeed, Indonesia'a first two presidents had many doubts over the virtue of democracy, as it appeared that each time they wanted to apply democracy as practised in the West, Indonesian society became unmanageable. This had been President Soeharto's main argument for deciding to stay away from Western-style democracy. It is possible that the majority of the Indonesian people had a hard time making a distinction between democracy and total liberalism, as the latter undoubtedly leads to anarchy. My father used to tell Pak Harto that after 1998, instead of "Guided Democracy", Indonesia had "Guided Anarchy".

From a young age, Bung Karno's crusade was to combine the country's varied and multiracial society into one nationalist movement. Bung Karno had been a firm believer that the absence of such unity would shatter the very nucleus of Indonesia's existence. Since then, Indonesia has shown a strong commitment towards supporting other nations, especially in Asia and Africa, to be free from their colonial masters. There had been reports that the Western powers, including Great Britain, had been very troubled and had tried to sabotage the gathering in Bandung of the Asia Africa Conference in 1955. As time went by and the Cold War ended, the Bandung Conference became the nucleus for the Non-Aligned Movement as followed by President Soeharto. A similar conference was organised in Belgrade from 1 to 6 September 1961 and it was attended by 24 countries. This was followed by the gathering in Cairo from 5 to 10 October 1964 with a presence of 47 nations. During Soeharto's government, there were a few more of these meetings, such as the one in Lusaka from 8 to 10 September 1970, where 53 countries attended, followed by the one in Algiers from 5 to 9 September 1973 with 75 attendees, in Colombo from 16 to 19 August 1976 with 85 countries, in Havana from 3 to 9 September 1979 with 92 nations, in New Delhi from 7 to 12 March 1983 with 100 participating countries, in Harare from 6 to 9 September 1986 with 101 countries, in Belgrade from 4 to 7 September 1989 with 104 states and in Jakarta from 1 to 6 September 1992 where 112 countries attended. The country was also under President Soeharto when ASEAN was established on 8 August 1967 in Bangkok. The primary objective of this association was to promote and increase economic, social and cultural growth of the member states. The member states wanted to protect the political and economic stability of the region and the association would serve as a venue for resolving inter-regional differences. The founding members were Thailand, Indonesia, Singapore, Malaysia and the Philippines. Asia (and Southeast Asian nations in particular) has come a long way since Indonesia's independence in 1945.

The Second World War signalled an end to centuries of colonial domination in Asia—some more gracefully done than others. Those countries under Britain were generally considered to have been in a better position than those colonised by the Dutch. The Dutch were considered to be one of the worst amongst the colonial masters, as being from a small country, they were more narrow-minded. Bung Karno had formulated the Non-Aligned concept together with the great world leaders of that time: Jawaharlal Nehru from India, U Nu from Burma, Joseph Broz Tito from Yugoslavia, Gamal Abdul Nasser from Egypt and Kwame Nkrumah from Ghana.

Pak Harto recalled his dialogue with President Soekarno in Semarang back in 1958 on the potential danger of PKI. President Soekarno had stood firm on his concept of Nasakom, believing that he would be able to convert PKI to the concept of Pancasila. As President Soekarno's subordinate, General Soeharto's approach had been a soft one. He quoted the Javanese verse, "*Sura dira jayaning rat lebur dening pangestuti*" ("Emotion and bravery should bend down to calmness and patience"). He recalled the period from 1965 to 1967 and said, "If you argue with someone who is agitated, he would be more upset; but if we demonstrate understanding and show respect, he would listen." That explained the nature of the birth of Supersemar. General Soeharto knew that President Soekarno would not be able to control the situation and President Soekarno knew that General Soeharto had the capability but would not do what he (President Soekarno) wanted. Dialogues went on between them until President Soekarno was convinced that General Soeharto would continue to use Pancasila and not harm him personally. In compliance with safeguarding President Soekarno's personal interest, after Pak Harto began his rule, there were reports that he had given petrol stations to Bung Karno's five children from Ibu Fatmawati to start their own business.

The colonial era gave rise to a strong sense of nationalism and it became the national identity of the modern Indonesian state. It is naive to believe that the authors of the 1945 Constitution were influenced by the centralised Japanese political model. Indonesia's nationalist movement started back in 1825 with Kebangkitan Nasional. That was the birth of nationalism as proclaimed by Indonesia's founding fathers. The Asian nations were in the midst of civil war as Indonesia emerged from colonial rule. The country had to fight hard to find its feet. It became worse with the Cold War and during the war that took place in Vietnam and Korea. However, consider Indonesia's position at the present time: in 2005, Indonesia was no longer comparable to Myanmar, Laos and Cambodia, as along with the other Southeast Asian nations, it has surged ahead. In a region of 500 million people, almost half are in Indonesia. President Soekarno and President Soeharto were forced to step down from power during the country's critical phases. For President Soekarno, it had been when inflation reached 600 per cent per annum and for President Soeharto when the currency collapsed. Both were at the centre of power and both had been too late to take action when the people became restless. Before President Soekarno fell out of power, he had suggested Kerukunan Nasional or national harmony. This reflected President Soekarno's concern for the disintegration of the nation's unity. Yet, Indonesians have killed their own to an estimated figure of at least 500,000 to a million after G30S. President Soeharto, too, had called for reformation during his final hours in power.

Sadly, although there is a general yearning for national reconciliation, what is continuing at present is, in fact, grouping according to political and shared interests. In addition, when Bung Karno and Pak Harto were out of the public's favour, many of their cronies turned their backs on them. Some members of their inner circle left them out in the cold. Another similarity is the demand to put Bung Karno and Pak Harto on trial, not only for political reasons but for allegations of corruption as well: Bung Karno for his *dana revolusi* or revolution funds and Pak Harto for his Yayasan or foundations. In Bung Karno's case, there had been no trial and Pak Harto's trial was halted due to his ill health; therefore, in both cases, the issues have never been clarified.

Pak Harto, the Person

Like in a game of poker, Pak Harto is not easily read, at least from the Westerners' point of view. My own experience is that once Pak Harto comes to know and trust someone, he emerges as an open and warm person. Pak Harto would never hesitate to come to a decision once he has made up his mind, even if it would be an unpopular one. This probably took root from his military background. He followed the rule of "attack enemies at their centre of power", that solutions to problems should be taken at their roots. In economic matters, he applied the same principles. He knew that the basis of improving trade and industry was rooted in efficiency, an efficiency which required the coordination and solidarity of all departments. To achieve this, Pak Harto took all important decision-making on a whole and not on a piecemeal basis as he felt that an iron hand was necessary in order to carry out his development programme effectively.

Pak Harto had looked at development within the whole context of governing the country. His first priority was security, without which there would be no stability. For this purpose, he did not have any qualms about applying military discipline with an iron fist. For those who tried to rock the boat, he did not hesitate in retaliating, with the level of response dependent on each situation. If the boat was rocked in a gentle manner, he would use a softer approach in responding; if the boat was shaken violently, he would hit back; if the boat was rocked to the point of it sinking, he would make the offender disappear. Ali Sadikin rocked the boat violently by signing *Petisi 50*. This was broadly publicised and, not surprisingly knowing Pak Harto's loathing of public confrontations, he retaliated by attacking Ali Sadikin hard.

For Pak Harto, one of the most important aspect of his job as the president was to improve the lives of the people. He knew that for the people at the grassroots level, having enough food, clothing and a roof over their heads was necessary to meet their basic requirements and to keep them happy. If there was happiness, peace would prevail. He could then focus on the next level of important basic needs, that is education and healthcare. However, he was also aware that material well-being was linked to spiritual contentment, without which greed, selfishness and a free-fighting liberalism would take place. For him, such a form of liberalism could not take place in the country while there was still a big gap in access to education and wealth distribution. The gap had to be narrowed or, at best, closed. Only then would Indonesian society be ready to take on the liberalism of the West. The leaders of the 2005 forum rightly blamed the world's ills on the way the news media interpreted events, rather than on any real shortcomings in the institutions of the governments which they presided over. "We are exposed to more opinion than at any time in our history," declared Prince Hasan bin-Talal of Jordan. "We have info-tainment, info-terror. I would like to see some info-wisdom." A statement very much in line with the sentiments of President Soekarno and President Soeharto.

President Soeharto clearly knows how to behave in a crisis, by closing defences and exercising the utmost restraint and discretion. An Australian leader once said, "Pak Harto was a president with a great deal of dignity and a great deal of pride whatever his critics may say of him."[4] Despite his simple background, Pak Harto had acquired the most important aspect of the Javanese upper class: the ability to maintain a gracious silence. In spite of his humble origins, he has the established manners of the Javanese *priyayi*, to which entry is guaranteed only by birth. He seemed to live with an awareness that he was never alone and that there was always someone watching him. Further, he is understanding by nature, although this is not always expressed. He also displays tolerance in an odd sort of way, almost like a form of compassion for the plight of the human condition, which is more visible in him now than before. Like most Javanese people, I believe that Pak Harto is a fatalist, in the sense that when he finds himself in a situation beyond his control, he is able to accept it and make the best of it under the circumstances.

The legacy of his time in power is a painful one that will not be quickly forgotten. Nevertheless, a wealthy Indonesian middle class has emerged, tourism has boomed and, most importantly, schoolchildren have hope. A bracing vitality has rejuvenated the nation. It is easy to comment only on the negative aspects of his administration, yet, how many Indonesian adults today would be where they are now without him? How did many of the young educated Indonesians today receive an education if their parents did not have sufficient funds to send them to school? How many Indonesians today have telephones, radios and television sets? All these were made possible through the infrastructure put in place during President Soeharto's time.

In contrast, after 1998, in the nation's pursuit of democracy, some of the people have been cast adrift, institutions have been weakened, the country's leaders divided and the nation's vulnerability to the threat of terrorism has never been greater. The people could have rebelled against President Soeharto's rule, if they had wanted to, so why did they not do so? In fact, during his rule, there had been conflicts resulting from religious differences and ethnic and regional interests. He had used a strong hand to manage these problems and it seemed to work. As a result of such decisive action, President Soeharto's administration could continue to concentrate on the development of Indonesia. On the issue of his weaknesses, it is difficult to find out whether his orders were conveyed or whether reports and relevant information were passed to him for his attention, either completely or after being censored. It was possible that only good things were reported to him and bad news were kept from him. His assistants and especially the ministers, were ultimately also responsible for what had happened, as the ministers were supposed to be accountable for everything that happened within the area of their authority.

Mahatma Gandhi could have been referring to Indonesia's situation when he said that appalling conditions will take place if politics is practised with no principles, if trade is conducted with no morals, if happiness is achieved with no deliberation, if education is taught with no character, if science is used with no humanity and if people believe in faith with no sacrifices.[5] After Pak Harto's downfall in May 1998, Indonesia had three presidents who survived a total of less than five years. The country is now under its sixth president in 60 years. The first two, President Soekarno and President Soeharto, were considered to have run non-democratic regimes that relied heavily on repression. On the other hand, it was due to their long stay in power that resulted in the international community's inability to disregard Indonesia.

How did Pak Harto manage to face the storm which surrounded his descent from power? An insight into his personal philosophy may be gleaned from his words when he said:[6]

> Do not be happy only when you are in power and desperate if you are not, since the two have their consequences. Do not be upset if you are no longer in power, because power is never eternal. And it does not mean everything in life. Those who feel frustrated when they are no longer in power are greedy. To the contrary, those who are happy when they are no longer in power are wise and heroic. Those who want to win at all times are selfish and not fit to be a leader since the nation would be divided when the leader is selfish. They are not genuine statesmen because a real statesman always thinks first of the national interest in the broadest context.

In this context, my father likes to quote a poem by Henrietta Roland Holst: "Why do you sing only for the flowers that bloom in the spring? Why not sing for the fallen leaves in autumn? Will the fallen leaves and flowers not turn into fertiliser for the next spring?" The message in this poem for the younger generation is that the past is a bridge between the present and the future, and one should not ignore the past in order to understand the present and face the future. The younger generation feels that they can do better as they feel smarter and often criticise the achievements of their elders. My father wanted to remind us that Pak Harto is human too; that he also bleeds when hurt and he has the capacity to feel and to love. Given the limitations of his own childhood and the formality of the presidency, he must have longed more than most for a happy and peaceful old age.

It seems cruel of fate to have denied Pak Harto the one thing he so badly wanted: a fair judgment of his achievements and failures. He no longer has Ibu Tien, his soulmate, by his side to console him in his darkest moments. It must be acknowledged that history tends to repeat itself and unless the

Indonesian people are willing to learn from past mistakes, the nation will remain stagnant. Through this book, I hope that the Indonesian people will gain sufficient awareness so as not to be mean spirited and to wish him a peaceful life in his final days. Great nations should respect their leaders. Pak Harto has handled his trials and tribulations with wisdom as he has accepted his fate with dignity. It is remarkable how someone in his position could have managed the criticisms, assaults and harassment that he has experienced to date. The Javanese call it a strong *bathin*, or inner strength that is achieved through unrelenting practice. This inner strength enables a person not to be perturbed by whatever happens in one's environment. It enables one to accept life and to know the right moment to act, as well as to be attuned to cosmic happenings.

LESSONS TO BE LEARNT

Each of Pak Harto's successors has promised to undertake reforms and make changes, to end corruption in politics and overhaul the economy in a new era of social justice. Each of them was supposed to change and improve on the conditions under President Soeharto's rule. However, the harsh reality is that Indonesia is still one of the most corrupt countries on this planet. Bribery is not new to the country but according to recent surveys and interviews, it has surged in scale and scope to touch just about every aspect of life. Corruption is still the biggest barrier to foreign investment. Corruption is no more than a virus infecting the system; it is not the system itself that is corrupt. I feel that it is an undeniable fact that during President Soeharto's era, development was visible and the common people were well-fed. Mortality rates went down while life expectancy went up.

Pak Harto gave up his presidency after mounting pressure from the students left him with no other choice. Ironically, it was the students' movement that had brought him to power in 1966. It was very similar to the downfall of Bung Karno. Students are the future of a nation and history tells us that it is usually the forces of youth—brave, fiery and full of hope for a better tomorrow—that are capable of making drastic changes in the government. However, the students' spirit and idealism do not stay true for good. The students too, would join a corrupt world as they develop a sense of self-interest.

Pak Harto, like Bung Karno, also became a controversial figure as he sailed into his sunset years. Strong leaders become notorious when they take decisive and unpopular actions, but it should be noted that leadership is not about a popularity contest. The heart of the matter lies in whether decisions are taken for personal or public interests. Thus, some would call Pak Harto and Bung Karno opportunists. In statesmanship, there is nothing wrong in being forceful and strong, and to use an iron fist when a situation calls for it. It is better than being indecisive or weak. As the saying goes, "no decision is a decision in itself".

What is good for one nation does not necessarily mean that it is good for another. The West uses its own values and principles in interpreting the situation in other countries. The trauma that Bung Karno and his generation had suffered during colonial times is not easily forgotten. In recent years, after the war in Afghanistan and Iraq, the image of the West has deteriorated. For Indonesia's older leaders, the memory of their long struggle for freedom has made them skeptical and more anxious about another form of colonialism. Slowly but surely, the so-called "economic colonialism" has started to creep into our lives.

From time to time, nationalist sentiments need revitalisation and new dreams have to be created. My father noted that as early as 1989, President Soeharto had sensed the need to revive the country's nationalist sentiments. It was time for Indonesia to develop the country's own resources. President Soeharto had planned that from 1993 onwards, the economy would take off and Indonesia would join the ranks of the developed countries. On the other hand, President Soeharto was pragmatic enough to accept the reality that the success of a country's development could not be solely dependent on external forces. The development of a nation had to rest on the skills of its own people and its capacity to mobilise its own resources. In other words, the essence of development was to upgrade the competence of a country's entire population or to develop its human resources.

In the eight years following Pak Harto's downfall, there have been some improvement in the transparency of the government, in economic and security matters, but there is still a lot more to be done. The positive aspects of President Soekarno and President Soeharto's leadership should not be swept conveniently under the carpet and their legacy should not be disregarded and discarded. Their roles and contributions should be studied and the positive elements and the similarities identified, so as to be able to perpetuate the good and avoid repeating the mistakes of the past. It is still fresh in our minds that President Soekarno had fallen out of power because he had been considered leftist oriented. During the Cold War, it had been more sinful to be a communist than to be an extremist Muslim. Therefore, in the eyes of the West, President Soekarno had to go. The West had supported President Soeharto enthusiastically from the beginning as he was very much anti-communist. However, as the years went by and the honeymoon period passed, they sharply criticised President Soeharto's government for being dictatorial. Rampant corruption was fuelled by the collusion of the "first families", thereby leading to a lot of harsh criticisms. President Soeharto himself became the sacrificial lamb. Today, the West has started to worry again, this time that Indonesia might become the training ground of Muslim extremists gathering their troops for *jihad*.

To my father, the past is the link between *das sein* and *das sollen*. One should not ignore the past or think that everything which took place in the past was wrong; after all, if President Soekarno and President Soeharto had been so wrong, how would one explain Indonesia's strong presence today? The younger generation should not make the same mistakes that the country's first two presidents did, but they should also have the grace to let bygones be bygones. The future generations should not lose sight of their primary aims and focus their energy into striving for a better tomorrow, especially in terms of achieving economic, social and cultural advancements. It is with this in mind that my father wanted me to write this book. It is indeed unfortunate that I did not get to know Bung Karno well as I was too young when my father was one of his loyalists. Fortunately, I have had the opportunity of getting to know Pak Harto and gaining his trust. He is a man who is ready to face the consequences of his actions. It is not difficult to admire his resilience and strength in accepting the life he has to deal with in his advanced years.

Having gotten to know Pak Harto after his exit from power, I came to the conclusion that he deserves a fair legacy. However, public scrutiny has, so far, only focused on his weaknesses and failures which have overshadowed his achievements. As part of a civilised nation, Indonesians have been taught to show respect to their elders and the elderly. Indonesians would never address their parents by their first names, as some do in America. We are taught to respect our teachers, as they are our source of guidance beyond our immediate family circle. Pak Harto's contributions to the country should not be forgotten, nor should he be judged solely as a friend of lost causes. My father had wished that Indonesia's new leaders would allow Pak Harto to live in serenity for the remainder of his life. It would require a big heart on the part of the new leadership to allow him to bow out of the controversies that have dogged him since his exit from office. I, for one, would like to see his life being placed in the appropriate context and to see it portrayed accurately. The economic growth of Indonesia during Pak Harto's reign was outstanding. However, there is no doubt that his time in power also featured numerous mistakes, but it would not be fair to assess his actions in politics and in government by today's standards, as he had taken over the country at a time when the political situation was volatile and there were many pressing issues which required urgent attention.

An important lesson for a leader holding high power is to be aware of cronies around him. How can one expect a president to fairly appraise his own judgment and performance when he is surrounded by "yes men"? It is unfair to lay blame on Bung Karno for putting Indonesia into misery and tragedy, as much as it is to accuse Pak Harto of milking the country of its wealth. Is there any real and substantial evidence that Pak Harto has accumulated billions of dollars? These billions in reality refer to the money given to the foundations which, as far as I know, are still kept deposited with the state banks. The fact that he has refused to go abroad for medical treatment even in serious ill health and has definitively refuted all speculations of intentions to live abroad shows that Pak Harto is a person who is not shadowed by the knowledge of his own intentional wrongdoing.

This reminded me of an 88-year-old Dutch gentleman, who had lived in Indonesia in early 1948 and worked for Shell in Balikpapan. In a personal letter to me, he wrote:

> And having had ourselves the Japanese occupation between 1940 and 1945, with the struggle to become free again, most of us could well understand that the Indonesian people would not accept the pre-war situation anymore. Personally, I supported the view of Dr Verkuyl, a theologian in Jakarta, who strongly rejected any attempt to restore the old dominant role of the Dutch.

He went on to say that in retrospect, and from perhaps a practical point of view, one could only add: "Imagine that the Netherlands could be held responsible for the well-being of the rapidly expanding population of Indonesia. It would have been a sheer impossibility."

For 30 years, President Soeharto managed to steer Indonesia through turbulent weather, violent storms and a capricious ocean. I feel that thousands of Indonesian children would not have been able to obtain an education abroad—in Australia, the United States and the like—if not for him. What would have happened to Shell, Exxon, Caltex, British Petroleum and others if Pak Harto had not been the president? In looking at the past, it is worth considering how many of the country's dreams have actually come true.

It is acknowledged that corruption is closely linked to bribery. The problem of corruption and bribery, a dangerous virus difficult to suppress, has pervaded many areas of this planet. Perhaps this problem occurs to a lesser degree in the Western nations or it is subtler and not as blatant as in Indonesia. Corruption has no prejudices, it does not discriminate against communists, atheists, animists or even staunchly religious nations, as corruption takes place everywhere. Businesses can easily take control of a country's economic life, and this usually leads to the creation of a few super-rich members in the community, while the majority live on minimum income. How many of the multinational companies operating in developing countries have been saints? How many of the companies practise double standards, so that whatever is taboo in their homeland is merely considered a cost of doing business in foreign lands? How many of them refrain from the temptation to bribe in order to turn quick profits? Let us not forget that it always takes two to tango.

Bung Karno and Pak Harto have been involved in the country's physical struggles against the communists and the Muslim extremists. One wonders how the history books would read if Indonesia had become a communist country under Muso in 1948 or Aidit in 1965, or if it had become an Islamic nation under Kartosuwiryo in 1950 or Abu Bakar Ba'asyir in 1998. Abu Bakar Ba'asyir had started a *pesantren* on 10 March 1972 that soon became the centre for hardline Muslims. Located in a village called Ngruki, 2.5 km from Solo, the full name of the *pesantren* was Pondok Pesantren Al-Mukmin. President Soeharto had captured him in 1983 and charged him with his rejection of Pancasila as the only foundation for the country. There had been reports that he had refused to salute the national flag. He received a nine-year sentence and while under house arrest, he managed to escape to Malaysia on 11 February 1985. Soon, his religious activities expanded to Singapore. At the same time, the Americans had also included his name as an activist in Jemaah Islamiah, which is related to Al-Qaeda. In 1999, a year after Pak Harto had stepped down from power, Ba'asyir saw a good opportunity to return. Since then, he has established Majelis Mujahidin Indonesia (MMI), an organisation with radical views to impose Syariah Islam (Islamic law). A few years down the road, his name has been constantly linked with terrorist activities, the most notorious having been the Bali bombing in 2003.

Was it wrong for General Soeharto to have been involved with smuggling? Yes, if the issue is considered within the context of a democratic society, but not if one argues that the Indonesian society is still feudalistic in nature. President Soeharto imposed tight military discipline as the army was supposed to stand above the different faiths, but he also demonstrated self-restraint; in Javanese, the term is *tepo sliro* or to think of the feelings of others. It is the need to protect the national interest and to put the country's interests above one's own personal interests. The discipline called for compliance with the majority and conformity with the laws. President Soeharto believed one had to be extremely cautious where there was a conflict of interests.

The tragedy that took place when President Soekarno was compelled to step down had been eerie to say the least but, to a certain degree, there were similarities with the conditions surrounding President Soeharto's stepping down in 1998. In May 1998, Jakarta was overwhelmed by such massive internal chaos that it felt like one was living in an inferno. The economy in both eras was in peril and worsened sharply after the political and economic crisis. The local currency devalued drastically, causing a shortage of foreign exchange and forced businesses to cease operations. Police officers and soldiers were called to put down the protests and riots. There was high tension where the soldiers drove around in panzers in empty streets. Property worth millions of dollars went up in flames. Families were forced out into the open without jobs and some even without shelter. In both situations, the country's two great leaders were seen as the cause of the state of affairs and both had become the most hated persons. Ironically, it was also the United States which was the first to cast harsh criticisms at President Soeharto for having neglected human rights.

There were accusations that General Soeharto had intended to use the Armed Forces Day celebrations on 5 October 1965 for a *coup*. This episode almost shattered the country. However, the two key players have chosen not to reveal the whole truth about the circumstances surrounding this major event. Personally, I do not believe that Bung Karno and Pak Harto had chosen silence for personal reasons, but out of their concern for national interest and unity. Therefore, the truth behind what had actually taken place during the abortive *coup* will remain untold. This, no doubt, provides an opportunity for academics, writers and observers to speculate on what had really happened and all books on this subject, in particular on the roles that Bung Karno and Pak Harto had played in the transition of power, will remain as conjecture and speculation.

President Soeharto's New Order achievements undoubtedly impressed the Western world. Indonesia became the focal point of interest for academics and political observers. More importantly, Indonesia became a viable place for investment. President Soekarno, known for his leftist orientation, had been unable to persuade Western investors to come to Indonesia. In contrast, when General Soeharto, who loathed communism, took over, the West poured the much needed funds into the country. Indonesia became a star performer in the eyes of the Western nations. President Soeharto, who used excellent strategies and brilliant tactical manoeuvres in his leadership, was always mindful of his limited education and humble background.

Indonesia's future generations should understand why Bung Karno, until the end of his life, "was fighting the ghosts of neo-colonialism".[7] The phantom of Dutch rule kept haunting him. The confrontation with Malaysia, the withdrawal from the United Nations and President Soekarno's dangerous dalliance with communism mirrored the trauma of someone who had spent his youth in and out of Dutch prisons. In the end, Bung Karno's suspicion was right, as the CIA was proven to have been involved in his removal from power. After President Soeharto came into power, an American documentary about the CIA revealed that the American Embassy had provided lists of PKI members to the Indonesian government in the absence of Indonesian intelligence capabilities at that time. Perhaps Bung Karno had been too late in recognising the changes that were taking place in the world, and in realising that there were new battles to fight and new enemies to defeat. Perhaps it was his mistake in believing that everything could be accomplished through political will.

Pak Harto learnt from Bung Karno by analysing his strengths and weaknesses, and this made him a wiser leader. However, Pak Harto did not consolidate his analyses by putting pen to paper, nor did he pinpoint accurately Bung Karno's faults; on the contrary, he showed his predecessor empathy and sympathy. In his time, Pak Harto had also failed to see that the world was changing, especially in the late 1990s. When globalisation swept through Southeast Asia, he failed to realise that there were new battles to fight and new enemies to defeat. President Soekarno had believed that political will alone could resolve all problems, while President Soeharto believed that everything could be accomplished through financial compensation. Both of them were proven wrong. President Soekarno had been fooled by the PKI and President Soeharto by the conglomerates and his cronies. Perhaps the greatest tragedy of their downfall was the fact that as soon as it happened, all their good work and positive contributions to the country counted for nothing.

In February 1970, Bung Karno's health deteriorated rapidly. On 16 June 1970, he was transported to RSPAD Gatot Subroto and admitted into intensive care. On Friday, 19 June, all eyes in the country were focused on two true friends who were meeting for the last time. These two friends had not only been true compatriots but they had also undergone a split at one point in time. Yet, these two men had the wisdom to know the difference between personal feelings and political outlook. Without these two wise men, Bung Karno and Bung Hatta, Indonesia would not be where it is today. They were two men of contrasting characters and personalities: one fiery and outgoing, the other quiet and introverted; one an orator, the other a thinker. Together, they had bulldozed Dutch supremacy and changed 20th century Asia for good.

Two days later, on 21 June 1970, Indonesia was in mourning. Bung Karno's remains were taken to Wisma Yaso, the home of his fourth Japanese wife, and President Soeharto came immediately to pay his last respects to this great man. A state funeral was arranged as President Soeharto called on all political leaders to pay their final respects to Bung Karno. President Soeharto went on to declare Bung Karno and Hatta the nation's proclamators. In 1980, a statue was erected in front of the building where they had proclaimed the nation's independence on 17 August 1945. In 1985, President Soeharto decided that in their honour, Cengkareng International Airport was to be renamed Soekarno-Hatta International Airport.

In his biography, Pak Harto had described his feelings about the person whom many had wanted to make his enemy. No matter what faults Bung Karno might have had, a traitor he was definitely not. It had never been his intention to put Indonesia in jeopardy. If it had appeared to be so, it could be attributed to President Soekarno having been too ambitious in maintaining his reputation as a world leader. Indeed, beyond Indonesia, President Soekarno's philosophy and charisma had inspired many, especially those from Third World countries. Leaders are usually the targets of criticism, hate, gossip, insults and innuendos, but they should equally be admired and respected, especially since they are willing to take the challenge of being at the centre of a power play, where intrigue and deceit is often the name of the game. Interestingly, as intelligent as they are, very few national leaders have learnt from past failures.

As the saying goes, "power corrupts and absolute power corrupts absolutely". There is much wisdom in these words, yet in most cases, they fall on deaf ears when offered to those holding great power. Leaders are likely to become blinded by adulation, deaf to criticisms and mute with the truth, and the longer they remain in power, the more the situation worsens. Factors such as old age, physical weakness and deteriorating mental abilities are also prime causes for long running leaders losing touch with reality. In some cases, the court players have changed, with new and younger ones replacing the old. The younger ones are more ambitious and they are more conscious of time running out. They are shrewd and not above taking advantage of an old and weakening ruler. The odds are that they will emerge the winner.

It is almost sinister that President Soekarno and President Soeharto's final hours in power ended seemingly in the same dramatic setting. The plot, the setting and the audience were the same, only the actors, of course, had changed. In 1998, President Soeharto was getting old, blinded by his cronies' request to hold on and deafened by empty and untrue praises. Pak Harto should have followed his first instincts when he had felt, some time previously, that the time was ripe for his departure and that he had already overstayed his welcome. Rosy but false pictures were regularly presented to him at the peak of his rule. His inner circle had covered up the truth for their own self-interests, like PKI had done in the case of President Soekarno. They had begun their first moves by intrigue, false or not, on the existence of the Council of Generals. Three decades later, President Soeharto's cronies begged him to stay on in power, on the pretext that the people still wanted him to govern. They claimed that corruption was not too bad and only the new PKI was stating otherwise. The re-emergence of PKI became the favoured front for covering up the rampant corruption. The unhappiness of many due to abuse of privilege hardly reached the ears at the top. Even if it did, his cronies would have denied them and claimed that the allegations were only being voiced by the minority. The same setting and background have clouded the successes of Indonesia's first two and longest-serving presidents.

At the time of writing, Pak Harto has fallen ill once again and has been hospitalised since 4 May 2006. On 7 May, he had to undergo an operation as his massive gastrointestinal bleeding would not stop. I called Dr Hari Sabardi the next day and he informed me that it had been necessary to remove close to 40cm of Pak Harto's intestinal tract in order to stop the bleeding. The operation lasted three hours, which was not easy on an 84-year-old man. When I called Suweden, he told me that Pak Harto had more than 30 spots of leakages in his intestinal tract. Since then, a few current Indonesian leaders have come forward to encourage the government to settle the issue of Pak Harto's court case. The government is trying hard to find ways of discontinuing his case. The solution lies in finding the most appropriate and elegant legal way out without compromising the integrity of the parties involved.

In the early morning of 19 May 2006, President Susilo Bambang Yudhoyono visited Pak Harto, whose condition was very critical. Persons such as Ali Sadikin, Des Alwi and Meutia Hatta had also visited him. I flew from Bangkok that day and late that evening, Tutut, Titiek and Mamiek allowed my sister, Lia, and me to see Pak Harto in the ICU. Probosutedjo, who had been granted 24 hours' leave from prison, was at the hospital to visit Pak Harto as well. Moerdiono now replaced the late Saadillah Mursjid in standing firmly with the family during Pak Harto's latest ailment: I have high regard for Moerdiono as he has demonstrated his reliability at this very trying time in Pak Harto's life. It is distressing that there are a few who refuse to let bygones be bygones and are demanding for the court case to continue even when Pak Harto's health is in such a critical state. On the other hand, Titiek said that even in his present grave condition, when Pak Harto was informed of Mount Merapi's eruption, he had immediately asked her to fly to Yogya on behalf of Yayasan Gotong Royong with a donation, which she did on 20 May. Even when he is fighting for his life, Pak Harto still thinks of the well-being of his fellow countrymen.

My father had, as early as in 2001, found the courage to voice his view on the approach that should be taken in relation to Pak Harto. On 20 December 2001, *Kompas*, the highest circulating local daily newspaper, printed this report: "He [my father] pleaded for the government to have a big heart and use humanitarian principles towards Soeharto, whom he [my father] said will face difficulty in recovering his health." On the same day, *Pelita*, another daily local newspaper, quoted my father as follows: "For the first 20 years, it was an extremely difficult time for HM Soeharto to lead our country. Hence, I do not agree with those who claimed that HM Soeharto's 32 years of rule had been all bad." If the government is able to make this move to end Pak Harto's court case, it would go a long way towards accomplishing our founding fathers' dreams for a united and prosperous nation. With Pak Harto's court case unresolved, the differing factions will remain, along with the risk of friction threatening the nation's unity and development.

Some Indonesians have suggested that, in view of Pak Harto's failing health and futility in proceeding further with a court trial, one of the ways to resolve his situation would be for him to offer a public apology for his past wrongdoings. This was done when Titiek flew to Yogya on behalf of Yayasan Gotong Royong with the donation for the Mount Merapi eruption victims. She had offered precisely such a public apology on behalf of her father and this was widely reported by the press. To this end, Pak Harto himself had said in his 1988 biography:[8]

> I know that I will not be free from mistakes. Thus, as I have often said and I want to repeat it now and here once again, I do hope that others will follow the good things that I have given to the country and the people, and stay away from the bad things that I might have done in performing my duties.

Johann Wolfgang von Goethe said, "Do your best to turn your life into a festival." I think Indonesia's founding fathers would be proud if the

Indonesian people not only manage to turn their lives into a festival worthy of celebration but, at the same time, find it within themselves to show compassion for their elderly former president who has spent 32 years of his life serving his country.

ENDNOTES

1 Ismail Saleh SH, *Proses Peradilan Soeharto Presiden RI ke 2. Penegakan Hukum atau Komoditi Politik* (Yayasan Dharmais, Indonesia, June 2001).

2 David Jenkins, *Suharto and His Generals—Military Politics 1975–1983* (Cornell Modern Indonesia Projects, South East Asia Program, Cornell University, Ithaca, New York, 1984), p 54.

3 H Hardiyanti Rukmana, *Butir-Butir Budaya Jawa* (Yayasan Purna Bhakti Pertiwi, Indonesia, 1996), p 189.

4 Alexander Downer, at the launch of *A Fading Dream* in 2004 and later published in the article "Indonesia means an enormous amount to us", Australian National University Newsletter, Issue 4, Second Quarter 2004, Australia.

5 These words were extracted from the translated speech of Kompas Gramedia Group's President Director, Jacob Utama, delivered on 11 December 2005 in Hotel Santika, Jakarta.

6 Pak Harto had quoted from a book by Hardiyanti Rukmana, *Butir-Butir Budaya Jawa* (Yayasan Purna Bhakti Pertiwi, Indonesia, 1996), p 189.

7 Roeslan Abdulgani, *Three Public Lectures in Australia*, 1972 (Yayasan Idayu, Indonesia, 1974).

8 G Dwipayana and Ramadhan KH, *Soeharto, Pikiran, Ucapan, dan Tindakan Saya* (PT Citra Lamtoro Gung Persada, 1988), p 566.

TIMELINE

1921	- 8 June	Born in Kemusuk (Central Jawa) from the marriage of Kertosudiro and Sukirah
1929-1935	-	Elementary School in Tiwir (Yogya), Wuryantoro and Solo (Central Jawa)
1935-1939	-	Junior High School and Islamic School in Wonogiri and Yogya
1940	- 1 June - 2 December	Joined the Royal Netherlands Indies Army (KNIL) Military Cadres School in Gombong
1941	-	Promoted to Corporal later as Sergeant and assigned to Battalion XIII at Rampal, near Malang; then duty in Gresik (East Jawa)
1942	- 1 November	Joined *Keibuho*, the Japanese sponsored police force in Yogya
1943	- October	Joined Peta, the Japanese sponsored voluntary army; undertaken platoon commander course in Yogya; commissioned to *Shodancho* as Platoon Leader
1944	- April	Undertaken company commander course in Bogor (West Jawa); promoted to the rank of *Chundancho* (Company Commander)
1945	- 17 August - 29 September - 5 October	Proclamation of Indonesia's Independence Arrival of Allied Forces in Jawa Assigned to Peta troops in Solo, Peta office in Madiun (East Jawa), then joined Battalion Peta in Blitar which rebelled against the Japanese and consequently removed to Brebek (East Jawa) Joined the People's Security Corps (BKR); elected Deputy Battalion Commander
1946	- January - 12 November - November	Appointed Lt Colonel and commander of Regiment III Linggarjati Agreement Became commander of 22nd Regiment, Division III (Yogya)
1947	- 21 July - 26 December	First Dutch "Police Action" Marriage to Siti Hartinah

1948	- 17 January	Renville Agreement
	- 18 September	Madiun revolt or PKI rebellion under Muso
	- 19 December	Second Dutch "Police Action"

1949	- 1 March	Indonesian assault to regain Yogya
	- 7 May	Rum-Van Royen or The Round Table agreement
	- 27 December	Dutch "de jure" recognition of Indonesia's Independence and transfer of its sovereignty to Republic of the United Sates of Indonesia

1950	- January	Confirmed as Lt Colonel of the Indonesian Army TNI
	- 26 April	Commander of Brigade Garuda Mataram on expedition to Makassar (South Sulawesi)
	- 17 August	Formation of the unitary Republic of Indonesia
	- September	Commander of Brigade Pangeran Mangkubumi, Yogya

| 1951 | - 15 November | Commander Brigade Pragola, Sub-Territorial IV, in Salatiga (Central Jawa) |

| 1953 | - 1 March | Commander, Infantry Regiment 15, Sub-Territorial IV, Solo |

1956	- 1 March	Chief of Staff Territorial IV/ Diponegoro Division, Semarang
	- 8 September	Assumed command of Territorial 1V/ Diponegoro Division
	- December	Regional military *coups* in Sumatra

| 1957 | - 1 January | Promoted to Colonel |
| | - 1 September | Appointed as member of the Curator Council, National Military Academy, Magelang (Central Jawa) |

| 1959 | - October | Removed from Territorial 1V/Diponegoro Division and sent to attend course at SESKOAD (Miltary School for Staff and Commander) in Bandung |

| 1960 | - 1 January | Promoted to Brigadier General |
| | - 18 December | Deputy 1 (operational) to army chief of staff |

1961	- 1 March	Commander of Army Reserve Corps 1 (CADUAD)
	- June	First overseas trip
	- 1 October	Commander of Army Air Defense Command (KOHANUDAD)

| 1962 | - 9 January | Promoted to Major General and appointed as Mandala commander to liberalise West Irian |

	- 23 January	Deputy Commander of East Indonesia Territory
1963	- 1 March	Appointed as Commander of The Army Strategic Command (KOSTRAD)
	- 2 May	Establishment of Yayasan Trikora
1965	- 1 January	Deputy Commander, Mandala Siaga (Kolaga)
	- 14 October	Appointed Army Commander and promoted as Lt General
1966	- 11 March	Supersemar
	- 12 March	PKI banned
	- 18 March	Arrest and dismissal of 15 cabinet ministers
	- 27 March	New cabinet, headed by 6-man team
	- 25 July	Ampera cabinet; appointed as chair of the presidium
	- 28 July	Promoted to General
	- 11 August	Normalisation of Indonesia-Malaysia relations
	- 28 September	Indonesia readmitted as member of the UN
	- 3 October	Undertaken economic stabilisation measures
1967	- 10 January	Foreign Investment Law introduced
	- 12 March	Appointed as acting president by MPRS
	- August	Indonesia became founding member of ASEAN
1968	- 27 March	Sworn in as full president, becoming Indonesia's 2nd President
	- 28-4 April	State visit to Japan and Cambodia
1969	- 6 September	Attended Non-Blok Movement Conference in Lusaka
	- 16 September	West Irian became a province of Indonesia
	- 22 November	General Elections Law passed by DPR-GR (Parliament)
1970	- 21 June	The passing of Bung Karno
1971	- 5 July	1st General Elections under the New Order
1973	- 23 March	Elected for the 2nd time as president by MPR
1974	- 15 January	Malari Affair
	- 16 May	Establishment of Yayasan Supersemar
1975	- 8 August	Establishment of Yayasan Dharmais

1977	- 2 May	2nd General Elections under the New Order
1978	- 22 March	Elected for the 3rd time as president by MPR
	- 15 November	Rupiah devalued
1980	- 14 March	The passing of Bung Hatta
	- 13 May	*Petisi 50*
1982	- 17 February	Establishment of YAMP
	- 4 May	3rd General Elections under the New Order
1983	- March	Petrus—Mysterious killings
	- 10 March	Named as "Bapak Pembangunan", "Father of Development" by MPR
	- 11 March	Elected for the 4th time as president by MPR
	- 30 March	Rupiah devalued
1984		Indonesia achieved self-sufficiency in rice
	- 12 September	Tanjung Priok shootings
1985	- 8 June	Establishment of Yayasan DAKAB
	- 14 November	Attended FAO meeting in Rome
1986	- 23 August	Establishment of Yayasan Gotong Royong Kemanusiaan
	- 12 September	Rupiah devalued
1987	- 23 April	4th General Elections under the New Order
1988	- 11 March	Elected for the 5th time as president by MPR
	- 27 October	Banking deregulation (PAKTO)
1989	- 23 February	Met with Chinese Foreign Minister, Qian Qichen
	- September	Visited Soviet Union
1990	- 5 December	Establishment of ICMI
1991	- June	*Hajj* pilgrimage to Mecca
	- September	Elected as Chairman of the Non-Blok Movement
1992	- 9 June	5th General Elections under the New Order
1993	- 11 March	Elected for the 6th time as president by MPR

1996	- 15 January	Establishment of Yayasan Damandiri
	- 28 April	The passing of Ibu Tien Soeharto
1997	- 29 May	6th General Elections under the New Order
	- July	Currency crisis and economic slump in Asia
	- October	1st IMF Bailout Financial Package
	- December	First mild stroke
1998	- 15 January	2nd IMF Bailout Financial Package
	- 11 March	Elected for the 7th time as president by MPR
	- 12 May	4 students shot and killed in Trisakti University, Jakarta
	- 13-15 May	Riots in Jakarta
	- 18 May	Students occupied DPR/MPR buildings; demanded President Soeharto's resignation
	- 21 May	Resigned from presidency and BJ Habibie sworn in as Indonesia's 3rd President
	- November	MPR called to investigate HM Soeharto's wealth
1999	- 20-30 July	Hospitalised in RSPP (CVD)
	- 12-17 September	Hospitalised in RSPP (1st massive GTI bleeding)
2000	- April	Under city arrest
	- 29 May	Under house arrest
	- 31 August	Charged with corruption
	- 28 September	Charges dismissed on ground of ill-health
2001	- 24 February-2 March	Hospitalised in RSPP (appendectomy)
	- 12-17 June	Hospitalised in RSPP (fitted with permanent pace maker)
	- 17-23 December	Hospitalised in RSPP (bronchopneumonia duplex)
2002	- 13-23 March	Hospitalised in RSPP (2nd massive GTI bleeding)
2004	- 16-20 April	Hospitalised in RSPP (3rd massive GTI bleeding)
2005	- 4-10 May	Hospitalised in RSPP (4th massive GTI bleeding)
	- 4-12 November	Hospitalised in RSPP (5th massive GTI bleeding)
2006	- 4 -31 May	Hospitalised in RSPP (6th massive GTI bleeding)

ABBREVIATIONS

ABRI	Angkatan Bersenjata Republik Indonesia—the armed forces of the Republic of Indonesia
ABS	Asal Bapak Senang—as long as it pleases Father
AFTA	ASEAN Free Trade Area
Ampera	Amanat Penderitaan Rakyat—Message of the People's Suffering
APEC	Asia-Pacific Economic Cooperation
APRA	Angkatan Perang Ratu Adil—Army of the Just Ruler
ASEAN	Association of South East Asian Nations
Aspri	Asisten Pribadi—Personal Assistant to President Soeharto
Banpres	Bantuan Presiden—Presidential Assistance
BAPINDO	Bank Pembangunan Indonesia—Indonesian Development Bank
Bappenas	Badan Perencanaan Pembangunan Nasional—National Development Planning Board
BBD	Bank Bumi Daya (a state bank)
BCA	Bank Central Asia (a private bank)
BDN	Bank Dagang Negara (a state bank)
BEII	Bank Ekspor Impor Indonesia (a state bank)
BEJ	Bursa Efek Jakarta—Jakarta Stock Exchange
BI	Bank Indonesia—Indonesian Central Bank
Bimas	Bimbingan Massal—mass guidance
BKKBN	Badan Koordinasi Keluarga Berencana Nasional—Family Planning Co-coordinating Board
BKPM	Badan Koordinasi Penanaman Modal—Indonesia's Investment Coordinating Board
BKR	Badan Keamanan Rakyat—People's Safety Organization
BKTN	Bank Koperasi Tani dan Nelayan—bank for farmers' and fishermans' cooperative
BNI	Bank Negara Indonesia (a state bank)
BPD	Bank Pembangunan Daerah—Regional Development Bank
BPK	Badan Pemeriksa Keuangan—The Audit Board of the Republic of Indonesia
BPR	Bank Perkreditan Rakyat—Bank for People's Small Credit
BRI	Bank Rakyat Indonesia (a state bank)
BTN	Bank Tabungan Negara—State Savings Bank

Bulog	Badan Urusan Logistik—National Logistic Board
BUMN	Badan Usaha Milik Negara (state-owned enterprises)
BUUD	Badan Usaha Unit Desa—village business unit
CIA	Central Intelligence Agency
CSIS	Centre for Strategic and International Studies
CTC	Central Trading Company
Dakab	Dana Abadi Karya Bakti (name of a Yayasan/foundation)
Damandiri	Dana Sejahtera Mandiri (name of a Yayasan/foundation)
Dekon	Deklarasi Ekonomi—Economic Declaration
Dharmais	Dharma Bhakti Sosial (name of a Yayasan/foundation)
DI/TII	Darul Islam/Tentara Islam Indonesia—Indonesian Military Islam (name of a rebellion movement)
DPA	Dewan Pertimbangan Agung—Supreme Advisory Council
DPR	Dewan Perwakilan Rakyat—People's Representative Council
Dwikora	Dwi Komando Rakyat—People's Dual Command
FAO	Food and Agriculture Organization
Fretilin	Revolucionária de Timor-Leste
G30S	Gerakan tiga puluh September—the 30 September Movement
GBHN	Garis-garis Besar Haluan Negara—Broad Outline of State Policies
Golkar	Golongan Karya—Functional Group
Gora	Gogo rancah—system used for land cultivation
HKTI	Himpunan Kerukunan Tani Indonesia—Association of Indonesian Farmers
HMI	Himpunan Mahasiswa Islam—Islamic Students Association
IAIN	Institut Agama Islam Negeri—Institute for Islamic Studies
IBRD	International Bank for Reconstruction and Development
ICMI	Ikatan Cendekiawan Muslim Indonesia—Association of Intellectual Muslim Indonesia
ICU	Intensive Care Unit
IDI	Ikatan Dokter Indonesia—Indonesian Doctors Association
IDT	Inpres Desa Tertinggal—Presidential Instruction for backward villages
IGGI	Inter-Governmental Group on Indonesia
IKKH	Ikatan Kesejahteraan Keluarga Hankam—Association of Armed Forces Family
IMF	International Monetary Fund
Inmas	Instruksi masyarakat—Mass Instruction

Inpres	Instruksi Presiden—Presidential Instruction
IPB	Institut Pertanian Bogor—Bogor Agriculture Institute
IPSX	Indonesian Parallel Stock Exchange
IPTN	Industri Pesawat Terbang Nusantara—indigenous aircraft industry
IRRI	International Rice Research Institute
ISC	Indonesian Service Company
KAMI	Kesatuan Aksi Mahasiswa Indonesia—Indonesian Student Action Front
KAPPI	Kesatuan Aksi Pemuda dan Pelajar Indonesia—Indonesian Youth and Student Action Front
KIK	Kredit Investasi Kecil—credit for small business investments
KKN	Korupsi, Kolusi dan Nepotisme—Corruption, Collusion and Nepotism
KKN	Kuliah Kerja Nyata—practical work experience while attending university
KMB	Konperensi Meja Bundar—Round Table Conference
KNIL	het Koninklijke Nederlands(ch)-Indische Leger—Royal Netherlands Indies Army
Kolognas	Komando Logistik Nasional—Commander for National Logistic
Kopkamtib	Komando Operasi Keamanan dan Ketertiban—Operational Command for the Restoration of Order and Security
KOPPN	Komando Operasi Kewaspadaan dan Tertiban Nasional—Operational Command for Alert and National Order
Korpri	Korps Pegawai Republik Indonesia—Civil Servants Professional Association
Kostrad	Komando Cadangan Strategis Angkatan Darat—Army Strategic Reserve Command
KPR	Kredit Pemilikan Rumah—Credit for Housing Loan
KTP	Kantor Tabungan Pos—Post Office Savings
KUD	Koperasi Unit Desa—Village Cooperatives Unit
Kukesra	Kredit Usaha Keluarga Sejahtera—Credit for Family Prosperity
Mahmilub	Mahkamah Militer Luar Biasa—Extraordinary Military Tribunal
Malari	Peristiwa Lima Belas Januari—15 January incident
Masyumi	Majelis Syuro Muslimin Indonesia—Council of Indonesian Syuro Muslim Association
MBAD	Markas Besar Angkatan Darat—Army Headquarter
MMI	Majelis Mujahidin Indonesia—Indonesian Muslim Mujahidin Council
MPR	Majelis Permusyawaratan Rakyat—People's Consultative Assembly
MPRS	Majelis Permusyawaratan Rakyat Sementara—Provisional Consultative People's Assembly
Mubestek	Musyawarah Besar Teknik—Grand Gathering for Technicians

MUI	Majelis Ulama Indonesia—Indonesian Mufti Council
Nasakom	Nasionalis, Agama, Komunis—Nationalist, Religion and Communism
NICA	Netherlands Indies Civil Administration
NU	Nahdlatul Ulama (name of a traditional Islamic association and political party)
Opsus	Operasi Khusus—Special Operations
ORI	Oeang Republik Indonesia—Indonesian Local Currency
Pakdes	Paket Desember—December Economic Package
Pakto	Paket Oktober—October Economic Package
PAN	Partai Amanat Nasional (name of a Muslim political party)
PBB	Partai Bulan Bintang (name of a Muslim political party)
PDIP	Partai Demokrasi Indonesia Perjuangan—The Indonesian Democratic Party-Struggle
Pelaju	Petik, olah, jual dan untung—pluck, treat, sell and profit
Pemaju	Proses, kemas, jual dan untung—proccessing, packaging, selling and make profit
Perapi	Perhimpunan Ahli Bedah Plastik Indonesia—Indonesian plastic surgeons
Perdami	Perhimpunan Dokter Spesialis Mata Indonesia—Indonesian Eye Specialist Doctors
Permesta	Piagam Perjuangan Semesta (name of a rebellion movement: Charter of Total Struggle)
Persit	Persatuan Isteri Tentara—Association of Military wives
PETA	Pembela Tanah Air—Defenders of Land and Water (note: Indonesians refer to their country as "Land and Water" because it is an archipelago)
Petrus	Pembunuhan misterius—mysterious killings
PKI	Partai Komunis Indonesia—Indonesian Communist Party
PKK	Pemberdayaan dan Kesejahteraan Keluarga—Family Empowerment for Welfare
PMA	Penanaman Modal Asing—Foreign Investment Law
PNI	Partai Nasional Indonesia—Indonesian National Party
Posyandu	Pos Pelayanan Terpadu—Centre for Combined Health Services
PP	Peraturan Pemerintah—Government Regulation
PRRI	Pemerintah Revolusioner Republik Indonesia—Revolutionary Government of the Republic of Indonesia (name of a rebellion movement)
PSI	Partai Sosialis Indonesia—Indonesian Socialist Party
Puskesmas	Pusat Kesehatan Masyarakat—Community Health Centre

Repelita	Rencana Pembangunan Lima Tahun—Five-Year Development Plan
RMS	Republik Maluku Selatan—Republic of South Moluccas (name of a rebellion movement)
RPKAD	Resimen Pasukan Komando Angkatan Darat—Army Commando Regiment (later Kopassus)
RRI	Radio Republic Indonesia
RSPAD	Rumah Sakit Pusat Angkatan Darat—Army Military Hospital
RSPP	Rumah Sakit Pusat Pertamina—Pertamina Hospital
SBI	Sertifikat Bank Indonesia—Bank Indonesia Certificate
SBPU	Surat Berharga Pasar Uang—government promissory notes
Sekber GOLKAR	Sekretariat Bersama Golongan Karya—Secretariat of Functional Group
SSKAD	Sekolah Staf dan Komando Angkatan Darat—Army Staff and Command School
SSX	Surabaya Stock Exchange
Supersemar	Surat Perintah Sebelas Maret—11 March Instruction
Takesra	Tabungan Keluarga Sejahtera—Saving for Family Prosperity
TKR	Tentara Keamanan Rakyat—People's Safety Army
TMII	Taman Mini Indonesia Indah—Indonesia Miniature Complex
TNI	Tentara Nasional Indonesia—Indonesian National Army
TRI	Tentara Republik Indonesia—Indonesian Republic Army
Trikora	Tri Komando Rakyat—Three People's Commands
Tritura	Tri Tuntutan Rakyat—Three Demands of the People
UNTEA	United Nations Temporary Executive Authority
Wanjakti	Dewan Jabatan dan Kepangkatan Perwira Tinggi—a committee to evaluate the promotion of army officers of higher ranks and positions
Wapangsar KOGAM	Wakil Panglima Besar Komando Ganjang Malaysia—Deputy Commander to Crush Malaysia
YAMP	Yayasan Amalbakti Muslim Pancasila (name of a Yayasan/foundation)
YPTE	Yayasan Pembangunan Teritorial Empat—Fourth Territory Development Foundations
YTE	Yayasan Teritorial Empat—Fourth Territory Foundation

GLOSSARY

Aja kagetan, aja gumunan, aja dumeh	do not be troubled (startled or shocked), do not be surprised and do not be arrogant
Alon-alon asal kelakon	slowly but surely
Azas kekeluargaan	family-style affairs
Azas keluarga	family affairs
Badan Pelaksana Urusan Pangan	organisation for food distribution
Cakrabirawa	personal bodyguard of President Soekarno
Cepat-cepat, tetapi kelewat	"In acting quickly one would bypass important matters."
Chudancho	Company Commander
Daidancho	Battalion Commandant
Daya luwih	Greater ability
Dewan Jenderal	Council of Generals
Dewan Revolusi	Revolutionary Council
Ganyang Malaysia	Crush Malaysia
Gotong royong	mutual cooperation and self-help
Heiho	the local Japanese army; a combination of volunteers and militia
Hormat kalawan Gusti, Guru, Ratu lan wong atuwo karo	respect the Almighty, teachers, the kings/queens/leaders and parents

Jihad	struggle
Kaigun	Japanese navy
Kerukunan Nasional	national harmony
Mikul dhuwur mendhem jero	placed highly and buried deeply
Musyawarah and mufakat	agreement reached through consultation and consensus
Nenek moyang	ancestors
Panca Amanat Revolusi	the Fifth Revolution Order
Pancasila	the five principles of Indonesian state ideology: belief in God, humanitarianism, nationalism through unity of the nation, consultative democracy and social justice
Pemimpin Besar Revolusi	The Great Revolutionary Leader
Rame ing gawe, sepi ing padudan	to work hard and stay away from arguments
Selametan	to offer gratitude
Sesajen	offerings
Shodancho	a platoon commander
Sing rukun karo sedulur	to live in accord with siblings
Tri Dharma	Three Good Deeds: *rumongso melu handarbeni, wajib melu hangrungkebi, mulat sarira hangrasawani*—a sense of mutual belonging, responsibility to preserve and uphold one's rights, and the courage to be introspective

REFERENCES

Abdulgani, Dr H Roeslan, *Three Public Lectures in Australia 1972*, Yayasan Idayu, Indonesia, 1974.

Abdulgani, Dr H Roeslan, *Catur Tutur tentang lahirnya Pancasila paska Orde Baru 1998–2001*, Cahaya Nusantara Foundation, 2003.

Abdulgani, Dr H Roeslan, *Indonesia dan Percaturan Politik Internasional*, Yayasan Keluarga Bhakti Surabaya dan Surabaya Post, November 1993

Abdulgani-Knapp, Retnowati, *A Fading Dream—The Story of Roeslan Abdulgani and Indonesia*, Times Books International, Singapore, 2003.

Aditjondro, Dr Goerge Junus, *Dari Suharto Ke Habibie*, Masyarakat Indonesia untuk Kemanusiaan, Pijar Indonesia, 1998.

Aly, Rum, *Titik Silang Jalan Kekuasaan Tahun 1965*, Kata Hasta Pustaka, Jakarta, 2006.

Antlov, Hans and Cederroth, Sven, *Leadership On Java, Gentle Hints, Authoritarian Rule*, Curzon Press, Richmond, Surrey, UK, 1994.

Aritonang, Diro, *Runtuhnya Rezim Soeharto*, Pustaka Hidayah, Bandung Indonesia, 1999.

Armstrong, Karen, *Islam, A Short History*, Phoenix Press, London, 2001.

Aspinall, Edward, Feith, Herb and van Klinken, Gerry (editors), *The Last Days of President Suharto*, Monash Asia Institute, 1999.

Brackman, Arnold C, Indonesia: Suharto's Road, USA American-Asian Educational Exchange, 1973.

Cak Roes Dalam Nuansa Pemikiran Nasionalisme di Usia 81 Tahun, Forum Komunikasi Alumni GMNI Jawa Timur, October 1995.

Djiwandono, J. Sudradjad, *Bank Indonesia and the Crisis—An Insider's View*, Institute of South East Asian Studies, ISEAS Publication, Singapore 2005.

Dwipayana, G and Sjamsuddin, Nazaruddin, *Among friends, Pak Harto at 70, a penetrating look at a unique leader by his closest associates*, Jakarta Citra Lamtoro Gung Persada, 1991.

Dwipayana, G and Ramadhan KH, *Soeharto, Pikiran, Ucapan, dan Tindakan Saya (otobiografi)*, Citra Lamtoro Gung Persada, 1989.

Elson, RE, Suharto, *A Political Biography*, Cambridge University Press, UK, 2001.

Fatah, Eep Saefulloh, Catatan Atas Gagalnya Politik Orde Baru, Pustaka Pelajar, 1998.

Feith, Herbert, and Castles, Lance, *Indonesian Political Thinking 1945–1965*, The Colonial Press, USA, 1970.

Fic, Victor M, *Anatomy of the Jakarta Coup: October 1, 1965*, Yayasan Cibor, Indonesia, Jakarta, 2005.

Forrester, Geoff and May, RJ, *Jatuhnya Soeharto*, Crawford House Publishing, Australia, 1999.

Friend, Theodore, *Indonesian Destinies*, The Belknap Press, Harvard University Press, Cambridge, Massachusetts and London, 2003.

Gemari, Tim Majalah, *Pengabdian Yayasan Supersemar Dalam Kepedulian Pendidikan Anak Bangsa*, Yayasan Supersemar, 2004.

Hendrowinoto, Nurinwa Ki S, dkk, *H Probosutedjo, Merindukan Kesejahteraan Rakyat Jelata (Refleksi Pers 1974–2005)*, Universitas Mercu Buana, Yayasan Biografi Indonesia, 2005.

Hendrowinoto, Nurinwa Ki S, dkk, *Ibu Indonesia Dalam Kenangan*, Bank Naskah Gramedia & Yayasan Biografi Indonesia, 2004.

Husaini, Adian, *Soeharto 1998*, Gema Insani Press, 1996.

Irvine, David, *Leather Gods & Wooden Heroes*, Times Editions, Singapore, 1996.

Jasin, M, *"Saya Tidak Pernah Minta Ampun Kepada Soeharto" Sebuah Memoar*, Pustaka Sinar Harapan, Jakarta, 1998.

Jenkins, David, *Suharto and his Generals—Indonesian Military Politics 1975–1983*, Cornell Modern Indonesia Projects, South East Asia Program, Cornell University, Ithaca, New York 1984.

Jones, Howard Palfrey, *Indonesia: The Possible Dream*, The Hoover Institution, New York, 1971.

Kahin, George McTurnan, *Nationalism and Revolution in Indonesia*, Cornell University Press, Ithaca, New York, 1952.

Kasdi, Aminuddin, and Wulan, G Ambar, *G 30 S PKI/1965 Bedah Caesar Dewan Revolusi Indonesia*, Java Pustaka, 2005.

Lane, Max, "Wedastera Suyasa in Balinese Politics, 1962–72: From Charismatic Politics to Socio-Educational Activities", a thesis presented as partial fulfillment of the requirements for the degree of Bachelor of Arts (Honours) at Sydney University, 1972.

Latief, Abdul, *Pledoi Kol A Latief, Soeharto Terlibat G 30 S*, Institut Studi Arus Informasi, 2000.

Latief, Heri, Miryanti, Ratih and Mahendra, Daniel (editors), *Tragedi Kemanusiaan 1965–2005 Antologi Puisi—Cerpen—Esai—Curhat*, Lembaga Sastra Pembebasan & Penerbit Malka, 2005.

Lee Kuan Yew, *From Third World to First, The Singapore Story 1965–2000*, Singapore Press Holdings and Times Editions, Singapore, 2000.

Legge, JD, *Indonesia*, Prentice Hall, New Jersey, 1965.

Lev, Daniel S, *Islamic Courts in Indonesia, A Study in the Political Bases of Legal Institutions*, University of California Press, USA, 1972.

Liddle, R William, *Leadership And Culture In Indonesian Politics*, Allen & Unwin, Sydney, Australia, 1996.

Loveard, Keith, *Suharto, Indonesia's Last Sultan*, Horizon Books, Singapore, 1999.

Lowry, Robert, *The Armed Forces of Indonesia*, Allen & Unwin, Australia, 1996.

Maarif, Prof Dr A Syafii, *Mencari Autentitas Dalam Kegalauan*, Pusat Studi Agama dan Peradaban (PSAP) Muhammadiyah, Jakarta, 2004.

Mann, Richard, *Indonesia Comes of Age, 50 Years of Independence*, Gateway Books, Canada, 1995.

Mann, Richard, *Plots & Schemes that brought down Soeharto*, Gateway Books, Jakarta, 1998.

McDonald, Hamish, *Suharto's Indonesia*, Fontana, Australia, 1980.

Mody, Nawaz B, *Indonesia under Suharto*, New Delhi Sterling Publishers, 1987.

Mubyarto, Penyunting, *Kisah-Kisah IDT*, Aditya Media, 1997.

Muller, Niels, *Mysticism in Java, Ideology in Indonesia*, The Pepin Press, Amsterdam/Singapore, 1998.

Naipospos, Bonar Tigor and Wiratama, Rahadi T (editors), *Plot TNI AD—Barat di Balik Tragedi '65*, Tapol—MIK—Solidamor, Juli 2000.

O'Rourke, Kevin, *Reformasi, The Struggle for Power in Post-Suharto Indonesia*, Allen & Unwin, Australia, 2002.

Patty, Servas Mario, *Kepemimpinan Soeharto Sebagai Benchmarking (19 Manajemen Presiden Soeharto)*, PT Penebar Swadaya, 1999.

Patty, Servas Mario, *Melihat Dengan Mata Hati Jasa-Jasa Pak Harto Bagi Bangsa dan Negara*, Yayasan Servas Mario, 1999.

Patty, Servas Mario, *Menggali Falsafah Pak Harto, Suatu Analisis Theologi Butir-Butir Budaya Jawa "Kitab Kebatinan dan Budi Pekerti"*, Yayasan Servas Mario, 2003.

Pejuang Yang Tidak Mengenal Akhir, Yayasan Bina Paraplegia Indonesia, 8 Juni 2001.

Perpustakaan Museum Purna Bhakti Pertiwi, *Dukungan dan Kebijakan-Kebijakan Pemerintah (Presiden Soeharto) Dalam Mengatasi Krisis Ekonomi & Moneter di Indonesia Jilid 1 Edisi ke-28*, 1998.

Prawiro, Radius, *Indonesia's Struggle for Economic Development—Pragmatism in Action*, Oxford University Press, Oxford Singapore/New York, 1998.

Priyatini, Erni, Harlinawati, Yuni, and Desigunawan, *Tak Surut Oleh Waktu, antara duka, harapan dan cinta*, Yayasan Dharmais, 2003.

Probosutedjo, H, *Kesaksian Sejarah H Probosutedjo Runtuhnya Pemerintahan Bung Karno—Pak Harto—BJ Habibie—Gus Dur*, Gemah Ripah, Jakarta, 2001.

Ramage, Douglas E, *Politics In Indonesia, Democracy, Islam and the ideology of Tolerance*, Routledge, London/New York, 1995.

Reid, Prof Anthony, *Early Modern History*, Archipelago Press, Singapore, 1996.

Rigg, Dr Jonathan, *The Human Environment*, Archipelago Press, Singapore, 1998.

Robison, Richard, Indonesia, *The Rise of Capital*, Allen & Unwin, Australia, 1986.

Roeder, OG, Anak Desa, *Biografi Presiden Soeharto*, Gunung Agung, Jakarta, 1976.

Rohwer, Jim, Asia Rising, *Why America Will Prosper as Asia's Economies Boom*, Simon & Schuster, New York, 1995.

Rose, La and Upi, *Pandangan Perempuan Tentang Soeharto*, Yayasan Rose, 1999.

Rukmana, H Hardiyanti, *Butir-Butir Budaya Jawa*, Yayasan Purna Bhakti Pertiwi, 1996.

Saidi, Zaim, *Soeharto Menjaring Matahari, Tarik-Ulur Ekonomi Orde Baru Pasca 1980*, Mizan Pustaka, Bandung, Indonesia, 1998.

Saleh, Ismail, *Bulir-Bulir Pikir Ismail Saleh*, Wedatama Widya Sastra, 2004.

Saleh, Ismail, *Ismail Saleh Yang Serius dan Yang Santai*, Perum Percetakan Negara RI, 2005.

Saleh, Ismail, SH, *Proses Peradilan Soeharto Presiden RI ke 2 Penegakan Hukum atau Komoditi Politik?*, Yayasan Dharmais, 2001.

Saleh, Ismail, *Taman Sari Pemikiran*, Perum Percetakan Negara RI, 2001.

Schwarz, Adam, *A Nation In Waiting*, Allen & Unwin, Australia, 1994.

Soebijono S.H., A.S.S. Tambunan S.H., Dr. Hidayat Mukmin, Drs. Roekmini

Koesoemo Astuti, *Dwifungsi ABRI. Perkembangan dan Peranannya dalam Kehidupan Politik di Indonesia*, Gajah Mada University Press, Yogya, 1992.

Soeharto, Soehartoisme dan Sumber Malapetaka, Pustaka GuGat, 1998.

Stewart, Ian Charles, *Indonesians, Portraits from an Archipelago*, Paramount Cipta, Indonesia and Concept Media, Singapore, 1983.

Sudarsono, Juwono (editor-in-chief), *The Movement Volume 1*, Publication Secretariat for the Non-Aligned Movement Book, August 1995.

Sulastomo, *Hari-Hari Yang Panjang 1963–1966*, Komapas, 2000.

Sulastomo, *Termination of A Power, An Analytical Perspective*, PT Raja Grafindo Persada, Jakarta, 2002.

Sumohardjono, Atmadji, *Jenderal M. Jusuf, Panglima Para Prajurit*, Kata Hasta Pustaka, Jakarta, 2006.

Suseno, Franz Magnis, *Etika Jawa, Sebuah Analisa Falsafi tentang Kebijaksanaan Hidup Jawa*, PT Gramedia Pustaka Utama, Jakarta, 2001.

Tabah, Anton, *Dua Jenderal Besar Bicara Tentang Gestapu/PKI*, CV Sahabat Klaten, 2000.

Tabah, Anton, *Empati di Tengah Badai Kumpulan Surat Kepada Pak Harto 21 Mei–31 Desember 1998*, Kharisma, 1999.

Thatcher, Margaret, *The Downing Street Years*, HarperCollins, 1993.

Vatikiotis, Michael RJ, *Indonesians Politics Under Suharto, Order, Development And Pressure For Change*, Routledge, London/New York, 1993.

Wangge, Mike and Wangge, Fr Wenyx, *Adili Soeharto, Jerat Dengan Kasus Pembunuhan Massal*, PT Permata Media Komunika, 1999.

Winters, Jeffrey A, *Power in Motion Capital Mobility and the Indonesian State*, Cornell University Press, USA, 1996.

YAMP, *Masjid YAMP, 22 tahun Yayasan Amalbakti Muslim Pancasila*, Yayasan Amalbakti Muslim Pancasila, 2004.

INDEX